Advance praise for
Java Concurrency in Practice

I was fortunate indeed to have worked with a fantastic team on the design and implementation of the concurrency features added to the Java platform in Java 5.0 and Java 6. Now this same team provides the best explanation yet of these new features, and of concurrency in general. Concurrency is no longer a subject for advanced users only. Every Java developer should read this book.

> —*Martin Buchholz*
> *JDK Concurrency Czar, Sun Microsystems*

For the past 30 years, computer performance has been driven by Moore's Law; from now on, it will be driven by Amdahl's Law. Writing code that effectively exploits multiple processors can be very challenging. *Java Concurrency in Practice* provides you with the concepts and techniques needed to write safe and scalable Java programs for today's—and tomorrow's—systems.

> —*Doron Rajwan*
> *Research Scientist, Intel Corp*

This is the book you need if you're writing—or designing, or debugging, or maintaining, or contemplating—multithreaded Java programs. If you've ever had to synchronize a method and you weren't sure why, you owe it to yourself and your users to read this book, cover to cover.

> —*Ted Neward*
> *Author of* Effective Enterprise Java

Brian addresses the fundamental issues and complexities of concurrency with uncommon clarity. This book is a must-read for anyone who uses threads and cares about performance.

> —*Kirk Pepperdine*
> *CTO, JavaPerformanceTuning.com*

This book covers a very deep and subtle topic in a very clear and concise way, making it the perfect Java Concurrency reference manual. Each page is filled with the problems (and solutions!) that programmers struggle with every day. Effectively exploiting concurrency is becoming more and more important now that Moore's Law is delivering more cores but not faster cores, and this book will show you how to do it.

> —*Dr. Cliff Click*
> *Senior Software Engineer, Azul Systems*

I have a strong interest in concurrency, and have probably written more thread deadlocks and made more synchronization mistakes than most programmers. Brian's book is the most readable on the topic of threading and concurrency in Java, and deals with this difficult subject with a wonderful hands-on approach. This is a book I am recommending to all my readers of The Java Specialists' Newsletter, because it is interesting, useful, and relevant to the problems facing Java developers today.

—Dr. Heinz Kabutz
The Java Specialists' Newsletter

I've focused a career on simplifying simple problems, but this book ambitiously and effectively works to simplify a complex but critical subject: concurrency. *Java Concurrency in Practice* is revolutionary in its approach, smooth and easy in style, and timely in its delivery—it's destined to be a very important book.

—Bruce Tate
Author of Beyond Java

Java Concurrency in Practice is an invaluable compilation of threading know-how for Java developers. I found reading this book intellectually exciting, in part because it is an excellent introduction to Java's concurrency API, but mostly because it captures in a thorough and accessible way expert knowledge on threading not easily found elsewhere.

—Bill Venners
Author of Inside the Java Virtual Machine

Java Concurrency in Practice

Java Concurrency in Practice

Brian Goetz
with
Tim Peierls
Joshua Bloch
Joseph Bowbeer
David Holmes
and Doug Lea

Upper Saddle River, NJ • Boston • Indianapolis • San Francisco
New York • Toronto • Montreal • London • Munich • Paris • Madrid
Capetown • Sydney • Tokyo • Singapore • Mexico City

This Book Is Safari Enabled

The Safari® Enabled icon on the cover of your favorite technology book means the book is available through Safari Bookshelf. When you buy this book, you get free access to the online edition for 45 days.

Safari Bookshelf is an electronic reference library that lets you easily search thousands of technical books, find code samples, download chapters, and access technical information whenever and wherever you need it.

To gain 45-day Safari Enabled access to this book:

- Go to http://www.awprofessional.com/safarienabled

- Complete the brief registration form

- Enter the coupon code UUIR-XRJG-JWWF-AHGM-137Z

If you have difficulty registering on Safari Bookshelf or accessing the online edition, please e-mail customer-service@safaribooksonline.com.

Library of Congress Cataloging-in-Publication Data

Goetz, Brian.
   Java Concurrency in Practice / Brian Goetz, with Tim Peierls. . . [et al.]
      p. cm.
   Includes bibliographical references and index.
   ISBN 0-321-34960-1 (pbk. : alk. paper)
  1. Java (Computer program language) 2. Parallel programming (Computer science) 3. Threads (Computer programs) I. Title.

QA76.73.J38G588 2006
005.13'3--dc22   2006012205

ISBN 0-321-34960-1
Text printed in the United States on recycled paper at Courier in Westford, Massachusetts.
Thirteenth printing, August 2014

To Jessica

Contents

Listings

Preface

At this writing, multicore processors are just now becoming inexpensive enough for midrange desktop systems. Not coincidentally, many development teams are noticing more and more threading-related bug reports in their projects. In a recent post on the NetBeans developer site, one of the core maintainers observed that a single class had been patched over 14 times to fix threading-related problems. Dion Almaer, former editor of TheServerSide, recently blogged (after a painful debugging session that ultimately revealed a threading bug) that most Java programs are so rife with concurrency bugs that they work only "by accident".

Indeed, developing, testing and debugging multithreaded programs can be extremely difficult because concurrency bugs do not manifest themselves predictably. And when they do surface, it is often at the worst possible time—in production, under heavy load.

One of the challenges of developing concurrent programs in Java is the mismatch between the concurrency features offered by the platform and how developers need to think about concurrency in their programs. The language provides low-level *mechanisms* such as synchronization and condition waits, but these mechanisms must be used consistently to implement application-level protocols or *policies*. Without such policies, it is all too easy to create programs that compile and appear to work but are nevertheless broken. Many otherwise excellent books on concurrency fall short of their goal by focusing excessively on low-level mechanisms and APIs rather than design-level policies and patterns.

Java 5.0 is a huge step forward for the development of concurrent applications in Java, providing new higher-level components and additional low-level mechanisms that make it easier for novices and experts alike to build concurrent applications. The authors are the primary members of the JCP Expert Group that created these facilities; in addition to describing their behavior and features, we present the underlying design patterns and anticipated usage scenarios that motivated their inclusion in the platform libraries.

Our goal is to give readers a set of design rules and mental models that make it easier—and more fun—to build correct, performant concurrent classes and applications in Java.

We hope you enjoy *Java Concurrency in Practice*.

Brian Goetz
Williston, VT
March 2006

How to use this book

To address the abstraction mismatch between Java's low-level mechanisms and the necessary design-level policies, we present a *simplified* set of rules for writing concurrent programs. Experts may look at these rules and say "Hmm, that's not entirely true: class *C* is thread-safe even though it violates rule *R*." While it is possible to write correct programs that break our rules, doing so requires a deep understanding of the low-level details of the Java Memory Model, and we want developers to be able to write correct concurrent programs *without* having to master these details. Consistently following our simplified rules will produce correct and maintainable concurrent programs.

We assume the reader already has some familiarity with the basic mechanisms for concurrency in Java. *Java Concurrency in Practice* is not an introduction to concurrency—for that, see the threading chapter of any decent introductory volume, such as *The Java Programming Language* (Arnold et al., 2005). Nor is it an encyclopedic reference for All Things Concurrency—for that, see *Concurrent Programming in Java* (Lea, 2000). Rather, it offers practical design rules to assist developers in the difficult process of creating safe and performant concurrent classes. Where appropriate, we cross-reference relevant sections of *The Java Programming Language*, *Concurrent Programming in Java*, *The Java Language Specification* (Gosling et al., 2005), and *Effective Java* (Bloch, 2001) using the conventions [JPL n.m], [CPJ n.m], [JLS n.m], and [EJ Item n].

After the introduction (Chapter 1), the book is divided into four parts:

Fundamentals. Part I (Chapters 2-5) focuses on the basic concepts of concurrency and thread safety, and how to compose thread-safe classes out of the concurrent building blocks provided by the class library. A "cheat sheet" summarizing the most important of the rules presented in Part I appears on page 110.

Chapters 2 (Thread Safety) and 3 (Sharing Objects) form the foundation for the book. Nearly all of the rules on avoiding concurrency hazards, constructing thread-safe classes, and verifying thread safety are here. Readers who prefer "practice" to "theory" may be tempted to skip ahead to Part II, but make sure to come back and read Chapters 2 and 3 before writing any concurrent code!

Chapter 4 (Composing Objects) covers techniques for composing thread-safe classes into larger thread-safe classes. Chapter 5 (Building Blocks) covers the concurrent building blocks—thread-safe collections and synchronizers—provided by the platform libraries.

Structuring Concurrent Applications. Part II (Chapters 6-9) describes how to exploit threads to improve the throughput or responsiveness of concurrent applications. Chapter 6 (Task Execution) covers identifying parallelizable tasks and executing them within the task-execution framework. Chapter 7 (Cancellation and Shutdown) deals with techniques for convincing tasks and threads to terminate before they would normally do so; how programs deal with cancellation and shutdown is often one of the factors that separates truly robust concurrent applications from those that merely work. Chapter 8 (Applying Thread Pools) addresses some of the more advanced features of the task-execution framework.

Chapter 9 (GUI Applications) focuses on techniques for improving responsiveness in single-threaded subsystems.

Liveness, Performance, and Testing. Part III (Chapters 10-12) concerns itself with ensuring that concurrent programs actually do what you want them to do and do so with acceptable performance. Chapter 10 (Avoiding Liveness Hazards) describes how to avoid liveness failures that can prevent programs from making forward progress. Chapter 11 (Performance and Scalability) covers techniques for improving the performance and scalability of concurrent code. Chapter 12 (Testing Concurrent Programs) covers techniques for testing concurrent code for both correctness and performance.

Advanced Topics. Part IV (Chapters 13-16) covers topics that are likely to be of interest only to experienced developers: explicit locks, atomic variables, nonblocking algorithms, and developing custom synchronizers.

Code examples

While many of the general concepts in this book are applicable to versions of Java prior to Java 5.0 and even to non-Java environments, most of the code examples (and all the statements about the Java Memory Model) assume Java 5.0 or later. Some of the code examples may use library features added in Java 6.

The code examples have been compressed to reduce their size and to high-light the relevant portions. The full versions of the code examples, as well as supplementary examples and errata, are available from the book's website, http://www.javaconcurrencyinpractice.com.

The code examples are of three sorts: "good" examples, "not so good" examples, and "bad" examples. Good examples illustrate techniques that should be emulated. Bad examples illustrate techniques that should definitely *not* be emulated, and are identified with a "Mr. Yuk" icon[1] to make it clear that this is "toxic" code (see Listing 1). Not-so-good examples illustrate techniques that are not *necessarily* wrong but are fragile, risky, or perform poorly, and are decorated with a "Mr. Could Be Happier" icon as in Listing 2.

```
public <T extends Comparable<? super T>> void sort(List<T> list) {
    // Never returns the wrong answer!
    System.exit(0);
}
```

Listing 1. Bad way to sort a list. *Don't do this.*

Some readers may question the role of the "bad" examples in this book; after all, a book should show how to do things right, not wrong. The bad examples have two purposes. They illustrate common pitfalls, but more importantly they demonstrate how to analyze a program for thread safety—and the best way to do that is to see the ways in which thread safety is compromised.

---

1. Mr. Yuk is a registered trademark of the Children's Hospital of Pittsburgh and appears by permission.

```
public <T extends Comparable<? super T>> void sort(List<T> list) {
    for (int i=0; i<1000000; i++)
        doNothing();
    Collections.sort(list);
}
```

LISTING 2. Less than optimal way to sort a list.

Acknowledgments

This book grew out of the development process for the `java.util.concurrent` package that was created by the Java Community Process JSR 166 for inclusion in Java 5.0. Many others contributed to JSR 166; in particular we thank Martin Buchholz for doing all the work related to getting the code into the JDK, and all the readers of the `concurrency-interest` mailing list who offered their suggestions and feedback on the draft APIs.

This book has been tremendously improved by the suggestions and assistance of a small army of reviewers, advisors, cheerleaders, and armchair critics. We would like to thank Dion Almaer, Tracy Bialik, Cindy Bloch, Martin Buchholz, Paul Christmann, Cliff Click, Stuart Halloway, David Hovemeyer, Jason Hunter, Michael Hunter, Jeremy Hylton, Heinz Kabutz, Robert Kuhar, Ramnivas Laddad, Jared Levy, Nicole Lewis, Victor Luchangco, Jeremy Manson, Paul Martin, Berna Massingill, Michael Maurer, Ted Neward, Kirk Pepperdine, Bill Pugh, Sam Pullara, Russ Rufer, Bill Scherer, Jeffrey Siegal, Bruce Tate, Gil Tene, Paul Tyma, and members of the Silicon Valley Patterns Group who, through many interesting technical conversations, offered guidance and made suggestions that helped make this book better.

We are especially grateful to Cliff Biffle, Barry Hayes, Dawid Kurzyniec, Angelika Langer, Doron Rajwan, and Bill Venners, who reviewed the entire manuscript in excruciating detail, found bugs in the code examples, and suggested numerous improvements.

We thank Katrina Avery for a great copy-editing job and Rosemary Simpson for producing the index under unreasonable time pressure. We thank Ami Dewar for doing the illustrations.

Thanks to the whole team at Addison-Wesley who helped make this book a reality. Ann Sellers got the project launched and Greg Doench shepherded it to a smooth completion; Elizabeth Ryan guided it through the production process.

We would also like to thank the thousands of software engineers who contributed indirectly by creating the software used to create this book, including TEX, LATEX, Adobe Acrobat, pic, grap, Adobe Illustrator, Perl, Apache Ant, IntelliJ IDEA, GNU emacs, Subversion, TortoiseSVN, and of course, the Java platform and class libraries.

Chapter 1

Introduction

Writing correct programs is hard; writing correct concurrent programs is harder. There are simply more things that can go wrong in a concurrent program than in a sequential one. So, why do we bother with concurrency? Threads are an inescapable feature of the Java language, and they can simplify the development of complex systems by turning complicated asynchronous code into simpler straight-line code. In addition, threads are the easiest way to tap the computing power of multiprocessor systems. And, as processor counts increase, exploiting concurrency effectively will only become more important.

1.1 A (very) brief history of concurrency

In the ancient past, computers didn't have operating systems; they executed a single program from beginning to end, and that program had direct access to all the resources of the machine. Not only was it difficult to write programs that ran on the bare metal, but running only a single program at a time was an inefficient use of expensive and scarce computer resources.

Operating systems evolved to allow more than one program to run at once, running individual programs in *processes*: isolated, independently executing programs to which the operating system allocates resources such as memory, file handles, and security credentials. If they needed to, processes could communicate with one another through a variety of coarse-grained communication mechanisms: sockets, signal handlers, shared memory, semaphores, and files.

Several motivating factors led to the development of operating systems that allowed multiple programs to execute simultaneously:

Resource utilization. Programs sometimes have to wait for external operations such as input or output, and while waiting can do no useful work. It is more efficient to use that wait time to let another program run.

Fairness. Multiple users and programs may have equal claims on the machine's resources. It is preferable to let them share the computer via finer-grained time slicing than to let one program run to completion and then start another.

Convenience. It is often easier or more desirable to write several programs that each perform a single task and have them coordinate with each other as necessary than to write a single program that performs all the tasks.

In early timesharing systems, each process was a virtual von Neumann computer; it had a memory space storing both instructions and data, executing instructions sequentially according to the semantics of the machine language, and interacting with the outside world via the operating system through a set of I/O primitives. For each instruction executed there was a clearly defined "next instruction", and control flowed through the program according to the rules of the instruction set. Nearly all widely used programming languages today follow this sequential programming model, where the language specification clearly defines "what comes next" after a given action is executed.

The sequential programming model is intuitive and natural, as it models the way humans work: do one thing at a time, in sequence—mostly. Get out of bed, put on your bathrobe, go downstairs and start the tea. As in programming languages, each of these real-world actions is an abstraction for a sequence of finer-grained actions—open the cupboard, select a flavor of tea, measure some tea into the pot, see if there's enough water in the teakettle, if not put some more water in, set it on the stove, turn the stove on, wait for the water to boil, and so on. This last step—waiting for the water to boil—also involves a degree of *asynchrony*. While the water is heating, you have a choice of what to do—just wait, or do other tasks in that time such as starting the toast (another asynchronous task) or fetching the newspaper, while remaining aware that your attention will soon be needed by the teakettle. The manufacturers of teakettles and toasters know their products are often used in an asynchronous manner, so they raise an audible signal when they complete their task. Finding the right balance of sequentiality and asynchrony is often a characteristic of efficient people—and the same is true of programs.

The same concerns (resource utilization, fairness, and convenience) that motivated the development of processes also motivated the development of *threads*. Threads allow multiple streams of program control flow to coexist within a process. They share process-wide resources such as memory and file handles, but each thread has its own program counter, stack, and local variables. Threads also provide a natural decomposition for exploiting hardware parallelism on multiprocessor systems; multiple threads within the same program can be scheduled simultaneously on multiple CPUs.

Threads are sometimes called *lightweight processes*, and most modern operating systems treat threads, not processes, as the basic units of scheduling. In the absence of explicit coordination, threads execute simultaneously and asynchronously with respect to one another. Since threads share the memory address space of their owning process, all threads within a process have access to the same variables and allocate objects from the same heap, which allows finer-grained data sharing than inter-process mechanisms. But without explicit synchronization to coordinate access to shared data, a thread may modify variables that another thread is in the middle of using, with unpredictable results.

1.2 Benefits of threads

When used properly, threads can reduce development and maintenance costs and improve the performance of complex applications. Threads make it easier to model how humans work and interact, by turning asynchronous workflows into mostly sequential ones. They can also turn otherwise convoluted code into straight-line code that is easier to write, read, and maintain.

Threads are useful in GUI applications for improving the responsiveness of the user interface, and in server applications for improving resource utilization and throughput. They also simplify the implementation of the JVM—the garbage collector usually runs in one or more dedicated threads. Most nontrivial Java applications rely to some degree on threads for their organization.

1.2.1 Exploiting multiple processors

Multiprocessor systems used to be expensive and rare, found only in large data centers and scientific computing facilities. Today they are cheap and plentiful; even low-end server and midrange desktop systems often have multiple processors. This trend will only accelerate; as it gets harder to scale up clock rates, processor manufacturers will instead put more processor cores on a single chip. All the major chip manufacturers have begun this transition, and we are already seeing machines with dramatically higher processor counts.

Since the basic unit of scheduling is the thread, a program with only one thread can run on at most one processor at a time. On a two-processor system, a single-threaded program is giving up access to half the available CPU resources; on a 100-processor system, it is giving up access to 99%. On the other hand, programs with multiple active threads can execute simultaneously on multiple processors. When properly designed, multithreaded programs can improve throughput by utilizing available processor resources more effectively.

Using multiple threads can also help achieve better throughput on single-processor systems. If a program is single-threaded, the processor remains idle while it waits for a synchronous I/O operation to complete. In a multithreaded program, another thread can still run while the first thread is waiting for the I/O to complete, allowing the application to still make progress during the blocking I/O. (This is like reading the newspaper while waiting for the water to boil, rather than waiting for the water to boil before starting to read.)

1.2.2 Simplicity of modeling

It is often easier to manage your time when you have only one type of task to perform (fix these twelve bugs) than when you have several (fix the bugs, interview replacement candidates for the system administrator, complete your team's performance evaluations, and create the slides for your presentation next week). When you have only one type of task to do, you can start at the top of the pile and keep working until the pile is exhausted (or you are); you don't have to spend any mental energy figuring out what to work on next. On the other hand, managing multiple priorities and deadlines and switching from task to task usually carries some overhead.

The same is true for software: a program that processes one type of task sequentially is simpler to write, less error-prone, and easier to test than one managing multiple different types of tasks at once. Assigning a thread to each type of task or to each element in a simulation affords the illusion of sequentiality and insulates domain logic from the details of scheduling, interleaved operations, asynchronous I/O, and resource waits. A complicated, asynchronous workflow can be decomposed into a number of simpler, synchronous workflows each running in a separate thread, interacting only with each other at specific synchronization points.

This benefit is often exploited by frameworks such as servlets or RMI (Remote Method Invocation). The framework handles the details of request management, thread creation, and load balancing, dispatching portions of the request handling to the appropriate application component at the appropriate point in the workflow. Servlet writers do not need to worry about how many other requests are being processed at the same time or whether the socket input and output streams block; when a servlet's `service` method is called in response to a web request, it can process the request synchronously as if it were a single-threaded program. This can simplify component development and reduce the learning curve for using such frameworks.

1.2.3   Simplified handling of asynchronous events

A server application that accepts socket connections from multiple remote clients may be easier to develop when each connection is allocated its own thread and allowed to use synchronous I/O.

If an application goes to read from a socket when no data is available, `read` blocks until some data is available. In a single-threaded application, this means that not only does processing the corresponding request stall, but processing of *all* requests stalls while the single thread is blocked. To avoid this problem, single-threaded server applications are forced to use nonblocking I/O, which is far more complicated and error-prone than synchronous I/O. However, if each request has its own thread, then blocking does not affect the processing of other requests.

Historically, operating systems placed relatively low limits on the number of threads that a process could create, as few as several hundred (or even less). As a result, operating systems developed efficient facilities for multiplexed I/O, such as the Unix `select` and `poll` system calls, and to access these facilities, the Java class libraries acquired a set of packages (`java.nio`) for nonblocking I/O. However, operating system support for larger numbers of threads has improved significantly, making the thread-per-client model practical even for large numbers of clients on some platforms.[1]

---

1. The NPTL threads package, now part of most Linux distributions, was designed to support hundreds of thousands of threads. Nonblocking I/O has its own benefits, but better OS support for threads means that there are fewer situations for which it is *essential*.

1.2.4 More responsive user interfaces

GUI applications used to be single-threaded, which meant that you had to either frequently poll throughout the code for input events (which is messy and intrusive) or execute all application code indirectly through a "main event loop". If code called from the main event loop takes too long to execute, the user interface appears to "freeze" until that code finishes, because subsequent user interface events cannot be processed until control is returned to the main event loop.

Modern GUI frameworks, such as the AWT and Swing toolkits, replace the main event loop with an *event dispatch thread* (EDT). When a user interface event such as a button press occurs, application-defined event handlers are called in the event thread. Most GUI frameworks are single-threaded subsystems, so the main event loop is effectively still present, but it runs in its own thread under the control of the GUI toolkit rather than the application.

If only short-lived tasks execute in the event thread, the interface remains responsive since the event thread is always able to process user actions reasonably quickly. However, processing a long-running task in the event thread, such as spell-checking a large document or fetching a resource over the network, impairs responsiveness. If the user performs an action while this task is running, there is a long delay before the event thread can process or even acknowledge it. To add insult to injury, not only does the UI become unresponsive, but it is impossible to cancel the offending task even if the UI provides a cancel button because the event thread is busy and cannot handle the cancel button-press event until the lengthy task completes! If, however, the long-running task is instead executed in a separate thread, the event thread remains free to process UI events, making the UI more responsive.

1.3 Risks of threads

Java's built-in support for threads is a double-edged sword. While it simplifies the development of concurrent applications by providing language and library support and a formal cross-platform memory model (it is this formal cross-platform memory model that makes possible the development of write-once, run-anywhere *concurrent* applications in Java), it also raises the bar for developers because more programs will use threads. When threads were more esoteric, concurrency was an "advanced" topic; now, mainstream developers must be aware of thread-safety issues.

1.3.1 Safety hazards

Thread safety can be unexpectedly subtle because, in the absence of sufficient synchronization, the ordering of operations in multiple threads is unpredictable and sometimes surprising. UnsafeSequence in Listing 1.1, which is supposed to generate a sequence of unique integer values, offers a simple illustration of how the interleaving of actions in multiple threads can lead to undesirable results. It behaves correctly in a single-threaded environment, but in a multithreaded environment does not.

```
@NotThreadSafe
public class UnsafeSequence {
    private int value;

    /** Returns a unique value. */
    public int getNext() {
        return value++;
    }
}
```

LISTING 1.1. Non-thread-safe sequence generator.

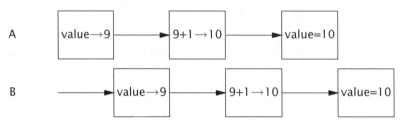

FIGURE 1.1. Unlucky execution of UnsafeSequence.getNext.

The problem with UnsafeSequence is that with some unlucky timing, two threads could call getNext and receive *the same value*. Figure 1.1 shows how this can happen. The increment notation, someVariable++, may *appear* to be a single operation, but is in fact three separate operations: read the value, add one to it, and write out the new value. Since operations in multiple threads may be arbitrarily interleaved by the runtime, it is possible for two threads to read the value at the same time, both see the same value, and then both add one to it. The result is that the same sequence number is returned from multiple calls in different threads.

> Diagrams like Figure 1.1 depict possible interleavings of operations in different threads. In these diagrams, time runs from left to right, and each line represents the activities of a different thread. These interleaving diagrams usually depict the worst case[2] and are intended to show the danger of incorrectly assuming things will happen in a particular order.

UnsafeSequence uses a nonstandard annotation: @NotThreadSafe. This is one of several custom annotations used throughout this book to document concurrency properties of classes and class members. (Other class-level annotations used

---

2. Actually, as we'll see in Chapter 3, the worst case can be even worse than these diagrams usually show because of the possibility of reordering.

in this way are @ThreadSafe and @Immutable; see Appendix A for details.) Annotations documenting thread safety are useful to multiple audiences. If a class is annotated with @ThreadSafe, users can use it with confidence in a multithreaded environment, maintainers are put on notice that it makes thread safety guarantees that must be preserved, and software analysis tools can identify possible coding errors.

UnsafeSequence illustrates a common concurrency hazard called a *race condition*. Whether or not getNext returns a unique value when called from multiple threads, as required by its specification, depends on how the runtime interleaves the operations—which is not a desirable state of affairs.

Because threads share the same memory address space and run concurrently, they can access or modify variables that other threads might be using. This is a tremendous convenience, because it makes data sharing much easier than would other inter-thread communications mechanisms. But it is also a significant risk: threads can be confused by having data change unexpectedly. Allowing multiple threads to access and modify the same variables introduces an element of nonsequentiality into an otherwise sequential programming model, which can be confusing and difficult to reason about. For a multithreaded program's behavior to be predictable, access to shared variables must be properly coordinated so that threads do not interfere with one another. Fortunately, Java provides synchronization mechanisms to coordinate such access.

UnsafeSequence can be fixed by making getNext a synchronized method, as shown in Sequence in Listing 1.2,[3] thus preventing the unfortunate interaction in Figure 1.1. (Exactly why this works is the subject of Chapters 2 and 3.)

```
@ThreadSafe
public class Sequence {
    @GuardedBy("this") private int value;

    public synchronized int getNext() {
        return value++;
    }
}
```

LISTING 1.2. Thread-safe sequence generator.

In the absence of synchronization, the compiler, hardware, and runtime are allowed to take substantial liberties with the timing and ordering of actions, such as caching variables in registers or processor-local caches where they are temporarily (or even permanently) invisible to other threads. These tricks are in aid of better performance and are generally desirable, but they place a burden on the developer to clearly identify where data is being shared across threads so that these optimizations do not undermine safety. (Chapter 16 gives the gory details on exactly what ordering guarantees the JVM makes and how synchronization

---

3. @GuardedBy is described in Section 2.4; it documents the *synchronization policy* for Sequence.

affects those guarantees, but if you follow the rules in Chapters 2 and 3, you can safely avoid these low-level details.)

1.3.2   Liveness hazards

It is critically important to pay attention to thread safety issues when developing concurrent code: safety cannot be compromised. The importance of safety is not unique to multithreaded programs—single-threaded programs also must take care to preserve safety and correctness—but the use of threads introduces additional safety hazards not present in single-threaded programs. Similarly, the use of threads introduces additional forms of *liveness failure* that do not occur in single-threaded programs.

While *safety* means "nothing bad ever happens", liveness concerns the complementary goal that "something good eventually happens". A liveness failure occurs when an activity gets into a state such that it is permanently unable to make forward progress. One form of liveness failure that can occur in sequential programs is an inadvertent infinite loop, where the code that follows the loop never gets executed. The use of threads introduces additional liveness risks. For example, if thread *A* is waiting for a resource that thread *B* holds exclusively, and *B* never releases it, *A* will wait forever. Chapter 10 describes various forms of liveness failures and how to avoid them, including deadlock (Section 10.1), starvation (Section 10.3.1), and livelock (Section 10.3.3). Like most concurrency bugs, bugs that cause liveness failures can be elusive because they depend on the relative timing of events in different threads, and therefore do not always manifest themselves in development or testing.

1.3.3   Performance hazards

Related to liveness is *performance*. While liveness means that something good *eventually* happens, eventually may not be good enough—we often want good things to happen quickly. Performance issues subsume a broad range of problems, including poor service time, responsiveness, throughput, resource consumption, or scalability. Just as with safety and liveness, multithreaded programs are subject to all the performance hazards of single-threaded programs, and to others as well that are introduced by the use of threads.

In well designed concurrent applications the use of threads is a net performance gain, but threads nevertheless carry some degree of runtime overhead. *Context switches*—when the scheduler suspends the active thread temporarily so another thread can run—are more frequent in applications with many threads, and have significant costs: saving and restoring execution context, loss of locality, and CPU time spent scheduling threads instead of running them. When threads share data, they must use synchronization mechanisms that can inhibit compiler optimizations, flush or invalidate memory caches, and create synchronization traffic on the shared memory bus. All these factors introduce additional performance costs; Chapter 11 covers techniques for analyzing and reducing these costs.

1.4 Threads are everywhere

Even if your program never explicitly creates a thread, frameworks may create threads on your behalf, and code called from these threads must be thread-safe. This can place a significant design and implementation burden on developers, since developing thread-safe classes requires more care and analysis than developing non-thread-safe classes.

Every Java application uses threads. When the JVM starts, it creates threads for JVM housekeeping tasks (garbage collection, finalization) and a main thread for running the main method. The AWT (Abstract Window Toolkit) and Swing user interface frameworks create threads for managing user interface events. Timer creates threads for executing deferred tasks. Component frameworks, such as servlets and RMI create pools of threads and invoke component methods in these threads.

If you use these facilities—as many developers do—you have to be familiar with concurrency and thread safety, because these frameworks create threads and call your components from them. It would be nice to believe that concurrency is an "optional" or "advanced" language feature, but the reality is that nearly all Java applications are multithreaded and these frameworks do not insulate you from the need to properly coordinate access to application state.

When concurrency is introduced into an application by a framework, it is usually impossible to restrict the concurrency-awareness to the framework code, because frameworks by their nature make callbacks to application components that in turn access application state. Similarly, the need for thread safety does not end with the components called by the framework—it extends to all code paths that access the program state accessed by those components. Thus, the need for thread safety is contagious.

> Frameworks introduce concurrency into applications by calling application components from framework threads. Components invariably access application state, thus requiring that *all* code paths accessing that state be thread-safe.

The facilities described below all cause application code to be called from threads not managed by the application. While the need for thread safety may start with these facilities, it rarely ends there; instead, it ripples through the application.

Timer. Timer is a convenience mechanism for scheduling tasks to run at a later time, either once or periodically. The introduction of a Timer can complicate an otherwise sequential program, because TimerTasks are executed in a thread managed by the Timer, not the application. If a TimerTask accesses data that is also accessed by other application threads, then not only must the TimerTask do so in a thread-safe manner, but *so must any other classes that access that data*. Often the easiest way to achieve this is to ensure that objects accessed by the `Timer-Task` are themselves thread-safe, thus encapsulating the thread safety within the shared objects.

Servlets and JavaServer Pages (JSPs).   The servlets framework is designed to handle all the infrastructure of deploying a web application and dispatching requests from remote HTTP clients. A request arriving at the server is dispatched, perhaps through a chain of filters, to the appropriate servlet or JSP. Each servlet represents a component of application logic, and in high-volume web sites, multiple clients may require the services of the same servlet at once. The servlets specification requires that a servlet be prepared to be called simultaneously from multiple threads. In other words, servlets need to be thread-safe.

Even if you could guarantee that a servlet was only called from one thread at a time, you would still have to pay attention to thread safety when building a web application. Servlets often access state information shared with other servlets, such as application-scoped objects (those stored in the `ServletContext`) or session-scoped objects (those stored in the per-client `HttpSession`). When a servlet accesses objects shared across servlets or requests, it must coordinate access to these objects properly, since multiple requests could be accessing them simultaneously from separate threads. Servlets and JSPs, as well as servlet filters and objects stored in scoped containers like `ServletContext` and `HttpSession`, simply have to be thread-safe.

Remote Method Invocation.   RMI lets you invoke methods on objects running in another JVM. When you call a remote method with RMI, the method arguments are packaged (marshaled) into a byte stream and shipped over the network to the remote JVM, where they are unpacked (unmarshaled) and passed to the remote method.

When the RMI code calls your remote object, in what thread does that call happen? You don't know, but it's definitely not in a thread you created—your object gets called in a thread managed by RMI. How many threads does RMI create? Could the same remote method on the same remote object be called simultaneously in multiple RMI threads?[4]

A remote object must guard against two thread safety hazards: properly coordinating access to state that may be shared with other objects, and properly coordinating access to the state of the remote object itself (since the same object may be called in multiple threads simultaneously). Like servlets, RMI objects should be prepared for multiple simultaneous calls and must provide their own thread safety.

Swing and AWT.   GUI applications are inherently asynchronous. Users may select a menu item or press a button at any time, and they expect that the application will respond promptly even if it is in the middle of doing something else. Swing and AWT address this problem by creating a separate thread for handling user-initiated events and updating the graphical view presented to the user.

---

4. Answer: yes, but it's not all that clear from the Javadoc—you have to read the RMI spec.

Swing components, such as JTable, are not thread-safe. Instead, Swing programs achieve their thread safety by confining all access to GUI components to the event thread. If an application wants to manipulate the GUI from outside the event thread, it must cause the code that will manipulate the GUI to run in the event thread instead.

When the user performs a UI action, an event handler is called in the event thread to perform whatever operation the user requested. If the handler needs to access application state that is also accessed from other threads (such as a document being edited), then the event handler, along with any other code that accesses that state, must do so in a thread-safe manner.

PART I

Fundamentals

Chapter 2

Thread Safety

Perhaps surprisingly, concurrent programming isn't so much about threads or locks, any more than civil engineering is about rivets and I-beams. Of course, building bridges that don't fall down requires the correct use of a lot of rivets and I-beams, just as building concurrent programs require the correct use of threads and locks. But these are just *mechanisms*—means to an end. Writing thread-safe code is, at its core, about managing access to *state*, and in particular to *shared, mutable state*.

Informally, an object's *state* is its data, stored in *state variables* such as instance or static fields. An object's state may include fields from other, dependent objects; a HashMap's state is partially stored in the HashMap object itself, but also in many Map.Entry objects. An object's state encompasses any data that can affect its externally visible behavior.

By *shared*, we mean that a variable could be accessed by multiple threads; by *mutable*, we mean that its value could change during its lifetime. We may talk about thread safety as if it were about *code*, but what we are really trying to do is protect *data* from uncontrolled concurrent access.

Whether an object needs to be thread-safe depends on whether it will be accessed from multiple threads. This is a property of how the object is *used* in a program, not what it *does*. Making an object thread-safe requires using synchronization to coordinate access to its mutable state; failing to do so could result in data corruption and other undesirable consequences.

Whenever more than one thread accesses a given state variable, and one of them might write to it, they all must coordinate their access to it using synchronization. The primary mechanism for synchronization in Java is the synchronized keyword, which provides exclusive locking, but the term "synchronization" also includes the use of volatile variables, explicit locks, and atomic variables.

You should avoid the temptation to think that there are "special" situations in which this rule does not apply. A program that omits needed synchronization might appear to work, passing its tests and performing well for years, but it is still broken and may fail at any moment.

> If multiple threads access the same mutable state variable without appro-
> priate synchronization, *your program is broken.* There are three ways to
> fix it:
>   • *Don't share* the state variable across threads;
>   • Make the state variable *immutable;* or
>   • Use *synchronization* whenever accessing the state variable.

If you haven't considered concurrent access in your class design, some of these approaches can require significant design modifications, so fixing the problem might not be as trivial as this advice makes it sound. *It is far easier to design a class to be thread-safe than to retrofit it for thread safety later.*

In a large program, identifying whether multiple threads might access a given variable can be complicated. Fortunately, the same object-oriented techniques that help you write well-organized, maintainable classes—such as encapsulation and data hiding—can also help you create thread-safe classes. The less code that has access to a particular variable, the easier it is to ensure that all of it uses the proper synchronization, and the easier it is to reason about the conditions under which a given variable might be accessed. The Java language doesn't force you to encapsulate state—it is perfectly allowable to store state in public fields (even public static fields) or publish a reference to an otherwise internal object—but the better encapsulated your program state, the easier it is to make your program thread-safe and to help maintainers keep it that way.

> When designing thread-safe classes, good object-oriented techniques—
> encapsulation, immutability, and clear specification of invariants—are
> your best friends.

There will be times when good object-oriented design techniques are at odds with real-world requirements; it may be necessary in these cases to compromise the rules of good design for the sake of performance or for the sake of back-ward compatibility with legacy code. Sometimes abstraction and encapsulation are at odds with performance—although not nearly as often as many developers believe—but it is always a good practice first to make your code right, and *then* make it fast. Even then, pursue optimization only if your performance measure-ments and requirements tell you that you must, and if those same measurements tell you that your optimizations actually made a difference under realistic condi-tions.[1]

If you decide that you simply must break encapsulation, all is not lost. It is still possible to make your program thread-safe, it is just a lot harder. Moreover, the

---

1. In concurrent code, this practice should be adhered to even more than usual. Because concur-rency bugs are so difficult to reproduce and debug, the benefit of a small performance gain on some infrequently used code path may well be dwarfed by the risk that the program will fail in the field.

thread safety of your program will be more fragile, increasing not only development cost and risk but maintenance cost and risk as well. Chapter 4 characterizes the conditions under which it is safe to relax encapsulation of state variables.

We've used the terms "thread-safe class" and "thread-safe program" nearly interchangeably thus far. Is a thread-safe program one that is constructed entirely of thread-safe classes? Not necessarily—a program that consists entirely of thread-safe classes may not be thread-safe, and a thread-safe program may contain classes that are not thread-safe. The issues surrounding the composition of thread-safe classes are also taken up in Chapter 4. In any case, the concept of a thread-safe class makes sense only if the class encapsulates its own state. Thread safety may be a term that is applied to *code*, but it is about *state*, and it can only be applied to the entire body of code that encapsulates its state, which may be an object or an entire program.

2.1 What is thread safety?

Defining thread safety is surprisingly tricky. The more formal attempts are so complicated as to offer little practical guidance or intuitive understanding, and the rest are informal descriptions that can seem downright circular. A quick Google search turns up numerous "definitions" like these:

> ...can be called from multiple program threads without unwanted interactions between the threads.

> ...may be called by more than one thread at a time without requiring any other action on the caller's part.

Given definitions like these, it's no wonder we find thread safety confusing! They sound suspiciously like "a class is thread-safe if it can be used safely from multiple threads." You can't really argue with such a statement, but it doesn't offer much practical help either. How do we tell a thread-safe class from an unsafe one? What do we even mean by "safe"?

At the heart of any reasonable definition of thread safety is the concept of *correctness*. If our definition of thread safety is fuzzy, it is because we lack a clear definition of correctness.

Correctness means that a class *conforms to its specification*. A good specification defines *invariants* constraining an object's state and *postconditions* describing the effects of its operations. Since we often don't write adequate specifications for our classes, how can we possibly know they are correct? We can't, but that doesn't stop us from using them anyway once we've convinced ourselves that "the code works". This "code confidence" is about as close as many of us get to correctness, so let's just assume that single-threaded correctness is something that "we know it when we see it". Having optimistically defined "correctness" as something that can be recognized, we can now define thread safety in a somewhat less circular way: a class is thread-safe when it continues to behave correctly when accessed from multiple threads.

A class is *thread-safe* if it behaves correctly when accessed from multiple threads, regardless of the scheduling or interleaving of the execution of those threads by the runtime environment, and with no additional synchronization or other coordination on the part of the calling code.

Since any single-threaded program is also a valid multithreaded program, it cannot be thread-safe if it is not even correct in a single-threaded environment.[2] If an object is correctly implemented, no sequence of operations—calls to public methods and reads or writes of public fields—should be able to violate any of its invariants or postconditions. *No set of operations performed sequentially or concurrently on instances of a thread-safe class can cause an instance to be in an invalid state.*

Thread-safe classes encapsulate any needed synchronization so that clients need not provide their own.

2.1.1   Example: a stateless servlet

In Chapter 1, we listed a number of frameworks that create threads and call your components from those threads, leaving you with the responsibility of making your components thread-safe. Very often, thread-safety requirements stem not from a decision to use threads directly but from a decision to use a facility like the Servlets framework. We're going to develop a simple example—a servlet-based factorization service—and slowly extend it to add features while preserving its thread safety.

Listing 2.1 shows our simple factorization servlet. It unpacks the number to be factored from the servlet request, factors it, and packages the results into the servlet response.

```
@ThreadSafe
public class StatelessFactorizer implements Servlet {
    public void service(ServletRequest req, ServletResponse resp) {
        BigInteger i = extractFromRequest(req);
        BigInteger[] factors = factor(i);
        encodeIntoResponse(resp, factors);
    }
}
```

LISTING 2.1. A stateless servlet.

---

2. If the loose use of "correctness" here bothers you, you may prefer to think of a thread-safe class as one that is no more broken in a concurrent environment than in a single-threaded environment.

StatelessFactorizer is, like most servlets, stateless: it has no fields and references no fields from other classes. The transient state for a particular computation exists solely in local variables that are stored on the thread's stack and are accessible only to the executing thread. One thread accessing a StatelessFactorizer cannot influence the result of another thread accessing the same StatelessFactorizer; because the two threads do not share state, it is as if they were accessing different instances. Since the actions of a thread accessing a stateless object cannot affect the correctness of operations in other threads, stateless objects are thread-safe.

> Stateless objects are always thread-safe.

The fact that most servlets can be implemented with no state greatly reduces the burden of making servlets thread-safe. It is only when servlets want to remember things from one request to another that the thread safety requirement becomes an issue.

2.2 Atomicity

What happens when we add one element of state to what was a stateless object? Suppose we want to add a "hit counter" that measures the number of requests processed. The obvious approach is to add a long field to the servlet and increment it on each request, as shown in UnsafeCountingFactorizer in Listing 2.2.

```
@NotThreadSafe
public class UnsafeCountingFactorizer implements Servlet {
    private long count = 0;

    public long getCount() { return count; }

    public void service(ServletRequest req, ServletResponse resp) {
        BigInteger i = extractFromRequest(req);
        BigInteger[] factors = factor(i);
        ++count;
        encodeIntoResponse(resp, factors);
    }
}
```

LISTING 2.2. Servlet that counts requests without the necessary synchronization. *Don't do this.*

Unfortunately, UnsafeCountingFactorizer is not thread-safe, even though it would work just fine in a single-threaded environment. Just like UnsafeSequence on page 6, it is susceptible to *lost updates*. While the increment operation, ++count, may look like a single action because of its compact syntax, it is not *atomic*, which means that it does not execute as a single, indivisible operation. Instead, it is a shorthand for a sequence of three discrete operations: fetch the current value, add one to it, and write the new value back. This is an example of a *read-modify-write* operation, in which the resulting state is derived from the previous state.

Figure 1.1 on page 6 shows what can happen if two threads try to increment a counter simultaneously without synchronization. If the counter is initially 9, with some unlucky timing each thread could read the value, see that it is 9, add one to it, and each set the counter to 10. This is clearly not what is supposed to happen; an increment got lost along the way, and the hit counter is now permanently off by one.

You might think that having a slightly inaccurate count of hits in a web-based service is an acceptable loss of accuracy, and sometimes it is. But if the counter is being used to generate sequences or unique object identifiers, returning the same value from multiple invocations could cause serious data integrity problems.[3] The possibility of incorrect results in the presence of unlucky timing is so important in concurrent programming that it has a name: a *race condition*.

2.2.1   Race conditions

UnsafeCountingFactorizer has several *race conditions* that make its results unreliable. A race condition occurs when the correctness of a computation depends on the relative timing or interleaving of multiple threads by the runtime; in other words, when getting the right answer relies on lucky timing.[4] The most common type of race condition is *check-then-act*, where a potentially stale observation is used to make a decision on what to do next.

We often encounter race conditions in real life. Let's say you planned to meet a friend at noon at the Starbucks on University Avenue. But when you get there, you realize there are *two* Starbucks on University Avenue, and you're not sure which one you agreed to meet at. At 12:10, you don't see your friend at Starbucks *A*, so you walk over to Starbucks *B* to see if he's there, but he isn't there either. There are a few possibilities: your friend is late and not at either Starbucks; your friend arrived at Starbucks *A* after you left; or your friend *was* at Starbucks *B*, but went to look for you, and is now en route to Starbucks *A*. Let's assume the worst and say it was the last possibility. Now it's 12:15, you've both been to both Starbucks, and you're both wondering if you've been stood up. What do you do now? Go back to the other Starbucks? How many times are you going to go back

---

3. The approach taken by UnsafeSequence and UnsafeCountingFactorizer has other serious problems, including the possibility of stale data (Section 3.1.1).

4. The term *race condition* is often confused with the related term *data race*, which arises when synchronization is not used to coordinate all access to a shared nonfinal field. You risk a data race whenever a thread writes a variable that might next be read by another thread or reads a variable that might have last been written by another thread if both threads do not use synchronization; code with data races has no useful defined semantics under the Java Memory Model. Not all race conditions are data races, and not all data races are race conditions, but they both can cause concurrent programs to fail in unpredictable ways. UnsafeCountingFactorizer has both race conditions and data races. See Chapter 16 for more on data races.

and forth? Unless you have agreed on a protocol, you could both spend the day walking up and down University Avenue, frustrated and undercaffeinated.

The problem with the "I'll just nip up the street and see if he's at the other one" approach is that while you're walking up the street, your friend might have moved. You look around Starbucks *A*, observe "he's not here", and go looking for him. And you can do the same for Starbucks *B*, but *not at the same time*. It takes a few minutes to walk up the street, and during those few minutes, *the state of the system may have changed*.

The Starbucks example illustrates a race condition because reaching the desired outcome (meeting your friend) depends on the relative timing of events (when each of you arrives at one Starbucks or the other, how long you wait there before switching, etc). The observation that he is not at Starbucks *A* becomes potentially invalid as soon as you walk out the front door; he could have come in through the back door and you wouldn't know. It is this invalidation of observations that characterizes most race conditions—using a potentially stale observation to make a decision or perform a computation. This type of race condition is called *check-then-act*: you observe something to be true (file *X* doesn't exist) and then take action based on that observation (create *X*); but in fact the observation could have become invalid between the time you observed it and the time you acted on it (someone else created *X* in the meantime), causing a problem (unexpected exception, overwritten data, file corruption).

2.2.2 Example: race conditions in lazy initialization

A common idiom that uses check-then-act is *lazy initialization*. The goal of lazy initialization is to defer initializing an object until it is actually needed while at the same time ensuring that it is initialized only once. `LazyInitRace` in Listing 2.3 illustrates the lazy initialization idiom. The `getInstance` method first checks whether the `ExpensiveObject` has already been initialized, in which case it returns the existing instance; otherwise it creates a new instance and returns it after retaining a reference to it so that future invocations can avoid the more expensive code path.

```
@NotThreadSafe
public class LazyInitRace {
    private ExpensiveObject instance = null;

    public ExpensiveObject getInstance() {
        if (instance == null)
            instance = new ExpensiveObject();
        return instance;
    }
}
```

LISTING 2.3. Race condition in lazy initialization. *Don't do this.*

LazyInitRace has race conditions that can undermine its correctness. Say that threads *A* and *B* execute getInstance at the same time. *A* sees that instance is null, and instantiates a new ExpensiveObject. *B* also checks if instance is null. Whether instance is null at this point depends unpredictably on timing, including the vagaries of scheduling and how long *A* takes to instantiate the ExpensiveObject and set the instance field. If instance is null when *B* examines it, the two callers to getInstance may receive two different results, even though getInstance is always supposed to return the same instance.

The hit-counting operation in UnsafeCountingFactorizer has another sort of race condition. Read-modify-write operations, like incrementing a counter, define a transformation of an object's state in terms of its previous state. To increment a counter, you have to know its previous value *and* make sure no one else changes or uses that value while you are in mid-update.

Like most concurrency errors, race conditions don't *always* result in failure: some unlucky timing is also required. But race conditions can cause serious problems. If LazyInitRace is used to instantiate an application-wide registry, having it return different instances from multiple invocations could cause registrations to be lost or multiple activities to have inconsistent views of the set of registered objects. If UnsafeSequence is used to generate entity identifiers in a persistence framework, two distinct objects could end up with the same ID, violating identity integrity constraints.

2.2.3 Compound actions

Both LazyInitRace and UnsafeCountingFactorizer contained a sequence of operations that needed to be *atomic*, or indivisible, relative to other operations on the same state. To avoid race conditions, there must be a way to prevent other threads from using a variable while we're in the middle of modifying it, so we can ensure that other threads can observe or modify the state only before we start or after we finish, but not in the middle.

> Operations *A* and *B* are *atomic* with respect to each other if, from the perspective of a thread executing *A*, when another thread executes *B*, either all of *B* has executed or none of it has. An *atomic operation* is one that is atomic with respect to all operations, including itself, that operate on the same state.

If the increment operation in UnsafeSequence were atomic, the race condition illustrated in Figure 1.1 on page 6 could not occur, and each execution of the increment operation would have the desired effect of incrementing the counter by exactly one. To ensure thread safety, check-then-act operations (like lazy initialization) and read-modify-write operations (like increment) must always be atomic. We refer collectively to check-then-act and read-modify-write sequences as *compound actions*: sequences of operations that must be executed atomically in order to remain thread-safe. In the next section, we'll consider *locking*, Java's built-in mechanism for ensuring atomicity. For now, we're going to fix the problem another way, by using an existing thread-safe class, as shown in CountingFactorizer in Listing 2.4.

```
@ThreadSafe
public class CountingFactorizer implements Servlet {
    private final AtomicLong count = new AtomicLong(0);

    public long getCount() { return count.get(); }

    public void service(ServletRequest req, ServletResponse resp) {
        BigInteger i = extractFromRequest(req);
        BigInteger[] factors = factor(i);
        count.incrementAndGet();
        encodeIntoResponse(resp, factors);
    }
}
```

LISTING 2.4. *Servlet that counts requests using* AtomicLong.

The java.util.concurrent.atomic package contains *atomic variable* classes for effecting atomic state transitions on numbers and object references. By replacing the long counter with an AtomicLong, we ensure that all actions that access the counter state are atomic.[5] Because the state of the servlet *is* the state of the counter and the counter is thread-safe, our servlet is once again thread-safe.

We were able to add a counter to our factoring servlet and maintain thread safety by using an existing thread-safe class to manage the counter state, AtomicLong. When a *single* element of state is added to a stateless class, the resulting class will be thread-safe if the state is entirely managed by a thread-safe object. But, as we'll see in the next section, going from one state variable to more than one is not necessarily as simple as going from zero to one.

> Where practical, use existing thread-safe objects, like AtomicLong, to manage your class's state. It is simpler to reason about the possible states and state transitions for existing thread-safe objects than it is for arbitrary state variables, and this makes it easier to maintain and verify thread safety.

2.3 Locking

We were able to add one state variable to our servlet while maintaining thread safety by using a thread-safe object to manage the entire state of the servlet. But if

---

5. CountingFactorizer calls incrementAndGet to increment the counter, which also returns the incremented value; in this case the return value is ignored.

we want to add more state to our servlet, can we just add more thread-safe state variables?

Imagine that we want to improve the performance of our servlet by caching the most recently computed result, just in case two consecutive clients request factorization of the same number. (This is unlikely to be an effective caching strategy; we offer a better one in Section 5.6.) To implement this strategy, we need to remember two things: the last number factored, and its factors.

We used `AtomicLong` to manage the counter state in a thread-safe manner; could we perhaps use its cousin, `AtomicReference`,[6] to manage the last number and its factors? An attempt at this is shown in `UnsafeCachingFactorizer` in Listing 2.5.

```
@NotThreadSafe
public class UnsafeCachingFactorizer implements Servlet {
    private final AtomicReference<BigInteger> lastNumber
        = new AtomicReference<BigInteger>();
    private final AtomicReference<BigInteger[]> lastFactors
        = new AtomicReference<BigInteger[]>();

    public void service(ServletRequest req, ServletResponse resp) {
        BigInteger i = extractFromRequest(req);
        if (i.equals(lastNumber.get()))
            encodeIntoResponse(resp, lastFactors.get());
        else {
            BigInteger[] factors = factor(i);
            lastNumber.set(i);
            lastFactors.set(factors);
            encodeIntoResponse(resp, factors);
        }
    }
}
```

LISTING 2.5. Servlet that attempts to cache its last result without adequate atomicity. *Don't do this.*

Unfortunately, this approach does not work. Even though the atomic references are individually thread-safe, `UnsafeCachingFactorizer` has race conditions that could make it produce the wrong answer.

The definition of thread safety requires that invariants be preserved regardless of timing or interleaving of operations in multiple threads. One invariant of `UnsafeCachingFactorizer` is that the product of the factors cached in `lastFactors` equal the value cached in `lastNumber`; our servlet is correct only if this invariant always holds. When multiple variables participate in an invariant, they are not

---

6. Just as `AtomicLong` is a thread-safe holder class for a `long` integer, `AtomicReference` is a thread-safe holder class for an object reference. Atomic variables and their benefits are covered in Chapter 15.

independent: the value of one constrains the allowed value(s) of the others. Thus when updating one, you must update the others *in the same atomic operation*.

With some unlucky timing, UnsafeCachingFactorizer can violate this invariant. Using atomic references, we cannot update both lastNumber and lastFactors simultaneously, even though each call to set is atomic; there is still a window of vulnerability when one has been modified and the other has not, and during that time other threads could see that the invariant does not hold. Similarly, the two values cannot be fetched simultaneously: between the time when thread *A* fetches the two values, thread *B* could have changed them, and again *A* may observe that the invariant does not hold.

> To preserve state consistency, update related state variables in a single atomic operation.

2.3.1 Intrinsic locks

Java provides a built-in locking mechanism for enforcing atomicity: the synchronized block. (There is also another critical aspect to locking and other synchronization mechanisms—visibility—which is covered in Chapter 3.) A synchronized block has two parts: a reference to an object that will serve as the *lock*, and a block of code to be guarded by that lock. A synchronized method is a shorthand for a synchronized block that spans an entire method body, and whose lock is the object on which the method is being invoked. (Static synchronized methods use the Class object for the lock.)

```
synchronized (lock) {
    // Access or modify shared state guarded by lock
}
```

Every Java object can implicitly act as a lock for purposes of synchronization; these built-in locks are called *intrinsic locks* or *monitor locks*. The lock is automatically acquired by the executing thread before entering a synchronized block and automatically released when control exits the synchronized block, whether by the normal control path or by throwing an exception out of the block. The only way to acquire an intrinsic lock is to enter a synchronized block or method guarded by that lock.

Intrinsic locks in Java act as *mutexes* (or *mutual exclusion locks*), which means that at most one thread may own the lock. When thread *A* attempts to acquire a lock held by thread *B*, *A* must wait, or *block*, until *B* releases it. If *B* never releases the lock, *A* waits forever.

Since only one thread at a time can execute a block of code guarded by a given lock, the synchronized blocks guarded by the same lock execute atomically with respect to one another. In the context of concurrency, atomicity means the same thing as it does in transactional applications—that a group of statements appear to execute as a single, indivisible unit. No thread executing a synchronized block

can observe another thread to be in the middle of a synchronized block guarded
by the same lock.

The machinery of synchronization makes it easy to restore thread safety to
the factoring servlet. Listing 2.6 makes the service method synchronized, so
only one thread may enter service at a time. SynchronizedFactorizer is now
thread-safe; however, this approach is fairly extreme, since it inhibits multiple
clients from using the factoring servlet simultaneously at all—resulting in unac-
ceptably poor responsiveness. This problem—which is a performance problem,
not a thread safety problem—is addressed in Section 2.5.

```
@ThreadSafe
public class SynchronizedFactorizer implements Servlet {
    @GuardedBy("this") private BigInteger lastNumber;
    @GuardedBy("this") private BigInteger[] lastFactors;

    public synchronized void service(ServletRequest req,
                                     ServletResponse resp) {
        BigInteger i = extractFromRequest(req);
        if (i.equals(lastNumber))
            encodeIntoResponse(resp, lastFactors);
        else {
            BigInteger[] factors = factor(i);
            lastNumber = i;
            lastFactors = factors;
            encodeIntoResponse(resp, factors);
        }
    }
}
```

LISTING 2.6. Servlet that caches last result, but with unnacceptably poor concurrency. *Don't do this.*

2.3.2 Reentrancy

When a thread requests a lock that is already held by another thread, the requesting thread blocks. But because intrinsic locks are *reentrant*, if a thread tries
to acquire a lock that *it* already holds, the request succeeds. Reentrancy means
that locks are acquired on a per-thread rather than per-invocation basis.[7] Reentrancy is implemented by associating with each lock an acquisition count and an
owning thread. When the count is zero, the lock is considered unheld. When a
thread acquires a previously unheld lock, the JVM records the owner and sets the
acquisition count to one. If that same thread acquires the lock again, the count

---

7. This differs from the default locking behavior for pthreads (POSIX threads) mutexes, which are
granted on a per-invocation basis.

is incremented, and when the owning thread exits the synchronized block, the count is decremented. When the count reaches zero, the lock is released.

Reentrancy facilitates encapsulation of locking behavior, and thus simplifies the development of object-oriented concurrent code. Without reentrant locks, the very natural-looking code in Listing 2.7, in which a subclass overrides a synchronized method and then calls the superclass method, would deadlock. Because the doSomething methods in Widget and LoggingWidget are both synchronized, each tries to acquire the lock on the Widget before proceeding. But if intrinsic locks were not reentrant, the call to super.doSomething would never be able to acquire the lock because it would be considered already held, and the thread would permanently stall waiting for a lock it can never acquire. Reentrancy saves us from deadlock in situations like this.

```
public class Widget {
    public synchronized void doSomething() {
        ...
    }
}

public class LoggingWidget extends Widget {
    public synchronized void doSomething() {
        System.out.println(toString() + ": calling doSomething");
        super.doSomething();
    }
}
```

LISTING 2.7. Code that would deadlock if intrinsic locks were not reentrant.

2.4 Guarding state with locks

Because locks enable serialized[8] access to the code paths they guard, we can use them to construct protocols for guaranteeing exclusive access to shared state. Following these protocols consistently can ensure state consistency.

Compound actions on shared state, such as incrementing a hit counter (read-modify-write) or lazy initialization (check-then-act), must be made atomic to avoid race conditions. Holding a lock for the *entire duration* of a compound action can make that compound action atomic. However, just wrapping the compound action with a synchronized block is not sufficient; if synchronization is used to coordinate access to a variable, it is needed *everywhere that variable is accessed*. Further, when using locks to coordinate access to a variable, the *same* lock must be used wherever that variable is accessed.

---

8. Serializing access to an object has nothing to do with object serialization (turning an object into a byte stream); serializing access means that threads take turns accessing the object exclusively, rather than doing so concurrently.

It is a common mistake to assume that synchronization needs to be used only when *writing* to shared variables; *this is simply not true.* (The reasons for this will become clearer in Section 3.1.)

> For each mutable state variable that may be accessed by more than one thread, *all* accesses to that variable must be performed with the *same* lock held. In this case, we say that the variable is *guarded by* that lock.

In SynchronizedFactorizer in Listing 2.6, lastNumber and lastFactors are guarded by the servlet object's intrinsic lock; this is documented by the @GuardedBy annotation.

There is no inherent relationship between an object's intrinsic lock and its state; an object's fields need not be guarded by its intrinsic lock, though this is a perfectly valid locking convention that is used by many classes. Acquiring the lock associated with an object does *not* prevent other threads from accessing that object—the only thing that acquiring a lock prevents any other thread from doing is acquiring that same lock. The fact that every object has a built-in lock is just a convenience so that you needn't explicitly create lock objects.[9] It is up to you to construct *locking protocols* or *synchronization policies* that let you access shared state safely, and to use them consistently throughout your program.

> Every shared, mutable variable should be guarded by exactly one lock. Make it clear to maintainers which lock that is.

A common locking convention is to encapsulate all mutable state within an object and to protect it from concurrent access by synchronizing any code path that accesses mutable state using the object's intrinsic lock. This pattern is used by many thread-safe classes, such as Vector and other synchronized collection classes. In such cases, all the variables in an object's state are guarded by the object's intrinsic lock. However, there is nothing special about this pattern, and neither the compiler nor the runtime enforces this (or any other) pattern of locking.[10] It is also easy to subvert this locking protocol accidentally by adding a new method or code path and forgetting to use synchronization.

Not all data needs to be guarded by locks—only mutable data that will be accessed from multiple threads. In Chapter 1, we described how adding a simple asynchronous event such as a TimerTask can create thread safety requirements that ripple throughout your program, especially if your program state is poorly encapsulated. Consider a single-threaded program that processes a large amount of data. Single-threaded programs require no synchronization, because no data is shared across threads. Now imagine you want to add a feature to create periodic

---

9. In retrospect, this design decision was probably a bad one: not only can it be confusing, but it forces JVM implementors to make tradeoffs between object size and locking performance.

10. Code auditing tools like FindBugs can identify when a variable is frequently but not always accessed with a lock held, which may indicate a bug.

snapshots of its progress, so that it does not have to start again from the beginning if it crashes or must be stopped. You might choose to do this with a `TimerTask` that goes off every ten minutes, saving the program state to a file.

Since the `TimerTask` will be called from another thread (one managed by `Timer`), any data involved in the snapshot is now accessed by two threads: the main program thread and the `Timer` thread. This means that not only must the `TimerTask` code use synchronization when accessing the program state, but so must any code path in the rest of the program that touches that same data. What used to require no synchronization now requires synchronization throughout the program.

When a variable is guarded by a lock—meaning that *every* access to that variable is performed with that lock held—you've ensured that only one thread at a time can access that variable. When a class has invariants that involve more than one state variable, there is an additional requirement: each variable participating in the invariant must be guarded by the *same* lock. This allows you to access or update them in a single atomic operation, preserving the invariant. Synchron-izedFactorizer demonstrates this rule: both the cached number and the cached factors are guarded by the servlet object's intrinsic lock.

> For every invariant that involves more than one variable, *all* the variables involved in that invariant must be guarded by the *same* lock.

If synchronization is the cure for race conditions, why not just declare every method `synchronized`? It turns out that such indiscriminate application of `synchronized` might be either too much or too little synchronization. Merely synchronizing every method, as `Vector` does, is not enough to render compound actions on a `Vector` atomic:

```
if (!vector.contains(element))
    vector.add(element);
```

This attempt at a put-if-absent operation has a race condition, even though both `contains` and `add` are atomic. While synchronized methods can make individual operations atomic, additional locking is required when multiple operations are combined into a compound action. (See Section 4.4 for some techniques for safely adding additional atomic operations to thread-safe objects.) At the same time, synchronizing every method can lead to liveness or performance problems, as we saw in `SynchronizedFactorizer`.

2.5 Liveness and performance

In `UnsafeCachingFactorizer`, we introduced some caching into our factoring servlet in the hope of improving performance. Caching required some shared state, which in turn required synchronization to maintain the integrity of that state. But the way we used synchronization in `SynchronizedFactorizer` makes it perform badly. The synchronization policy for `SynchronizedFactorizer` is to

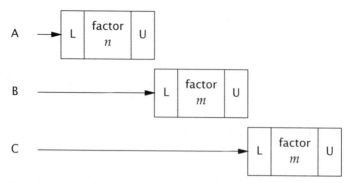

FIGURE 2.1. Poor concurrency of SynchronizedFactorizer.

guard each state variable with the servlet object's intrinsic lock, and that policy was implemented by synchronizing the entirety of the service method. This simple, coarse-grained approach restored safety, but at a high price.

Because service is synchronized, only one thread may execute it at once. This subverts the intended use of the servlet framework—that servlets be able to handle multiple requests simultaneously—and can result in frustrated users if the load is high enough. If the servlet is busy factoring a large number, other clients have to wait until the current request is complete before the servlet can start on the new number. If the system has multiple CPUs, processors may remain idle even if the load is high. In any case, even short-running requests, such as those for which the value is cached, may take an unexpectedly long time because they must wait for previous long-running requests to complete.

Figure 2.1 shows what happens when multiple requests arrive for the synchronized factoring servlet: they queue up and are handled sequentially. We would describe this web application as exhibiting *poor concurrency*: the number of simultaneous invocations is limited not by the availability of processing resources, but by the structure of the application itself. Fortunately, it is easy to improve the concurrency of the servlet while maintaining thread safety by narrowing the scope of the synchronized block. You should be careful not to make the scope of the synchronized block *too* small; you would not want to divide an operation that should be atomic into more than one synchronized block. But it is reasonable to try to exclude from synchronized blocks long-running operations that do not affect shared state, so that other threads are not prevented from accessing the shared state while the long-running operation is in progress.

CachedFactorizer in Listing 2.8 restructures the servlet to use two separate synchronized blocks, each limited to a short section of code. One guards the check-then-act sequence that tests whether we can just return the cached result, and the other guards updating both the cached number and the cached factors. As a bonus, we've reintroduced the hit counter and added a "cache hit" counter as well, updating them within the initial synchronized block. Because these counters constitute shared mutable state as well, we must use synchronization everywhere they are accessed. The portions of code that are outside the synchronized blocks operate exclusively on local (stack-based) variables, which are not shared across threads and therefore do not require synchronization.

```
@ThreadSafe
public class CachedFactorizer implements Servlet {
    @GuardedBy("this") private BigInteger lastNumber;
    @GuardedBy("this") private BigInteger[] lastFactors;
    @GuardedBy("this") private long hits;
    @GuardedBy("this") private long cacheHits;

    public synchronized long getHits() { return hits; }
    public synchronized double getCacheHitRatio() {
        return (double) cacheHits / (double) hits;
    }

    public void service(ServletRequest req, ServletResponse resp) {
        BigInteger i = extractFromRequest(req);
        BigInteger[] factors = null;
        synchronized (this) {
            ++hits;
            if (i.equals(lastNumber)) {
                ++cacheHits;
                factors = lastFactors.clone();
            }
        }
        if (factors == null) {
            factors = factor(i);
            synchronized (this) {
                lastNumber = i;
                lastFactors = factors.clone();
            }
        }
        encodeIntoResponse(resp, factors);
    }
}
```

LISTING 2.8. Servlet that caches its last request and result.

CachedFactorizer no longer uses AtomicLong for the hit counter, instead reverting to using a long field. It would be safe to use AtomicLong here, but there is less benefit than there was in CountingFactorizer. Atomic variables are useful for effecting atomic operations on a single variable, but since we are already using synchronized blocks to construct atomic operations, using two different synchronization mechanisms would be confusing and would offer no performance or safety benefit.

The restructuring of CachedFactorizer provides a balance between simplicity (synchronizing the entire method) and concurrency (synchronizing the shortest possible code paths). Acquiring and releasing a lock has some overhead, so it is undesirable to break down synchronized blocks *too* far (such as factoring ++hits into its own synchronized block), even if this would not compromise atomicity. CachedFactorizer holds the lock when accessing state variables and for the duration of compound actions, but releases it before executing the potentially long-running factorization operation. This preserves thread safety without unduly affecting concurrency; the code paths in each of the synchronized blocks are "short enough".

Deciding how big or small to make synchronized blocks may require tradeoffs among competing design forces, including safety (which must not be compromised), simplicity, and performance. Sometimes simplicity and performance are at odds with each other, although as CachedFactorizer illustrates, a reasonable balance can usually be found.

> There is frequently a tension between simplicity and performance. When implementing a synchronization policy, resist the temptation to prematurely sacrifice simplicity (potentially compromising safety) for the sake of performance.

Whenever you use locking, you should be aware of what the code in the block is doing and how likely it is to take a long time to execute. Holding a lock for a long time, either because you are doing something compute-intensive or because you execute a potentially blocking operation, introduces the risk of liveness or performance problems.

> Avoid holding locks during lengthy computations or operations at risk of not completing quickly such as network or console I/O.

CHAPTER 3

Sharing Objects

We stated at the beginning of Chapter 2 that writing correct concurrent programs is primarily about managing access to shared, mutable state. That chapter was about using synchronization to prevent multiple threads from accessing the same data at the same time; this chapter examines techniques for sharing and publishing objects so they can be safely accessed by multiple threads. Together, they lay the foundation for building thread-safe classes and safely structuring concurrent applications using the java.util.concurrent library classes.

We have seen how synchronized blocks and methods can ensure that operations execute atomically, but it is a common misconception that synchronized is *only* about atomicity or demarcating "critical sections". Synchronization also has another significant, and subtle, aspect: *memory visibility*. We want not only to prevent one thread from modifying the state of an object when another is using it, but also to ensure that when a thread modifies the state of an object, other threads can actually *see* the changes that were made. But without synchronization, this may not happen. You can ensure that objects are published safely either by using explicit synchronization or by taking advantage of the synchronization built into library classes.

3.1 Visibility

Visibility is subtle because the things that can go wrong are so counterintuitive. In a single-threaded environment, if you write a value to a variable and later read that variable with no intervening writes, you can expect to get the same value back. This seems only natural. It may be hard to accept at first, but when the reads and writes occur in different threads, *this is simply not the case*. In general, there is *no* guarantee that the reading thread will see a value written by another thread on a timely basis, or even at all. In order to ensure visibility of memory writes across threads, you must use synchronization.

NoVisibility in Listing 3.1 illustrates what can go wrong when threads share data without synchronization. Two threads, the main thread and the reader thread, access the shared variables ready and number. The main thread starts the reader thread and then sets number to 42 and ready to true. The reader thread spins until it sees ready is true, and then prints out number. While it may seem obvious that NoVisibility will print 42, it is in fact possible that it will print zero, or never terminate at all! Because it does not use adequate synchronization, there is no guarantee that the values of ready and number written by the main thread will be visible to the reader thread.

```java
public class NoVisibility {
    private static boolean ready;
    private static int number;

    private static class ReaderThread extends Thread {
        public void run() {
            while (!ready)
                Thread.yield();
            System.out.println(number);
        }
    }

    public static void main(String[] args) {
        new ReaderThread().start();
        number = 42;
        ready = true;
    }
}
```

LISTING 3.1. Sharing variables without synchronization. *Don't do this.*

NoVisibility could loop forever because the value of ready might never become visible to the reader thread. Even more strangely, NoVisibility could print zero because the write to ready might be made visible to the reader thread *before* the write to number, a phenomenon known as *reordering*. There is no guarantee that operations in one thread will be performed in the order given by the program, as long as the reordering is not detectable from within *that* thread—*even if the reordering is apparent to other threads.*[1] When the main thread writes first to number and then to ready without synchronization, the reader thread could see those writes happen in the opposite order—or not at all.

---

1. This may seem like a broken design, but it is meant to allow JVMs to take full advantage of the performance of modern multiprocessor hardware. For example, in the absence of synchronization, the Java Memory Model permits the compiler to reorder operations and cache values in registers, and permits CPUs to reorder operations and cache values in processor-specific caches. For more details, see Chapter 16.

> In the absence of synchronization, the compiler, processor, and runtime can do some downright weird things to the order in which operations appear to execute. Attempts to reason about the order in which memory actions "must" happen in insufficiently synchronized multithreaded programs will almost certainly be incorrect.

NoVisibility is about as simple as a concurrent program can get—two threads and two shared variables—and yet it is still all too easy to come to the wrong conclusions about what it does or even whether it will terminate. Reasoning about insufficiently synchronized concurrent programs is prohibitively difficult.

This may all sound a little scary, and it should. Fortunately, there's an easy way to avoid these complex issues: *always use the proper synchronization whenever data is shared across threads.*

3.1.1 Stale data

NoVisibility demonstrated one of the ways that insufficiently synchronized programs can cause surprising results: *stale data*. When the reader thread examines ready, it may see an out-of-date value. Unless synchronization is used *every time a variable is accessed*, it is possible to see a stale value for that variable. Worse, staleness is not all-or-nothing: a thread can see an up-to-date value of one variable but a stale value of another variable that was written first.

When food is stale, it is usually still edible—just less enjoyable. But stale data can be more dangerous. While an out-of-date hit counter in a web application might not be so bad,[2] stale values can cause serious safety or liveness failures. In NoVisibility, stale values could cause it to print the wrong value or prevent the program from terminating. Things can get even more complicated with stale values of object references, such as the link pointers in a linked list implementation. *Stale data can cause serious and confusing failures such as unexpected exceptions, corrupted data structures, inaccurate computations, and infinite loops.*

MutableInteger in Listing 3.2 is not thread-safe because the value field is accessed from both get and set without synchronization. Among other hazards, it is susceptible to stale values: if one thread calls set, other threads calling get may or may not see that update.

We can make MutableInteger thread safe by synchronizing the getter and setter as shown in SynchronizedInteger in Listing 3.3. Synchronizing only the setter would not be sufficient: threads calling get would still be able to see stale values.

---

2. Reading data without synchronization is analogous to using the READ_UNCOMMITTED isolation level in a database, where you are willing to trade accuracy for performance. However, in the case of unsynchronized reads, you are trading away a greater degree of accuracy, since the visible value for a shared variable can be arbitrarily stale.

```
@NotThreadSafe
public class MutableInteger {
    private int value;

    public int  get() { return value; }
    public void set(int value) { this.value = value; }
}
```

LISTING 3.2. Non-thread-safe mutable integer holder.

```
@ThreadSafe
public class SynchronizedInteger {
    @GuardedBy("this") private int value;

    public synchronized int get() { return value; }
    public synchronized void set(int value) { this.value = value; }
}
```

LISTING 3.3. Thread-safe mutable integer holder.

3.1.2   Nonatomic 64-bit operations

When a thread reads a variable without synchronization, it may see a stale value, but at least it sees a value that was actually placed there by some thread rather than some random value. This safety guarantee is called *out-of-thin-air safety*.

Out-of-thin-air safety applies to all variables, with one exception: 64-bit numeric variables (double and long) that are not declared volatile (see Section 3.1.4). The Java Memory Model requires fetch and store operations to be atomic, but for nonvolatile long and double variables, the JVM is permitted to treat a 64-bit read or write as two separate 32-bit operations. If the reads and writes occur in different threads, it is therefore possible to read a nonvolatile long and get back the high 32 bits of one value and the low 32 bits of another.[3] Thus, even if you don't care about stale values, it is not safe to use shared mutable long and double variables in multithreaded programs unless they are declared volatile or guarded by a lock.

3.1.3   Locking and visibility

Intrinsic locking can be used to guarantee that one thread sees the effects of another in a predictable manner, as illustrated by Figure 3.1. When thread *A* executes a synchronized block, and subsequently thread *B* enters a synchronized block guarded by the same lock, the values of variables that were visible to *A* prior to releasing the lock are guaranteed to be visible to *B* upon acquiring the

---

3. When the Java Virtual Machine Specification was written, many widely used processor architectures could not efficiently provide atomic 64-bit arithmetic operations.

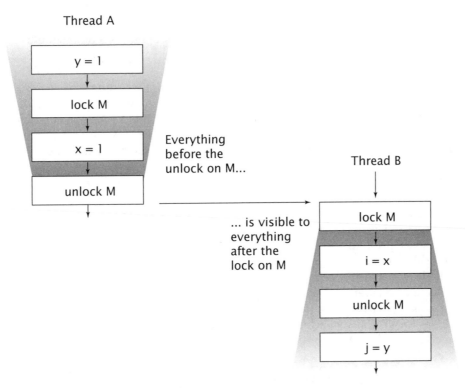

FIGURE 3.1. Visibility guarantees for synchronization.

lock. In other words, everything *A* did in or prior to a `synchronized` block is visible to *B* when it executes a `synchronized` block guarded by the same lock. *Without synchronization, there is no such guarantee.*

We can now give the other reason for the rule requiring all threads to synchronize on the *same* lock when accessing a shared mutable variable—to guarantee that values written by one thread are made visible to other threads. Otherwise, if a thread reads a variable without holding the appropriate lock, it might see a stale value.

> Locking is not just about mutual exclusion; it is also about memory visibility. To ensure that all threads see the most up-to-date values of shared mutable variables, the reading and writing threads must synchronize on a common lock.

3.1.4 Volatile variables

The Java language also provides an alternative, weaker form of synchronization, *volatile variables*, to ensure that updates to a variable are propagated predictably to other threads. When a field is declared `volatile`, the compiler and runtime are put on notice that this variable is shared and that operations on it should not be reordered with other memory operations. Volatile variables are not cached in registers or in caches where they are hidden from other processors, so a read of a volatile variable always returns the most recent write by any thread.

A good way to think about volatile variables is to imagine that they behave roughly like the `SynchronizedInteger` class in Listing 3.3, replacing reads and writes of the volatile variable with calls to `get` and `set`.[4] Yet accessing a volatile variable performs no locking and so cannot cause the executing thread to block, making volatile variables a lighter-weight synchronization mechanism than `synchronized`.[5]

The visibility effects of volatile variables extend beyond the value of the volatile variable itself. When thread *A* writes to a volatile variable and subsequently thread *B* reads that same variable, the values of *all* variables that were visible to *A* prior to writing to the volatile variable become visible to *B* after reading the volatile variable. So from a memory visibility perspective, writing a volatile variable is like exiting a `synchronized` block and reading a volatile variable is like entering a `synchronized` block. However, we do not recommend relying too heavily on volatile variables for visibility; code that relies on volatile variables for visibility of arbitrary state is more fragile and harder to understand than code that uses locking.

> Use `volatile` variables only when they simplify implementing and verifying your synchronization policy; avoid using `volatile` variables when veryfing correctness would require subtle reasoning about visibility. Good uses of `volatile` variables include ensuring the visibility of their own state, that of the object they refer to, or indicating that an important lifecycle event (such as initialization or shutdown) has occurred.

Listing 3.4 illustrates a typical use of volatile variables: checking a status flag to determine when to exit a loop. In this example, our anthropomorphized thread is trying to get to sleep by the time-honored method of counting sheep. For this example to work, the `asleep` flag must be volatile. Otherwise, the thread might not notice when `asleep` has been set by another thread.[6] We could instead have

---

4. This analogy is not exact; the memory visibility effects of `SynchronizedInteger` are actually slightly stronger than those of volatile variables. See Chapter 16.

5. Volatile reads are only slightly more expensive than nonvolatile reads on most current processor architectures.

6. Debugging tip: For server applications, be sure to always specify the `-server` JVM command line switch when invoking the JVM, even for development and testing. The server JVM performs more optimization than the client JVM, such as hoisting variables out of a loop that are not modified in the loop; code that might appear to work in the development environment (client JVM) can break in the deployment environment (server JVM). For example, had we "forgotten" to declare the variable `asleep` as `volatile` in Listing 3.4, the server JVM could hoist the test out of the loop (turning it into an infinite loop), but the client JVM would not. An infinite loop that shows up in development is far less costly than one that only shows up in production.

used locking to ensure visibility of changes to `asleep`, but that would have made the code more cumbersome.

```
volatile boolean asleep;
...
    while (!asleep)
        countSomeSheep();
```

LISTING 3.4. *Counting sheep.*

Volatile variables are convenient, but they have limitations. The most common use for volatile variables is as a completion, interruption, or status flag, such as the `asleep` flag in Listing 3.4. Volatile variables can be used for other kinds of state information, but more care is required when attempting this. For example, the semantics of `volatile` are not strong enough to make the increment operation (`count++`) atomic, unless you can guarantee that the variable is written only from a single thread. (Atomic variables do provide atomic read-modify-write support and can often be used as "better volatile variables"; see Chapter 15.)

> Locking can guarantee both visibility and atomicity; volatile variables can only guarantee visibility.

You can use volatile variables only when all the following criteria are met:

- Writes to the variable do not depend on its current value, or you can ensure that only a single thread ever updates the value;

- The variable does not participate in invariants with other state variables; and

- Locking is not required for any other reason while the variable is being accessed.

3.2 Publication and escape

Publishing an object means making it available to code outside of its current scope, such as by storing a reference to it where other code can find it, returning it from a nonprivate method, or passing it to a method in another class. In many situations, we want to ensure that objects and their internals are *not* published. In other situations, we do want to publish an object for general use, but doing so in a thread-safe manner may require synchronization. Publishing internal state variables can compromise encapsulation and make it more difficult to preserve invariants; publishing objects before they are fully constructed can compromise thread safety. An object that is published when it should not have been is said to have *escaped*. Section 3.5 covers idioms for safe publication; right now, we look at how an object can escape.

The most blatant form of publication is to store a reference in a public static field, where any class and thread could see it, as in Listing 3.5. The `initialize` method instantiates a new `HashSet` and publishes it by storing a reference to it into `knownSecrets`.

```
public static Set<Secret> knownSecrets;

public void initialize() {
    knownSecrets = new HashSet<Secret>();
}
```

LISTING 3.5. Publishing an object.

Publishing one object may indirectly publish others. If you add a `Secret` to the published `knownSecrets` set, you've also published that `Secret`, because any code can iterate the `Set` and obtain a reference to the new `Secret`. Similarly, returning a reference from a nonprivate method also publishes the returned object. `UnsafeStates` in Listing 3.6 publishes the supposedly private array of state abbreviations.

```
class UnsafeStates {
    private String[] states = new String[] {
        "AK", "AL" ...
    };
    public String[] getStates() { return states; }
}
```

LISTING 3.6. Allowing internal mutable state to escape. *Don't do this.*

Publishing `states` in this way is problematic because any caller can modify its contents. In this case, the `states` array has escaped its intended scope, because what was supposed to be private state has been effectively made public.

Publishing an object also publishes any objects referred to by its nonprivate fields. More generally, any object that is *reachable* from a published object by following some chain of nonprivate field references and method calls has also been published.

From the perspective of a class *C*, an *alien* method is one whose behavior is not fully specified by *C*. This includes methods in other classes as well as overrideable methods (neither `private` nor `final`) in *C* itself. Passing an object to an alien method must also be considered publishing that object. Since you can't know what code will actually be invoked, you don't know that the alien method won't publish the object or retain a reference to it that might later be used from another thread.

Whether another thread actually does something with a published reference doesn't really matter, because the risk of misuse is still present.[7] Once an ob-

7. If someone steals your password and posts it on the `alt.free-passwords` newsgroup, that infor-

ject escapes, you have to assume that another class or thread may, maliciously or carelessly, misuse it. This is a compelling reason to use encapsulation: it makes it practical to analyze programs for correctness and harder to violate design constraints accidentally.

A final mechanism by which an object or its internal state can be published is to publish an inner class instance, as shown in ThisEscape in Listing 3.7. When ThisEscape publishes the EventListener, it implicitly publishes the enclosing ThisEscape instance as well, because inner class instances contain a hidden reference to the enclosing instance.

```
public class ThisEscape {
    public ThisEscape(EventSource source) {
        source.registerListener(
            new EventListener() {
                public void onEvent(Event e) {
                    doSomething(e);
                }
            });
    }
}
```

LISTING 3.7. Implicitly allowing the this reference to escape. *Don't do this.*

3.2.1 Safe construction practices

ThisEscape illustrates an important special case of escape—when the this references escapes during construction. When the inner EventListener instance is published, so is the enclosing ThisEscape instance. But an object is in a predictable, consistent state only after its constructor returns, so publishing an object from within its constructor can publish an incompletely constructed object. This is true *even if the publication is the last statement in the constructor.* If the this reference escapes during construction, the object is considered *not properly constructed.*[8]

> Do not allow the this reference to escape during construction.

A common mistake that can let the this reference escape during construction is to start a thread from a constructor. When an object creates a thread from its constructor, it almost always shares its this reference with the new thread, either explicitly (by passing it to the constructor) or implicitly (because the Thread or

---

mation has escaped: whether or not someone has (yet) used those credentials to create mischief, your account has still been compromised. Publishing a reference poses the same sort of risk.

8. More specifically, the this reference should not escape from the *thread* until after the constructor returns. The this reference can be stored somewhere by the constructor so long as it is not *used* by another thread until after construction. SafeListener in Listing 3.8 uses this technique.

Runnable is an inner class of the owning object). The new thread might then be able to see the owning object before it is fully constructed. There's nothing wrong with *creating* a thread in a constructor, but it is best not to *start* the thread immediately. Instead, expose a start or initialize method that starts the owned thread. (See Chapter 7 for more on service lifecycle issues.) Calling an override-able instance method (one that is neither private nor final) from the constructor can also allow the this reference to escape.

If you are tempted to register an event listener or start a thread from a constructor, you can avoid the improper construction by using a private constructor and a public factory method, as shown in SafeListener in Listing 3.8.

```
public class SafeListener {
    private final EventListener listener;

    private SafeListener() {
        listener = new EventListener() {
            public void onEvent(Event e) {
                doSomething(e);
            }
        };
    }

    public static SafeListener newInstance(EventSource source) {
        SafeListener safe = new SafeListener();
        source.registerListener(safe.listener);
        return safe;
    }
}
```

LISTING 3.8. Using a factory method to prevent the this reference from escaping during construction.

3.3 Thread confinement

Accessing shared, mutable data requires using synchronization; one way to avoid this requirement is to *not share*. If data is only accessed from a single thread, no synchronization is needed. This technique, *thread confinement*, is one of the simplest ways to achieve thread safety. When an object is confined to a thread, such usage is automatically thread-safe even if the confined object itself is not [CPJ 2.3.2].

Swing uses thread confinement extensively. The Swing visual components and data model objects are not thread safe; instead, safety is achieved by confining them to the Swing event dispatch thread. To use Swing properly, code running in threads other than the event thread should not access these objects. (To make this easier, Swing provides the invokeLater mechanism to schedule a Runnable for execution in the event thread.) Many concurrency errors in Swing applications stem from improper use of these confined objects from another thread.

Another common application of thread confinement is the use of pooled JDBC (Java Database Connectivity) Connection objects. The JDBC specification does not require that Connection objects be thread-safe.[9] In typical server applications, a thread acquires a connection from the pool, uses it for processing a single request, and returns it. Since most requests, such as servlet requests or EJB (Enterprise JavaBeans) calls, are processed synchronously by a single thread, and the pool will not dispense the same connection to another thread until it has been returned, this pattern of connection management implicitly confines the Connection to that thread for the duration of the request.

Just as the language has no mechanism for enforcing that a variable is guarded by a lock, it has no means of confining an object to a thread. Thread confinement is an element of your program's design that must be enforced by its implementation. The language and core libraries provide mechanisms that can help in maintaining thread confinement—local variables and the ThreadLocal class—but even with these, it is still the programmer's responsibility to ensure that thread-confined objects do not escape from their intended thread.

3.3.1 Ad-hoc thread confinement

Ad-hoc thread confinement describes when the responsibility for maintaining thread confinement falls entirely on the implementation. Ad-hoc thread confinement can be fragile because none of the language features, such as visibility modifiers or local variables, helps confine the object to the target thread. In fact, references to thread-confined objects such as visual components or data models in GUI applications are often held in public fields.

The decision to use thread confinement is often a consequence of the decision to implement a particular subsystem, such as the GUI, as a single-threaded subsystem. Single-threaded subsystems can sometimes offer a simplicity benefit that outweighs the fragility of ad-hoc thread confinement.[10]

A special case of thread confinement applies to volatile variables. It is safe to perform read-modify-write operations on shared volatile variables as long as you ensure that the volatile variable is only written from a single thread. In this case, you are confining the *modification* to a single thread to prevent race conditions, and the visibility guarantees for volatile variables ensure that other threads see the most up-to-date value.

Because of its fragility, ad-hoc thread confinement should be used sparingly; if possible, use one of the stronger forms of thread confinment (stack confinement or ThreadLocal) instead.

---

9. The connection *pool* implementations provided by application servers are thread-safe; connection pools are necessarily accessed from multiple threads, so a non-thread-safe implementation would not make sense.

10. Another reason to make a subsystem single-threaded is deadlock avoidance; this is one of the primary reasons most GUI frameworks are single-threaded. Single-threaded subsystems are covered in Chapter 9.

3.3.2   Stack confinement

Stack confinement is a special case of thread confinement in which an object can only be reached through local variables. Just as encapsulation can make it easier to preserve invariants, local variables can make it easier to confine objects to a thread. Local variables are intrinsically confined to the executing thread; they exist on the executing thread's stack, which is not accessible to other threads. Stack confinement (also called *within-thread* or *thread-local* usage, but not to be confused with the ThreadLocal library class) is simpler to maintain and less fragile than ad-hoc thread confinement.

For primitively typed local variables, such as numPairs in loadTheArk in Listing 3.9, you cannot violate stack confinement even if you tried. There is no way to obtain a reference to a primitive variable, so the language semantics ensure that primitive local variables are always stack confined.

```
public int loadTheArk(Collection<Animal> candidates) {
    SortedSet<Animal> animals;
    int numPairs = 0;
    Animal candidate = null;

    // animals confined to method, don't let them escape!
    animals = new TreeSet<Animal>(new SpeciesGenderComparator());
    animals.addAll(candidates);
    for (Animal a : animals) {
        if (candidate == null || !candidate.isPotentialMate(a))
            candidate = a;
        else {
            ark.load(new AnimalPair(candidate, a));
            ++numPairs;
            candidate = null;
        }
    }
    return numPairs;
}
```

LISTING 3.9. Thread confinement of local primitive and reference variables.

Maintaining stack confinement for object references requires a little more assistance from the programmer to ensure that the referent does not escape. In loadTheArk, we instantiate a TreeSet and store a reference to it in animals. At this point, there is exactly one reference to the Set, held in a local variable and therefore confined to the executing thread. However, if we were to publish a reference to the Set (or any of its internals), the confinement would be violated and the animals would escape.

Using a non-thread-safe object in a within-thread context is still thread-safe. However, be careful: the design requirement that the object be confined to the executing thread, or the awareness that the confined object is not thread-safe, often exists only in the head of the developer when the code is written. If the assumption of within-thread usage is not clearly documented, future maintainers might mistakenly allow the object to escape.

3.3.3 ThreadLocal

A more formal means of maintaining thread confinement is ThreadLocal, which allows you to associate a per-thread value with a value-holding object. Thread-Local provides get and set accessor methods that maintain a separate copy of the value for each thread that uses it, so a get returns the most recent value passed to set *from the currently executing thread.*

Thread-local variables are often used to prevent sharing in designs based on mutable Singletons or global variables. For example, a single-threaded application might maintain a global database connection that is initialized at startup to avoid having to pass a Connection to every method. Since JDBC connections may not be thread-safe, a multithreaded application that uses a global connection without additional coordination is not thread-safe either. By using a ThreadLocal to store the JDBC connection, as in ConnectionHolder in Listing 3.10, each thread will have its own connection.

```
private static ThreadLocal<Connection> connectionHolder
    = new ThreadLocal<Connection>() {
        public Connection initialValue() {
            return DriverManager.getConnection(DB_URL);
        }
    };

public static Connection getConnection() {
    return connectionHolder.get();
}
```

LISTING 3.10. Using ThreadLocal to ensure thread confinement.

This technique can also be used when a frequently used operation requires a temporary object such as a buffer and wants to avoid reallocating the temporary object on each invocation. For example, before Java 5.0, Integer.toString used a ThreadLocal to store the 12-byte buffer used for formatting its result, rather than using a shared static buffer (which would require locking) or allocating a new buffer for each invocation.[11]

When a thread calls ThreadLocal.get for the first time, initialValue is consulted to provide the initial value for that thread. Conceptually, you can think of a ThreadLocal<T> as holding a Map<Thread,T> that stores the thread-specific

---

11. This technique is unlikely to be a performance win unless the operation is performed very frequently or the allocation is unusually expensive. In Java 5.0, it was replaced with the more straightforward approach of allocating a new buffer for every invocation, suggesting that for something as mundane as a temporary buffer, it is not a performance win.

values, though this is not how it is actually implemented. The thread-specific values are stored in the `Thread` object itself; when the thread terminates, the thread-specific values can be garbage collected.

If you are porting a single-threaded application to a multithreaded environment, you can preserve thread safety by converting shared global variables into `ThreadLocals`, if the semantics of the shared globals permits this; an application-wide cache would not be as useful if it were turned into a number of thread-local caches.

`ThreadLocal` is widely used in implementing application frameworks. For example, J2EE containers associate a transaction context with an executing thread for the duration of an EJB call. This is easily implemented using a static `Thread-Local` holding the transaction context: when framework code needs to determine what transaction is currently running, it fetches the transaction context from this `ThreadLocal`. This is convenient in that it reduces the need to pass execution context information into every method, but couples any code that uses this mechanism to the framework.

It is easy to abuse `ThreadLocal` by treating its thread confinement property as a license to use global variables or as a means of creating "hidden" method arguments. Like global variables, thread-local variables can detract from reusability and introduce hidden couplings among classes, and should therefore be used with care.

3.4 Immutability

The other end-run around the need to synchronize is to use *immutable* objects [EJ Item 13]. Nearly all the atomicity and visibility hazards we've described so far, such as seeing stale values, losing updates, or observing an object to be in an inconsistent state, have to do with the vagaries of multiple threads trying to access the same mutable state at the same time. If an object's state cannot be modified, these risks and complexities simply go away.

An immutable object is one whose state cannot be changed after construction. Immutable objects are inherently thread-safe; their invariants are established by the constructor, and if their state cannot be changed, these invariants always hold.

> Immutable objects are always thread-safe.

Immutable objects are *simple*. They can only be in one state, which is carefully controlled by the constructor. One of the most difficult elements of program design is reasoning about the possible states of complex objects. Reasoning about the state of immutable objects, on the other hand, is trivial.

Immutable objects are also *safer*. Passing a mutable object to untrusted code, or otherwise publishing it where untrusted code could find it, is dangerous—the untrusted code might modify its state, or, worse, retain a reference to it and modify its state later from another thread. On the other hand, immutable objects cannot be subverted in this manner by malicious or buggy code, so they are safe to share and publish freely without the need to make defensive copies [EJ Item 24].

Neither the Java Language Specification nor the Java Memory Model formally defines immutability, but immutability is *not* equivalent to simply declaring all fields of an object final. An object whose fields are all final may still be mutable, since final fields can hold references to mutable objects.

> An object is *immutable* if:
> - Its state cannot be modified after construction;
> - All its fields are final;[12] and
> - It is *properly constructed* (the this reference does not escape during construction).

Immutable objects can still use mutable objects internally to manage their state, as illustrated by ThreeStooges in Listing 3.11. While the Set that stores the names is mutable, the design of ThreeStooges makes it impossible to modify that Set after construction. The stooges reference is final, so all object state is reached through a final field. The last requirement, proper construction, is easily met since the constructor does nothing that would cause the this reference to become accessible to code other than the constructor and its caller.

```
@Immutable
public final class ThreeStooges {
    private final Set<String> stooges = new HashSet<String>();

    public ThreeStooges() {
        stooges.add("Moe");
        stooges.add("Larry");
        stooges.add("Curly");
    }

    public boolean isStooge(String name) {
        return stooges.contains(name);
    }
}
```

LISTING 3.11. Immutable class built out of mutable underlying objects.

Because program state changes all the time, you might be tempted to think that immutable objects are of limited use, but this is not the case. There is a dif-

---

12. It is technically possible to have an immutable object without all fields being final—String is such a class—but this relies on delicate reasoning about benign data races that requires a deep understanding of the Java Memory Model. (For the curious: String lazily computes the hash code the first time hashCode is called and caches it in a nonfinal field, but this works only because that field can take on only one nondefault value that is the same every time it is computed because it is derived deterministically from immutable state. Don't try this at home.)

ference between an *object* being immutable and the *reference* to it being immutable. Program state stored in immutable objects can still be updated by "replacing" immutable objects with a new instance holding new state; the next section offers an example of this technique.[13]

3.4.1 Final fields

The final keyword, a more limited version of the const mechanism from C++, supports the construction of immutable objects. Final fields can't be modified (although the objects they refer to can be modified if they are mutable), but they also have special semantics under the Java Memory Model. It is the use of final fields that makes possible the guarantee of *initialization safety* (see Section 3.5.2) that lets immutable objects be freely accessed and shared without synchronization.

Even if an object is mutable, making some fields final can still simplify reasoning about its state, since limiting the mutability of an object restricts its set of possible states. An object that is "mostly immutable" but has one or two mutable state variables is still simpler than one that has many mutable variables. Declaring fields final also documents to maintainers that these fields are not expected to change.

> Just as it is a good practice to make all fields private unless they need greater visibility [EJ Item 12], it is a good practice to make all fields final unless they need to be mutable.

3.4.2 Example: Using volatile to publish immutable objects

In UnsafeCachingFactorizer on page 24, we tried to use two AtomicReferences to store the last number and last factors, but this was not thread-safe because we could not fetch or update the two related values atomically. Using volatile variables for these values would not be thread-safe for the same reason. However, immutable objects can sometimes provide a weak form of atomicity.

The factoring servlet performs two operations that must be atomic: updating the cached result and conditionally fetching the cached factors if the cached number matches the requested number. Whenever a group of related data items must be acted on atomically, consider creating an immutable holder class for them, such as OneValueCache[14] in Listing 3.12.

Race conditions in accessing or updating multiple related variables can be eliminated by using an immutable object to hold all the variables. With a mutable

---

13. Many developers fear that this approach will create performance problems, but these fears are usually unwarranted. Allocation is cheaper than you might think, and immutable objects offer additional performance advantages such as reduced need for locking or defensive copies and reduced impact on generational garbage collection.

14. OneValueCache wouldn't be immutable without the copyOf calls in the constructor and getter. Arrays.copyOf was added as a convenience in Java 6; clone would also work.

```
@Immutable
class OneValueCache {
    private final BigInteger lastNumber;
    private final BigInteger[] lastFactors;

    public OneValueCache(BigInteger i,
                            BigInteger[] factors) {
        lastNumber = i;
        lastFactors = Arrays.copyOf(factors, factors.length);
    }

    public BigInteger[] getFactors(BigInteger i) {
        if (lastNumber == null || !lastNumber.equals(i))
            return null;
        else
            return Arrays.copyOf(lastFactors, lastFactors.length);
    }
}
```

LISTING 3.12. Immutable holder for caching a number and its factors.

holder object, you would have to use locking to ensure atomicity; with an immutable one, once a thread acquires a reference to it, it need never worry about another thread modifying its state. If the variables are to be updated, a new holder object is created, but any threads working with the previous holder still see it in a consistent state.

VolatileCachedFactorizer in Listing 3.13 uses a OneValueCache to store the cached number and factors. When a thread sets the volatile cache field to reference a new OneValueCache, the new cached data becomes immediately visible to other threads.

The cache-related operations cannot interfere with each other because One-ValueCache is immutable and the cache field is accessed only once in each of the relevant code paths. This combination of an immutable holder object for multiple state variables related by an invariant, and a volatile reference used to ensure its timely visibility, allows VolatileCachedFactorizer to be thread-safe even though it does no explicit locking.

3.5 Safe publication

So far we have focused on ensuring that an object *not* be published, such as when it is supposed to be confined to a thread or within another object. Of course, sometimes we *do* want to share objects across threads, and in this case we must do so safely. Unfortunately, simply storing a reference to an object into a public field, as in Listing 3.14, is *not* enough to publish that object safely.

```
@ThreadSafe
public class VolatileCachedFactorizer implements Servlet {
    private volatile OneValueCache cache =
        new OneValueCache(null, null);

    public void service(ServletRequest req, ServletResponse resp) {
        BigInteger i = extractFromRequest(req);
        BigInteger[] factors = cache.getFactors(i);
        if (factors == null) {
            factors = factor(i);
            cache = new OneValueCache(i, factors);
        }
        encodeIntoResponse(resp, factors);
    }
}
```

LISTING 3.13. *Caching the last result using a volatile reference to an immutable holder object.*

```
// Unsafe publication
public Holder holder;

public void initialize() {
    holder = new Holder(42);
}
```

LISTING 3.14. *Publishing an object without adequate synchronization.* Don't do this.

You may be surprised at how badly this harmless-looking example could fail. Because of visibility problems, the Holder could appear to another thread to be in an inconsistent state, even though its invariants were properly established by its constructor! This improper publication could allow another thread to observe a *partially constructed object*.

3.5.1 Improper publication: when good objects go bad

You cannot rely on the integrity of partially constructed objects. An observing thread could see the object in an inconsistent state, and then later see its state suddenly change, even though it has not been modified since publication. In fact, if the Holder in Listing 3.15 is published using the unsafe publication idiom in Listing 3.14, and a thread other than the publishing thread were to call assertSanity, it could throw AssertionError![15]

---

15. The problem here is not the Holder class itself, but that the Holder is not properly published. However, Holder can be made immune to improper publication by declaring the n field to be final,

```
public class Holder {
    private int n;

    public Holder(int n) { this.n = n; }

    public void assertSanity() {
        if (n != n)
            throw new AssertionError("This statement is false.");
    }
}
```

LISTING 3.15. *Class at risk of failure if not properly published.*

Because synchronization was not used to make the `Holder` visible to other threads, we say the `Holder` was *not properly published*. Two things can go wrong with improperly published objects. Other threads could see a stale value for the `holder` field, and thus see a `null` reference or other older value even though a value has been placed in `holder`. But far worse, other threads could see an up-to-date value for the `holder` reference, but stale values for the *state* of the `Holder`.[16] To make things even less predictable, a thread may see a stale value the first time it reads a field and then a more up-to-date value the next time, which is why `assertSanity` can throw `AssertionError`.

At the risk of repeating ourselves, some very strange things can happen when data is shared across threads without sufficient synchronization.

3.5.2 Immutable objects and initialization safety

Because immutable objects are so important, the Java Memory Model offers a special guarantee of *initialization safety* for sharing immutable objects. As we've seen, that an object reference becomes visible to another thread does not necessarily mean that the state of that object is visible to the consuming thread. In order to guarantee a consistent view of the object's state, synchronization is needed.

Immutable objects, on the other hand, can be safely accessed *even when synchronization is not used to publish the object reference*. For this guarantee of initialization safety to hold, all of the requirements for immutability must be met: unmodifiable state, all fields are `final`, and proper construction. (If `Holder` in Listing 3.15 were immutable, `assertSanity` could not throw `AssertionError`, even if the `Holder` was not properly published.)

---

which would make `Holder` immutable; see Section 3.5.2.

16. While it may seem that field values set in a constructor are the first values written to those fields and therefore that there are no "older" values to see as stale values, the `Object` constructor first writes the default values to all fields before subclass constructors run. It is therefore possible to see the default value for a field as a stale value.

Immutable objects can be used safely by any thread without additional synchronization, even when synchronization is not used to publish them.

This guarantee extends to the values of all final fields of properly constructed objects; final fields can be safely accessed without additional synchronization. However, if final fields refer to mutable objects, synchronization is still required to access the state of the objects they refer to.

3.5.3 Safe publication idioms

Objects that are not immutable must be *safely published*, which usually entails synchronization by both the publishing and the consuming thread. For the moment, let's focus on ensuring that the consuming thread can see the object in its as-published state; we'll deal with visibility of modifications made after publication soon.

To publish an object safely, both the reference to the object and the object's state must be made visible to other threads at the same time. A properly constructed object can be safely published by:
- Initializing an object reference from a static initializer;
- Storing a reference to it into a `volatile` field or `AtomicReference`;
- Storing a reference to it into a `final` field of a properly constructed object; or
- Storing a reference to it into a field that is properly guarded by a lock.

The internal synchronization in thread-safe collections means that placing an object in a thread-safe collection, such as a `Vector` or `synchronizedList`, fulfills the last of these requirements. If thread *A* places object *X* in a thread-safe collection and thread *B* subsequently retrieves it, *B* is guaranteed to see the state of *X* as *A* left it, even though the application code that hands *X* off in this manner has no *explicit* synchronization. The thread-safe library collections offer the following safe publication guarantees, even if the Javadoc is less than clear on the subject:

- Placing a key or value in a `Hashtable`, `synchronizedMap`, or `Concurrent-Map` safely publishes it to any thread that retrieves it from the `Map` (whether directly or via an iterator);

- Placing an element in a `Vector`, `CopyOnWriteArrayList`, `CopyOnWrite-ArraySet`, `synchronizedList`, or `synchronizedSet` safely publishes it to any thread that retrieves it from the collection;

- Placing an element on a `BlockingQueue` or a `ConcurrentLinkedQueue` safely publishes it to any thread that retrieves it from the queue.

Other handoff mechanisms in the class library (such as `Future` and `Exchanger`) also constitute safe publication; we will identify these as providing safe publication as they are introduced.

Using a static initializer is often the easiest and safest way to publish objects that can be statically constructed:

```
public static Holder holder = new Holder(42);
```

Static initializers are executed by the JVM at class initialization time; because of internal synchronization in the JVM, this mechanism is guaranteed to safely publish any objects initialized in this way [JLS 12.4.2].

3.5.4   Effectively immutable objects

Safe publication is sufficient for other threads to safely access objects that are not going to be modified after publication without additional synchronization. The safe publication mechanisms all guarantee that the as-published state of an object is visible to all accessing threads as soon as the reference to it is visible, and if that state is not going to be changed again, this is sufficient to ensure that any access is safe.

Objects that are not technically immutable, but whose state will not be modified after publication, are called *effectively immutable*. They do not need to meet the strict definition of immutability in Section 3.4; they merely need to be treated by the program as if they were immutable after they are published. Using effectively immutable objects can simplify development and improve performance by reducing the need for synchronization.

> Safely published *effectively immutable* objects can be used safely by any thread without additional synchronization.

For example, `Date` is mutable,[17] but if you use it as if it were immutable, you may be able to eliminate the locking that would otherwise be required when sharing a `Date` across threads. Suppose you want to maintain a `Map` storing the last login time of each user:

```
public Map<String, Date> lastLogin =
    Collections.synchronizedMap(new HashMap<String, Date>());
```

If the `Date` values are not modified after they are placed in the `Map`, then the synchronization in the `synchronizedMap` implementation is sufficient to publish the `Date` values safely, and no additional synchronization is needed when accessing them.

---

17. This was probably a mistake in the class library design.

3.5.5   Mutable objects

If an object may be modified after construction, safe publication ensures only the visibility of the as-published state. Synchronization must be used not only to publish a mutable object, but also every time the object is accessed to ensure visibility of subsequent modifications. To share mutable objects safely, they must be safely published *and* be either thread-safe or guarded by a lock.

> The publication requirements for an object depend on its mutability:
> - *Immutable objects* can be published through any mechanism;
> - *Effectively immutable objects* must be safely published;
> - *Mutable objects* must be safely published, and must be either thread-safe or guarded by a lock.

3.5.6   Sharing objects safely

Whenever you acquire a reference to an object, you should know what you are allowed to do with it. Do you need to acquire a lock before using it? Are you allowed to modify its state, or only to read it? Many concurrency errors stem from failing to understand these "rules of engagement" for a shared object. When you publish an object, you should document how the object can be accessed.

> The most useful policies for using and sharing objects in a concurrent program are:
>
> **Thread-confined.** A thread-confined object is owned exclusively by and confined to one thread, and can be modified by its owning thread.
>
> **Shared read-only.** A shared read-only object can be accessed concurrently by multiple threads without additional synchronization, but cannot be modified by any thread. Shared read-only objects include immutable and effectively immutable objects.
>
> **Shared thread-safe.** A thread-safe object performs synchronization internally, so multiple threads can freely access it through its public interface without further synchronization.
>
> **Guarded.** A guarded object can be accessed only with a specific lock held. Guarded objects include those that are encapsulated within other thread-safe objects and published objects that are known to be guarded by a specific lock.

CHAPTER 4

Composing Objects

So far, we've covered the low-level basics of thread safety and synchronization. But we don't want to have to analyze each memory access to ensure that our program is thread-safe; we want to be able to take thread-safe components and safely compose them into larger components or programs. This chapter covers patterns for structuring classes that can make it easier to make them thread-safe and to maintain them without accidentally undermining their safety guarantees.

4.1 Designing a thread-safe class

While it is possible to write a thread-safe program that stores all its state in public static fields, it is a lot harder to verify its thread safety or to modify it so that it remains thread-safe than one that uses encapsulation appropriately. Encapsulation makes it possible to determine that a class is thread-safe without having to examine the entire program.

> The design process for a thread-safe class should include these three basic elements:
> - Identify the variables that form the object's state;
> - Identify the invariants that constrain the state variables;
> - Establish a policy for managing concurrent access to the object's state.

An object's state starts with its fields. If they are all of primitive type, the fields comprise the entire state. Counter in Listing 4.1 has only one field, so the value field comprises its entire state. The state of an object with n primitive fields is just the n-tuple of its field values; the state of a 2D Point is its (x, y) value. If the object has fields that are references to other objects, its state will encompass fields from the referenced objects as well. For example, the state of a LinkedList includes the state of all the link node objects belonging to the list.

The *synchronization policy* defines how an object coordinates access to its state without violating its invariants or postconditions. It specifies what combination of

```
@ThreadSafe
public final class Counter {
    @GuardedBy("this") private long value = 0;

    public synchronized long getValue() {
        return value;
    }
    public synchronized long increment() {
        if (value == Long.MAX_VALUE)
            throw new IllegalStateException("counter overflow");
        return ++value;
    }
}
```

LISTING 4.1. Simple thread-safe counter using the Java monitor pattern.

immutability, thread confinement, and locking is used to maintain thread safety, and which variables are guarded by which locks. To ensure that the class can be analyzed and maintained, document the synchronization policy.

4.1.1 Gathering synchronization requirements

Making a class thread-safe means ensuring that its invariants hold under concurrent access; this requires reasoning about its state. Objects and variables have a *state space*: the range of possible states they can take on. The smaller this state space, the easier it is to reason about. By using final fields wherever practical, you make it simpler to analyze the possible states an object can be in. (In the extreme case, immutable objects can only be in a single state.)

Many classes have invariants that identify certain states as *valid* or *invalid*. The value field in Counter is a long. The state space of a long ranges from Long.MIN_VALUE to Long.MAX_VALUE, but Counter places constraints on value; negative values are not allowed.

Similarly, operations may have postconditions that identify certain *state transitions* as invalid. If the current state of a Counter is 17, the *only* valid next state is 18. When the next state is derived from the current state, the operation is necessarily a compound action. Not all operations impose state transition constraints; when updating a variable that holds the current temperature, its previous state does not affect the computation.

Constraints placed on states or state transitions by invariants and postconditions create additional synchronization or encapsulation requirements. If certain states are invalid, then the underlying state variables must be encapsulated, otherwise client code could put the object into an invalid state. If an operation has invalid state transitions, it must be made atomic. On the other hand, if the class does not impose any such constraints, we may be able to relax encapsulation or serialization requirements to obtain greater flexibility or better performance.

A class can also have invariants that constrain multiple state variables. A number range class, like `NumberRange` in Listing 4.10, typically maintains state variables for the lower and upper bounds of the range. These variables must obey the constraint that the lower bound be less than or equal to the upper bound. Multivariable invariants like this one create atomicity requirements: related variables must be fetched or updated in a single atomic operation. You cannot update one, release and reacquire the lock, and then update the others, since this could involve leaving the object in an invalid state when the lock was released. When multiple variables participate in an invariant, the lock that guards them must be held for the duration of any operation that accesses the related variables.

> You cannot ensure thread safety without understanding an object's invariants and postconditions. Constraints on the valid values or state transitions for state variables can create atomicity and encapsulation requirements.

4.1.2 State-dependent operations

Class invariants and method postconditions constrain the valid states and state transitions for an object. Some objects also have methods with state-based *preconditions*. For example, you cannot remove an item from an empty queue; a queue must be in the "nonempty" state before you can remove an element. Operations with state-based preconditions are called *state-dependent* [CPJ 3].

In a single-threaded program, if a precondition does not hold, the operation has no choice but to fail. But in a concurrent program, the precondition may become true later due to the action of another thread. Concurrent programs add the possibility of waiting until the precondition becomes true, and then proceeding with the operation.

The built-in mechanisms for efficiently waiting for a condition to become true—`wait` and `notify`—are tightly bound to intrinsic locking, and can be difficult to use correctly. To create operations that wait for a precondition to become true before proceeding, it is often easier to use existing library classes, such as blocking queues or semaphores, to provide the desired state-dependent behavior. Blocking library classes such as `BlockingQueue`, `Semaphore`, and other *synchronizers* are covered in Chapter 5; creating state-dependent classes using the low-level mechanisms provided by the platform and class library is covered in Chapter 14.

4.1.3 State ownership

We implied in Section 4.1 that an object's state could be a subset of the fields in the object graph rooted at that object. Why might it be a subset? Under what conditions are fields reachable from a given object *not* part of that object's state?

When defining which variables form an object's state, we want to consider only the data that object *owns*. Ownership is not embodied explicitly in the language, but is instead an element of class design. If you allocate and populate a `HashMap`, you are creating multiple objects: the `HashMap` object, a number of `Map.Entry` objects used by the implementation of `HashMap`, and perhaps other internal objects as well. The logical state of a `HashMap` includes the state of all its `Map.Entry` and internal objects, even though they are implemented as separate objects.

For better or worse, garbage collection lets us avoid thinking carefully about ownership. When passing an object to a method in C++, you have to think fairly carefully about whether you are transferring ownership, engaging in a short-term loan, or envisioning long-term joint ownership. In Java, all these same ownership models are possible, but the garbage collector reduces the cost of many of the common errors in reference sharing, enabling less-than-precise thinking about ownership.

In many cases, ownership and encapsulation go together—the object encapsulates the state it owns and owns the state it encapsulates. It is the owner of a given state variable that gets to decide on the locking protocol used to maintain the integrity of that variable's state. Ownership implies control, but once you publish a reference to a mutable object, you no longer have exclusive control; at best, you might have "shared ownership". A class usually does not own the objects passed to its methods or constructors, unless the method is designed to explicitly transfer ownership of objects passed in (such as the synchronized collection wrapper factory methods).

Collection classes often exhibit a form of "split ownership", in which the collection owns the state of the collection infrastructure, but client code owns the objects stored in the collection. An example is `ServletContext` from the servlet framework. `ServletContext` provides a `Map`-like object container service to servlets where they can register and retrieve application objects by name with `setAttribute` and `getAttribute`. The `ServletContext` object implemented by the servlet container must be thread-safe, because it will necessarily be accessed by multiple threads. Servlets need not use synchronization when calling `set-Attribute` and `getAttribute`, but they may have to use synchronization when *using* the objects stored in the `ServletContext`. These objects are owned by the application; they are being stored for safekeeping by the servlet container on the application's behalf. Like all shared objects, they must be shared safely; in order to prevent interference from multiple threads accessing the same object concurrently, they should either be thread-safe, effectively immutable, or explicitly guarded by a lock.[1]

4.2   Instance confinement

If an object is not thread-safe, several techniques can still let it be used safely in a multithreaded program. You can ensure that it is only accessed from a single thread (thread confinement), or that all access to it is properly guarded by a lock.

---

[1]. Interestingly, the `HttpSession` object, which performs a similar function in the servlet framework, may have stricter requirements. Because the servlet container may access the objects in the `HttpSession` so they can be serialized for replication or passivation, they must be thread-safe because the container will be accessing them as well as the web application. (We say "may have" since replication and passivation is outside of the servlet specification but is a common feature of servlet containers.)

Encapsulation simplifies making classes thread-safe by promoting *instance confinement*, often just called *confinement* [CPJ 2.3.3]. When an object is encapsulated within another object, all code paths that have access to the encapsulated object are known and can be therefore be analyzed more easily than if that object were accessible to the entire program. Combining confinement with an appropriate locking discipline can ensure that otherwise non-thread-safe objects are used in a thread-safe manner.

> Encapsulating data within an object confines access to the data to the object's methods, making it easier to ensure that the data is always accessed with the appropriate lock held.

Confined objects must not escape their intended scope. An object may be confined to a class instance (such as a private class member), a lexical scope (such as a local variable), or a thread (such as an object that is passed from method to method within a thread, but not supposed to be shared across threads). Objects don't escape on their own, of course—they need help from the developer, who assists by publishing the object beyond its intended scope.

PersonSet in Listing 4.2 illustrates how confinement and locking can work together to make a class thread-safe even when its component state variables are not. The state of PersonSet is managed by a HashSet, which is not thread-safe. But because mySet is private and not allowed to escape, the HashSet is confined to the PersonSet. The only code paths that can access mySet are addPerson and containsPerson, and each of these acquires the lock on the PersonSet. All its state is guarded by its intrinsic lock, making PersonSet thread-safe.

```
@ThreadSafe
public class PersonSet {
    @GuardedBy("this")
    private final Set<Person> mySet = new HashSet<Person>();

    public synchronized void addPerson(Person p) {
        mySet.add(p);
    }

    public synchronized boolean containsPerson(Person p) {
        return mySet.contains(p);
    }
}
```

LISTING 4.2. Using confinement to ensure thread safety.

This example makes no assumptions about the thread-safety of Person, but if it is mutable, additional synchronization will be needed when accessing a Person retrieved from a PersonSet. The most reliable way to do this would be to make

Person thread-safe; less reliable would be to guard the Person objects with a lock and ensure that all clients follow the protocol of acquiring the appropriate lock before accessing the Person.

Instance confinement is one of the easiest ways to build thread-safe classes. It also allows flexibility in the choice of locking strategy; PersonSet happened to use its own intrinsic lock to guard its state, but any lock, consistently used, would do just as well. Instance confinement also allows different state variables to be guarded by different locks. (For an example of a class that uses multiple lock objects to guard its state, see ServerStatus on page 236.)

There are many examples of confinement in the platform class libraries, including some classes that exist solely to turn non-thread-safe classes into thread-safe ones. The basic collection classes such as ArrayList and HashMap are not thread-safe, but the class library provides wrapper factory methods (Collections.synchronizedList and friends) so they can be used safely in multi-threaded environments. These factories use the Decorator pattern (Gamma et al., 1995) to wrap the collection with a synchronized wrapper object; the wrapper implements each method of the appropriate interface as a synchronized method that forwards the request to the underlying collection object. So long as the wrapper object holds the only reachable reference to the underlying collection (i.e., the underlying collection is confined to the wrapper), the wrapper object is then thread-safe. The Javadoc for these methods warns that all access to the underlying collection must be made through the wrapper.

Of course, it is still possible to violate confinement by publishing a supposedly confined object; if an object is intended to be confined to a specific scope, then letting it escape from that scope is a bug. Confined objects can also escape by publishing other objects such as iterators or inner class instances that may indirectly publish the confined objects.

> Confinement makes it easier to build thread-safe classes because a class that confines its state can be analyzed for thread safety without having to examine the whole program.

4.2.1 The Java monitor pattern

Following the principle of instance confinement to its logical conclusion leads you to the *Java monitor pattern*.[2] An object following the Java monitor pattern encapsulates all its mutable state and guards it with the object's own intrinsic lock.

Counter in Listing 4.1 shows a typical example of this pattern. It encapsulates one state variable, value, and all access to that state variable is through the methods of Counter, which are all synchronized.

---

2. The Java monitor pattern is inspired by Hoare's work on *monitors* (Hoare, 1974), though there are significant differences between this pattern and a true monitor. The bytecode instructions for entering and exiting a synchronized block are even called monitorenter and monitorexit, and Java's built-in (intrinsic) locks are sometimes called *monitor locks* or *monitors*.

The Java monitor pattern is used by many library classes, such as `Vector` and `Hashtable`. Sometimes a more sophisticated synchronization policy is needed; Chapter 11 shows how to improve scalability through finer-grained locking strategies. The primary advantage of the Java monitor pattern is its simplicity.

The Java monitor pattern is merely a convention; any lock object could be used to guard an object's state so long as it is used consistently. Listing 4.3 illustrates a class that uses a private lock to guard its state.

```
public class PrivateLock {
    private final Object myLock = new Object();
    @GuardedBy("myLock") Widget widget;

    void someMethod() {
        synchronized(myLock) {
            // Access or modify the state of widget
        }
    }
}
```

LISTING 4.3. Guarding state with a private lock.

There are advantages to using a private lock object instead of an object's intrinsic lock (or any other publicly accessible lock). Making the lock object private encapsulates the lock so that client code cannot acquire it, whereas a publicly accessible lock allows client code to participate in its synchronization policy—correctly or incorrectly. Clients that improperly acquire another object's lock could cause liveness problems, and verifying that a publicly accessible lock is properly used requires examining the entire program rather than a single class.

4.2.2   Example: tracking fleet vehicles

`Counter` in Listing 4.1 is a concise, but trivial, example of the Java monitor pattern. Let's build a slightly less trivial example: a "vehicle tracker" for dispatching fleet vehicles such as taxicabs, police cars, or delivery trucks. We'll build it first using the monitor pattern, and then see how to relax some of the encapsulation requirements while retaining thread safety.

Each vehicle is identified by a `String` and has a location represented by (x, y) coordinates. The `VehicleTracker` classes encapsulate the identity and locations of the known vehicles, making them well-suited as a data model in a model-view-controller GUI application where it might be shared by a view thread and multiple updater threads. The view thread would fetch the names and locations of the vehicles and render them on a display:

```
Map<String, Point> locations = vehicles.getLocations();
for (String key : locations.keySet())
    renderVehicle(key, locations.get(key));
```

Similarly, the updater threads would modify vehicle locations with data received from GPS devices or entered manually by a dispatcher through a GUI interface:

```
void vehicleMoved(VehicleMovedEvent evt) {
    Point loc = evt.getNewLocation();
    vehicles.setLocation(evt.getVehicleId(), loc.x, loc.y);
}
```

Since the view thread and the updater threads will access the data model concurrently, it must be thread-safe. Listing 4.4 shows an implementation of the vehicle tracker using the Java monitor pattern that uses `MutablePoint` in Listing 4.5 for representing the vehicle locations.

Even though `MutablePoint` is not thread-safe, the tracker class is. Neither the map nor any of the mutable points it contains is ever published. When we need to return vehicle locations to callers, the appropriate values are copied using either the `MutablePoint` copy constructor or `deepCopy`, which creates a new `Map` whose values are copies of the keys and values from the old `Map`.[3]

This implementation maintains thread safety in part by copying mutable data before returning it to the client. This is usually not a performance issue, but could become one *if* the set of vehicles is very large.[4] Another consequence of copying the data on each call to `getLocation` is that the contents of the returned collection do not change even if the underlying locations change. Whether this is good or bad depends on your requirements. It could be a benefit if there are internal consistency requirements on the location set, in which case returning a consistent snapshot is critical, or a drawback if callers require up-to-date information for each vehicle and therefore need to refresh their snapshot more often.

4.3 Delegating thread safety

All but the most trivial objects are composite objects. The Java monitor pattern is useful when building classes from scratch or composing classes out of objects that are not thread-safe. But what if the components of our class are already thread-safe? Do we need to add an additional layer of thread safety? The answer is ... "it depends". In some cases a composite made of thread-safe components is thread-safe (Listings 4.7 and 4.9), and in others it is merely a good start (Listing 4.10).

In `CountingFactorizer` on page 23, we added an `AtomicLong` to an otherwise stateless object, and the resulting composite object was still thread-safe. Since the state of `CountingFactorizer` *is* the state of the thread-safe `AtomicLong`, and since `CountingFactorizer` imposes no additional validity constraints on the state of the

---

3. Note that `deepCopy` can't just wrap the Map with an `unmodifiableMap`, because that protects only the *collection* from modification; it does not prevent callers from modifying the mutable objects stored in it. For the same reason, populating the `HashMap` in `deepCopy` via a copy constructor wouldn't work either, because only the *references* to the points would be copied, not the point objects themselves.

4. Because `deepCopy` is called from a `synchronized` method, the tracker's intrinsic lock is held for the duration of what might be a long-running copy operation, and this could degrade the responsiveness of the user interface when many vehicles are being tracked.

```java
@ThreadSafe
public class MonitorVehicleTracker {
    @GuardedBy("this")
    private final Map<String, MutablePoint> locations;

    public MonitorVehicleTracker(
            Map<String, MutablePoint> locations) {
        this.locations = deepCopy(locations);
    }

    public synchronized Map<String, MutablePoint> getLocations() {
        return deepCopy(locations);
    }

    public synchronized MutablePoint getLocation(String id) {
        MutablePoint loc = locations.get(id);
        return loc == null ? null : new MutablePoint(loc);
    }

    public synchronized void setLocation(String id, int x, int y) {
        MutablePoint loc = locations.get(id);
        if (loc == null)
            throw new IllegalArgumentException("No such ID: " + id);
        loc.x = x;
        loc.y = y;
    }

    private static Map<String, MutablePoint> deepCopy(
            Map<String, MutablePoint> m) {
        Map<String, MutablePoint> result =
                new HashMap<String, MutablePoint>();
        for (String id : m.keySet())
            result.put(id, new MutablePoint(m.get(id)));
        return Collections.unmodifiableMap(result);
    }
}

public class MutablePoint { /* Listing 4.5 */ }
```

LISTING 4.4. Monitor-based vehicle tracker implementation.

```
@NotThreadSafe
public class MutablePoint {
    public int x, y;

    public MutablePoint() { x = 0; y = 0; }
    public MutablePoint(MutablePoint p) {
        this.x = p.x;
        this.y = p.y;
    }
}
```

LISTING 4.5. *Mutable point class similar to* java.awt.Point.

counter, it is easy to see that CountingFactorizer is thread-safe. We could say that CountingFactorizer *delegates* its thread safety responsibilities to the AtomicLong: CountingFactorizer is thread-safe because AtomicLong is.[5]

4.3.1 Example: vehicle tracker using delegation

As a more substantial example of delegation, let's construct a version of the vehicle tracker that delegates to a thread-safe class. We store the locations in a Map, so we start with a thread-safe Map implementation, ConcurrentHashMap. We also store the location using an immutable Point class instead of MutablePoint, shown in Listing 4.6.

```
@Immutable
public class Point {
    public final int x, y;

    public Point(int x, int y) {
        this.x = x;
        this.y = y;
    }
}
```

LISTING 4.6. *Immutable* Point *class used by* DelegatingVehicleTracker.

Point is thread-safe because it is immutable. Immutable values can be freely shared and published, so we no longer need to copy the locations when returning them.

---

5. If count were not final, the thread safety analysis of CountingFactorizer would be more complicated. If CountingFactorizer could modify count to reference a different AtomicLong, we would then have to ensure that this update was visible to all threads that might access the count, and that there were no race conditions regarding the value of the count reference. This is another good reason to use final fields wherever practical.

DelegatingVehicleTracker in Listing 4.7 does not use any explicit synchronization; all access to state is managed by ConcurrentHashMap, and all the keys and values of the Map are immutable.

```
@ThreadSafe
public class DelegatingVehicleTracker {
    private final ConcurrentMap<String, Point> locations;
    private final Map<String, Point> unmodifiableMap;

    public DelegatingVehicleTracker(Map<String, Point> points) {
        locations = new ConcurrentHashMap<String, Point>(points);
        unmodifiableMap = Collections.unmodifiableMap(locations);
    }

    public Map<String, Point> getLocations() {
        return unmodifiableMap;
    }

    public Point getLocation(String id) {
        return locations.get(id);
    }

    public void setLocation(String id, int x, int y) {
        if (locations.replace(id, new Point(x, y)) == null)
            throw new IllegalArgumentException(
                "invalid vehicle name: " + id);
    }
}
```

LISTING 4.7. *Delegating thread safety to a* ConcurrentHashMap.

If we had used the original MutablePoint class instead of Point, we would be breaking encapsulation by letting getLocations publish a reference to mutable state that is not thread-safe. Notice that we've changed the behavior of the vehicle tracker class slightly; while the monitor version returned a snapshot of the locations, the delegating version returns an unmodifiable but "live" view of the vehicle locations. This means that if thread *A* calls getLocations and thread *B* later modifies the location of some of the points, those changes are reflected in the Map returned to thread *A*. As we remarked earlier, this can be a benefit (more up-to-date data) or a liability (potentially inconsistent view of the fleet), depending on your requirements.

If an unchanging view of the fleet is required, getLocations could instead return a shallow copy of the locations map. Since the contents of the Map are immutable, only the structure of the Map, not the contents, must be copied, as shown in Listing 4.8 (which returns a plain HashMap, since getLocations did not promise to return a thread-safe Map).

```
public Map<String, Point> getLocations() {
    return Collections.unmodifiableMap(
            new HashMap<String, Point>(locations));
}
```

LISTING 4.8. Returning a static copy of the location set instead of a "live" one.

4.3.2   Independent state variables

The delegation examples so far delegate to a single, thread-safe state variable. We can also delegate thread safety to more than one underlying state variable as long as those underlying state variables are *independent*, meaning that the composite class does not impose any invariants involving the multiple state variables.

VisualComponent in Listing 4.9 is a graphical component that allows clients to register listeners for mouse and keystroke events. It maintains a list of registered listeners of each type, so that when an event occurs the appropriate listeners can be invoked. But there is no relationship between the set of mouse listeners and key listeners; the two are independent, and therefore VisualComponent can delegate its thread safety obligations to two underlying thread-safe lists.

```
public class VisualComponent {
    private final List<KeyListener> keyListeners
        = new CopyOnWriteArrayList<KeyListener>();
    private final List<MouseListener> mouseListeners
        = new CopyOnWriteArrayList<MouseListener>();

    public void addKeyListener(KeyListener listener) {
        keyListeners.add(listener);
    }

    public void addMouseListener(MouseListener listener) {
        mouseListeners.add(listener);
    }

    public void removeKeyListener(KeyListener listener) {
        keyListeners.remove(listener);
    }

    public void removeMouseListener(MouseListener listener) {
        mouseListeners.remove(listener);
    }
}
```

LISTING 4.9. Delegating thread safety to multiple underlying state variables.

VisualComponent uses a CopyOnWriteArrayList to store each listener list; this is a thread-safe List implementation particularly suited for managing listener lists (see Section 5.2.3). Each List is thread-safe, and because there are no constraints coupling the state of one to the state of the other, VisualComponent can delegate its thread safety responsibilities to the underlying mouseListeners and keyListeners objects.

4.3.3 When delegation fails

Most composite classes are not as simple as VisualComponent: they have invariants that relate their component state variables. NumberRange in Listing 4.10 uses two AtomicIntegers to manage its state, but imposes an additional constraint—that the first number be less than or equal to the second.

```
public class NumberRange {
    // INVARIANT: lower <= upper
    private final AtomicInteger lower = new AtomicInteger(0);
    private final AtomicInteger upper = new AtomicInteger(0);

    public void setLower(int i) {
        // Warning -- unsafe check-then-act
        if (i > upper.get())
            throw new IllegalArgumentException(
                    "can't set lower to " + i + " > upper");
        lower.set(i);
    }

    public void setUpper(int i) {
        // Warning -- unsafe check-then-act
        if (i < lower.get())
            throw new IllegalArgumentException(
                    "can't set upper to " + i + " < lower");
        upper.set(i);
    }

    public boolean isInRange(int i) {
        return (i >= lower.get() && i <= upper.get());
    }
}
```

LISTING 4.10. Number range class that does not sufficiently protect its invariants. *Don't do this.*

NumberRange is not thread-safe; it does not preserve the invariant that constrains lower and upper. The setLower and setUpper methods *attempt* to respect this invariant, but do so poorly. Both setLower and setUpper are check-then-act sequences, but they do not use sufficient locking to make them atomic. If the number range holds $(0, 10)$, and one thread calls setLower(5) while another thread calls `setUpper(4)`, with some unlucky timing both will pass the checks in the setters and both modifications will be applied. The result is that the range now holds (5, 4)—an invalid state. So while the underlying `AtomicIntegers` are thread-safe, the composite class is not. Because the underlying state variables `lower` and `upper` are not independent, `NumberRange` cannot simply delegate thread safety to its thread-safe state variables.

`NumberRange` could be made thread-safe by using locking to maintain its invariants, such as guarding `lower` and `upper` with a common lock. It must also avoid publishing `lower` and `upper` to prevent clients from subverting its invariants.

If a class has compound actions, as `NumberRange` does, delegation alone is again not a suitable approach for thread safety. In these cases, the class must provide its own locking to ensure that compound actions are atomic, unless the entire compound action can also be delegated to the underlying state variables.

> If a class is composed of multiple *independent* thread-safe state variables and has no operations that have any invalid state transitions, then it can delegate thread safety to the underlying state variables.

The problem that prevented `NumberRange` from being thread-safe even though its state components were thread-safe is very similar to one of the rules about volatile variables described in Section 3.1.4: a variable is suitable for being declared `volatile` only if it does not participate in invariants involving other state variables.

4.3.4 Publishing underlying state variables

When you delegate thread safety to an object's underlying state variables, under what conditions can you publish those variables so that other classes can modify them as well? Again, the answer depends on what invariants your class imposes on those variables. While the underlying `value` field in `Counter` could take on any integer value, `Counter` constrains it to take on only positive values, and the increment operation constrains the set of valid next states given any current state. If you were to make the `value` field public, clients could change it to an invalid value, so publishing it would render the class incorrect. On the other hand, if a variable represents the current temperature or the ID of the last user to log on, then having another class modify this value at any time probably would not violate any invariants, so publishing this variable might be acceptable. (It still may not be a good idea, since publishing mutable variables constrains future development and opportunities for subclassing, but it would not *necessarily* render the class not thread-safe.)

> If a state variable is thread-safe, does not participate in any invariants that constrain its value, and has no prohibited state transitions for any of its operations, then it can safely be published.

For example, it would be safe to publish `mouseListeners` or `keyListeners` in `VisualComponent`. Because `VisualComponent` does not impose any constraints on the valid states of its listener lists, these fields could be made public or otherwise published without compromising thread safety.

4.3.5 Example: vehicle tracker that publishes its state

Let's construct another version of the vehicle tracker that publishes its underlying mutable state. Again, we need to modify the interface a little bit to accommodate this change, this time using mutable but thread-safe points.

```
@ThreadSafe
public class SafePoint {
    @GuardedBy("this") private int x, y;

    private SafePoint(int[] a) { this(a[0], a[1]); }

    public SafePoint(SafePoint p) { this(p.get()); }

    public SafePoint(int x, int y) {
        this.x = x;
        this.y = y;
    }

    public synchronized int[] get() {
        return new int[] { x, y };
    }

    public synchronized void set(int x, int y) {
        this.x = x;
        this.y = y;
    }
}
```

LISTING 4.11. Thread-safe mutable point class.

`SafePoint` in Listing 4.11 provides a getter that retrieves both the x and y values at once by returning a two-element array.[6] If we provided separate getters

---

6. The private constructor exists to avoid the race condition that would occur if the copy constructor were implemented as `this(p.x, p.y)`; this is an example of the *private constructor capture idiom* (Bloch and Gafter, 2005).

for x and y, then the values could change between the time one coordinate is
retrieved and the other, resulting in a caller seeing an inconsistent value: an (x, y)
location where the vehicle never was. Using SafePoint, we can construct a vehicle
tracker that publishes the underlying mutable state without undermining thread
safety, as shown in the PublishingVehicleTracker class in Listing 4.12.

```
@ThreadSafe
public class PublishingVehicleTracker {
    private final Map<String, SafePoint> locations;
    private final Map<String, SafePoint> unmodifiableMap;

    public PublishingVehicleTracker(
                            Map<String, SafePoint> locations) {
        this.locations
            = new ConcurrentHashMap<String, SafePoint>(locations);
        this.unmodifiableMap
            = Collections.unmodifiableMap(this.locations);
    }

    public Map<String, SafePoint> getLocations() {
        return unmodifiableMap;
    }

    public SafePoint getLocation(String id) {
        return locations.get(id);
    }

    public void setLocation(String id, int x, int y) {
        if (!locations.containsKey(id))
            throw new IllegalArgumentException(
                "invalid vehicle name: " + id);
        locations.get(id).set(x, y);
    }
}
```

LISTING 4.12. *Vehicle tracker that safely publishes underlying state.*

PublishingVehicleTracker derives its thread safety from delegation to an underlying ConcurrentHashMap, but this time the contents of the Map are thread-safe
mutable points rather than immutable ones. The getLocation method returns an
unmodifiable copy of the underlying Map. Callers cannot add or remove vehicles,
but could change the location of one of the vehicles by mutating the SafePoint
values in the returned Map. Again, the "live" nature of the Map may be a benefit
or a drawback, depending on the requirements. PublishingVehicleTracker is
thread-safe, but would not be so if it imposed any additional constraints on the
valid values for vehicle locations. If it needed to be able to "veto" changes to

vehicle locations or to take action when a location changes, the approach taken by `PublishingVehicleTracker` would not be appropriate.

4.4 Adding functionality to existing thread-safe classes

The Java class library contains many useful "building block" classes. Reusing existing classes is often preferable to creating new ones: reuse can reduce development effort, development risk (because the existing components are already tested), and maintenance cost. Sometimes a thread-safe class that supports all of the operations we want already exists, but often the best we can find is a class that supports *almost* all the operations we want, and then we need to add a new operation to it without undermining its thread safety.

As an example, let's say we need a thread-safe `List` with an atomic put-if-absent operation. The synchronized `List` implementations nearly do the job, since they provide the `contains` and `add` methods from which we can construct a put-if-absent operation.

The concept of put-if-absent is straightforward enough—check to see if an element is in the collection before adding it, and do not add it if it is already there. (Your "check-then-act" warning bells should be going off now.) The requirement that the class be thread-safe implicitly adds another requirement—that operations like put-if-absent be *atomic*. Any reasonable interpretation suggests that, if you take a `List` that does not contain object X, and add X twice with put-if-absent, the resulting collection contains only one copy of X. But, if put-if-absent were not atomic, with some unlucky timing two threads could both see that X was not present and both add X, resulting in two copies of X.

The safest way to add a new atomic operation is to modify the original class to support the desired operation, but this is not always possible because you may not have access to the source code or may not be free to modify it. If you can modify the original class, you need to understand the implementation's synchronization policy so that you can enhance it in a manner consistent with its original design. Adding the new method directly to the class means that all the code that implements the synchronization policy for that class is still contained in one source file, facilitating easier comprehension and maintenance.

Another approach is to extend the class, assuming it was designed for extension. `BetterVector` in Listing 4.13 extends `Vector` to add a `putIfAbsent` method. Extending `Vector` is straightforward enough, but not all classes expose enough of their state to subclasses to admit this approach.

Extension is more fragile than adding code directly to a class, because the implementation of the synchronization policy is now distributed over multiple, separately maintained source files. If the underlying class were to change its synchronization policy by choosing a different lock to guard its state variables, the subclass would subtly and silently break, because it no longer used the right lock to control concurrent access to the base class's state. (The synchronization policy of `Vector` is fixed by its specification, so `BetterVector` would not suffer from this problem.)

```
@ThreadSafe
public class BetterVector<E> extends Vector<E> {
    public synchronized boolean putIfAbsent(E x) {
        boolean absent = !contains(x);
        if (absent)
            add(x);
        return absent;
    }
}
```

LISTING 4.13. Extending Vector to have a put-if-absent method.

4.4.1 Client-side locking

For an ArrayList wrapped with a Collections.synchronizedList wrapper, neither of these approaches—adding a method to the original class or extending the
class—works because the client code does not even know the class of the List
object returned from the synchronized wrapper factories. A third strategy is to
extend the functionality of the class without extending the class itself by placing
extension code in a "helper" class.

Listing 4.14 shows a failed attempt to create a helper class with an atomic
put-if-absent operation for operating on a thread-safe List.

```
@NotThreadSafe
public class ListHelper<E> {
    public List<E> list =
        Collections.synchronizedList(new ArrayList<E>());
    ...
    public synchronized boolean putIfAbsent(E x) {
        boolean absent = !list.contains(x);
        if (absent)
            list.add(x);
        return absent;
    }
}
```

LISTING 4.14. Non-thread-safe attempt to implement put-if-absent. *Don't do this.*

Why wouldn't this work? After all, putIfAbsent is synchronized, right? The
problem is that it synchronizes on the *wrong lock*. Whatever lock the List uses
to guard its state, it sure isn't the lock on the ListHelper. ListHelper provides
only the *illusion of synchronization*; the various list operations, while all synchronized, use different locks, which means that putIfAbsent is *not* atomic relative to
other operations on the List. So there is no guarantee that another thread won't
modify the list while putIfAbsent is executing.

To make this approach work, we have to use the *same* lock that the List uses by using *client-side locking* or *external locking*. Client-side locking entails guarding client code that uses some object *X* with the lock *X* uses to guard its own state. In order to use client-side locking, you must know what lock *X* uses.

The documentation for Vector and the synchronized wrapper classes states, albeit obliquely, that they support client-side locking, by using the intrinsic lock for the Vector or the wrapper collection (not the wrapped collection). Listing 4.15 shows a putIfAbsent operation on a thread-safe List that correctly uses client-side locking.

```
@ThreadSafe
public class ListHelper<E> {
    public List<E> list =
        Collections.synchronizedList(new ArrayList<E>());
    ...
    public boolean putIfAbsent(E x) {
        synchronized (list) {
            boolean absent = !list.contains(x);
            if (absent)
                list.add(x);
            return absent;
        }
    }
}
```

LISTING 4.15. Implementing put-if-absent with client-side locking.

If extending a class to add another atomic operation is fragile because it distributes the locking code for a class over multiple classes in an object hierarchy, client-side locking is even more fragile because it entails putting locking code for class *C* into classes that are totally unrelated to *C*. Exercise care when using client-side locking on classes that do not commit to their locking strategy.

Client-side locking has a lot in common with class extension—they both couple the behavior of the derived class to the implementation of the base class. Just as extension violates encapsulation of implementation [EJ Item 14], client-side locking violates encapsulation of synchronization policy.

4.4.2 Composition

There is a less fragile alternative for adding an atomic operation to an existing class: *composition*. ImprovedList in Listing 4.16 implements the List operations by delegating them to an underlying List instance, and adds an atomic put-IfAbsent method. (Like Collections.synchronizedList and other collections wrappers, ImprovedList assumes that once a list is passed to its constructor, the client will not use the underlying list directly again, accessing it only through the ImprovedList.)

```
@ThreadSafe
public class ImprovedList<T> implements List<T> {
    private final List<T> list;

    public ImprovedList(List<T> list) { this.list = list; }

    public synchronized boolean putIfAbsent(T x) {
        boolean contains = list.contains(x);
        if (contains)
            list.add(x);
        return !contains;
    }

    public synchronized void clear() { list.clear(); }
    // ... similarly delegate other List methods
}
```

LISTING 4.16. Implementing put-if-absent using composition.

ImprovedList adds an additional level of locking using its own intrinsic lock. It does not care whether the underlying List is thread-safe, because it provides its own consistent locking that provides thread safety even if the List is not thread-safe or changes its locking implementation. While the extra layer of synchronization may add some small performance penalty,[7] the implementation in ImprovedList is less fragile than attempting to mimic the locking strategy of another object. In effect, we've used the Java monitor pattern to encapsulate an existing List, and this is guaranteed to provide thread safety so long as our class holds the only outstanding reference to the underlying List.

4.5 Documenting synchronization policies

Documentation is one of the most powerful (and, sadly, most underutilized) tools for managing thread safety. Users look to the documentation to find out if a class is thread-safe, and maintainers look to the documentation to understand the implementation strategy so they can maintain it without inadvertently compromising safety. Unfortunately, both of these constituencies usually find less information in the documentation than they'd like.

> Document a class's thread safety guarantees for its clients; document its synchronization policy for its maintainers.

---

7. The penalty will be small because the synchronization on the underlying List is guaranteed to be uncontended and therefore fast; see Chapter 11.

Each use of synchronized, volatile, or any thread-safe class reflects a *synchronization policy* defining a strategy for ensuring the integrity of data in the face of concurrent access. That policy is an element of your program's design, and should be documented. Of course, the best time to document design decisions is at design time. Weeks or months later, the details may be a blur—so write it down before you forget.

Crafting a synchronization policy requires a number of decisions: which variables to make volatile, which variables to guard with locks, which lock(s) guard which variables, which variables to make immutable or confine to a thread, which operations must be atomic, etc. Some of these are strictly implementation details and should be documented for the sake of future maintainers, but some affect the publicly observable locking behavior of your class and should be documented as part of its specification.

At the very least, document the thread safety guarantees made by a class. Is it thread-safe? Does it make callbacks with a lock held? Are there any specific locks that affect its behavior? Don't force clients to make risky guesses. If you don't want to commit to supporting client-side locking, that's fine, but say so. If you want clients to be able to create new atomic operations on your class, as we did in Section 4.4, you need to document which locks they should acquire to do so safely. If you use locks to guard state, document this for future maintainers, because it's so easy—the @GuardedBy annotation will do the trick. If you use more subtle means to maintain thread safety, document them because they may not be obvious to maintainers.

The current state of affairs in thread safety documentation, even in the platform library classes, is not encouraging. How many times have you looked at the Javadoc for a class and wondered whether it was thread-safe?[8] Most classes don't offer any clue either way. Many official Java technology specifications, such as servlets and JDBC, woefully underdocument their thread safety promises and requirements.

While prudence suggests that we not assume behaviors that aren't part of the specification, we have work to get done, and we are often faced with a choice of bad assumptions. Should we assume an object is thread-safe because it seems that it ought to be? Should we assume that access to an object can be made thread-safe by acquiring its lock first? (This risky technique works only if we control *all* the code that accesses that object; otherwise, it provides only the illusion of thread safety.) Neither choice is very satisfying.

To make matters worse, our intuition may often be wrong on which classes are "probably thread-safe" and which are not. As an example, java.text.SimpleDateFormat isn't thread-safe, but the Javadoc neglected to mention this until JDK 1.4. That this particular class isn't thread-safe comes as a surprise to many developers. How many programs mistakenly create a shared instance of a non-thread-safe object and used it from multiple threads, unaware that this might cause erroneous results under heavy load?

The problem with SimpleDateFormat could be avoided by not assuming a class is thread-safe if it doesn't say so. On the other hand, it is impossible to

---

8. If you've never wondered this, we admire your optimism.

develop a servlet-based application without making some pretty questionable assumptions about the thread safety of container-provided objects like HttpSession. Don't make your customers or colleagues have to make guesses like this.

4.5.1 Interpreting vague documentation

Many Java technology specifications are silent, or at least unforthcoming, about thread safety guarantees and requirements for interfaces such as ServletContext, HttpSession, or DataSource.[9] Since these interfaces are implemented by your container or database vendor, you often can't look at the code to see what it does. Besides, you don't want to rely on the implementation details of one particular JDBC driver—you want to be compliant with the standard so your code works properly with any JDBC driver. But the words "thread" and "concurrent" do not appear at all in the JDBC specification, and appear frustratingly rarely in the servlet specification. So what do you do?

You are going to have to guess. One way to improve the quality of your guess is to interpret the specification from the perspective of someone who will *implement* it (such as a container or database vendor), as opposed to someone who will merely use it. Servlets are always called from a container-managed thread, and it is safe to assume that if there is more than one such thread, the container knows this. The servlet container makes available certain objects that provide service to multiple servlets, such as HttpSession or ServletContext. So the servlet container should expect to have these objects accessed concurrently, since it has created multiple threads and called methods like Servlet.service from them that could reasonably be expected to access the ServletContext.

Since it is impossible to imagine a single-threaded context in which these objects would be useful, one has to assume that they have been made thread-safe, even though the specification does not explicitly require this. Besides, if they required client-side locking, on what lock should the client code synchronize? The documentation doesn't say, and it seems absurd to guess. This "reasonable assumption" is further bolstered by the examples in the specification and official tutorials that show how to access ServletContext or HttpSession and do not use any client-side synchronization.

On the other hand, the objects placed in the ServletContext or HttpSession with setAttribute are owned by the web application, not the servlet container. The servlet specification does not suggest any mechanism for coordinating concurrent access to shared attributes. So attributes stored by the container on behalf of the web application should be thread-safe or effectively immutable. If all the container did was store these attributes on behalf of the web application, another option would be to ensure that they are consistently guarded by a lock when accessed from servlet application code. But because the container may want to serialize objects in the HttpSession for replication or passivation purposes, and the servlet container can't possibly know your locking protocol, you should make them thread-safe.

---

9. We find it particularly frustrating that these omissions persist despite multiple major revisions of the specifications.

One can make a similar inference about the JDBC `DataSource` interface, which represents a pool of reusable database connections. A `DataSource` provides service to an application, and it doesn't make much sense in the context of a single-threaded application. It is hard to imagine a use case that doesn't involve calling `getConnection` from multiple threads. And, as with servlets, the examples in the JDBC specification do not suggest the need for any client-side locking in the many code examples using `DataSource`. So, even though the specification doesn't promise that `DataSource` is thread-safe or require container vendors to provide a thread-safe implementation, by the same "it would be absurd if it weren't" argument, we have no choice but to assume that `DataSource.getConnection` does not require additional client-side locking.

On the other hand, we would not make the same argument about the JDBC `Connection` objects dispensed by the `DataSource`, since these are not necessarily intended to be shared by other activities until they are returned to the pool. So if an activity that obtains a JDBC `Connection` spans multiple threads, it must take responsibility for ensuring that access to the `Connection` is properly guarded by synchronization. (In most applications, activities that use a JDBC `Connection` are implemented so as to confine the `Connection` to a specific thread anyway.)

CHAPTER 5

Building Blocks

The last chapter explored several techniques for constructing thread-safe classes, including delegating thread safety to existing thread-safe classes. Where practical, delegation is one of the most effective strategies for creating thread-safe classes: just let existing thread-safe classes manage all the state.

The platform libraries include a rich set of concurrent building blocks, such as thread-safe collections and a variety of *synchronizers* that can coordinate the control flow of cooperating threads. This chapter covers the most useful concurrent building blocks, especially those introduced in Java 5.0 and Java 6, and some patterns for using them to structure concurrent applications.

5.1 Synchronized collections

The *synchronized collection classes* include Vector and Hashtable, part of the original JDK, as well as their cousins added in JDK 1.2, the synchronized wrapper classes created by the Collections.synchronizedXxx factory methods. These classes achieve thread safety by encapsulating their state and synchronizing every public method so that only one thread at a time can access the collection state.

5.1.1 Problems with synchronized collections

The synchronized collections are thread-safe, but you may sometimes need to use additional client-side locking to guard compound actions. Common compound actions on collections include iteration (repeatedly fetch elements until the collection is exhausted), navigation (find the next element after this one according to some order), and conditional operations such as put-if-absent (check if a Map has a mapping for key K, and if not, add the mapping (K, V)). With a synchronized collection, these compound actions are still technically thread-safe even without client-side locking, but they may not behave as you might expect when other threads can concurrently modify the collection.

Listing 5.1 shows two methods that operate on a Vector, getLast and delete-Last, both of which are check-then-act sequences. Each calls size to determine the size of the array and uses the resulting value to retrieve or remove the last element.

```
public static Object getLast(Vector list) {
    int lastIndex = list.size() - 1;
    return list.get(lastIndex);
}

public static void deleteLast(Vector list) {
    int lastIndex = list.size() - 1;
    list.remove(lastIndex);
}
```

LISTING 5.1. Compound actions on a `Vector` that may produce confusing results.

These methods seem harmless, and in a sense they are—they can't corrupt the `Vector`, no matter how many threads call them simultaneously. But the caller of these methods might have a different opinion. If thread *A* calls `getLast` on a `Vector` with ten elements, thread *B* calls `deleteLast` on the same `Vector`, and the operations are interleaved as shown in Figure 5.1, `getLast` throws `ArrayIndexOutOfBoundsException`. Between the call to `size` and the subsequent call to `get` in `getLast`, the `Vector` shrank and the index computed in the first step is no longer valid. This is perfectly consistent with the specification of `Vector`—it throws an exception if asked for a nonexistent element. But this is not what a caller expects `getLast` to do, even in the face of concurrent modification, unless perhaps the `Vector` was empty to begin with.

Because the synchronized collections commit to a synchronization policy that supports client-side locking,[1] it is possible to create new operations that are atomic with respect to other collection operations as long as we know which lock to use. The synchronized collection classes guard each method with the lock on the synchronized collection object itself. By acquiring the collection lock we can make `getLast` and `deleteLast` atomic, ensuring that the size of the `Vector` does not change between calling `size` and `get`, as shown in Listing 5.2.

The risk that the size of the list might change between a call to `size` and the corresponding call to `get` is also present when we iterate through the elements of a `Vector` as shown in Listing 5.3.

This iteration idiom relies on a leap of faith that other threads will not modify the `Vector` between the calls to `size` and `get`. In a single-threaded environment, this assumption is perfectly valid, but when other threads may concurrently modify the `Vector` it can lead to trouble. Just as with `getLast`, if another thread deletes an element while you are iterating through the `Vector` and the operations are interleaved unluckily, this iteration idiom throws `ArrayIndexOutOfBoundsException`.

---

1. This is documented only obliquely in the Java 5.0 Javadoc, as an example of the correct iteration idiom.

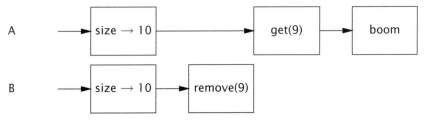

FIGURE 5.1. Interleaving of getLast and deleteLast that throws ArrayIndexOut-
OfBoundsException.

```
public static Object getLast(Vector list) {
    synchronized (list) {
        int lastIndex = list.size() - 1;
        return list.get(lastIndex);
    }
}

public static void deleteLast(Vector list) {
    synchronized (list) {
        int lastIndex = list.size() - 1;
        list.remove(lastIndex);
    }
}
```

LISTING 5.2. Compound actions on Vector using client-side locking.

```
for (int i = 0; i < vector.size(); i++)
    doSomething(vector.get(i));
```

LISTING 5.3. Iteration that may throw ArrayIndexOutOfBoundsException.

Even though the iteration in Listing 5.3 can throw an exception, this doesn't
mean Vector isn't thread-safe. The state of the Vector is still valid and the exception is in fact in conformance with its specification. However, that something
as mundane as fetching the last element or iteration throw an exception is clearly
undesirable.

The problem of unreliable iteration can again be addressed by client-side locking, at some additional cost to scalability. By holding the Vector lock for the duration of iteration, as shown in Listing 5.4, we prevent other threads from modifying
the Vector while we are iterating it. Unfortunately, we also prevent other threads
from accessing it at all during this time, impairing concurrency.

```
synchronized (vector) {
    for (int i = 0; i < vector.size(); i++)
        doSomething(vector.get(i));
}
```

LISTING 5.4. Iteration with client-side locking.

5.1.2 Iterators and `ConcurrentModificationException`

We use `Vector` for the sake of clarity in many of our examples, even though it is considered a "legacy" collection class. But the more "modern" collection classes do not eliminate the problem of compound actions. The standard way to iterate a `Collection` is with an `Iterator`, either explicitly or through the for-each loop syntax introduced in Java 5.0, but using iterators does not obviate the need to lock the collection during iteration if other threads can concurrently modify it. The iterators returned by the synchronized collections are not designed to deal with concurrent modification, and they are *fail-fast*—meaning that if they detect that the collection has changed since iteration began, they throw the unchecked `ConcurrentModificationException`.

These fail-fast iterators are not designed to be foolproof—they are designed to catch concurrency errors on a "good-faith-effort" basis and thus act only as early-warning indicators for concurrency problems. They are implemented by associating a modification count with the collection: if the modification count changes during iteration, `hasNext` or `next` throws `ConcurrentModificationException`. However, this check is done without synchronization, so there is a risk of seeing a stale value of the modification count and therefore that the iterator does not realize a modification has been made. This was a deliberate design tradeoff to reduce the performance impact of the concurrent modification detection code.[2]

Listing 5.5 illustrates iterating a collection with the for-each loop syntax. Internally, `javac` generates code that uses an `Iterator`, repeatedly calling `hasNext` and `next` to iterate the `List`. Just as with iterating the `Vector`, the way to prevent `ConcurrentModificationException` is to hold the collection lock for the duration of the iteration.

```
List<Widget> widgetList
    = Collections.synchronizedList(new ArrayList<Widget>());
...
// May throw ConcurrentModificationException
for (Widget w : widgetList)
    doSomething(w);
```

LISTING 5.5. Iterating a `List` with an `Iterator`.

---

2. `ConcurrentModificationException` can arise in single-threaded code as well; this happens when objects are removed from the collection directly rather than through `Iterator.remove`.

There are several reasons, however, why locking a collection during iteration may be undesirable. Other threads that need to access the collection will block until the iteration is complete; if the collection is large or the task performed for each element is lengthy, they could wait a long time. Also, if the collection is locked as in Listing 5.4, doSomething is being called with a lock held, which is a risk factor for deadlock (see Chapter 10). Even in the absence of starvation or deadlock risk, locking collections for significant periods of time hurts application scalability. The longer a lock is held, the more likely it is to be contended, and if many threads are blocked waiting for a lock throughput and CPU utilization can suffer (see Chapter 11).

An alternative to locking the collection during iteration is to clone the collection and iterate the copy instead. Since the clone is thread-confined, no other thread can modify it during iteration, eliminating the possibility of Concurrent-ModificationException. (The collection still must be locked during the clone operation itself.) Cloning the collection has an obvious performance cost; whether this is a favorable tradeoff depends on many factors including the size of the collection, how much work is done for each element, the relative frequency of iteration compared to other collection operations, and responsiveness and throughput requirements.

5.1.3 Hidden iterators

While locking can prevent iterators from throwing ConcurrentModificationException, you have to remember to use locking everywhere a shared collection might be iterated. This is trickier than it sounds, as iterators are sometimes hidden, as in HiddenIterator in Listing 5.6. There is no explicit iteration in Hidden-Iterator, but the code in bold entails iteration just the same. The string concatenation gets turned by the compiler into a call to StringBuilder.append(Object), which in turn invokes the collection's toString method—and the implementation of toString in the standard collections iterates the collection and calls toString on each element to produce a nicely formatted representation of the collection's contents.

The addTenThings method could throw ConcurrentModificationException, because the collection is being iterated by toString in the process of preparing the debugging message. Of course, the real problem is that HiddenIterator is not thread-safe; the HiddenIterator lock should be acquired before using set in the println call, but debugging and logging code commonly neglect to do this.

The real lesson here is that the greater the distance between the state and the synchronization that guards it, the more likely that someone will forget to use proper synchronization when accessing that state. If HiddenIterator wrapped the HashSet with a synchronizedSet, encapsulating the synchronization, this sort of error would not occur.

Just as encapsulating an object's state makes it easier to preserve its invariants, encapsulating its synchronization makes it easier to enforce its synchronization policy.

```
public class HiddenIterator {
    @GuardedBy("this")
    private final Set<Integer> set = new HashSet<Integer>();

    public synchronized void add(Integer i) { set.add(i); }
    public synchronized void remove(Integer i) { set.remove(i); }

    public void addTenThings() {
        Random r = new Random();
        for (int i = 0; i < 10; i++)
            add(r.nextInt());
        System.out.println("DEBUG: added ten elements to " + set);
    }
}
```

LISTING 5.6. Iteration hidden within string concatenation. *Don't do this.*

Iteration is also indirectly invoked by the collection's `hashCode` and `equals` methods, which may be called if the collection is used as an element or key of another collection. Similarly, the `containsAll`, `removeAll`, and `retainAll` methods, as well as the constructors that take collections as arguments, also iterate the collection. All of these indirect uses of iteration can cause `ConcurrentModificationException`.

5.2 Concurrent collections

Java 5.0 improves on the synchronized collections by providing several *concurrent* collection classes. Synchronized collections achieve their thread safety by serializing all access to the collection's state. The cost of this approach is poor concurrency; when multiple threads contend for the collection-wide lock, throughput suffers.

The concurrent collections, on the other hand, are designed for concurrent access from multiple threads. Java 5.0 adds `ConcurrentHashMap`, a replacement for synchronized hash-based `Map` implementations, and `CopyOnWriteArrayList`, a replacement for synchronized `List` implementations for cases where traversal is the dominant operation. The new `ConcurrentMap` interface adds support for common compound actions such as put-if-absent, replace, and conditional remove.

> Replacing synchronized collections with concurrent collections can offer dramatic scalability improvements with little risk.

Java 5.0 also adds two new collection types, `Queue` and `BlockingQueue`. A Queue is intended to hold a set of elements temporarily while they await processing. Several implementations are provided, including `ConcurrentLinkedQueue`, a traditional FIFO queue, and `PriorityQueue`, a (non concurrent) priority ordered queue. Queue operations do not block; if the queue is empty, the retrieval operation returns `null`. While you can simulate the behavior of a `Queue` with a `List`—in fact, `LinkedList` also implements `Queue`—the Queue classes were added because eliminating the random-access requirements of `List` admits more efficient concurrent implementations.

`BlockingQueue` extends `Queue` to add blocking insertion and retrieval operations. If the queue is empty, a retrieval blocks until an element is available, and if the queue is full (for bounded queues) an insertion blocks until there is space available. Blocking queues are extremely useful in producer-consumer designs, and are covered in greater detail in Section 5.3.

Just as `ConcurrentHashMap` is a concurrent replacement for a synchronized hash-based `Map`, Java 6 adds `ConcurrentSkipListMap` and `ConcurrentSkipList-Set`, which are concurrent replacements for a synchronized `SortedMap` or `Sort-edSet` (such as `TreeMap` or `TreeSet` wrapped with `synchronizedMap`).

5.2.1 ConcurrentHashMap

The synchronized collections classes hold a lock for the duration of each operation. Some operations, such as `HashMap.get` or `List.contains`, may involve more work than is initially obvious: traversing a hash bucket or list to find a specific object entails calling `equals` (which itself may involve a fair amount of computation) on a number of candidate objects. In a hash-based collection, if `hashCode` does not spread out hash values well, elements may be unevenly distributed among buckets; in the degenerate case, a poor hash function will turn a hash table into a linked list. Traversing a long list and calling `equals` on some or all of the elements can take a long time, and during that time no other thread can access the collection.

`ConcurrentHashMap` is a hash-based `Map` like `HashMap`, but it uses an entirely different locking strategy that offers better concurrency and scalability. Instead of synchronizing every method on a common lock, restricting access to a single thread at a time, it uses a finer-grained locking mechanism called *lock striping* (see Section 11.4.3) to allow a greater degree of shared access. Arbitrarily many reading threads can access the map concurrently, readers can access the map concurrently with writers, and a limited number of writers can modify the map concurrently. The result is far higher throughput under concurrent access, with little performance penalty for single-threaded access.

`ConcurrentHashMap`, along with the other concurrent collections, further improve on the synchronized collection classes by providing iterators that do not throw `ConcurrentModificationException`, thus eliminating the need to lock the collection during iteration. The iterators returned by `ConcurrentHashMap` are *weakly consistent* instead of fail-fast. A weakly consistent iterator can tolerate concurrent modification, traverses elements as they existed when the iterator was constructed, and may (but is not guaranteed to) reflect modifications to the collection after the construction of the iterator.

As with all improvements, there are still a few tradeoffs. The semantics of methods that operate on the entire `Map`, such as `size` and `isEmpty`, have been slightly weakened to reflect the concurrent nature of the collection. Since the result of `size` could be out of date by the time it is computed, it is really only an estimate, so `size` is allowed to return an approximation instead of an exact count. While at first this may seem disturbing, in reality methods like `size` and `isEmpty` are far less useful in concurrent environments because these quantities are moving targets. So the requirements for these operations were weakened to enable performance optimizations for the most important operations, primarily `get`, `put`, `containsKey`, and `remove`.

The one feature offered by the synchronized `Map` implementations but not by `ConcurrentHashMap` is the ability to lock the map for exclusive access. With `Hashtable` and `synchronizedMap`, acquiring the `Map` lock prevents any other thread from accessing it. This might be necessary in unusual cases such as adding several mappings atomically, or iterating the `Map` several times and needing to see the same elements in the same order. On the whole, though, this is a reasonable tradeoff: concurrent collections should be expected to change their contents continuously.

Because it has so many advantages and so few disadvantages compared to `Hashtable` or `synchronizedMap`, replacing synchronized `Map` implementations with `ConcurrentHashMap` in most cases results only in better scalability. Only if your application needs to lock the map for exclusive access[3] is `Concurrent-HashMap` not an appropriate drop-in replacement.

5.2.2 Additional atomic `Map` operations

Since a `ConcurrentHashMap` cannot be locked for exclusive access, we cannot use client-side locking to create new atomic operations such as put-if-absent, as we did for `Vector` in Section 4.4.1. Instead, a number of common compound operations such as put-if-absent, remove-if-equal, and replace-if-equal are implemented as atomic operations and specified by the `ConcurrentMap` interface, shown in Listing 5.7. If you find yourself adding such functionality to an existing synchronized `Map` implementation, it is probably a sign that you should consider using a `ConcurrentMap` instead.

5.2.3 `CopyOnWriteArrayList`

`CopyOnWriteArrayList` is a concurrent replacement for a synchronized `List` that offers better concurrency in some common situations and eliminates the need to lock or copy the collection during iteration. (Similarly, `CopyOnWriteArraySet` is a concurrent replacement for a synchronized `Set`.)

The copy-on-write collections derive their thread safety from the fact that as long as an effectively immutable object is properly published, no further synchronization is required when accessing it. They implement mutability by creating and republishing a new copy of the collection every time it is modified. Iterators for the copy-on-write collections retain a reference to the backing array that was current at the start of iteration, and since this will never change, they need to

---

3. Or if you are relying on the synchronization side effects of the synchronized `Map` implementations.

```
public interface ConcurrentMap<K,V> extends Map<K,V> {
    // Insert into map only if no value is mapped from K
    V putIfAbsent(K key, V value);

    // Remove only if K is mapped to V
    boolean remove(K key, V value);

    // Replace value only if K is mapped to oldValue
    boolean replace(K key, V oldValue, V newValue);

    // Replace value only if K is mapped to some value
    V replace(K key, V newValue);
}
```

LISTING 5.7. ConcurrentMap interface.

synchronize only briefly to ensure visibility of the array contents. As a result, multiple threads can iterate the collection without interference from one another or from threads wanting to modify the collection. The iterators returned by the copy-on-write collections do not throw ConcurrentModificationException and return the elements exactly as they were at the time the iterator was created, regardless of subsequent modifications.

Obviously, there is some cost to copying the backing array every time the collection is modified, especially if the collection is large; the copy-on-write collections are reasonable to use only when iteration is far more common than modification. This criterion exactly describes many event-notification systems: delivering a notification requires iterating the list of registered listeners and calling each one of them, and in most cases registering or unregistering an event listener is far less common than receiving an event notification. (See [CPJ 2.4.4] for more information on copy-on-write.)

5.3 Blocking queues and the producer-consumer pattern

Blocking queues provide blocking put and take methods as well as the timed equivalents offer and poll. If the queue is full, put blocks until space becomes available; if the queue is empty, take blocks until an element is available. Queues can be bounded or unbounded; unbounded queues are never full, so a put on an unbounded queue never blocks.

Blocking queues support the *producer-consumer* design pattern. A producer-consumer design separates the identification of work to be done from the execution of that work by placing work items on a "to do" list for later processing, rather than processing them immediately as they are identified. The producer-consumer pattern simplifies development because it removes code dependencies between producer and consumer classes, and simplifies workload management by decoupling activities that may produce or consume data at different or variable rates.

In a producer-consumer design built around a blocking queue, producers place data onto the queue as it becomes available, and consumers retrieve data from the queue when they are ready to take the appropriate action. Producers don't need to know anything about the identity or number of consumers, or even whether they are the only producer—all they have to do is place data items on the queue. Similarly, consumers need not know who the producers are or where the work came from. BlockingQueue simplifies the implementation of producer-consumer designs with any number of producers and consumers. One of the most common producer-consumer designs is a thread pool coupled with a work queue; this pattern is embodied in the Executor task execution framework that is the subject of Chapters 6 and 8.

The familiar division of labor for two people washing the dishes is an example of a producer-consumer design: one person washes the dishes and places them in the dish rack, and the other person retrieves the dishes from the rack and dries them. In this scenario, the dish rack acts as a blocking queue; if there are no dishes in the rack, the consumer waits until there are dishes to dry, and if the rack fills up, the producer has to stop washing until there is more space. This analogy extends to multiple producers (though there may be contention for the sink) and multiple consumers; each worker interacts only with the dish rack. No one needs to know how many producers or consumers there are, or who produced a given item of work.

The labels "producer" and "consumer" are relative; an activity that acts as a consumer in one context may act as a producer in another. Drying the dishes "consumes" clean wet dishes and "produces" clean dry dishes. A third person wanting to help might put away the dry dishes, in which case the drier is both a consumer and a producer, and there are now two shared work queues (each of which may block the drier from proceeding.)

Blocking queues simplify the coding of consumers, since take blocks until data is available. If the producers don't generate work fast enough to keep the consumers busy, the consumers just wait until more work is available. Sometimes this is perfectly acceptable (as in a server application when no client is requesting service), and sometimes it indicates that the ratio of producer threads to consumer threads should be adjusted to achieve better utilization (as in a web crawler or other application in which there is effectively infinite work to do).

If the producers consistently generate work faster than the consumers can process it, eventually the application will run out of memory because work items will queue up without bound. Again, the blocking nature of put greatly simplifies coding of producers; if we use a *bounded queue*, then when the queue fills up the producers block, giving the consumers time to catch up because a blocked producer cannot generate more work.

Blocking queues also provide an offer method, which returns a failure status if the item cannot be enqueued. This enables you to create more flexible policies for dealing with overload, such as shedding load, serializing excess work items and writing them to disk, reducing the number of producer threads, or throttling producers in some other manner.

Bounded queues are a powerful resource management tool for building reliable applications: they make your program more robust to overload by throttling activities that threaten to produce more work than can be handled.

While the producer-consumer pattern enables producer and consumer *code* to be decoupled from each other, their *behavior* is still coupled indirectly through the shared work queue. It is tempting to assume that the consumers will always keep up, so that you need not place any bounds on the size of work queues, but this is a prescription for rearchitecting your system later. *Build resource management into your design early using blocking queues—it is a lot easier to do this up front than to retrofit it later.* Blocking queues make this easy for a number of situations, but if blocking queues don't fit easily into your design, you can create other blocking data structures using Semaphore (see Section 5.5.3).

The class library contains several implementations of BlockingQueue. LinkedBlockingQueue and ArrayBlockingQueue are FIFO queues, analogous to LinkedList and ArrayList but with better concurrent performance than a synchronized List. PriorityBlockingQueue is a priority-ordered queue, which is useful when you want to process elements in an order other than FIFO. Just like other sorted collections, PriorityBlockingQueue can compare elements according to their natural order (if they implement Comparable) or using a Comparator.

The last BlockingQueue implementation, SynchronousQueue, is not really a queue at all, in that it maintains no storage space for queued elements. Instead, it maintains a list of queued *threads* waiting to enqueue or dequeue an element. In the dish-washing analogy, this would be like having no dish rack, but instead handing the washed dishes directly to the next available dryer. While this may seem a strange way to implement a queue, it reduces the latency associated with moving data from producer to consumer because the work can be handed off directly. (In a traditional queue, the enqueue and dequeue operations must complete sequentially before a unit of work can be handed off.) The direct handoff also feeds back more information about the state of the task to the producer; when the handoff is accepted, it knows a consumer has taken responsibility for it, rather than simply letting it sit on a queue somewhere—much like the difference between handing a document to a colleague and merely putting it in her mailbox and hoping she gets it soon. Since a SynchronousQueue has no storage capacity, put and take will block unless another thread is already waiting to participate in the handoff. Synchronous queues are generally suitable only when there are enough consumers that there nearly always will be one ready to take the handoff.

5.3.1 Example: desktop search

One type of program that is amenable to decomposition into producers and consumers is an agent that scans local drives for documents and indexes them for later searching, similar to Google Desktop or the Windows Indexing service. DiskCrawler in Listing 5.8 shows a producer task that searches a file hierarchy for files meeting an indexing criterion and puts their names on the work queue; Indexer in Listing 5.8 shows the consumer task that takes file names from the queue and indexes them.

The producer-consumer pattern offers a thread-friendly means of decomposing the desktop search problem into simpler components. Factoring file-crawling and indexing into separate activities results in code that is more readable and reusable than with a monolithic activity that does both; each of the activities has only a single task to do, and the blocking queue handles all the flow control, so the code for each is simpler and clearer.

The producer-consumer pattern also enables several performance benefits. Producers and consumers can execute concurrently; if one is I/O-bound and the other is CPU-bound, executing them concurrently yields better overall through-put than executing them sequentially. If the producer and consumer activities are parallelizable to different degrees, tightly coupling them reduces parallelizability to that of the less parallelizable activity.

Listing 5.9 starts several crawlers and indexers, each in their own thread. As written, the consumer threads never exit, which prevents the program from terminating; we examine several techniques for addressing this problem in Chapter 7. While this example uses explicitly managed threads, many producer-consumer designs can be expressed using the Executor task execution framework, which itself uses the producer-consumer pattern.

5.3.2 Serial thread confinement

The blocking queue implementations in java.util.concurrent all contain sufficient internal synchronization to safely publish objects from a producer thread to the consumer thread.

For mutable objects, producer-consumer designs and blocking queues facilitate *serial thread confinement* for handing off ownership of objects from producers to consumers. A thread-confined object is owned exclusively by a single thread, but that ownership can be "transferred" by publishing it safely where only one other thread will gain access to it and ensuring that the publishing thread does not access it after the handoff. The safe publication ensures that the object's state is visible to the new owner, and since the original owner will not touch it again, it is now confined to the new thread. The new owner may modify it freely since it has exclusive access.

Object pools exploit serial thread confinement, "lending" an object to a requesting thread. As long as the pool contains sufficient internal synchronization to publish the pooled object safely, and as long as the clients do not themselves publish the pooled object or use it after returning it to the pool, ownership can be transferred safely from thread to thread.

One could also use other publication mechanisms for transferring ownership of a mutable object, but it is necessary to ensure that only one thread receives the object being handed off. Blocking queues make this easy; with a little more work, it could also done with the atomic remove method of ConcurrentMap or the compareAndSet method of AtomicReference.

```java
public class FileCrawler implements Runnable {
    private final BlockingQueue<File> fileQueue;
    private final FileFilter fileFilter;
    private final File root;
    ...
    public void run() {
        try {
            crawl(root);
        } catch (InterruptedException e) {
            Thread.currentThread().interrupt();
        }
    }

    private void crawl(File root) throws InterruptedException {
        File[] entries = root.listFiles(fileFilter);
        if (entries != null) {
            for (File entry : entries)
                if (entry.isDirectory())
                    crawl(entry);
                else if (!alreadyIndexed(entry))
                    fileQueue.put(entry);
        }
    }
}

public class Indexer implements Runnable {
    private final BlockingQueue<File> queue;

    public Indexer(BlockingQueue<File> queue) {
        this.queue = queue;
    }

    public void run() {
        try {
            while (true)
                indexFile(queue.take());
        } catch (InterruptedException e) {
            Thread.currentThread().interrupt();
        }
    }
}
```

LISTING 5.8. Producer and consumer tasks in a desktop search application.

```
public static void startIndexing(File[] roots) {
    BlockingQueue<File> queue = new LinkedBlockingQueue<File>(BOUND);
    FileFilter filter = new FileFilter() {
        public boolean accept(File file) { return true; }
    };

    for (File root : roots)
        new Thread(new FileCrawler(queue, filter, root)).start();

    for (int i = 0; i < N_CONSUMERS; i++)
        new Thread(new Indexer(queue)).start();
}
```

LISTING 5.9. Starting the desktop search.

5.3.3 Deques and work stealing

Java 6 also adds another two collection types, Deque (pronounced "deck") and BlockingDeque, that extend Queue and BlockingQueue. A Deque is a double-ended queue that allows efficient insertion and removal from both the head and the tail. Implementations include ArrayDeque and LinkedBlockingDeque.

Just as blocking queues lend themselves to the producer-consumer pattern, deques lend themselves to a related pattern called *work stealing*. A producer-consumer design has one shared work queue for all consumers; in a work stealing design, every consumer has its own deque. If a consumer exhausts the work in its own deque, it can steal work from the *tail* of someone else's deque. Work stealing can be more scalable than a traditional producer-consumer design because workers don't contend for a shared work queue; most of the time they access only their own deque, reducing contention. When a worker has to access another's queue, it does so from the tail rather than the head, further reducing contention.

Work stealing is well suited to problems in which consumers are also producers—when performing a unit of work is likely to result in the identification of more work. For example, processing a page in a web crawler usually results in the identification of new pages to be crawled. Similarly, many graph-exploring algorithms, such as marking the heap during garbage collection, can be efficiently parallelized using work stealing. When a worker identifies a new unit of work, it places it at the end of its own deque (or alternatively, in a *work sharing* design, on that of another worker); when its deque is empty, it looks for work at the end of someone else's deque, ensuring that each worker stays busy.

5.4 Blocking and interruptible methods

Threads may *block*, or pause, for several reasons: waiting for I/O completion, waiting to acquire a lock, waiting to wake up from Thread.sleep, or waiting for the result of a computation in another thread. When a thread blocks, it is usually suspended and placed in one of the blocked thread states (BLOCKED, WAITING, or

TIMED_WAITING). The distinction between a blocking operation and an ordinary operation that merely takes a long time to finish is that a blocked thread must wait for an event that is beyond its control before it can proceed—the I/O completes, the lock becomes available, or the external computation finishes. When that external event occurs, the thread is placed back in the RUNNABLE state and becomes eligible again for scheduling.

The put and take methods of BlockingQueue throw the checked InterruptedException, as do a number of other library methods such as Thread.sleep. When a method can throw InterruptedException, it is telling you that it is a blocking method, and further that if it is *interrupted*, it will make an effort to stop blocking early.

Thread provides the interrupt method for interrupting a thread and for querying whether a thread has been interrupted. Each thread has a boolean property that represents its interrupted status; interrupting a thread sets this status.

Interruption is a *cooperative* mechanism. One thread cannot force another to stop what it is doing and do something else; when thread *A* interrupts thread *B*, *A* is merely requesting that *B* stop what it is doing when it gets to a convenient stopping point—if it feels like it. While there is nothing in the API or language specification that demands any specific application-level semantics for interruption, the most sensible use for interruption is to cancel an activity. Blocking methods that are responsive to interruption make it easier to cancel long-running activities on a timely basis.

When your code calls a method that throws InterruptedException, then your method is a blocking method too, and must have a plan for responding to interruption. For library code, there are basically two choices:

Propagate the InterruptedException. This is often the most sensible policy if you can get away with it—just propagate the InterruptedException to your caller. This could involve not catching InterruptedException, or catching it and throwing it again after performing some brief activity-specific cleanup.

Restore the interrupt. Sometimes you cannot throw InterruptedException, for instance when your code is part of a Runnable. In these situations, you must catch InterruptedException and restore the interrupted status by calling interrupt on the current thread, so that code higher up the call stack can see that an interrupt was issued, as demonstrated in Listing 5.10.

You can get much more sophisticated with interruption, but these two approaches should work in the vast majority of situations. But there is one thing you should *not* do with InterruptedException—catch it and do nothing in response. This deprives code higher up on the call stack of the opportunity to act on the interruption, because the evidence that the thread was interrupted is lost. *The only situation in which it is acceptable to swallow an interrupt is when you are extending Thread and therefore control all the code higher up on the call stack.* Cancellation and interruption are covered in greater detail in Chapter 7.

```
public class TaskRunnable implements Runnable {
    BlockingQueue<Task> queue;
    ...
    public void run() {
        try {
            processTask(queue.take());
        } catch (InterruptedException e) {
            // restore interrupted status
            Thread.currentThread().interrupt();
        }
    }
}
```

LISTING 5.10. Restoring the interrupted status so as not to swallow the interrupt.

5.5   Synchronizers

Blocking queues are unique among the collections classes: not only do they act as containers for objects, but they can also coordinate the control flow of producer and consumer threads because take and put block until the queue enters the desired state (not empty or not full).

A *synchronizer* is any object that coordinates the control flow of threads based on its state. Blocking queues can act as synchronizers; other types of synchronizers include semaphores, barriers, and latches. There are a number of synchronizer classes in the platform library; if these do not meet your needs, you can also create your own using the mechanisms described in Chapter 14.

All synchronizers share certain structural properties: they encapsulate state that determines whether threads arriving at the synchronizer should be allowed to pass or forced to wait, provide methods to manipulate that state, and provide methods to wait efficiently for the synchronizer to enter the desired state.

5.5.1   Latches

A *latch* is a synchronizer that can delay the progress of threads until it reaches its *terminal* state [CPJ 3.4.2]. A latch acts as a gate: until the latch reaches the terminal state the gate is closed and no thread can pass, and in the terminal state the gate opens, allowing all threads to pass. Once the latch reaches the terminal state, it cannot change state again, so it remains open forever. Latches can be used to ensure that certain activities do not proceed until other one-time activities complete, such as:

- Ensuring that a computation does not proceed until resources it needs have been initialized. A simple binary (two-state) latch could be used to indicate "Resource R has been initialized", and any activity that requires R would wait first on this latch.

- Ensuring that a service does not start until other services on which it depends have started. Each service would have an associated binary latch; starting service *S* would involve first waiting on the latches for other services on which *S* depends, and then releasing the *S* latch after startup completes so any services that depend on *S* can then proceed.

- Waiting until all the parties involved in an activity, for instance the players in a multi-player game, are ready to proceed. In this case, the latch reaches the terminal state after all the players are ready.

CountDownLatch is a flexible latch implementation that can be used in any of these situations; it allows one or more threads to wait for a set of events to occur. The latch state consists of a counter initialized to a positive number, representing the number of events to wait for. The countDown method decrements the counter, indicating that an event has occurred, and the await methods wait for the counter to reach zero, which happens when all the events have occurred. If the counter is nonzero on entry, await blocks until the counter reaches zero, the waiting thread is interrupted, or the wait times out.

TestHarness in Listing 5.11 illustrates two common uses for latches. Test-Harness creates a number of threads that run a given task concurrently. It uses two latches, a "starting gate" and an "ending gate". The starting gate is initialized with a count of one; the ending gate is initialized with a count equal to the number of worker threads. The first thing each worker thread does is wait on the starting gate; this ensures that none of them starts working until they all are ready to start. The last thing each does is count down on the ending gate; this allows the master thread to wait efficiently until the last of the worker threads has finished, so it can calculate the elapsed time.

Why did we bother with the latches in TestHarness instead of just starting the threads immediately after they are created? Presumably, we wanted to measure how long it takes to run a task *n* times *concurrently*. If we simply created and started the threads, the threads started earlier would have a "head start" on the later threads, and the degree of contention would vary over time as the number of active threads increased or decreased. Using a starting gate allows the master thread to release all the worker threads at once, and the ending gate allows the master thread to wait for the *last* thread to finish rather than waiting sequentially for each thread to finish.

5.5.2 FutureTask

FutureTask also acts like a latch. (FutureTask implements Future, which describes an abstract result-bearing computation [CPJ 4.3.3].) A computation represented by a FutureTask is implemented with a Callable, the result-bearing equivalent of Runnable, and can be in one of three states: waiting to run, running, or completed. Completion subsumes all the ways a computation can complete, including normal completion, cancellation, and exception. Once a FutureTask enters the completed state, it stays in that state forever.

The behavior of Future.get depends on the state of the task. If it is completed, get returns the result immediately, and otherwise blocks until the task transitions

```java
public class TestHarness {
    public long timeTasks(int nThreads, final Runnable task)
            throws InterruptedException {
        final CountDownLatch startGate = new CountDownLatch(1);
        final CountDownLatch endGate = new CountDownLatch(nThreads);

        for (int i = 0; i < nThreads; i++) {
            Thread t = new Thread() {
                public void run() {
                    try {
                        startGate.await();
                        try {
                            task.run();
                        } finally {
                            endGate.countDown();
                        }
                    } catch (InterruptedException ignored) { }
                }
            };
            t.start();
        }

        long start = System.nanoTime();
        startGate.countDown();
        endGate.await();
        long end = System.nanoTime();
        return end-start;
    }
}
```

LISTING 5.11. Using CountDownLatch for starting and stopping threads in timing tests.

to the completed state and then returns the result or throws an exception. `Fut-`
`ureTask` conveys the result from the thread executing the computation to the
thread(s) retrieving the result; the specification of `FutureTask` guarantees that
this transfer constitutes a safe publication of the result.

FutureTask is used by the `Executor` framework to represent asynchronous
tasks, and can also be used to represent any potentially lengthy computation that
can be started before the results are needed. `Preloader` in Listing 5.12 uses `Fut-`
`ureTask` to perform an expensive computation whose results are needed later; by
starting the computation early, you reduce the time you would have to wait later
when you actually need the results.

```
public class Preloader {
    private final FutureTask<ProductInfo> future =
        new FutureTask<ProductInfo>(new Callable<ProductInfo>() {
            public ProductInfo call() throws DataLoadException {
                return loadProductInfo();
            }
        });
    private final Thread thread = new Thread(future);

    public void start() { thread.start(); }

    public ProductInfo get()
            throws DataLoadException, InterruptedException {
        try {
            return future.get();
        } catch (ExecutionException e) {
            Throwable cause = e.getCause();
            if (cause instanceof DataLoadException)
                throw (DataLoadException) cause;
            else
                throw launderThrowable(cause);
        }
    }
}
```

LISTING 5.12. *Using* FutureTask *to preload data that is needed later.*

Preloader creates a `FutureTask` that describes the task of loading product
information from a database and a thread in which the computation will be performed. It provides a `start` method to start the thread, since it is inadvisable
to start a thread from a constructor or static initializer. When the program later
needs the `ProductInfo`, it can call `get`, which returns the loaded data if it is ready,
or waits for the load to complete if not.

Tasks described by `Callable` can throw checked and unchecked exceptions,
and any code can throw an `Error`. Whatever the task code may throw, it is

wrapped in an ExecutionException and rethrown from Future.get. This complicates code that calls get, not only because it must deal with the possibility of ExecutionException (and the unchecked CancellationException), but also because the cause of the ExecutionException is returned as a Throwable, which is inconvenient to deal with.

When get throws an ExecutionException in Preloader, the cause will fall into one of three categories: a checked exception thrown by the Callable, a RuntimeException, or an Error. We must handle each of these cases separately, but we will use the launderThrowable utility method in Listing 5.13 to encapsulate some of the messier exception-handling logic. Before calling launderThrowable, Preloader tests for the known checked exceptions and rethrows them. That leaves only unchecked exceptions, which Preloader handles by calling launderThrowable and throwing the result. If the Throwable passed to launderThrowable is an Error, launderThrowable rethrows it directly; if it is not a RuntimeException, it throws an IllegalStateException to indicate a logic error. That leaves only RuntimeException, which launderThrowable returns to its caller, and which the caller generally rethrows.

```
/** If the Throwable is an Error, throw it; if it is a
 *  RuntimeException return it, otherwise throw IllegalStateException
 */
public static RuntimeException launderThrowable(Throwable t) {
    if (t instanceof RuntimeException)
        return (RuntimeException) t;
    else if (t instanceof Error)
        throw (Error) t;
    else
        throw new IllegalStateException("Not unchecked", t);
}
```

LISTING 5.13. Coercing an unchecked Throwable to a RuntimeException.

5.5.3 Semaphores

Counting semaphores are used to control the number of activities that can access a certain resource or perform a given action at the same time [CPJ 3.4.1]. Counting semaphores can be used to implement resource pools or to impose a bound on a collection.

A Semaphore manages a set of virtual *permits*; the initial number of permits is passed to the Semaphore constructor. Activities can acquire permits (as long as some remain) and release permits when they are done with them. If no permit is available, acquire blocks until one is (or until interrupted or the operation times out). The release method returns a permit to the semaphore.[4] A degenerate case

4. The implementation has no actual permit objects, and Semaphore does not associate dispensed permits with threads, so a permit acquired in one thread can be released from another thread. You

of a counting semaphore is a binary semaphore, a `Semaphore` with an initial count of one. A binary semaphore can be used as a *mutex* with nonreentrant locking semantics; whoever holds the sole permit holds the mutex.

Semaphores are useful for implementing resource pools such as database connection pools. While it is easy to construct a fixed-sized pool that fails if you request a resource from an empty pool, what you really want is to *block* if the pool is empty and unblock when it becomes nonempty again. If you initialize a `Semaphore` to the pool size, `acquire` a permit before trying to fetch a resource from the pool, and `release` the permit after putting a resource back in the pool, `acquire` blocks until the pool becomes nonempty. This technique is used in the bounded buffer class in Chapter 12. (An easier way to construct a blocking object pool would be to use a `BlockingQueue` to hold the pooled resources.)

Similarly, you can use a `Semaphore` to turn any collection into a blocking bounded collection, as illustrated by `BoundedHashSet` in Listing 5.14. The semaphore is initialized to the desired maximum size of the collection. The add operation acquires a permit before adding the item into the underlying collection. If the underlying add operation does not actually add anything, it releases the permit immediately. Similarly, a successful `remove` operation releases a permit, enabling more elements to be added. The underlying `Set` implementation knows nothing about the bound; this is handled by `BoundedHashSet`.

5.5.4 Barriers

We have seen how latches can facilitate starting a group of related activities or waiting for a group of related activities to complete. Latches are single-use objects; once a latch enters the terminal state, it cannot be reset.

Barriers are similar to latches in that they block a group of threads until some event has occurred [CPJ 4.4.3]. The key difference is that with a barrier, all the threads must come together at a barrier point *at the same time* in order to proceed. Latches are for waiting for *events*; barriers are for waiting for *other threads*. A barrier implements the protocol some families use to rendezvous during a day at the mall: "Everyone meet at McDonald's at 6:00; once you get there, stay there until everyone shows up, and then we'll figure out what we're doing next."

`CyclicBarrier` allows a fixed number of parties to rendezvous repeatedly at a *barrier point* and is useful in parallel iterative algorithms that break down a problem into a fixed number of independent subproblems. Threads call `await` when they reach the barrier point, and `await` blocks until *all* the threads have reached the barrier point. If all threads meet at the barrier point, the barrier has been successfully passed, in which case all threads are released and the barrier is reset so it can be used again. If a call to `await` times out or a thread blocked in `await` is interrupted, then the barrier is considered *broken* and all outstanding calls to `await` terminate with `BrokenBarrierException`. If the barrier is successfully passed, `await` returns a unique arrival index for each thread, which can be used to "elect" a leader that takes some special action in the next iteration. `CyclicBar-`

---

can think of `acquire` as consuming a permit and `release` as creating one; a `Semaphore` is not limited to the number of permits it was created with.

```
public class BoundedHashSet<T> {
    private final Set<T> set;
    private final Semaphore sem;

    public BoundedHashSet(int bound) {
        this.set = Collections.synchronizedSet(new HashSet<T>());
        sem = new Semaphore(bound);
    }

    public boolean add(T o) throws InterruptedException {
        sem.acquire();
        boolean wasAdded = false;
        try {
            wasAdded = set.add(o);
            return wasAdded;
        }
        finally {
            if (!wasAdded)
                sem.release();
        }
    }

    public boolean remove(Object o) {
        boolean wasRemoved = set.remove(o);
        if (wasRemoved)
            sem.release();
        return wasRemoved;
    }
}
```

LISTING 5.14. Using Semaphore to bound a collection.

rier also lets you pass a *barrier action* to the constructor; this is a `Runnable` that is executed (in one of the subtask threads) when the barrier is successfully passed but before the blocked threads are released.

Barriers are often used in simulations, where the work to calculate one step can be done in parallel but all the work associated with a given step must complete before advancing to the next step. For example, in n-body particle simulations, each step calculates an update to the position of each particle based on the locations and other attributes of the other particles. Waiting on a barrier between each update ensures that all updates for step k have completed before moving on to step $k + 1$.

`CellularAutomata` in Listing 5.15 demonstrates using a barrier to compute a cellular automata simulation, such as Conway's Life game (Gardner, 1970). When parallelizing a simulation, it is generally impractical to assign a separate thread to each element (in the case of Life, a cell); this would require too many threads, and the overhead of coordinating them would dwarf the computation. Instead, it makes sense to *partition* the problem into a number of subparts, let each thread solve a subpart, and then merge the results. `CellularAutomata` partitions the board into N_{cpu} parts, where N_{cpu} is the number of CPUs available, and assigns each part to a thread.[5] At each step, the worker threads calculate new values for all the cells in their part of the board. When all worker threads have reached the barrier, the barrier action commits the new values to the data model. After the barrier action runs, the worker threads are released to compute the next step of the calculation, which includes consulting an `isDone` method to determine whether further iterations are required.

Another form of barrier is `Exchanger`, a two-party barrier in which the parties exchange data at the barrier point [CPJ 3.4.3]. Exchangers are useful when the parties perform asymmetric activities, for example when one thread fills a buffer with data and the other thread consumes the data from the buffer; these threads could use an `Exchanger` to meet and exchange a full buffer for an empty one. When two threads exchange objects via an `Exchanger`, the exchange constitutes a safe publication of both objects to the other party.

The timing of the exchange depends on the responsiveness requirements of the application. The simplest approach is that the filling task exchanges when the buffer is full, and the emptying task exchanges when the buffer is empty; this minimizes the number of exchanges but can delay processing of some data if the arrival rate of new data is unpredictable. Another approach would be that the filler exchanges when the buffer is full, but also when the buffer is partially filled and a certain amount of time has elapsed.

5.6 Building an efficient, scalable result cache

Nearly every server application uses some form of caching. Reusing the results of a previous computation can reduce latency and increase throughput, at the cost

---

5. For computational problems like this that do no I/O and access no shared data, N_{cpu} or $N_{cpu} + 1$ threads yield optimal throughput; more threads do not help, and may in fact degrade performance as the threads compete for CPU and memory resources.

```
public class CellularAutomata {
    private final Board mainBoard;
    private final CyclicBarrier barrier;
    private final Worker[] workers;

    public CellularAutomata(Board board) {
        this.mainBoard = board;
        int count = Runtime.getRuntime().availableProcessors();
        this.barrier = new CyclicBarrier(count,
                new Runnable() {
                    public void run() {
                        mainBoard.commitNewValues();
                    }});
        this.workers = new Worker[count];
        for (int i = 0; i < count; i++)
            workers[i] = new Worker(mainBoard.getSubBoard(count, i));
    }

    private class Worker implements Runnable {
        private final Board board;

        public Worker(Board board) { this.board = board; }
        public void run() {
            while (!board.hasConverged()) {
                for (int x = 0; x < board.getMaxX(); x++)
                    for (int y = 0; y < board.getMaxY(); y++)
                        board.setNewValue(x, y, computeValue(x, y));
                try {
                    barrier.await();
                } catch (InterruptedException ex) {
                    return;
                } catch (BrokenBarrierException ex) {
                    return;
                }
            }
        }
    }

    public void start() {
        for (int i = 0; i < workers.length; i++)
            new Thread(workers[i]).start();
        mainBoard.waitForConvergence();
    }
}
```

LISTING 5.15. Coordinating computation in a cellular automaton with `CyclicBar-
rier`.

of some additional memory usage.

Like many other frequently reinvented wheels, caching often looks simpler than it is. A naive cache implementation is likely to turn a performance bottleneck into a scalability bottleneck, even if it does improve single-threaded performance. In this section we develop an efficient and scalable result cache for a computationally expensive function. Let's start with the obvious approach—a simple HashMap—and then look at some of its concurrency disadvantages and how to fix them.

The Computable<A,V> interface in Listing 5.16 describes a function with input of type *A* and result of type *V*. ExpensiveFunction, which implements Computable, takes a long time to compute its result; we'd like to create a Computable wrapper that remembers the results of previous computations and encapsulates the caching process. (This technique is known as *memoization*.)

```
public interface Computable<A, V> {
    V compute(A arg) throws InterruptedException;
}

public class ExpensiveFunction
        implements Computable<String, BigInteger> {
    public BigInteger compute(String arg) {
        // after deep thought...
        return new BigInteger(arg);
    }
}

public class Memoizer1<A, V> implements Computable<A, V> {
    @GuardedBy("this")
    private final Map<A, V> cache = new HashMap<A, V>();
    private final Computable<A, V> c;

    public Memoizer1(Computable<A, V> c) {
        this.c = c;
    }

    public synchronized V compute(A arg) throws InterruptedException {
        V result = cache.get(arg);
        if (result == null) {
            result = c.compute(arg);
            cache.put(arg, result);
        }
        return result;
    }
}
```

LISTING 5.16. Initial cache attempt using HashMap and synchronization.

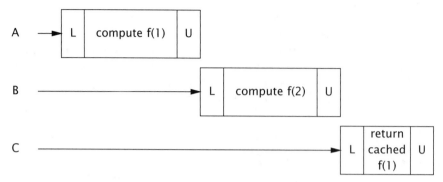

FIGURE 5.2. Poor concurrency of `Memoizer1`.

`Memoizer1` in Listing 5.16 shows a first attempt: using a HashMap to store the results of previous computations. The `compute` method first checks whether the desired result is already cached, and returns the precomputed value if it is. Otherwise, the result is computed and cached in the HashMap before returning.

HashMap is not thread-safe, so to ensure that two threads do not access the HashMap at the same time, `Memoizer1` takes the conservative approach of synchronizing the entire `compute` method. This ensures thread safety but has an obvious scalability problem: only one thread at a time can execute `compute` at all. If another thread is busy computing a result, other threads calling `compute` may be blocked for a long time. If multiple threads are queued up waiting to compute values not already computed, `compute` may actually take longer than it would have without memoization. Figure 5.2 illustrates what could happen when several threads attempt to use a function memoized with this approach. This is not the sort of performance improvement we had hoped to achieve through caching.

`Memoizer2` in Listing 5.17 improves on the awful concurrent behavior of `Memoizer1` by replacing the HashMap with a `ConcurrentHashMap`. Since ConcurrentHashMap is thread-safe, there is no need to synchronize when accessing the backing Map, thus eliminating the serialization induced by synchronizing `compute` in `Memoizer1`.

`Memoizer2` certainly has better concurrent behavior than `Memoizer1`: multiple threads can actually use it concurrently. But it still has some defects as a cache—there is a window of vulnerability in which two threads calling `compute` at the same time could end up computing the same value. In the case of memoization, this is merely inefficient—the purpose of a cache is to prevent the same data from being calculated multiple times. For a more general-purpose caching mechanism, it is far worse; for an object cache that is supposed to provide once-and-only-once initialization, this vulnerability would also pose a safety risk.

The problem with `Memoizer2` is that if one thread starts an expensive computation, other threads are not aware that the computation is in progress and so may start the same computation, as illustrated in Figure 5.3. We'd like to somehow represent the notion that "thread X is currently computing $f(27)$", so that if another thread arrives looking for $f(27)$, it knows that the most efficient way to find it is to head over to Thread X's house, hang out there until X is finished, and

```
public class Memoizer2<A, V> implements Computable<A, V> {
    private final Map<A, V> cache = new ConcurrentHashMap<A, V>();
    private final Computable<A, V> c;

    public Memoizer2(Computable<A, V> c) { this.c = c; }

    public V compute(A arg) throws InterruptedException {
        V result = cache.get(arg);
        if (result == null) {
            result = c.compute(arg);
            cache.put(arg, result);
        }
        return result;
    }
}
```

LISTING 5.17. Replacing HashMap with ConcurrentHashMap.

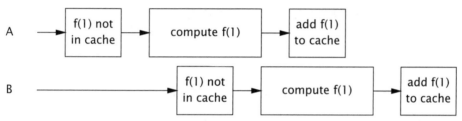

FIGURE 5.3. Two threads computing the same value when using Memoizer2.

then ask "Hey, what did you get for $f(27)$?"

We've already seen a class that does almost exactly this: FutureTask. FutureTask represents a computational process that may or may not already have completed. FutureTask.get returns the result of the computation immediately if it is available; otherwise it blocks until the result has been computed and then returns it.

Memoizer3 in Listing 5.18 redefines the backing Map for the value cache as a ConcurrentHashMap<A,Future<V>> instead of a ConcurrentHashMap<A,V>. Memoizer3 first checks to see if the appropriate calculation has been started (as opposed to finished, as in Memoizer2). If not, it creates a FutureTask, registers it in the Map, and starts the computation; otherwise it waits for the result of the existing computation. The result might be available immediately or might be in the process of being computed—but this is transparent to the caller of Future.get.

The Memoizer3 implementation is almost perfect: it exhibits very good concurrency (mostly derived from the excellent concurrency of ConcurrentHashMap), the result is returned efficiently if it is already known, and if the computation is in progress by another thread, newly arriving threads wait patiently for the result. It has only one defect—there is still a small window of vulnerability in which

```
public class Memoizer3<A, V> implements Computable<A, V> {
    private final Map<A, Future<V>> cache
            = new ConcurrentHashMap<A, Future<V>>();
    private final Computable<A, V> c;

    public Memoizer3(Computable<A, V> c) { this.c = c; }

    public V compute(final A arg) throws InterruptedException {
        Future<V> f = cache.get(arg);
        if (f == null) {
            Callable<V> eval = new Callable<V>() {
                public V call() throws InterruptedException {
                    return c.compute(arg);
                }
            };
            FutureTask<V> ft = new FutureTask<V>(eval);
            f = ft;
            cache.put(arg, ft);
            ft.run(); // call to c.compute happens here
        }
        try {
            return f.get();
        } catch (ExecutionException e) {
            throw launderThrowable(e.getCause());
        }
    }
}
```

LISTING 5.18. *Memoizing wrapper using FutureTask.*

two threads might compute the same value. This window is far smaller than in
`Memoizer2`, but because the `if` block in `compute` is still a nonatomic check-then-
act sequence, it is possible for two threads to call `compute` with the same value at
roughly the same time, both see that the cache does not contain the desired value,
and both start the computation. This unlucky timing is illustrated in Figure 5.4.

`Memoizer3` is vulnerable to this problem because a compound action (put-
if-absent) is performed on the backing map that cannot be made atomic using
locking. `Memoizer` in Listing 5.19 takes advantage of the atomic `putIfAbsent`
method of `ConcurrentMap`, closing the window of vulnerability in `Memoizer3`.

Caching a `Future` instead of a value creates the possibility of *cache pollution*:
if a computation is cancelled or fails, future attempts to compute the result will
also indicate cancellation or failure. To avoid this, `Memoizer` removes the `Fut`-
`ure` from the cache if it detects that the computation was cancelled; it might also
be desirable to remove the `Future` upon detecting a `RuntimeException` if the
computation might succeed on a future attempt. `Memoizer` also does not address

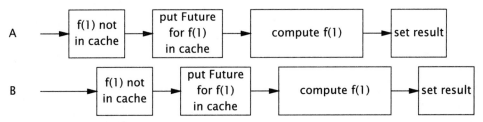

FIGURE 5.4. Unlucky timing that could cause `Memoizer3` to calculate the same value twice.

cache expiration, but this could be accomplished by using a subclass of `Future-Task` that associates an expiration time with each result and periodically scanning the cache for expired entries. (Similarly, it does not address cache eviction, where old entries are removed to make room for new ones so that the cache does not consume too much memory.)

With our concurrent cache implementation complete, we can now add real caching to the factorizing servlet from Chapter 2, as promised. `Factorizer` in Listing 5.20 uses `Memoizer` to cache previously computed values efficiently and scalably.

```
public class Memoizer<A, V> implements Computable<A, V> {
    private final ConcurrentMap<A, Future<V>> cache
        = new ConcurrentHashMap<A, Future<V>>();
    private final Computable<A, V> c;

    public Memoizer(Computable<A, V> c) { this.c = c; }

    public V compute(final A arg) throws InterruptedException {
        while (true) {
            Future<V> f = cache.get(arg);
            if (f == null) {
                Callable<V> eval = new Callable<V>() {
                    public V call() throws InterruptedException {
                        return c.compute(arg);
                    }
                };
                FutureTask<V> ft = new FutureTask<V>(eval);
                f = cache.putIfAbsent(arg, ft);
                if (f == null) { f = ft; ft.run(); }
            }
            try {
                return f.get();
            } catch (CancellationException e) {
                cache.remove(arg, f);
            } catch (ExecutionException e) {
                throw launderThrowable(e.getCause());
            }
        }
    }
}
```

LISTING 5.19. Final implementation of Memoizer.

```
@ThreadSafe
public class Factorizer implements Servlet {
    private final Computable<BigInteger, BigInteger[]> c =
        new Computable<BigInteger, BigInteger[]>() {
            public BigInteger[] compute(BigInteger arg) {
                return factor(arg);
            }
        };
    private final Computable<BigInteger, BigInteger[]> cache
        = new Memoizer<BigInteger, BigInteger[]>(c);

    public void service(ServletRequest req,
                        ServletResponse resp) {
        try {
            BigInteger i = extractFromRequest(req);
            encodeIntoResponse(resp, cache.compute(i));
        } catch (InterruptedException e) {
            encodeError(resp, "factorization interrupted");
        }
    }
}
```

LISTING 5.20. Factorizing servlet that caches results using Memoizer.

Summary of Part I

We've covered a lot of material so far! The following "concurrency cheat sheet" summarizes the main concepts and rules presented in Part I.

- *It's the mutable state, stupid.*[1]

  All concurrency issues boil down to coordinating access to mutable state. The less mutable state, the easier it is to ensure thread safety.

- *Make fields final unless they need to be mutable.*

- *Immutable objects are automatically thread-safe.*

  Immutable objects simplify concurrent programming tremendously. They are simpler and safer, and can be shared freely without locking or defensive copying.

- *Encapsulation makes it practical to manage the complexity.*

  You could write a thread-safe program with all data stored in global variables, but why would you want to? Encapsulating data within objects makes it easier to preserve their invariants; encapsulating synchronization within objects makes it easier to comply with their synchronization policy.

- *Guard each mutable variable with a lock.*

- *Guard all variables in an invariant with the same lock.*

- *Hold locks for the duration of compound actions.*

- *A program that accesses a mutable variable from multiple threads without synchronization is a broken program.*

- *Don't rely on clever reasoning about why you don't need to synchronize.*

- *Include thread safety in the design process—or explicitly document that your class is not thread-safe.*

- *Document your synchronization policy.*

---

1. During the 1992 U.S. presidential election, electoral strategist James Carville hung a sign in Bill Clinton's campaign headquarters reading "The economy, stupid", to keep the campaign on message.

Part II

Structuring Concurrent Applications

CHAPTER 6

Task Execution

Most concurrent applications are organized around the execution of *tasks*: abstract, discrete units of work. Dividing the work of an application into tasks simplifies program organization, facilitates error recovery by providing natural transaction boundaries, and promotes concurrency by providing a natural structure for parallelizing work.

6.1 Executing tasks in threads

The first step in organizing a program around task execution is identifying sensible *task boundaries*. Ideally, tasks are *independent* activities: work that doesn't depend on the state, result, or side effects of other tasks. Independence facilitates concurrency, as independent tasks can be executed in parallel if there are adequate processing resources. For greater flexibility in scheduling and load balancing tasks, each task should also represent a small fraction of your application's processing capacity.

Server applications should exhibit both *good throughput* and *good responsiveness* under normal load. Application providers want applications to support as many users as possible, so as to reduce provisioning costs per user; users want to get their response quickly. Further, applications should exhibit *graceful degradation* as they become overloaded, rather than simply falling over under heavy load. Choosing good task boundaries, coupled with a sensible *task execution policy* (see Section 6.2.2), can help achieve these goals.

Most server applications offer a natural choice of task boundary: individual client requests. Web servers, mail servers, file servers, EJB containers, and database servers all accept requests via network connections from remote clients. Using individual requests as task boundaries usually offers both independence and appropriate task sizing. For example, the result of submitting a message to a mail server is not affected by the other messages being processed at the same time, and handling a single message usually requires a very small percentage of the server's total capacity.

6.1.1 Executing tasks sequentially

There are a number of possible policies for scheduling tasks within an application, some of which exploit the potential for concurrency better than others. The simplest is to execute tasks sequentially in a single thread. `SingleThreadWeb-Server` in Listing 6.1 processes its tasks—HTTP requests arriving on port 80—sequentially. The details of the request processing aren't important; we're interested in characterizing the concurrency of various scheduling policies.

```
class SingleThreadWebServer {
    public static void main(String[] args) throws IOException {
        ServerSocket socket = new ServerSocket(80);
        while (true) {
            Socket connection = socket.accept();
            handleRequest(connection);
        }
    }
}
```

LISTING 6.1. Sequential web server.

`SingleThreadedWebServer` is simple and theoretically correct, but would perform poorly in production because it can handle only one request at a time. The main thread alternates between accepting connections and processing the associated request. While the server is handling a request, new connections must wait until it finishes the current request and calls `accept` again. This might work if request processing were so fast that `handleRequest` effectively returned immediately, but this doesn't describe any web server in the real world.

Processing a web request involves a mix of computation and I/O. The server must perform socket I/O to read the request and write the response, which can block due to network congestion or connectivity problems. It may also perform file I/O or make database requests, which can also block. In a single-threaded server, blocking not only delays completing the current request, but prevents pending requests from being processed at all. If one request blocks for an unusually long time, users might think the server is unavailable because it appears unresponsive. At the same time, resource utilization is poor, since the CPU sits idle while the single thread waits for its I/O to complete.

In server applications, sequential processing rarely provides either good throughput or good responsiveness. There are exceptions—such as when tasks are few and long-lived, or when the server serves a single client that makes only a single request at a time—but most server applications do not work this way.[1]

---

1. In some situations, sequential processing may offer a simplicity or safety advantage; most GUI frameworks process tasks sequentially using a single thread. We return to the sequential model in Chapter 9.

6.1.2 Explicitly creating threads for tasks

A more responsive approach is to create a new thread for servicing each request, as shown in ThreadPerTaskWebServer in Listing 6.2.

```
class ThreadPerTaskWebServer {
    public static void main(String[] args) throws IOException {
        ServerSocket socket = new ServerSocket(80);
        while (true) {
            final Socket connection = socket.accept();
            Runnable task = new Runnable() {
                    public void run() {
                        handleRequest(connection);
                    }
                };
            new Thread(task).start();
        }
    }
}
```

LISTING 6.2. Web server that starts a new thread for each request.

ThreadPerTaskWebServer is similar in structure to the single-threaded version—the main thread still alternates between accepting an incoming connection and dispatching the request. The difference is that for each connection, the main loop creates a new thread to process the request instead of processing it within the main thread. This has three main consequences:

- Task processing is offloaded from the main thread, enabling the main loop to resume waiting for the next incoming connection more quickly. This enables new connections to be accepted before previous requests complete, improving responsiveness.

- Tasks can be processed in parallel, enabling multiple requests to be serviced simultaneously. This may improve throughput if there are multiple processors, or if tasks need to block for any reason such as I/O completion, lock acquisition, or resource availability.

- Task-handling code must be thread-safe, because it may be invoked concurrently for multiple tasks.

Under light to moderate load, the thread-per-task approach is an improvement over sequential execution. As long as the request arrival rate does not exceed the server's capacity to handle requests, this approach offers better responsiveness and throughput.

6.1.3   Disadvantages of unbounded thread creation

For production use, however, the thread-per-task approach has some practical drawbacks, especially when a large number of threads may be created:

Thread lifecycle overhead. Thread creation and teardown are not free. The actual overhead varies across platforms, but thread creation takes time, introducing latency into request processing, and requires some processing activity by the JVM and OS. If requests are frequent and lightweight, as in most server applications, creating a new thread for each request can consume significant computing resources.

Resource consumption. Active threads consume system resources, especially memory. When there are more runnable threads than available processors, threads sit idle. Having many idle threads can tie up a lot of memory, putting pressure on the garbage collector, and having many threads competing for the CPUs can impose other performance costs as well. If you have enough threads to keep all the CPUs busy, creating more threads won't help and may even hurt.

Stability. There is a limit on how many threads can be created. The limit varies by platform and is affected by factors including JVM invocation parameters, the requested stack size in the Thread constructor, and limits on threads placed by the underlying operating system.[2] When you hit this limit, the most likely result is an OutOfMemoryError. Trying to recover from such an error is very risky; it is far easier to structure your program to avoid hitting this limit.

Up to a certain point, more threads can improve throughput, but beyond that point creating more threads just slows down your application, and creating one thread too many can cause your entire application to crash horribly. The way to stay out of danger is to place some bound on how many threads your application creates, and to test your application thoroughly to ensure that, even when this bound is reached, it does not run out of resources.

The problem with the thread-per-task approach is that nothing places any limit on the number of threads created except the rate at which remote users can throw HTTP requests at it. Like other concurrency hazards, unbounded thread creation may *appear* to work just fine during prototyping and development, with problems surfacing only when the application is deployed and under heavy load. So a malicious user, or enough ordinary users, can make your web server crash if the traffic load ever reaches a certain threshold. For a server application that is supposed to provide high availability and graceful degradation under load, this is a serious failing.

---

2. On 32-bit machines, a major limiting factor is address space for thread stacks. Each thread maintains two execution stacks, one for Java code and one for native code. Typical JVM defaults yield a combined stack size of around half a megabyte. (You can change this with the -Xss JVM flag or through the Thread constructor.) If you divide the per-thread stack size into 2^{32}, you get a limit of a few thousands or tens of thousands of threads. Other factors, such as OS limitations, may impose stricter limits.

6.2 The Executor framework

Tasks are logical units of work, and threads are a mechanism by which tasks can run asynchronously. We've examined two policies for executing tasks using threads—execute tasks sequentially in a single thread, and execute each task in its own thread. Both have serious limitations: the sequential approach suffers from poor responsiveness and throughput, and the thread-per-task approach suffers from poor resource management.

In Chapter 5, we saw how to use *bounded queues* to prevent an overloaded application from running out of memory. *Thread pools* offer the same benefit for thread management, and `java.util.concurrent` provides a flexible thread pool implementation as part of the Executor framework. The primary abstraction for task execution in the Java class libraries is *not* Thread, but Executor, shown in Listing 6.3.

```
public interface Executor {
    void execute(Runnable command);
}
```

LISTING 6.3. Executor interface.

Executor may be a simple interface, but it forms the basis for a flexible and powerful framework for asynchronous task execution that supports a wide variety of task execution policies. It provides a standard means of decoupling *task submission* from *task execution*, describing tasks with Runnable. The Executor implementations also provide lifecycle support and hooks for adding statistics gathering, application management, and monitoring.

Executor is based on the producer-consumer pattern, where activities that submit tasks are the producers (producing units of work to be done) and the threads that execute tasks are the consumers (consuming those units of work). *Using an Executor is usually the easiest path to implementing a producer-consumer design in your application.*

6.2.1 Example: web server using Executor

Building a web server with an Executor is easy. TaskExecutionWebServer in Listing 6.4 replaces the hard-coded thread creation with an Executor. In this case, we use one of the standard Executor implementations, a fixed-size thread pool with 100 threads.

In TaskExecutionWebServer, submission of the request-handling task is decoupled from its execution using an Executor, and its behavior can be changed merely by substituting a different Executor implementation. Changing Executor implementations or configuration is far less invasive than changing the way tasks are submitted; Executor configuration is generally a one-time event and can easily be exposed for deployment-time configuration, whereas task submission code tends to be strewn throughout the program and harder to expose.

```
class TaskExecutionWebServer {
    private static final int NTHREADS = 100;
    private static final Executor exec
        = Executors.newFixedThreadPool(NTHREADS);

    public static void main(String[] args) throws IOException {
        ServerSocket socket = new ServerSocket(80);
        while (true) {
            final Socket connection = socket.accept();
            Runnable task = new Runnable() {
                public void run() {
                    handleRequest(connection);
                }
            };
            exec.execute(task);
        }
    }
}
```

LISTING 6.4. Web server using a thread pool.

We can easily modify `TaskExecutionWebServer` to behave like `ThreadPer-TaskWebServer` by substituting an `Executor` that creates a new thread for each request. Writing such an `Executor` is trivial, as shown in `ThreadPerTaskExecutor` in Listing 6.5.

```
public class ThreadPerTaskExecutor implements Executor {
    public void execute(Runnable r) {
        new Thread(r).start();
    };
}
```

LISTING 6.5. Executor that starts a new thread for each task.

Similarly, it is also easy to write an `Executor` that would make `TaskExecutionWebServer` behave like the single-threaded version, executing each task synchronously before returning from `execute`, as shown in `WithinThreadExecutor` in Listing 6.6.

6.2.2 Execution policies

The value of decoupling submission from execution is that it lets you easily specify, and subsequently change without great difficulty, the *execution policy* for a given class of tasks. An execution policy specifies the "what, where, when, and how" of task execution, including:

```
public class WithinThreadExecutor implements Executor {
    public void execute(Runnable r) {
        r.run();
    };
}
```

LISTING 6.6. Executor that executes tasks synchronously in the calling thread.

- In what thread will tasks be executed?

- In what order should tasks be executed (FIFO, LIFO, priority order)?

- How many tasks may execute concurrently?

- How many tasks may be queued pending execution?

- If a task has to be rejected because the system is overloaded, which task should be selected as the victim, and how should the application be notified?

- What actions should be taken before or after executing a task?

Execution policies are a resource management tool, and the optimal policy depends on the available computing resources and your quality-of-service requirements. By limiting the number of concurrent tasks, you can ensure that the application does not fail due to resource exhaustion or suffer performance problems due to contention for scarce resources.[3] Separating the specification of execution policy from task submission makes it practical to select an execution policy at deployment time that is matched to the available hardware.

> Whenever you see code of the form:
>   `new Thread(runnable).start()`
> and you think you might at some point want a more flexible execution policy, seriously consider replacing it with the use of an Executor.

6.2.3   Thread pools

A thread pool, as its name suggests, manages a homogeneous pool of worker threads. A thread pool is tightly bound to a *work queue* holding tasks waiting to be executed. Worker threads have a simple life: request the next task from the work queue, execute it, and go back to waiting for another task.

---

3. This is analogous to one of the roles of a transaction monitor in an enterprise application: it can throttle the rate at which transactions are allowed to proceed so as not to exhaust or overstress limited resources.

Executing tasks in pool threads has a number of advantages over the thread-per-task approach. Reusing an existing thread instead of creating a new one amortizes thread creation and teardown costs over multiple requests. As an added bonus, since the worker thread often already exists at the time the request arrives, the latency associated with thread creation does not delay task execution, thus improving responsiveness. By properly tuning the size of the thread pool, you can have enough threads to keep the processors busy while not having so many that your application runs out of memory or thrashes due to competition among threads for resources.

The class library provides a flexible thread pool implementation along with some useful predefined configurations. You can create a thread pool by calling one of the static factory methods in `Executors`:

newFixedThreadPool. A fixed-size thread pool creates threads as tasks are submitted, up to the maximum pool size, and then attempts to keep the pool size constant (adding new threads if a thread dies due to an unexpected `Exception`).

newCachedThreadPool. A cached thread pool has more flexibility to reap idle threads when the current size of the pool exceeds the demand for processing, and to add new threads when demand increases, but places no bounds on the size of the pool.

newSingleThreadExecutor. A single-threaded executor creates a single worker thread to process tasks, replacing it if it dies unexpectedly. Tasks are guaranteed to be processed sequentially according to the order imposed by the task queue (FIFO, LIFO, priority order).[4]

newScheduledThreadPool. A fixed-size thread pool that supports delayed and periodic task execution, similar to `Timer`. (See Section 6.2.5.)

The `newFixedThreadPool` and `newCachedThreadPool` factories return instances of the general-purpose `ThreadPoolExecutor`, which can also be used directly to construct more specialized executors. We discuss thread pool configuration options in depth in Chapter 8.

The web server in `TaskExecutionWebServer` uses an `Executor` with a bounded pool of worker threads. Submitting a task with `execute` adds the task to the work queue, and the worker threads repeatedly dequeue tasks from the work queue and execute them.

Switching from a thread-per-task policy to a pool-based policy has a big effect on application stability: the web server will no longer fail under heavy load.[5]

---

4. Single-threaded executors also provide sufficient internal synchronization to guarantee that any memory writes made by tasks are visible to subsequent tasks; this means that objects can be safely confined to the "task thread" even though that thread may be replaced with another from time to time.

5. While the server may not fail due to the creation of too many threads, if the task arrival rate exceeds the task service rate for long enough it is still possible (just harder) to run out of memory because of the growing queue of `Runnables` awaiting execution. This can be addressed within the `Executor` framework by using a bounded work queue—see Section 8.3.2.

It also degrades more gracefully, since it does not create thousands of threads that compete for limited CPU and memory resources. And using an Executor opens the door to all sorts of additional opportunities for tuning, management, monitoring, logging, error reporting, and other possibilities that would have been far more difficult to add without a task execution framework.

6.2.4 Executor lifecycle

We've seen how to create an Executor but not how to shut one down. An Executor implementation is likely to create threads for processing tasks. But the JVM can't exit until all the (nondaemon) threads have terminated, so failing to shut down an Executor could prevent the JVM from exiting.

Because an Executor processes tasks asynchronously, at any given time the state of previously submitted tasks is not immediately obvious. Some may have completed, some may be currently running, and others may be queued awaiting execution. In shutting down an application, there is a spectrum from graceful shutdown (finish what you've started but don't accept any new work) to abrupt shutdown (turn off the power to the machine room), and various points in between. Since Executors provide a service to applications, they should be able to be shut down as well, both gracefully and abruptly, and feed back information to the application about the status of tasks that were affected by the shutdown.

To address the issue of execution service lifecycle, the ExecutorService interface extends Executor, adding a number of methods for lifecycle management (as well as some convenience methods for task submission). The lifecycle management methods of ExecutorService are shown in Listing 6.7.

```java
public interface ExecutorService extends Executor {
    void shutdown();
    List<Runnable> shutdownNow();
    boolean isShutdown();
    boolean isTerminated();
    boolean awaitTermination(long timeout, TimeUnit unit)
        throws InterruptedException;
    // ... additional convenience methods for task submission
}
```

LISTING 6.7. Lifecycle methods in ExecutorService.

The lifecycle implied by ExecutorService has three states—*running, shutting down,* and *terminated.* ExecutorServices are initially created in the *running* state. The shutdown method initiates a graceful shutdown: no new tasks are accepted but previously submitted tasks are allowed to complete—including those that have not yet begun execution. The shutdownNow method initiates an abrupt shutdown: it attempts to cancel outstanding tasks and does not start any tasks that are queued but not begun.

Tasks submitted to an ExecutorService after it has been shut down are handled by the *rejected execution handler* (see Section 8.3.3), which might silently dis-

card the task or might cause execute to throw the unchecked RejectedExecu-
tionException. Once all tasks have completed, the ExecutorService transitions
to the *terminated* state. You can wait for an ExecutorService to reach the terminated state with awaitTermination, or poll for whether it has yet terminated with
isTerminated. It is common to follow shutdown immediately by awaitTermination, creating the effect of synchronously shutting down the ExecutorService.
(Executor shutdown and task cancellation are covered in more detail in Chapter
7.)

LifecycleWebServer in Listing 6.8 extends our web server with lifecycle support. It can be shut down in two ways: programmatically by calling stop, and
through a client request by sending the web server a specially formatted HTTP
request.

```
class LifecycleWebServer {
    private final ExecutorService exec = ...;

    public void start() throws IOException {
        ServerSocket socket = new ServerSocket(80);
        while (!exec.isShutdown()) {
            try {
                final Socket conn = socket.accept();
                exec.execute(new Runnable() {
                    public void run() { handleRequest(conn); }
                });
            } catch (RejectedExecutionException e) {
                if (!exec.isShutdown())
                    log("task submission rejected", e);
            }
        }
    }

    public void stop() { exec.shutdown(); }

    void handleRequest(Socket connection) {
        Request req = readRequest(connection);
        if (isShutdownRequest(req))
            stop();
        else
            dispatchRequest(req);
    }
}
```

LISTING 6.8. Web server with shutdown support.

6.2.5 Delayed and periodic tasks

The Timer facility manages the execution of deferred ("run this task in 100 ms") and periodic ("run this task every 10 ms") tasks. However, Timer has some drawbacks, and ScheduledThreadPoolExecutor should be thought of as its replacement.[6] You can construct a ScheduledThreadPoolExecutor through its constructor or through the newScheduledThreadPool factory.

A Timer creates only a single thread for executing timer tasks. If a timer task takes too long to run, the timing accuracy of other TimerTasks can suffer. If a recurring TimerTask is scheduled to run every 10 ms and another Timer-Task takes 40 ms to run, the recurring task either (depending on whether it was scheduled at fixed rate or fixed delay) gets called four times in rapid succession after the long-running task completes, or "misses" four invocations completely. Scheduled thread pools address this limitation by letting you provide multiple threads for executing deferred and periodic tasks.

Another problem with Timer is that it behaves poorly if a TimerTask throws an unchecked exception. The Timer thread doesn't catch the exception, so an unchecked exception thrown from a TimerTask terminates the timer thread. Timer also doesn't resurrect the thread in this situation; instead, it erroneously assumes the entire Timer was cancelled. In this case, TimerTasks that are already scheduled but not yet executed are never run, and new tasks cannot be scheduled. (This problem, called "thread leakage" is described in Section 7.3, along with techniques for avoiding it.)

OutOfTime in Listing 6.9 illustrates how a Timer can become confused in this manner and, as confusion loves company, how the Timer shares its confusion with the next hapless caller that tries to submit a TimerTask. You might expect the program to run for six seconds and exit, but what actually happens is that it terminates after one second with an IllegalStateException whose message text is "Timer already cancelled". ScheduledThreadPoolExecutor deals properly with ill-behaved tasks; there is little reason to use Timer in Java 5.0 or later.

If you need to build your own scheduling service, you may still be able to take advantage of the library by using a DelayQueue, a BlockingQueue implementation that provides the scheduling functionality of ScheduledThreadPoolExecutor. A DelayQueue manages a collection of Delayed objects. A Delayed has a delay time associated with it: DelayQueue lets you take an element only if its delay has expired. Objects are returned from a DelayQueue ordered by the time associated with their delay.

6.3 Finding exploitable parallelism

The Executor framework makes it easy to specify an execution policy, but in order to use an Executor, you have to be able to describe your task as a Runnable. In most server applications, there is an obvious task boundary: a single client request. But sometimes good task boundaries are not quite so obvious, as

---

6. Timer does have support for scheduling based on absolute, not relative time, so that tasks can be sensitive to changes in the system clock; ScheduledThreadPoolExecutor supports only relative time.

```
public class OutOfTime {
    public static void main(String[] args) throws Exception {
        Timer timer = new Timer();
        timer.schedule(new ThrowTask(), 1);
        SECONDS.sleep(1);
        timer.schedule(new ThrowTask(), 1);
        SECONDS.sleep(5);
    }

    static class ThrowTask extends TimerTask {
        public void run() { throw new RuntimeException(); }
    }
}
```

LISTING 6.9. Class illustrating confusing Timer behavior.

in many desktop applications. There may also be exploitable parallelism within
a single client request in server applications, as is sometimes the case in database
servers. (For a further discussion of the competing design forces in choosing task
boundaries, see [CPJ 4.4.1.1].)

In this section we develop several versions of a component that admit varying
degrees of concurrency. Our sample component is the page-rendering portion of
a browser application, which takes a page of HTML and renders it into an image
buffer. To keep it simple, we assume that the HTML consists only of marked up
text interspersed with image elements with pre-specified dimensions and URLs.

6.3.1 Example: sequential page renderer

The simplest approach is to process the HTML document sequentially. As text
markup is encountered, render it into the image buffer; as image references are
encountered, fetch the image over the network and draw it into the image buffer
as well. This is easy to implement and requires touching each element of the
input only once (it doesn't even require buffering the document), but is likely to
annoy the user, who may have to wait a long time before all the text is rendered.

A less annoying but still sequential approach involves rendering the text elements first, leaving rectangular placeholders for the images, and after completing
the initial pass on the document, going back and downloading the images and
drawing them into the associated placeholder. This approach is shown in Sin-
gleThreadRenderer in Listing 6.10.

Downloading an image mostly involves waiting for I/O to complete, and during this time the CPU does little work. So the sequential approach may under-
utilize the CPU, and also makes the user wait longer than necessary to see the
finished page. We can achieve better utilization and responsiveness by breaking
the problem into independent tasks that can execute concurrently.

```
public class SingleThreadRenderer {
    void renderPage(CharSequence source) {
        renderText(source);
        List<ImageData> imageData = new ArrayList<ImageData>();
        for (ImageInfo imageInfo : scanForImageInfo(source))
            imageData.add(imageInfo.downloadImage());
        for (ImageData data : imageData)
            renderImage(data);
    }
}
```

LISTING 6.10. Rendering page elements sequentially.

6.3.2   Result-bearing tasks: `Callable` and `Future`

The `Executor` framework uses `Runnable` as its basic task representation. `Runnable` is a fairly limiting abstraction; `run` cannot return a value or throw checked exceptions, although it can have side effects such as writing to a log file or placing a result in a shared data structure.

Many tasks are effectively deferred computations—executing a database query, fetching a resource over the network, or computing a complicated function. For these types of tasks, `Callable` is a better abstraction: it expects that the main entry point, `call`, will return a value and anticipates that it might throw an exception.[7] `Executors` includes several utility methods for wrapping other types of tasks, including `Runnable` and `java.security.PrivilegedAction`, with a `Callable`.

`Runnable` and `Callable` describe abstract computational tasks. Tasks are usually finite: they have a clear starting point and they eventually terminate. The lifecycle of a task executed by an `Executor` has four phases: *created*, *submitted*, *started*, and *completed*. Since tasks can take a long time to run, we also want to be able to cancel a task. In the `Executor` framework, tasks that have been submitted but not yet started can always be cancelled, and tasks that have started can sometimes be cancelled if they are responsive to interruption. Cancelling a task that has already completed has no effect. (Cancellation is covered in greater detail in Chapter 7.)

`Future` represents the lifecycle of a task and provides methods to test whether the task has completed or been cancelled, retrieve its result, and cancel the task. `Callable` and `Future` are shown in Listing 6.11. Implicit in the specification of `Future` is that task lifecycle can only move forwards, not backwards—just like the `ExecutorService` lifecycle. Once a task is completed, it stays in that state forever.

The behavior of `get` varies depending on the task state (not yet started, running, completed). It returns immediately or throws an `Exception` if the task has already completed, but if not it blocks until the task completes. If the task completes by throwing an exception, `get` rethrows it wrapped in an `Execution-`

---

7. To express a non-value-returning task with `Callable`, use `Callable<Void>`.

```
public interface Callable<V> {
    V call() throws Exception;
}

public interface Future<V> {
    boolean cancel(boolean mayInterruptIfRunning);
    boolean isCancelled();
    boolean isDone();
    V get() throws InterruptedException, ExecutionException,
                   CancellationException;
    V get(long timeout, TimeUnit unit)
        throws InterruptedException, ExecutionException,
               CancellationException, TimeoutException;
}
```

LISTING 6.11. Callable and Future interfaces.

Exception; if it was cancelled, get throws CancellationException. If get throws
ExecutionException, the underlying exception can be retrieved with getCause.

There are several ways to create a Future to describe a task. The submit
methods in ExecutorService all return a Future, so that you can submit a Runnable or a Callable to an executor and get back a Future that can be used to
retrieve the result or cancel the task. You can also explicitly instantiate a FutureTask for a given Runnable or Callable. (Because FutureTask implements
Runnable, it can be submitted to an Executor for execution or executed directly
by calling its run method.)

As of Java 6, ExecutorService implementations can override newTaskFor in
AbstractExecutorService to control instantiation of the Future corresponding
to a submitted Callable or Runnable. The default implementation just creates a
new FutureTask, as shown in Listing 6.12.

```
protected <T> RunnableFuture<T> newTaskFor(Callable<T> task) {
    return new FutureTask<T>(task);
}
```

LISTING 6.12. Default implementation of newTaskFor in ThreadPoolExecutor.

Submitting a Runnable or Callable to an Executor constitutes a safe publication (see Section 3.5) of the Runnable or Callable from the submitting thread to
the thread that will eventually execute the task. Similarly, setting the result value
for a Future constitutes a safe publication of the result from the thread in which
it was computed to any thread that retrieves it via get.

6.3.3 Example: page renderer with Future

As a first step towards making the page renderer more concurrent, let's divide it into two tasks, one that renders the text and one that downloads all the images. (Because one task is largely CPU-bound and the other is largely I/O-bound, this approach may yield improvements even on single-CPU systems.)

Callable and Future can help us express the interaction between these cooperating tasks. In FutureRenderer in Listing 6.13, we create a Callable to download all the images, and submit it to an ExecutorService. This returns a Future describing the task's execution; when the main task gets to the point where it needs the images, it waits for the result by calling Future.get. If we're lucky, the results will already be ready by the time we ask; otherwise, at least we got a head start on downloading the images.

The state-dependent nature of get means that the caller need not be aware of the state of the task, and the safe publication properties of task submission and result retrieval make this approach thread-safe. The exception handling code surrounding Future.get deals with two possible problems: that the task encountered an Exception, or the thread calling get was interrupted before the results were available. (See Sections 5.5.2 and 5.4.)

FutureRenderer allows the text to be rendered concurrently with downloading the image data. When all the images are downloaded, they are rendered onto the page. This is an improvement in that the user sees a result quickly and it exploits some parallelism, but we can do considerably better. There is no need for users to wait for *all* the images to be downloaded; they would probably prefer to see individual images drawn as they become available.

6.3.4 Limitations of parallelizing heterogeneous tasks

In the last example, we tried to execute two different types of tasks in parallel—downloading the images and rendering the page. But obtaining significant performance improvements by trying to parallelize sequential heterogeneous tasks can be tricky.

Two people can divide the work of cleaning the dinner dishes fairly effectively: one person washes while the other dries. However, assigning a different type of task to each worker does not scale well; if several more people show up, it is not obvious how they can help without getting in the way or significantly restructuring the division of labor. Without finding finer-grained parallelism among similar tasks, this approach will yield diminishing returns.

A further problem with dividing heterogeneous tasks among multiple workers is that the tasks may have disparate sizes. If you divide tasks A and B between two workers but A takes ten times as long as B, you've only speeded up the total process by 9%. Finally, dividing a task among multiple workers always involves some amount of coordination overhead; for the division to be worthwhile, this overhead must be more than compensated by productivity improvements due to parallelism.

FutureRenderer uses two tasks: one for rendering text and one for downloading the images. If rendering the text is much faster than downloading the images,

```
public class FutureRenderer {
    private final ExecutorService executor = ...;

    void renderPage(CharSequence source) {
        final List<ImageInfo> imageInfos = scanForImageInfo(source);
        Callable<List<ImageData>> task =
                new Callable<List<ImageData>>() {
                    public List<ImageData> call() {
                        List<ImageData> result
                                = new ArrayList<ImageData>();
                        for (ImageInfo imageInfo : imageInfos)
                            result.add(imageInfo.downloadImage());
                        return result;
                    }
                };

        Future<List<ImageData>> future = executor.submit(task);
        renderText(source);

        try {
            List<ImageData> imageData = future.get();
            for (ImageData data : imageData)
                renderImage(data);
        } catch (InterruptedException e) {
            // Re-assert the thread's interrupted status
            Thread.currentThread().interrupt();
            // We don't need the result, so cancel the task too
            future.cancel(true);
        } catch (ExecutionException e) {
            throw launderThrowable(e.getCause());
        }
    }
}
```

LISTING 6.13. Waiting for image download with Future.

as is entirely possible, the resulting performance is not much different from the sequential version, but the code is a lot more complicated. And the best we can do with two threads is speed things up by a factor of two. Thus, trying to increase concurrency by parallelizing heterogeneous activities can be a lot of work, and there is a limit to how much additional concurrency you can get out of it. (See Sections 11.4.2 and 11.4.3 for another example of the same phenomenon.)

> The real performance payoff of dividing a program's workload into tasks comes when there are a large number of independent, *homogeneous* tasks that can be processed concurrently.

6.3.5 CompletionService: Executor meets BlockingQueue

If you have a batch of computations to submit to an Executor and you want to retrieve their results as they become available, you could retain the Future associated with each task and repeatedly poll for completion by calling get with a timeout of zero. This is possible, but tedious. Fortunately there is a better way: a *completion service*.

CompletionService combines the functionality of an Executor and a BlockingQueue. You can submit Callable tasks to it for execution and use the queue-like methods take and poll to retrieve completed results, packaged as Futures, as they become available. ExecutorCompletionService implements Completion-Service, delegating the computation to an Executor.

The implementation of ExecutorCompletionService is quite straightforward. The constructor creates a BlockingQueue to hold the completed results. Future-Task has a done method that is called when the computation completes. When a task is submitted, it is wrapped with a QueueingFuture, a subclass of FutureTask that overrides done to place the result on the BlockingQueue, as shown in Listing 6.14. The take and poll methods delegate to the BlockingQueue, blocking if results are not yet available.

```
private class QueueingFuture<V> extends FutureTask<V> {
    QueueingFuture(Callable<V> c) { super(c); }
    QueueingFuture(Runnable t, V r) { super(t, r); }

    protected void done() {
        completionQueue.add(this);
    }
}
```

Listing 6.14. QueueingFuture class used by ExecutorCompletionService.

6.3.6 Example: page renderer with CompletionService

We can use a CompletionService to improve the performance of the page renderer in two ways: shorter total runtime and improved responsiveness. We
can create a separate task for downloading *each* image and execute them in a
thread pool, turning the sequential download into a parallel one: this reduces the
amount of time to download all the images. And by fetching results from the
CompletionService and rendering each image as soon as it is available, we can
give the user a more dynamic and responsive user interface. This implementation
is shown in Renderer in Listing 6.15.

```java
public class Renderer {
    private final ExecutorService executor;

    Renderer(ExecutorService executor) { this.executor = executor; }

    void renderPage(CharSequence source) {
        List<ImageInfo> info = scanForImageInfo(source);
        CompletionService<ImageData> completionService =
            new ExecutorCompletionService<ImageData>(executor);
        for (final ImageInfo imageInfo : info)
            completionService.submit(new Callable<ImageData>() {
                public ImageData call() {
                    return imageInfo.downloadImage();
                }
            });

        renderText(source);

        try {
            for (int t = 0, n = info.size(); t < n; t++) {
                Future<ImageData> f = completionService.take();
                ImageData imageData = f.get();
                renderImage(imageData);
            }
        } catch (InterruptedException e) {
            Thread.currentThread().interrupt();
        } catch (ExecutionException e) {
            throw launderThrowable(e.getCause());
        }
    }
}
```

LISTING 6.15. Using CompletionService to render page elements as they become
available.

Multiple ExecutorCompletionServices can share a single Executor, so it is perfectly sensible to create an `ExecutorCompletionService` that is private to a particular computation while sharing a common `Executor`. When used in this way, a `CompletionService` acts as a handle for a batch of computations in much the same way that a `Future` acts as a handle for a single computation. By remembering how many tasks were submitted to the `CompletionService` and counting how many completed results are retrieved, you can know when all the results for a given batch have been retrieved, even if you use a shared `Executor`.

6.3.7 Placing time limits on tasks

Sometimes, if an activity does not complete within a certain amount of time, the result is no longer needed and the activity can be abandoned. For example, a web application may fetch its advertisements from an external ad server, but if the ad is not available within two seconds, it instead displays a default advertisement so that ad unavailability does not undermine the site's responsiveness requirements. Similarly, a portal site may fetch data in parallel from multiple data sources, but may be willing to wait only a certain amount of time for data to be available before rendering the page without it.

The primary challenge in executing tasks within a time budget is making sure that you don't wait longer than the time budget to get an answer or find out that one is not forthcoming. The timed version of `Future.get` supports this requirement: it returns as soon as the result is ready, but throws `TimeoutException` if the result is not ready within the timeout period.

A secondary problem when using timed tasks is to stop them when they run out of time, so they do not waste computing resources by continuing to compute a result that will not be used. This can be accomplished by having the task strictly manage its own time budget and abort if it runs out of time, or by cancelling the task if the timeout expires. Again, `Future` can help; if a timed `get` completes with a `TimeoutException`, you can cancel the task through the `Future`. If the task is written to be cancellable (see Chapter 7), it can be terminated early so as not to consume excessive resources. This technique is used in Listings 6.13 and 6.16.

Listing 6.16 shows a typical application of a timed `Future.get`. It generates a composite web page that contains the requested content plus an advertisement fetched from an ad server. It submits the ad-fetching task to an executor, computes the rest of the page content, and then waits for the ad until its time budget runs out.[8] If the `get` times out, it cancels[9] the ad-fetching task and uses a default advertisement instead.

6.3.8 Example: a travel reservations portal

The time-budgeting approach in the previous section can be easily generalized to an arbitrary number of tasks. Consider a travel reservation portal: the user en-

---

8. The timeout passed to `get` is computed by subtracting the current time from the deadline; this may in fact yield a negative number, but all the timed methods in `java.util.concurrent` treat negative timeouts as zero, so no extra code is needed to deal with this case.
9. The `true` parameter to `Future.cancel` means that the task thread can be interrupted if the task is currently running; see Chapter 7.

```
Page renderPageWithAd() throws InterruptedException {
    long endNanos = System.nanoTime() + TIME_BUDGET;
    Future<Ad> f = exec.submit(new FetchAdTask());
    // Render the page while waiting for the ad
    Page page = renderPageBody();
    Ad ad;
    try {
        // Only wait for the remaining time budget
        long timeLeft = endNanos - System.nanoTime();
        ad = f.get(timeLeft, NANOSECONDS);
    } catch (ExecutionException e) {
        ad = DEFAULT_AD;
    } catch (TimeoutException e) {
        ad = DEFAULT_AD;
        f.cancel(true);
    }
    page.setAd(ad);
    return page;
}
```

LISTING 6.16. Fetching an advertisement with a time budget.

ters travel dates and requirements and the portal fetches and displays bids from a number of airlines, hotels or car rental companies. Depending on the company, fetching a bid might involve invoking a web service, consulting a database, performing an EDI transaction, or some other mechanism. Rather than have the response time for the page be driven by the slowest response, it may be preferable to present only the information available within a given time budget. For providers that do not respond in time, the page could either omit them completely or display a placeholder such as "Did not hear from Air Java in time."

Fetching a bid from one company is independent of fetching bids from another, so fetching a single bid is a sensible task boundary that allows bid retrieval to proceed concurrently. It would be easy enough to create *n* tasks, submit them to a thread pool, retain the Futures, and use a timed get to fetch each result sequentially via its Future, but there is an even easier way—invokeAll.

Listing 6.17 uses the timed version of invokeAll to submit multiple tasks to an ExecutorService and retrieve the results. The invokeAll method takes a collection of tasks and returns a collection of Futures. The two collections have identical structures; invokeAll adds the Futures to the returned collection in the order imposed by the task collection's iterator, thus allowing the caller to associate a Future with the Callable it represents. The timed version of invokeAll will return when all the tasks have completed, the calling thread is interrupted, or the timeout expires. Any tasks that are not complete when the timeout expires are cancelled. On return from invokeAll, each task will have either completed normally or been cancelled; the client code can call get or isCancelled to find out which.

Summary

Structuring applications around the execution of *tasks* can simplify development and facilitate concurrency. The `Executor` framework permits you to decouple task submission from execution policy and supports a rich variety of execution policies; whenever you find yourself creating threads to perform tasks, consider using an `Executor` instead. To maximize the benefit of decomposing an application into tasks, you must identify sensible task boundaries. In some applications, the obvious task boundaries work well, whereas in others some analysis may be required to uncover finer-grained exploitable parallelism.

```
private class QuoteTask implements Callable<TravelQuote> {
    private final TravelCompany company;
    private final TravelInfo travelInfo;
    ...
    public TravelQuote call() throws Exception {
        return company.solicitQuote(travelInfo);
    }
}

public List<TravelQuote> getRankedTravelQuotes(
        TravelInfo travelInfo, Set<TravelCompany> companies,
        Comparator<TravelQuote> ranking, long time, TimeUnit unit)
        throws InterruptedException {
    List<QuoteTask> tasks = new ArrayList<QuoteTask>();
    for (TravelCompany company : companies)
        tasks.add(new QuoteTask(company, travelInfo));

    List<Future<TravelQuote>> futures =
        exec.invokeAll(tasks, time, unit);

    List<TravelQuote> quotes =
        new ArrayList<TravelQuote>(tasks.size());
    Iterator<QuoteTask> taskIter = tasks.iterator();
    for (Future<TravelQuote> f : futures) {
        QuoteTask task = taskIter.next();
        try {
            quotes.add(f.get());
        } catch (ExecutionException e) {
            quotes.add(task.getFailureQuote(e.getCause()));
        } catch (CancellationException e) {
            quotes.add(task.getTimeoutQuote(e));
        }
    }

    Collections.sort(quotes, ranking);
    return quotes;
}
```

LISTING 6.17. Requesting travel quotes under a time budget.

CHAPTER 7

Cancellation and Shutdown

It is easy to start tasks and threads. Most of the time we allow them to decide when to stop by letting them run to completion. Sometimes, however, we want to stop tasks or threads earlier than they would on their own, perhaps because the user cancelled an operation or the application needs to shut down quickly.

Getting tasks and threads to stop safely, quickly, and reliably is not always easy. Java does not provide any mechanism for safely forcing a thread to stop what it is doing.[1] Instead, it provides *interruption*, a cooperative mechanism that lets one thread ask another to stop what it is doing.

The cooperative approach is required because we rarely want a task, thread, or service to stop *immediately*, since that could leave shared data structures in an inconsistent state. Instead, tasks and services can be coded so that, when requested, they clean up any work currently in progress and *then* terminate. This provides greater flexibility, since the task code itself is usually better able to assess the cleanup required than is the code requesting cancellation.

End-of-lifecycle issues can complicate the design and implementation of tasks, services, and applications, and this important element of program design is too often ignored. Dealing well with failure, shutdown, and cancellation is one of the characteristics that distinguishes a well-behaved application from one that merely works. This chapter addresses mechanisms for cancellation and interruption, and how to code tasks and services to be responsive to cancellation requests.

7.1 Task cancellation

An activity is *cancellable* if external code can move it to completion before its normal completion. There are a number of reasons why you might want to cancel an activity:

---

1. The deprecated `Thread.stop` and `suspend` methods were an attempt to provide such a mechanism, but were quickly realized to be seriously flawed and should be avoided. See `http://java.sun.com/j2se/1.5.0/docs/guide/misc/threadPrimitiveDeprecation.html` for an explanation of the problems with these methods.

User-requested cancellation. The user clicked on the "cancel" button in a GUI application, or requested cancellation through a management interface such as JMX (Java Management Extensions).

Time-limited activities. An application searches a problem space for a finite amount of time and chooses the best solution found within that time. When the timer expires, any tasks still searching are cancelled.

Application events. An application searches a problem space by decomposing it so that different tasks search different regions of the problem space. When one task finds a solution, all other tasks still searching are cancelled.

Errors. A web crawler searches for relevant pages, storing pages or summary data to disk. When a crawler task encounters an error (for example, the disk is full), other crawling tasks are cancelled, possibly recording their current state so that they can be restarted later.

Shutdown. When an application or service is shut down, something must be done about work that is currently being processed or queued for processing. In a graceful shutdown, tasks currently in progress might be allowed to complete; in a more immediate shutdown, currently executing tasks might be cancelled.

There is no safe way to preemptively stop a thread in Java, and therefore no safe way to preemptively stop a task. There are only cooperative mechanisms, by which the task and the code requesting cancellation follow an agreed-upon protocol.

One such cooperative mechanism is setting a "cancellation requested" flag that the task checks periodically; if it finds the flag set, the task terminates early. `PrimeGenerator` in Listing 7.1, which enumerates prime numbers until it is cancelled, illustrates this technique. The `cancel` method sets the `cancelled` flag, and the main loop polls this flag before searching for the next prime number. (For this to work reliably, `cancelled` must be `volatile`.)

Listing 7.2 shows a sample use of this class that lets the prime generator run for one second before cancelling it. The generator won't necessarily stop after exactly one second, since there may be some delay between the time that cancellation is requested and the time that the `run` loop next checks for cancellation. The `cancel` method is called from a `finally` block to ensure that the prime generator is cancelled even if the the call to `sleep` is interrupted. If `cancel` were not called, the prime-seeking thread would run forever, consuming CPU cycles and preventing the JVM from exiting.

A task that wants to be cancellable must have a *cancellation policy* that specifies the "how", "when", and "what" of cancellation—how other code can request cancellation, when the task checks whether cancellation has been requested, and what actions the task takes in response to a cancellation request.

Consider the real-world example of stopping payment on a check. Banks have rules about how to submit a stop-payment request, what responsiveness guarantees it makes in processing such requests, and what procedures it follows when

```
@ThreadSafe
public class PrimeGenerator implements Runnable {
    @GuardedBy("this")
    private final List<BigInteger> primes
            = new ArrayList<BigInteger>();
    private volatile boolean cancelled;

    public void run() {
        BigInteger p = BigInteger.ONE;
        while (!cancelled) {
            p = p.nextProbablePrime();
            synchronized (this) {
                primes.add(p);
            }
        }
    }

    public void cancel() { cancelled = true; }

    public synchronized List<BigInteger> get() {
        return new ArrayList<BigInteger>(primes);
    }
}
```

LISTING 7.1. Using a volatile field to hold cancellation state.

```
List<BigInteger> aSecondOfPrimes() throws InterruptedException {
    PrimeGenerator generator = new PrimeGenerator();
    new Thread(generator).start();
    try {
        SECONDS.sleep(1);
    } finally {
        generator.cancel();
    }
    return generator.get();
}
```

LISTING 7.2. Generating a second's worth of prime numbers.

payment is actually stopped (such as notifying the other bank involved in the transaction and assessing a fee against the payor's account). Taken together, these procedures and guarantees comprise the cancellation policy for check payment.

PrimeGenerator uses a simple cancellation policy: client code requests cancellation by calling cancel, PrimeGenerator checks for cancellation once per prime found and exits when it detects cancellation has been requested.

7.1.1 Interruption

The cancellation mechanism in PrimeGenerator will eventually cause the prime-seeking task to exit, but it might take a while. If, however, a task that uses this approach calls a blocking method such as BlockingQueue.put, we could have a more serious problem—the task might never check the cancellation flag and therefore might never terminate.

BrokenPrimeProducer in Listing 7.3 illustrates this problem. The producer thread generates primes and places them on a blocking queue. If the producer gets ahead of the consumer, the queue will fill up and put will block. What happens if the consumer tries to cancel the producer task while it is blocked in put? It can call cancel which will set the cancelled flag—but the producer will never check the flag because it will never emerge from the blocking put (because the consumer has stopped retrieving primes from the queue).

As we hinted in Chapter 5, certain blocking library methods support *interruption*. Thread interruption is a cooperative mechanism for a thread to signal another thread that it should, at its convenience and if it feels like it, stop what it is doing and do something else.

> There is nothing in the API or language specification that ties interruption to any specific cancellation semantics, but in practice, using interruption for anything but cancellation is fragile and difficult to sustain in larger applications.

Each thread has a boolean *interrupted status*; interrupting a thread sets its interrupted status to true. Thread contains methods for interrupting a thread and querying the interrupted status of a thread, as shown in Listing 7.4. The interrupt method interrupts the target thread, and isInterrupted returns the interrupted status of the target thread. The poorly named static interrupted method *clears* the interrupted status of the current thread and returns its previous value; this is the only way to clear the interrupted status.

Blocking library methods like Thread.sleep and Object.wait try to detect when a thread has been interrupted and return early. They respond to interruption by clearing the interrupted status and throwing InterruptedException, indicating that the blocking operation completed early due to interruption. The JVM makes no guarantees on how quickly a blocking method will detect interruption, but in practice this happens reasonably quickly.

```
class BrokenPrimeProducer extends Thread {
    private final BlockingQueue<BigInteger> queue;
    private volatile boolean cancelled = false;

    BrokenPrimeProducer(BlockingQueue<BigInteger> queue) {
        this.queue = queue;
    }

    public void run() {
        try {
            BigInteger p = BigInteger.ONE;
            while (!cancelled)
                queue.put(p = p.nextProbablePrime());
        } catch (InterruptedException consumed) { }
    }

    public void cancel() { cancelled = true; }
}

void consumePrimes() throws InterruptedException {
    BlockingQueue<BigInteger> primes = ...;
    BrokenPrimeProducer producer = new BrokenPrimeProducer(primes);
    producer.start();
    try {
        while (needMorePrimes())
            consume(primes.take());
    } finally {
        producer.cancel();
    }
}
```

LISTING 7.3. Unreliable cancellation that can leave producers stuck in a blocking operation. *Don't do this.*

```
public class Thread {
    public void interrupt() { ... }
    public boolean isInterrupted() { ... }
    public static boolean interrupted() { ... }
    ...
}
```

LISTING 7.4. Interruption methods in Thread.

If a thread is interrupted when it is *not* blocked, its interrupted status is set, and it is up to the activity being cancelled to poll the interrupted status to detect interruption. In this way interruption is "sticky"—if it doesn't trigger an `InterruptedException`, evidence of interruption persists until someone deliberately clears the interrupted status.

> Calling `interrupt` does not necessarily stop the target thread from doing what it is doing; it merely delivers the message that interruption has been requested.

A good way to think about interruption is that it does not actually interrupt a running thread; it just *requests* that the thread interrupt itself at the next convenient opportunity. (These opportunities are called *cancellation points.*) Some methods, such as `wait`, `sleep`, and `join`, take such requests seriously, throwing an exception when they receive an interrupt request or encounter an already set interrupt status upon entry. Well behaved methods may totally ignore such requests so long as they leave the interruption request in place so that calling code can do something with it. Poorly behaved methods swallow the interrupt request, thus denying code further up the call stack the opportunity to act on it.

The static `interrupted` method should be used with caution, because it clears the current thread's interrupted status. If you call `interrupted` and it returns `true`, unless you are planning to swallow the interruption, you should do something with it—either throw `InterruptedException` or restore the interrupted status by calling `interrupt` again, as in Listing 5.10 on page 94.

`BrokenPrimeProducer` illustrates how custom cancellation mechanisms do not always interact well with blocking library methods. If you code your tasks to be responsive to interruption, you can use interruption as your cancellation mechanism and take advantage of the interruption support provided by many library classes.

> Interruption is usually the most sensible way to implement cancellation.

`BrokenPrimeProducer` can be easily fixed (and simplified) by using interruption instead of a boolean flag to request cancellation, as shown in Listing 7.5. There are two points in each loop iteration where interruption may be detected: in the blocking `put` call, and by explicitly polling the interrupted status in the loop header. The explicit test is not strictly necessary here because of the blocking `put` call, but it makes `PrimeProducer` more responsive to interruption because it checks for interruption *before* starting the lengthy task of searching for a prime, rather than after. When calls to interruptible blocking methods are not frequent enough to deliver the desired responsiveness, explicitly testing the interrupted status can help.

```
class PrimeProducer extends Thread {
    private final BlockingQueue<BigInteger> queue;

    PrimeProducer(BlockingQueue<BigInteger> queue) {
        this.queue = queue;
    }

    public void run() {
        try {
            BigInteger p = BigInteger.ONE;
            while (!Thread.currentThread().isInterrupted())
                queue.put(p = p.nextProbablePrime());
        } catch (InterruptedException consumed) {
            /* Allow thread to exit */
        }
    }
    public void cancel() { interrupt(); }
}
```

LISTING 7.5. Using interruption for cancellation.

7.1.2 Interruption policies

Just as tasks should have a cancellation policy, threads should have an *interruption policy*. An interruption policy determines how a thread interprets an interruption request—what it does (if anything) when one is detected, what units of work are considered atomic with respect to interruption, and how quickly it reacts to interruption.

The most sensible interruption policy is some form of thread-level or service-level cancellation: exit as quickly as practical, cleaning up if necessary, and possibly notifying some owning entity that the thread is exiting. It is possible to establish other interruption policies, such as pausing or resuming a service, but threads or thread pools with nonstandard interruption policies may need to be restricted to tasks that have been written with an awareness of the policy.

It is important to distinguish between how *tasks* and *threads* should react to interruption. A single interrupt request may have more than one desired recipient—interrupting a worker thread in a thread pool can mean both "cancel the current task" and "shut down the worker thread".

Tasks do not execute in threads they own; they borrow threads owned by a service such as a thread pool. Code that doesn't own the thread (for a thread pool, any code outside of the thread pool implementation) should be careful to preserve the interrupted status so that the owning code can eventually act on it, even if the "guest" code acts on the interruption as well. (If you are house-sitting for someone, you don't throw out the mail that comes while they're away—you save it and let them deal with it when they get back, even if you do read their magazines.)

This is why most blocking library methods simply throw `InterruptedException` in response to an interrupt. They will never execute in a thread they own, so they implement the most reasonable cancellation policy for task or library code: get out of the way as quickly as possible and communicate the interruption back to the caller so that code higher up on the call stack can take further action.

A task needn't necessarily drop everything when it detects an interruption request—it can choose to postpone it until a more opportune time by remembering that it was interrupted, finishing the task it was performing, and *then* throwing `InterruptedException` or otherwise indicating interruption. This technique can protect data structures from corruption when an activity is interrupted in the middle of an update.

A task should not assume anything about the interruption policy of its executing thread unless it is explicitly designed to run within a service that has a specific interruption policy. Whether a task interprets interruption as cancellation or takes some other action on interruption, it should take care to preserve the executing thread's interruption status. If it is not simply going to propagate `InterruptedException` to its caller, it should restore the interruption status after catching `InterruptedException`:

```
Thread.currentThread().interrupt();
```

Just as task code should not make assumptions about what interruption means to its executing thread, cancellation code should not make assumptions about the interruption policy of arbitrary threads. A thread should be interrupted only by its owner; the owner can encapsulate knowledge of the thread's interruption policy in an appropriate cancellation mechanism such as a shutdown method.

> Because each thread has its own interruption policy, you should not interrupt a thread unless you know what interruption means to that thread.

Critics have derided the Java interruption facility because it does not provide a preemptive interruption capability and yet forces developers to handle `InterruptedException`. However, the ability to postpone an interruption request enables developers to craft flexible interruption policies that balance responsiveness and robustness as appropriate for the application.

7.1.3 Responding to interruption

As mentioned in Section 5.4, when you call an interruptible blocking method such as `Thread.sleep` or `BlockingQueue.put`, there are two practical strategies for handling `InterruptedException`:

- Propagate the exception (possibly after some task-specific cleanup), making your method an interruptible blocking method, too; or

- Restore the interruption status so that code higher up on the call stack can deal with it.

Propagating `InterruptedException` can be as easy as adding `Interrupted-Exception` to the throws clause, as shown by `getNextTask` in Listing 7.6.

```
BlockingQueue<Task> queue;
...
public Task getNextTask() throws InterruptedException {
    return queue.take();
}
```

LISTING 7.6. Propagating `InterruptedException` to callers.

If you don't want to or cannot propagate `InterruptedException` (perhaps because your task is defined by a `Runnable`), you need to find another way to preserve the interruption request. The standard way to do this is to restore the interrupted status by calling `interrupt` again. What you should *not* do is swallow the `InterruptedException` by catching it and doing nothing in the `catch` block, unless your code is actually implementing the interruption policy for a thread. `PrimeProducer` swallows the interrupt, but does so with the knowledge that the thread is about to terminate and that therefore there is no code higher up on the call stack that needs to know about the interruption. Most code does not know what thread it will run in and so should preserve the interrupted status.

> Only code that implements a thread's interruption policy may swallow an interruption request. General-purpose task and library code should never swallow interruption requests.

Activities that do not support cancellation but still call interruptible blocking methods will have to call them in a loop, retrying when interruption is detected. In this case, they should save the interruption status locally and restore it just before returning, as shown in Listing 7.7, rather than immediately upon catching `InterruptedException`. Setting the interrupted status too early could result in an infinite loop, because most interruptible blocking methods check the interrupted status on entry and throw `InterruptedException` immediately if it is set. (Interruptible methods usually poll for interruption before blocking or doing any significant work, so as to be as responsive to interruption as possible.)

If your code does not call interruptible blocking methods, it can still be made responsive to interruption by polling the current thread's interrupted status throughout the task code. Choosing a polling frequency is a tradeoff between efficiency and responsiveness. If you have high responsiveness requirements, you cannot call potentially long-running methods that are not themselves responsive to interruption, potentially restricting your options for calling library code.

Cancellation can involve state other than the interruption status; interruption can be used to get the thread's attention, and information stored elsewhere by the interrupting thread can be used to provide further instructions for the interrupted thread. (Be sure to use synchronization when accessing that information.)

```
public Task getNextTask(BlockingQueue<Task> queue) {
    boolean interrupted = false;
    try {
        while (true) {
            try {
                return queue.take();
            } catch (InterruptedException e) {
                interrupted = true;
                // fall through and retry
            }
        }
    } finally {
        if (interrupted)
            Thread.currentThread().interrupt();
    }
}
```

LISTING 7.7. *Noncancelable task that restores interruption before exit.*

For example, when a worker thread owned by a ThreadPoolExecutor detects interruption, it checks whether the pool is being shut down. If so, it performs some pool cleanup before terminating; otherwise it may create a new thread to restore the thread pool to the desired size.

7.1.4 Example: timed run

Many problems can take forever to solve (e.g., enumerate all the prime numbers); for others, the answer might be found reasonably quickly but also might take forever. Being able to say "spend up to ten minutes looking for the answer" or "enumerate all the answers you can in ten minutes" can be useful in these situations.

The aSecondOfPrimes method in Listing 7.2 starts a PrimeGenerator and interrupts it after a second. While the PrimeGenerator might take somewhat longer than a second to stop, it will eventually notice the interrupt and stop, allowing the thread to terminate. But another aspect of executing a task is that you want to find out if the task throws an exception. If PrimeGenerator throws an unchecked exception before the timeout expires, it will probably go unnoticed, since the prime generator runs in a separate thread that does not explicitly handle exceptions.

Listing 7.8 shows an attempt at running an arbitrary Runnable for a given amount of time. It runs the task in the calling thread and schedules a cancellation task to interrupt it after a given time interval. This addresses the problem of unchecked exceptions thrown from the task, since they can then be caught by the caller of timedRun.

This is an appealingly simple approach, but it violates the rules: you should know a thread's interruption policy before interrupting it. Since timedRun can be called from an arbitrary thread, it cannot know the calling thread's interrup-

```
private static final ScheduledExecutorService cancelExec = ...;

public static void timedRun(Runnable r,
                            long timeout, TimeUnit unit) {
    final Thread taskThread = Thread.currentThread();
    cancelExec.schedule(new Runnable() {
        public void run() { taskThread.interrupt(); }
    }, timeout, unit);
    r.run();
}
```

LISTING 7.8. *Scheduling an interrupt on a borrowed thread.* Don't do this.

tion policy. If the task completes before the timeout, the cancellation task that interrupts the thread in which timedRun was called could go off *after* timedRun has returned to its caller. We don't know what code will be running when that happens, but the result won't be good. (It is possible but surprisingly tricky to eliminate this risk by using the ScheduledFuture returned by schedule to cancel the cancellation task.)

Further, if the task is not responsive to interruption, timedRun will not return until the task finishes, which may be long after the desired timeout (or even not at all). A timed run service that doesn't return after the specified time is likely to be irritating to its callers.

Listing 7.9 addresses the exception-handling problem of aSecondOfPrimes and the problems with the previous attempt. The thread created to run the task can have its own execution policy, and even if the task doesn't respond to the interrupt, the timed run method can still return to its caller. After starting the task thread, timedRun executes a timed join with the newly created thread. After join returns, it checks if an exception was thrown from the task and if so, rethrows it in the thread calling timedRun. The saved Throwable is shared between the two threads, and so is declared volatile to safely publish it from the task thread to the timedRun thread.

This version addresses the problems in the previous examples, but because it relies on a timed join, it shares a deficiency with join: we don't know if control was returned because the thread exited normally or because the join timed out.[2]

7.1.5   Cancellation via Future

We've already used an abstraction for managing the lifecycle of a task, dealing with exceptions, and facilitating cancellation—Future. Following the general principle that it is better to use existing library classes than to roll your own, let's build timedRun using Future and the task execution framework.

---

2. This is a flaw in the Thread API, because whether or not the join completes successfully has memory visibility consequences in the Java Memory Model, but join does not return a status indicating whether it was successful.

```
public static void timedRun(final Runnable r,
                           long timeout, TimeUnit unit)
                           throws InterruptedException {
    class RethrowableTask implements Runnable {
        private volatile Throwable t;
        public void run() {
            try { r.run(); }
            catch (Throwable t) { this.t = t; }
        }
        void rethrow() {
            if (t != null)
                throw launderThrowable(t);
        }
    }

    RethrowableTask task = new RethrowableTask();
    final Thread taskThread = new Thread(task);
    taskThread.start();
    cancelExec.schedule(new Runnable() {
        public void run() { taskThread.interrupt(); }
    }, timeout, unit);
    taskThread.join(unit.toMillis(timeout));
    task.rethrow();
}
```

LISTING 7.9. *Interrupting a task in a dedicated thread.*

ExecutorService.submit returns a Future describing the task. Future has
a cancel method that takes a boolean argument, mayInterruptIfRunning, and
returns a value indicating whether the cancellation attempt was successful. (This
tells you only whether it was able to deliver the interruption, not whether the task
detected and acted on it.) When mayInterruptIfRunning is true and the task is
currently running in some thread, then that thread is interrupted. Setting this
argument to false means "don't run this task if it hasn't started yet", and should
be used for tasks that are not designed to handle interruption.

Since you shouldn't interrupt a thread unless you know its interruption policy, when is it OK to call cancel with an argument of true? The task execution
threads created by the standard Executor implementations implement an interruption policy that lets tasks be cancelled using interruption, so it is safe to set
mayInterruptIfRunning when cancelling tasks through their Futures when they
are running in a standard Executor. You should not interrupt a pool thread directly when attempting to cancel a task, because you won't know what task is
running when the interrupt request is delivered—do this only through the task's
Future. This is yet another reason to code tasks to treat interruption as a cancellation request: then they can be cancelled through their Futures.

Listing 7.10 shows a version of timedRun that submits the task to an Executor-Service and retrieves the result with a timed Future.get. If get terminates with a TimeoutException, the task is cancelled via its Future. (To simplify coding, this version calls Future.cancel unconditionally in a finally block, taking advantage of the fact that cancelling a completed task has no effect.) If the underlying computation throws an exception prior to cancellation, it is rethrown from timed-Run, which is the most convenient way for the caller to deal with the exception. Listing 7.10 also illustrates another good practice: cancelling tasks whose result is no longer needed. (This technique was also used in Listing 6.13 on page 128 and Listing 6.16 on page 132.)

```
public static void timedRun(Runnable r,
                            long timeout, TimeUnit unit)
                            throws InterruptedException {
    Future<?> task = taskExec.submit(r);
    try {
        task.get(timeout, unit);
    } catch (TimeoutException e) {
        // task will be cancelled below
    } catch (ExecutionException e) {
        // exception thrown in task; rethrow
        throw launderThrowable(e.getCause());
    } finally {
        // Harmless if task already completed
        task.cancel(true); // interrupt if running
    }
}
```

LISTING 7.10. Cancelling a task using Future.

When Future.get throws InterruptedException or TimeoutException and you know that the result is no longer needed by the program, cancel the task with Future.cancel.

7.1.6 Dealing with non-interruptible blocking

Many blocking library methods respond to interruption by returning early and throwing InterruptedException, which makes it easier to build tasks that are responsive to cancellation. However, not all blocking methods or blocking mechanisms are responsive to interruption; if a thread is blocked performing synchronous socket I/O or waiting to acquire an intrinsic lock, interruption has no effect other than setting the thread's interrupted status. We can sometimes convince threads blocked in noninterruptible activities to stop by means similar to interruption, but this requires greater awareness of why the thread is blocked.

Synchronous socket I/O in java.io. The common form of blocking I/O in server applications is reading or writing to a socket. Unfortunately, the read and write methods in InputStream and OutputStream are not responsive to interruption, but closing the underlying socket makes any threads blocked in read or write throw a SocketException.

Synchronous I/O in java.nio. Interrupting a thread waiting on an InterruptibleChannel causes it to throw ClosedByInterruptException and close the channel (and also causes all other threads blocked on the channel to throw ClosedByInterruptException). Closing an InterruptibleChannel causes threads blocked on channel operations to throw AsynchronousCloseException. Most standard Channels implement InterruptibleChannel.

Asynchronous I/O with Selector. If a thread is blocked in Selector.select (in java.nio.channels), calling close or wakeup causes it to return prematurely.

Lock acquisition. If a thread is blocked waiting for an intrinsic lock, there is nothing you can do to stop it short of ensuring that it eventually acquires the lock and makes enough progress that you can get its attention some other way. However, the explicit Lock classes offer the lockInterruptibly method, which allows you to wait for a lock and still be responsive to interrupts—see Chapter 13.

ReaderThread in Listing 7.11 shows a technique for encapsulating nonstandard cancellation. ReaderThread manages a single socket connection, reading synchronously from the socket and passing any data received to processBuffer. To facilitate terminating a user connection or shutting down the server, ReaderThread overrides interrupt to both deliver a standard interrupt and close the underlying socket; thus interrupting a ReaderThread makes it stop what it is doing whether it is blocked in read or in an interruptible blocking method.

7.1.7 Encapsulating nonstandard cancellation with newTaskFor

The technique used in ReaderThread to encapsulate nonstandard cancellation can be refined using the newTaskFor hook added to ThreadPoolExecutor in Java 6. When a Callable is submitted to an ExecutorService, submit returns a Future that can be used to cancel the task. The newTaskFor hook is a factory method that creates the Future representing the task. It returns a RunnableFuture, an interface that extends both Future and Runnable (and is implemented by FutureTask).

Customizing the task Future allows you to override Future.cancel. Custom cancellation code can perform logging or gather statistics on cancellation, and can also be used to cancel activities that are not responsive to interruption. ReaderThread encapsulates cancellation of socket-using threads by overriding interrupt; the same can be done for tasks by overriding Future.cancel.

CancellableTask in Listing 7.12 defines a CancellableTask interface that extends Callable and adds a cancel method and a newTask factory method for

```java
public class ReaderThread extends Thread {
    private final Socket socket;
    private final InputStream in;

    public ReaderThread(Socket socket) throws IOException {
        this.socket = socket;
        this.in = socket.getInputStream();
    }

    public void interrupt() {
        try {
            socket.close();
        }
        catch (IOException ignored) { }
        finally {
            super.interrupt();
        }
    }

    public void run() {
        try {
            byte[] buf = new byte[BUFSZ];
            while (true) {
                int count = in.read(buf);
                if (count < 0)
                    break;
                else if (count > 0)
                    processBuffer(buf, count);
            }
        } catch (IOException e) { /* Allow thread to exit */ }
    }
}
```

LISTING 7.11. Encapsulating nonstandard cancellation in a Thread by overriding interrupt.

constructing a `RunnableFuture`. `CancellingExecutor` extends `ThreadPoolExecutor`, and overrides `newTaskFor` to let a `CancellableTask` create its own `Future`.

`SocketUsingTask` implements `CancellableTask` and defines `Future.cancel` to close the socket as well as call `super.cancel`. If a `SocketUsingTask` is cancelled through its `Future`, the socket is closed *and* the executing thread is interrupted. This increases the task's responsiveness to cancellation: not only can it safely call interruptible blocking methods while remaining responsive to cancellation, but it can also call blocking socket I/O methods.

7.2   Stopping a thread-based service

Applications commonly create services that own threads, such as thread pools, and the lifetime of these services is usually longer than that of the method that creates them. If the application is to shut down gracefully, the threads owned by these services need to be terminated. Since there is no preemptive way to stop a thread, they must instead be persuaded to shut down on their own.

Sensible encapsulation practices dictate that you should not manipulate a thread—interrupt it, modify its priority, etc.—unless you own it. The thread API has no formal concept of thread ownership: a thread is represented with a `Thread` object that can be freely shared like any other object. However, it makes sense to think of a thread as having an owner, and this is usually the class that created the thread. So a thread pool owns its worker threads, and if those threads need to be interrupted, the thread pool should take care of it.

As with any other encapsulated object, thread ownership is not transitive: the application may own the service and the service may own the worker threads, but the application doesn't own the worker threads and therefore should not attempt to stop them directly. Instead, the service should provide *lifecycle methods* for shutting itself down that also shut down the owned threads; then the application can shut down the service, and the service can shut down the threads. `ExecutorService` provides the `shutdown` and `shutdownNow` methods; other thread-owning services should provide a similar shutdown mechanism.

> Provide lifecycle methods whenever a thread-owning service has a lifetime longer than that of the method that created it.

7.2.1   Example: a logging service

Most server applications use logging, which can be as simple as inserting `println` statements into the code. Stream classes like `PrintWriter` are thread-safe, so this simple approach would require no explicit synchronization.[3] However, as

---

3. If you are logging multiple lines as part of a single log message, you may need to use additional client-side locking to prevent undesirable interleaving of output from multiple threads. If two threads logged multiline stack traces to the same stream with one `println` call per line, the results would be interleaved unpredictably, and could easily look like one large but meaningless stack trace.

```java
public interface CancellableTask<T> extends Callable<T> {
    void cancel();
    RunnableFuture<T> newTask();
}

@ThreadSafe
public class CancellingExecutor extends ThreadPoolExecutor {
    ...
    protected<T> RunnableFuture<T> newTaskFor(Callable<T> callable) {
        if (callable instanceof CancellableTask)
            return ((CancellableTask<T>) callable).newTask();
        else
            return super.newTaskFor(callable);
    }
}

public abstract class SocketUsingTask<T>
        implements CancellableTask<T> {
    @GuardedBy("this") private Socket socket;

    protected synchronized void setSocket(Socket s) { socket = s; }

    public synchronized void cancel() {
        try {
            if (socket != null)
                socket.close();
        } catch (IOException ignored) { }
    }

    public RunnableFuture<T> newTask() {
        return new FutureTask<T>(this) {
            public boolean cancel(boolean mayInterruptIfRunning) {
                try {
                    SocketUsingTask.this.cancel();
                } finally {
                    return super.cancel(mayInterruptIfRunning);
                }
            }
        };
    }
}
```

LISTING 7.12. *Encapsulating nonstandard cancellation in a task with newTaskFor.*

we'll see in Section 11.6, inline logging can have some performance costs in high-volume applications. Another alternative is have the log call queue the log message for processing by another thread.

LogWriter in Listing 7.13 shows a simple logging service in which the logging activity is moved to a separate logger thread. Instead of having the thread that produces the message write it directly to the output stream, LogWriter hands it off to the logger thread via a BlockingQueue and the logger thread writes it out. This is a multiple-producer, single-consumer design: any activity calling log is acting as a producer, and the background logger thread is the consumer. If the logger thread falls behind, the BlockingQueue eventually blocks the producers until the logger thread catches up.

```java
public class LogWriter {
    private final BlockingQueue<String> queue;
    private final LoggerThread logger;

    public LogWriter(Writer writer) {
        this.queue = new LinkedBlockingQueue<String>(CAPACITY);
        this.logger = new LoggerThread(writer);
    }

    public void start() { logger.start(); }

    public void log(String msg) throws InterruptedException {
        queue.put(msg);
    }

    private class LoggerThread extends Thread {
        private final PrintWriter writer;
        ...
        public void run() {
            try {
                while (true)
                    writer.println(queue.take());
            } catch(InterruptedException ignored) {
            } finally {
                writer.close();
            }
        }
    }
}
```

LISTING 7.13. Producer-consumer logging service with no shutdown support.

For a service like LogWriter to be useful in production, we need a way to terminate the logger thread so it does not prevent the JVM from shutting down normally. Stopping the logger thread is easy enough, since it repeatedly calls take, which is responsive to interruption; if the logger thread is modified to exit on catching InterruptedException, then interrupting the logger thread stops the service.

However, simply making the logger thread exit is not a very satisfying shutdown mechanism. Such an abrupt shutdown discards log messages that might be waiting to be written to the log, but, more importantly, threads blocked in log because the queue is full *will never become unblocked*. Cancelling a producer-consumer activity requires cancelling both the producers and the consumers. Interrupting the logger thread deals with the consumer, but because the producers in this case are not dedicated threads, cancelling them is harder.

Another approach to shutting down LogWriter would be to set a "shutdown requested" flag to prevent further messages from being submitted, as shown in Listing 7.14. The consumer could then drain the queue upon being notified that shutdown has been requested, writing out any pending messages and unblocking any producers blocked in log. However, this approach has race conditions that make it unreliable. The implementation of log is a check-then-act sequence: producers could observe that the service has not yet been shut down but still queue messages after the shutdown, again with the risk that the producer might get blocked in log and never become unblocked. There are tricks that reduce the likelihood of this (like having the consumer wait several seconds before declaring the queue drained), but these do not change the fundamental problem, merely the likelihood that it will cause a failure.

```
public void log(String msg) throws InterruptedException {
    if (!shutdownRequested)
        queue.put(msg);
    else
        throw new IllegalStateException("logger is shut down");
}
```

LISTING 7.14. Unreliable way to add shutdown support to the logging service.

The way to provide reliable shutdown for LogWriter is to fix the race condition, which means making the submission of a new log message atomic. But we don't want to hold a lock while trying to enqueue the message, since put could block. Instead, we can atomically check for shutdown and conditionally increment a counter to "reserve" the right to submit a message, as shown in Log-Service in Listing 7.15.

7.2.2 ExecutorService shutdown

In Section 6.2.4, we saw that ExecutorService offers two ways to shut down: graceful shutdown with shutdown, and abrupt shutdown with shutdownNow. In an abrupt shutdown, shutdownNow returns the list of tasks that had not yet started after attempting to cancel all actively executing tasks.

```java
public class LogService {
    private final BlockingQueue<String> queue;
    private final LoggerThread loggerThread;
    private final PrintWriter writer;
    @GuardedBy("this") private boolean isShutdown;
    @GuardedBy("this") private int reservations;

    public void start() { loggerThread.start(); }

    public void stop() {
        synchronized (this) { isShutdown = true; }
        loggerThread.interrupt();
    }

    public void log(String msg) throws InterruptedException {
        synchronized (this) {
            if (isShutdown)
                throw new IllegalStateException(...);
            ++reservations;
        }
        queue.put(msg);
    }

    private class LoggerThread extends Thread {
        public void run() {
            try {
                while (true) {
                    try {
                        synchronized (LogService.this) {
                            if (isShutdown && reservations == 0)
                                break;
                        }
                        String msg = queue.take();
                        synchronized (LogService.this) {
                            --reservations;
                        }
                        writer.println(msg);
                    } catch (InterruptedException e) { /* retry */ }
                }
            } finally {
                writer.close();
            }
        }
    }
}
```

LISTING 7.15. Adding reliable cancellation to LogWriter.

The two different termination options offer a tradeoff between safety and responsiveness: abrupt termination is faster but riskier because tasks may be interrupted in the middle of execution, and normal termination is slower but safer because the ExecutorService does not shut down until all queued tasks are processed. Other thread-owning services should consider providing a similar choice of shutdown modes.

Simple programs can get away with starting and shutting down a global ExecutorService from main. More sophisticated programs are likely to encapsulate an ExecutorService behind a higher-level service that provides its own lifecycle methods, such as the variant of LogService in Listing 7.16 that delegates to an ExecutorService instead of managing its own threads. Encapsulating an ExecutorService extends the ownership chain from application to service to thread by adding another link; each member of the chain manages the lifecycle of the services or threads it owns.

```java
public class LogService {
    private final ExecutorService exec = newSingleThreadExecutor();
    ...
    public void start() { }

    public void stop() throws InterruptedException {
        try {
            exec.shutdown();
            exec.awaitTermination(TIMEOUT, UNIT);
        } finally {
            writer.close();
        }
    }
    public void log(String msg) {
        try {
            exec.execute(new WriteTask(msg));
        } catch (RejectedExecutionException ignored) { }
    }
}
```

LISTING 7.16. Logging service that uses an ExecutorService.

7.2.3 Poison pills

Another way to convince a producer-consumer service to shut down is with a *poison pill*: a recognizable object placed on the queue that means "when you get this, stop." With a FIFO queue, poison pills ensure that consumers finish the work on their queue before shutting down, since any work submitted prior to submitting the poison pill will be retrieved before the pill; producers should not submit any work after putting a poison pill on the queue. IndexingService in Listings 7.17, 7.18, and 7.19 shows a single-producer, single-consumer version of

```
public class IndexingService {
    private static final File POISON = new File("");
    private final IndexerThread consumer = new IndexerThread();
    private final CrawlerThread producer = new CrawlerThread();
    private final BlockingQueue<File> queue;
    private final FileFilter fileFilter;
    private final File root;

    class CrawlerThread extends Thread { /* Listing 7.18 */ }
    class IndexerThread extends Thread { /* Listing 7.19 */ }

    public void start() {
        producer.start();
        consumer.start();
    }

    public void stop() { producer.interrupt(); }

    public void awaitTermination() throws InterruptedException {
        consumer.join();
    }
}
```

LISTING 7.17. Shutdown with poison pill.

the desktop search example from Listing 5.8 on page 91 that uses a poison pill to shut down the service.

Poison pills work only when the number of producers and consumers is known. The approach in IndexingService can be extended to multiple producers by having each producer place a pill on the queue and having the consumer stop only when it receives $N_{producers}$ pills. It can be extended to multiple consumers by having each producer place $N_{consumers}$ pills on the queue, though this can get unwieldy with large numbers of producers and consumers. Poison pills work reliably only with unbounded queues.

7.2.4 Example: a one-shot execution service

If a method needs to process a batch of tasks and does not return until all the tasks are finished, it can simplify service lifecycle management by using a private Executor whose lifetime is bounded by that method. (The invokeAll and invokeAny methods can often be useful in such situations.)

The checkMail method in Listing 7.20 checks for new mail in parallel on a number of hosts. It creates a private executor and submits a task for each host: it then shuts down the executor and waits for termination, which occurs when all

```
public class CrawlerThread extends Thread {
    public void run() {
        try {
            crawl(root);
        } catch (InterruptedException e) { /* fall through */ }
        finally {
            while (true) {
                try {
                    queue.put(POISON);
                    break;
                } catch (InterruptedException e1) { /* retry */ }
            }
        }
    }

    private void crawl(File root) throws InterruptedException {
        ...
    }
}
```

LISTING 7.18. Producer thread for IndexingService.

```
public class IndexerThread extends Thread {
    public void run() {
        try {
            while (true) {
                File file = queue.take();
                if (file == POISON)
                    break;
                else
                    indexFile(file);
            }
        } catch (InterruptedException consumed) { }
    }
}
```

LISTING 7.19. Consumer thread for IndexingService.

the mail-checking tasks have completed.[4]

```
boolean checkMail(Set<String> hosts, long timeout, TimeUnit unit)
        throws InterruptedException {
    ExecutorService exec = Executors.newCachedThreadPool();
    final AtomicBoolean hasNewMail = new AtomicBoolean(false);
    try {
        for (final String host : hosts)
            exec.execute(new Runnable() {
                public void run() {
                    if (checkMail(host))
                        hasNewMail.set(true);
                }
            });
    } finally {
        exec.shutdown();
        exec.awaitTermination(timeout, unit);
    }
    return hasNewMail.get();
}
```

LISTING 7.20. Using a private Executor whose lifetime is bounded by a method call.

7.2.5   Limitations of shutdownNow

When an ExecutorService is shut down abruptly with shutdownNow, it attempts to cancel the tasks currently in progress and returns a list of tasks that were submitted but never started so that they can be logged or saved for later processing.[5]

However, there is no general way to find out which tasks started but did not complete. This means that there is no way of knowing the state of the tasks in progress at shutdown time unless the tasks themselves perform some sort of checkpointing. To know which tasks have not completed, you need to know not only which tasks didn't start, but also which tasks were in progress when the executor was shut down.[6]

TrackingExecutor in Listing 7.21 shows a technique for determining which tasks were in progress at shutdown time. By encapsulating an ExecutorService and instrumenting execute (and similarly submit, not shown) to remember

---

4. The reason an AtomicBoolean is used instead of a volatile boolean is that in order to access the hasNewMail flag from the inner Runnable, it would have to be final, which would preclude modifying it.
5. The Runnable objects returned by shutdownNow might not be the same objects that were submitted to the ExecutorService: they might be *wrapped* instances of the submitted tasks.
6. Unfortunately, there is no shutdown option in which tasks not yet started are returned to the caller but tasks in progress are allowed to complete; such an option would eliminate this uncertain intermediate state.

which tasks were cancelled after shutdown, TrackingExecutor can identify which tasks started but did not complete normally. After the executor terminates, get-CancelledTasks returns the list of cancelled tasks. In order for this technique to work, the tasks must preserve the thread's interrupted status when they return, which well behaved tasks will do anyway.

```java
public class TrackingExecutor extends AbstractExecutorService {
    private final ExecutorService exec;
    private final Set<Runnable> tasksCancelledAtShutdown =
        Collections.synchronizedSet(new HashSet<Runnable>());
    ...
    public List<Runnable> getCancelledTasks() {
        if (!exec.isTerminated())
            throw new IllegalStateException(...);
        return new ArrayList<Runnable>(tasksCancelledAtShutdown);
    }

    public void execute(final Runnable runnable) {
        exec.execute(new Runnable() {
            public void run() {
                try {
                    runnable.run();
                } finally {
                    if (isShutdown()
                        && Thread.currentThread().isInterrupted())
                        tasksCancelledAtShutdown.add(runnable);
                }
            }
        });
    }

    // delegate other ExecutorService methods to exec
}
```

LISTING 7.21. ExecutorService that keeps track of cancelled tasks after shutdown.

WebCrawler in Listing 7.22 shows an application of TrackingExecutor. The work of a web crawler is often unbounded, so if a crawler must be shut down we might want to save its state so it can be restarted later. CrawlTask provides a getPage method that identifies what page it is working on. When the crawler is shut down, both the tasks that did not start and those that were cancelled are scanned and their URLs recorded, so that page-crawling tasks for those URLs can be added to the queue when the crawler restarts.

TrackingExecutor has an unavoidable race condition that could make it yield false positives: tasks that are identified as cancelled but actually completed. This

```
public abstract class WebCrawler {
    private volatile TrackingExecutor exec;
    @GuardedBy("this")
    private final Set<URL> urlsToCrawl = new HashSet<URL>();
    ...
    public synchronized void start() {
        exec = new TrackingExecutor(
                Executors.newCachedThreadPool());
        for (URL url : urlsToCrawl) submitCrawlTask(url);
        urlsToCrawl.clear();
    }

    public synchronized void stop() throws InterruptedException {
        try {
            saveUncrawled(exec.shutdownNow());
            if (exec.awaitTermination(TIMEOUT, UNIT))
                saveUncrawled(exec.getCancelledTasks());
        } finally {
            exec = null;
        }
    }

    protected abstract List<URL> processPage(URL url);

    private void saveUncrawled(List<Runnable> uncrawled) {
        for (Runnable task : uncrawled)
            urlsToCrawl.add((((CrawlTask) task).getPage());
    }
    private void submitCrawlTask(URL u) {
        exec.execute(new CrawlTask(u));
    }
    private class CrawlTask implements Runnable {
        private final URL url;
        ...
        public void run() {
            for (URL link : processPage(url)) {
                if (Thread.currentThread().isInterrupted())
                    return;
                submitCrawlTask(link);
            }
        }
        public URL getPage() { return url; }
    }
}
```

LISTING 7.22. Using `TrackingExecutorService` to save unfinished tasks for later execution.

arises because the thread pool could be shut down between when the last instruction of the task executes and when the pool records the task as complete. This is not a problem if tasks are *idempotent* (if performing them twice has the same effect as performing them once), as they typically are in a web crawler. Otherwise, the application retrieving the cancelled tasks must be aware of this risk and be prepared to deal with false positives.

7.3 Handling abnormal thread termination

It is obvious when a single-threaded console application terminates due to an uncaught exception—the program stops running and produces a stack trace that is very different from typical program output. Failure of a thread in a concurrent application is not always so obvious. The stack trace may be printed on the console, but no one may be watching the console. Also, when a thread fails, the application may appear to continue to work, so its failure could go unnoticed. Fortunately, there are means of both detecting and preventing threads from "leaking" from an application.

The leading cause of premature thread death is `RuntimeException`. Because these exceptions indicate a programming error or other unrecoverable problem, they are generally not caught. Instead they propagate all the way up the stack, at which point the default behavior is to print a stack trace on the console and let the thread terminate.

The consequences of abnormal thread death range from benign to disastrous, depending on the thread's role in the application. Losing a thread from a thread pool can have performance consequences, but an application that runs well with a 50-thread pool will probably run fine with a 49-thread pool too. But losing the event dispatch thread in a GUI application would be quite noticeable—the application would stop processing events and the GUI would freeze. `OutOf-Time` on page 124 showed a serious consequence of thread leakage: the service represented by the `Timer` is permanently out of commission.

Just about any code can throw a `RuntimeException`. Whenever you call another method, you are taking a leap of faith that it will return normally or throw one of the checked exceptions its signature declares. The less familiar you are with the code being called, the more skeptical you should be about its behavior.

Task-processing threads such as the worker threads in a thread pool or the Swing event dispatch thread spend their whole life calling unknown code through an abstraction barrier like `Runnable`, and these threads should be very skeptical that the code they call will be well behaved. It would be very bad if a service like the Swing event thread failed just because some poorly written event handler threw a `NullPointerException`. Accordingly, these facilities should call tasks within a `try-catch` block that catches unchecked exceptions, or within a `try-finally` block to ensure that if the thread exits abnormally the framework is informed of this and can take corrective action. This is one of the few times when you might want to consider catching `RuntimeException`—when you are calling unknown, untrusted code through an abstraction such as `Runnable`.[7]

---

7. There is some controversy over the safety of this technique; when a thread throws an unchecked

Listing 7.23 illustrates a way to structure a worker thread within a thread pool. If a task throws an unchecked exception, it allows the thread to die, but not before notifying the framework that the thread has died. The framework may then replace the worker thread with a new thread, or may choose not to because the thread pool is being shut down or there are already enough worker threads to meet current demand. ThreadPoolExecutor and Swing use this technique to ensure that a poorly behaved task doesn't prevent subsequent tasks from executing. If you are writing a worker thread class that executes submitted tasks, or calling untrusted external code (such as dynamically loaded plugins), use one of these approaches to prevent a poorly written task or plugin from taking down the thread that happens to call it.

```
public void run() {
    Throwable thrown = null;
    try {
        while (!isInterrupted())
            runTask(getTaskFromWorkQueue());
    } catch (Throwable e) {
        thrown = e;
    } finally {
        threadExited(this, thrown);
    }
}
```

LISTING 7.23. Typical thread-pool worker thread structure.

7.3.1 Uncaught exception handlers

The previous section offered a proactive approach to the problem of unchecked exceptions. The Thread API also provides the UncaughtExceptionHandler facility, which lets you detect when a thread dies due to an uncaught exception. The two approaches are complementary: taken together, they provide defense-in-depth against thread leakage.

When a thread exits due to an uncaught exception, the JVM reports this event to an application-provided UncaughtExceptionHandler (see Listing 7.24); if no handler exists, the default behavior is to print the stack trace to System.err.[8]

exception, the entire application may possibly be compromised. But the alternative—shutting down the entire application—is usually not practical.

8. Before Java 5.0, the only way to control the UncaughtExceptionHandler was by subclassing ThreadGroup. In Java 5.0 and later, you can set an UncaughtExceptionHandler on a per-thread basis with Thread.setUncaughtExceptionHandler, and can also set the default UncaughtExceptionHandler with Thread.setDefaultUncaughtExceptionHandler. However, only one of these handlers is called—first the JVM looks for a per-thread handler, then for a ThreadGroup handler. The default handler implementation in ThreadGroup delegates to its parent thread group, and so on up the chain until one of the ThreadGroup handlers deals with the uncaught exception or it bubbles up to the top-level thread group. The top-level thread group handler delegates to the default system handler (if one exists; the default is none) and otherwise prints the stack trace to the console.

```
public interface UncaughtExceptionHandler {
    void uncaughtException(Thread t, Throwable e);
}
```

LISTING 7.24. UncaughtExceptionHandler interface.

What the handler should do with an uncaught exception depends on your quality-of-service requirements. The most common response is to write an error message and stack trace to the application log, as shown in Listing 7.25. Handlers can also take more direct action, such as trying to restart the thread, shutting down the application, paging an operator, or other corrective or diagnostic action.

```
public class UEHLogger implements Thread.UncaughtExceptionHandler {
    public void uncaughtException(Thread t, Throwable e) {
        Logger logger = Logger.getAnonymousLogger();
        logger.log(Level.SEVERE,
            "Thread terminated with exception: " + t.getName(),
            e);
    }
}
```

LISTING 7.25. UncaughtExceptionHandler that logs the exception.

In long-running applications, always use uncaught exception handlers for all threads that at least log the exception.

To set an UncaughtExceptionHandler for pool threads, provide a ThreadFactory to the ThreadPoolExecutor constructor. (As with all thread manipulation, only the thread's owner should change its UncaughtExceptionHandler.) The standard thread pools allow an uncaught task exception to terminate the pool thread, but use a try-finally block to be notified when this happens so the thread can be replaced. Without an uncaught exception handler or other failure notification mechanism, tasks can appear to fail silently, which can be very confusing. If you want to be notified when a task fails due to an exception so that you can take some task-specific recovery action, either wrap the task with a Runnable or Callable that catches the exception or override the afterExecute hook in ThreadPoolExecutor.

Somewhat confusingly, exceptions thrown from tasks make it to the uncaught exception handler only for tasks submitted with execute; for tasks submitted with submit, *any* thrown exception, checked or not, is considered to be part of the task's return status. If a task submitted with submit terminates with an exception, it is rethrown by Future.get, wrapped in an ExecutionException.

7.4 JVM shutdown

The JVM can shut down in either an *orderly* or *abrupt* manner. An orderly shutdown is initiated when the last "normal" (nondaemon) thread terminates, someone calls System.exit, or by other platform-specific means (such as sending a SIGINT or hitting Ctrl-C). While this is the standard and preferred way for the JVM to shut down, it can also be shut down abruptly by calling Runtime.halt or by killing the JVM process through the operating system (such as sending a SIGKILL).

7.4.1 Shutdown hooks

In an orderly shutdown, the JVM first starts all registered *shutdown hooks*. Shutdown hooks are unstarted threads that are registered with Runtime.addShutdownHook. The JVM makes no guarantees on the order in which shutdown hooks are started. If any application threads (daemon or nondaemon) are still running at shutdown time, they continue to run concurrently with the shutdown process. When all shutdown hooks have completed, the JVM may choose to run finalizers if runFinalizersOnExit is true, and then halts. The JVM makes no attempt to stop or interrupt any application threads that are still running at shutdown time; they are abruptly terminated when the JVM eventually halts. If the shutdown hooks or finalizers don't complete, then the orderly shutdown process "hangs" and the JVM must be shut down abruptly. In an abrupt shutdown, the JVM is not required to do anything other than halt the JVM; shutdown hooks will not run.

Shutdown hooks should be thread-safe: they must use synchronization when accessing shared data and should be careful to avoid deadlock, just like any other concurrent code. Further, they should not make assumptions about the state of the application (such as whether other services have shut down already or all normal threads have completed) or about why the JVM is shutting down, and must therefore be coded extremely defensively. Finally, they should exit as quickly as possible, since their existence delays JVM termination at a time when the user may be expecting the JVM to terminate quickly.

Shutdown hooks can be used for service or application cleanup, such as deleting temporary files or cleaning up resources that are not automatically cleaned up by the OS. Listing 7.26 shows how LogService in Listing 7.16 could register a shutdown hook from its start method to ensure the log file is closed on exit.

Because shutdown hooks all run concurrently, closing the log file could cause trouble for other shutdown hooks who want to use the logger. To avoid this problem, shutdown hooks should not rely on services that can be shut down by the application or other shutdown hooks. One way to accomplish this is to use a single shutdown hook for all services, rather than one for each service, and have it call a series of shutdown actions. This ensures that shutdown actions execute sequentially in a single thread, thus avoiding the possibility of race conditions or deadlock between shutdown actions. This technique can be used whether or not you use shutdown hooks; executing shutdown actions sequentially rather than concurrently eliminates many potential sources of failure. In applications

```
public void start() {
    Runtime.getRuntime().addShutdownHook(new Thread() {
        public void run() {
            try { LogService.this.stop(); }
            catch (InterruptedException ignored) {}
        }
    });
}
```

LISTING 7.26. Registering a shutdown hook to stop the logging service.

that maintain explicit dependency information among services, this technique can also ensure that shutdown actions are performed in the right order.

7.4.2 Daemon threads

Sometimes you want to create a thread that performs some helper function but you don't want the existence of this thread to prevent the JVM from shutting down. This is what *daemon threads* are for.

Threads are divided into two types: normal threads and daemon threads. When the JVM starts up, all the threads it creates (such as garbage collector and other housekeeping threads) are daemon threads, except the main thread. When a new thread is created, it inherits the daemon status of the thread that created it, so by default any threads created by the main thread are also normal threads.

Normal threads and daemon threads differ only in what happens when they exit. When a thread exits, the JVM performs an inventory of running threads, and if the only threads that are left are daemon threads, it initiates an orderly shutdown. When the JVM halts, any remaining daemon threads are abandoned—`finally` blocks are not executed, stacks are not unwound—the JVM just exits.

Daemon threads should be used sparingly—few processing activities can be safely abandoned at any time with no cleanup. In particular, it is dangerous to use daemon threads for tasks that might perform any sort of I/O. Daemon threads are best saved for "housekeeping" tasks, such as a background thread that periodically removes expired entries from an in-memory cache.

> Daemon threads are not a good substitute for properly managing the life-cycle of services within an application.

7.4.3 Finalizers

The garbage collector does a good job of reclaiming memory resources when they are no longer needed, but some resources, such as file or socket handles, must be explicitly returned to the operating system when no longer needed. To assist in this, the garbage collector treats objects that have a nontrivial `finalize` method specially: after they are reclaimed by the collector, `finalize` is called so that persistent resources can be released.

Since finalizers can run in a thread managed by the JVM, any state accessed by a finalizer will be accessed by more than one thread and therefore must be accessed with synchronization. Finalizers offer no guarantees on when or even if they run, and they impose a significant performance cost on objects with nontrivial finalizers. They are also extremely difficult to write correctly.[9] In most cases, the combination of `finally` blocks and explicit `close` methods does a better job of resource management than finalizers; the sole exception is when you need to manage objects that hold resources acquired by native methods. For these reasons and others, work hard to avoid writing or using classes with finalizers (other than the platform library classes) [EJ Item 6].

> Avoid finalizers.

Summary

End-of-lifecycle issues for tasks, threads, services, and applications can add complexity to their design and implementation. Java does not provide a preemptive mechanism for cancelling activities or terminating threads. Instead, it provides a cooperative interruption mechanism that can be used to facilitate cancellation, but it is up to you to construct protocols for cancellation and use them consistently. Using `FutureTask` and the `Executor` framework simplifies building cancellable tasks and services.

---

9. See (Boehm, 2005) for some of the challenges involved in writing finalizers.

CHAPTER 8

Applying Thread Pools

Chapter 6 introduced the task execution framework, which simplifies management of task and thread lifecycles and provides a simple and flexible means for decoupling task submission from execution policy. Chapter 7 covered some of the messy details of service lifecycle that arise from using the task execution framework in real applications. This chapter looks at advanced options for configuring and tuning thread pools, describes hazards to watch for when using the task execution framework, and offers some more advanced examples of using Executor.

8.1 Implicit couplings between tasks and execution policies

We claimed earlier that the Executor framework decouples task submission from task execution. Like many attempts at decoupling complex processes, this was a bit of an overstatement. While the Executor framework offers substantial flexibility in specifying and modifying execution policies, not all tasks are compatible with all execution policies. Types of tasks that require specific execution policies include:

Dependent tasks. The most well behaved tasks are *independent*: those that do not depend on the timing, results, or side effects of other tasks. When executing independent tasks in a thread pool, you can freely vary the pool size and configuration without affecting anything but performance. On the other hand, when you submit tasks that depend on other tasks to a thread pool, you implicitly create constraints on the execution policy that must be carefully managed to avoid liveness problems (see Section 8.1.1).

Tasks that exploit thread confinement. Single-threaded executors make stronger promises about concurrency than do arbitrary thread pools. They guarantee that tasks are not executed concurrently, which allows you to relax the thread safety of task code. Objects can be confined to the task thread, thus enabling tasks designed to run in that thread to access those objects without synchronization, even if those resources are not thread-safe. This forms an implicit coupling between the task and the execution policy—the tasks require their executor to be single-threaded.[1] In this case, if you changed the `Executor` from a single-threaded one to a thread pool, thread safety could be lost.

Response-time-sensitive tasks. GUI applications are sensitive to response time: users are annoyed at long delays between a button click and the corresponding visual feedback. Submitting a long-running task to a single-threaded executor, or submitting several long-running tasks to a thread pool with a small number of threads, may impair the responsiveness of the service managed by that `Executor`.

Tasks that use `ThreadLocal`. `ThreadLocal` allows each thread to have its own private "version" of a variable. However, executors are free to reuse threads as they see fit. The standard `Executor` implementations may reap idle threads when demand is low and add new ones when demand is high, and also replace a worker thread with a fresh one if an unchecked exception is thrown from a task. `ThreadLocal` makes sense to use in pool threads only if the thread-local value has a lifetime that is bounded by that of a task; `ThreadLocal` should not be used in pool threads to communicate values between tasks.

Thread pools work best when tasks are *homogeneous* and *independent*. Mixing long-running and short-running tasks risks "clogging" the pool unless it is very large; submitting tasks that depend on other tasks risks deadlock unless the pool is unbounded. Fortunately, requests in typical network-based server applications—web servers, mail servers, file servers—usually meet these guidelines.

> Some tasks have characteristics that require or preclude a specific execution policy. Tasks that depend on other tasks require that the thread pool be large enough that tasks are never queued or rejected; tasks that exploit thread confinement require sequential execution. Document these requirements so that future maintainers do not undermine safety or liveness by substituting an incompatible execution policy.

8.1.1 Thread starvation deadlock

If tasks that depend on other tasks execute in a thread pool, they can deadlock. In a single-threaded executor, a task that submits another task to the same executor and waits for its result will always deadlock. The second task sits on the work queue until the first task completes, but the first will not complete because it is

---

1. The requirement is not quite this strong; it would be enough to ensure only that tasks not execute concurrently and provide enough synchronization so that the memory effects of one task are guaranteed to be visible to the next task—which is precisely the guarantee offered by `newSingleThreadExecutor`.

waiting for the result of the second task. The same thing can happen in larger thread pools if all threads are executing tasks that are blocked waiting for other tasks still on the work queue. This is called *thread starvation deadlock*, and can occur whenever a pool task initiates an unbounded blocking wait for some resource or condition that can succeed only through the action of another pool task, such as waiting for the return value or side effect of another task, unless you can guarantee that the pool is large enough.

ThreadDeadlock in Listing 8.1 illustrates thread starvation deadlock. Render-PageTask submits two additional tasks to the Executor to fetch the page header and footer, renders the page body, waits for the results of the header and footer tasks, and then combines the header, body, and footer into the finished page. With a single-threaded executor, ThreadDeadlock will always deadlock. Similarly, tasks coordinating amongst themselves with a barrier could also cause thread starvation deadlock if the pool is not big enough.

> Whenever you submit to an Executor tasks that are not independent, be aware of the possibility of thread starvation deadlock, and document any pool sizing or configuration constraints in the code or configuration file where the Executor is configured.

In addition to any explicit bounds on the size of a thread pool, there may also be implicit limits because of constraints on other resources. If your application uses a JDBC connection pool with ten connections and each task needs a database connection, it is as if your thread pool only has ten threads because tasks in excess of ten will block waiting for a connection.

```
public class ThreadDeadlock {
    ExecutorService exec = Executors.newSingleThreadExecutor();

    public class RenderPageTask implements Callable<String> {
        public String call() throws Exception {
            Future<String> header, footer;
            header = exec.submit(new LoadFileTask("header.html"));
            footer = exec.submit(new LoadFileTask("footer.html"));
            String page = renderBody();
            // Will deadlock -- task waiting for result of subtask
            return header.get() + page + footer.get();
        }
    }
}
```

LISTING 8.1. Task that deadlocks in a single-threaded Executor. *Don't do this.*

8.1.2   Long-running tasks

Thread pools can have responsiveness problems if tasks can block for extended periods of time, even if deadlock is not a possibility. A thread pool can become clogged with long-running tasks, increasing the service time even for short tasks. If the pool size is too small relative to the expected steady-state number of long-running tasks, eventually all the pool threads will be running long-running tasks and responsiveness will suffer.

One technique that can mitigate the ill effects of long-running tasks is for tasks to use timed resource waits instead of unbounded waits. Most blocking methods in the plaform libraries come in both untimed and timed versions, such as `Thread.join`, `BlockingQueue.put`, `CountDownLatch.await`, and `Selector.select`. If the wait times out, you can mark the task as failed and abort it or requeue it for execution later. This guarantees that each task eventually makes progress towards either successful or failed completion, freeing up threads for tasks that might complete more quickly. If a thread pool is frequently full of blocked tasks, this may also be a sign that the pool is too small.

8.2   Sizing thread pools

The ideal size for a thread pool depends on the types of tasks that will be submitted and the characteristics of the deployment system. Thread pool sizes should rarely be hard-coded; instead pool sizes should be provided by a configuration mechanism or computed dynamically by consulting `Runtime.availableProcessors`.

Sizing thread pools is not an exact science, but fortunately you need only avoid the extremes of "too big" and "too small". If a thread pool is too big, then threads compete for scarce CPU and memory resources, resulting in higher memory usage and possible resource exhaustion. If it is too small, throughput suffers as processors go unused despite available work.

To size a thread pool properly, you need to understand your computing environment, your resource budget, and the nature of your tasks. How many processors does the deployment system have? How much memory? Do tasks perform mostly computation, I/O, or some combination? Do they require a scarce resource, such as a JDBC connection? If you have different categories of tasks with very different behaviors, consider using multiple thread pools so each can be tuned according to its workload.

For compute-intensive tasks, an N_{cpu}-processor system usually achieves optimum utilization with a thread pool of $N_{cpu} + 1$ threads. (Even compute-intensive threads occasionally take a page fault or pause for some other reason, so an "extra" runnable thread prevents CPU cycles from going unused when this happens.) For tasks that also include I/O or other blocking operations, you want a larger pool, since not all of the threads will be schedulable at all times. In order to size the pool properly, you must estimate the ratio of waiting time to compute time for your tasks; this estimate need not be precise and can be obtained through profiling or instrumentation. Alternatively, the size of the thread pool can be tuned by running the application using several different pool sizes under a benchmark load and observing the level of CPU utilization.

Given these definitions:

$$N_{cpu} \ = \ \text{\textit{number of CPUs}}$$
$$U_{cpu} \ = \ \text{\textit{target CPU utilization}}, 0 \leq U_{cpu} \leq 1$$
$$\frac{W}{C} \ = \ \text{\textit{ratio of wait time to compute time}}$$

The optimal pool size for keeping the processors at the desired utilization is:

$$N_{threads} = N_{cpu} * U_{cpu} * \left(1 + \frac{W}{C}\right)$$

You can determine the number of CPUs using `Runtime`:

```
int N_CPUS = Runtime.getRuntime().availableProcessors();
```

Of course, CPU cycles are not the only resource you might want to manage using thread pools. Other resources that can contribute to sizing constraints are memory, file handles, socket handles, and database connections. Calculating pool size constraints for these types of resources is easier: just add up how much of that resource each task requires and divide that into the total quantity available. The result will be an upper bound on the pool size.

When tasks require a pooled resource such as database connections, thread pool size and resource pool size affect each other. If each task requires a connection, the effective size of the thread pool is limited by the connection pool size. Similarly, when the only consumers of connections are pool tasks, the effective size of the connection pool is limited by the thread pool size.

8.3   Configuring `ThreadPoolExecutor`

`ThreadPoolExecutor` provides the base implementation for the executors returned by the `newCachedThreadPool`, `newFixedThreadPool`, and `newScheduled-ThreadExecutor` factories in `Executors`. `ThreadPoolExecutor` is a flexible, robust pool implementation that allows a variety of customizations.

If the default execution policy does not meet your needs, you can instantiate a `ThreadPoolExecutor` through its constructor and customize it as you see fit; you can consult the source code for `Executors` to see the execution policies for the default configurations and use them as a starting point. `ThreadPoolExecutor` has several constructors, the most general of which is shown in Listing 8.2.

8.3.1   Thread creation and teardown

The core pool size, maximum pool size, and keep-alive time govern thread creation and teardown. The core size is the target size; the implementation attempts to maintain the pool at this size even when there are no tasks to execute,[2] and will

---

2. When a `ThreadPoolExecutor` is initially created, the core threads are not started immediately but instead as tasks are submitted, unless you call `prestartAllCoreThreads`.

```
public ThreadPoolExecutor(int corePoolSize,
                          int maximumPoolSize,
                          long keepAliveTime,
                          TimeUnit unit,
                          BlockingQueue<Runnable> workQueue,
                          ThreadFactory threadFactory,
                          RejectedExecutionHandler handler) { ... }
```

LISTING 8.2. General constructor for ThreadPoolExecutor.

not create more threads than this unless the work queue is full.[3] The maximum pool size is the upper bound on how many pool threads can be active at once. A thread that has been idle for longer than the keep-alive time becomes a candidate for reaping and can be terminated if the current pool size exceeds the core size.

By tuning the core pool size and keep-alive times, you can encourage the pool to reclaim resources used by otherwise idle threads, making them available for more useful work. (Like everything else, this is a tradeoff: reaping idle threads incurs additional latency due to thread creation if threads must later be created when demand increases.)

The newFixedThreadPool factory sets both the core pool size and the maximum pool size to the requested pool size, creating the effect of infinite timeout; the newCachedThreadPool factory sets the maximum pool size to Integer.MAX_- VALUE and the core pool size to zero with a timeout of one minute, creating the effect of an infinitely expandable thread pool that will contract again when demand decreases. Other combinations are possible using the explicit ThreadPool-Executor constructor.

8.3.2 Managing queued tasks

Bounded thread pools limit the number of tasks that can be executed concurrently. (The single-threaded executors are a notable special case: they guarantee that no tasks will execute concurrently, offering the possibility of achieving thread safety through thread confinement.)

We saw in Section 6.1.2 how unbounded thread creation could lead to instability, and addressed this problem by using a fixed-sized thread pool instead of creating a new thread for every request. However, this is only a partial solution; it is still possible for the application to run out of resources under heavy load, just harder. If the arrival rate for new requests exceeds the rate at which they can be

---

3. Developers are sometimes tempted to set the core size to zero so that the worker threads will eventually be torn down and therefore won't prevent the JVM from exiting, but this can cause some strange-seeming behavior in thread pools that don't use a SynchronousQueue for their work queue (as newCachedThreadPool does). If the pool is already at the core size, ThreadPoolExecutor creates a new thread only if the work queue is full. So tasks submitted to a thread pool with a work queue that has any capacity and a core size of zero will not execute until the queue fills up, which is usually not what is desired. In Java 6, allowCoreThreadTimeOut allows you to request that all pool threads be able to time out; enable this feature with a core size of zero if you want a bounded thread pool with a bounded work queue but still have all the threads torn down when there is no work to do.

handled, requests will still queue up. With a thread pool, they wait in a queue of Runnables managed by the Executor instead of queueing up as threads contending for the CPU. Representing a waiting task with a Runnable and a list node is certainly a lot cheaper than with a thread, but the risk of resource exhaustion still remains if clients can throw requests at the server faster than it can handle them.

Requests often arrive in bursts even when the average request rate is fairly stable. Queues can help smooth out transient bursts of tasks, but if tasks continue to arrive too quickly you will eventually have to throttle the arrival rate to avoid running out of memory.[4] Even before you run out of memory, response time will get progressively worse as the task queue grows.

ThreadPoolExecutor allows you to supply a BlockingQueue to hold tasks awaiting execution. There are three basic approaches to task queueing: unbounded queue, bounded queue, and synchronous handoff. The choice of queue interacts with other configuration parameters such as pool size.

The default for newFixedThreadPool and newSingleThreadExecutor is to use an unbounded LinkedBlockingQueue. Tasks will queue up if all worker threads are busy, but the queue could grow without bound if the tasks keep arriving faster than they can be executed.

A more stable resource management strategy is to use a bounded queue, such as an ArrayBlockingQueue or a bounded LinkedBlockingQueue or PriorityBlockingQueue. Bounded queues help prevent resource exhaustion but introduce the question of what to do with new tasks when the queue is full. (There are a number of possible *saturation policies* for addressing this problem; see Section 8.3.3.) With a bounded work queue, the queue size and pool size must be tuned together. A large queue coupled with a small pool can help reduce memory usage, CPU usage, and context switching, at the cost of potentially constraining throughput.

For very large or unbounded pools, you can also bypass queueing entirely and instead hand off tasks directly from producers to worker threads using a SynchronousQueue. A SynchronousQueue is not really a queue at all, but a mechanism for managing handoffs between threads. In order to put an element on a SynchronousQueue, another thread must already be waiting to accept the handoff. If no thread is waiting but the current pool size is less than the maximum, ThreadPoolExecutor creates a new thread; otherwise the task is rejected according to the saturation policy. Using a direct handoff is more efficient because the task can be handed right to the thread that will execute it, rather than first placing it on a queue and then having the worker thread fetch it from the queue. SynchronousQueue is a practical choice only if the pool is unbounded or if rejecting excess tasks is acceptable. The newCachedThreadPool factory uses a SynchronousQueue.

Using a FIFO queue like LinkedBlockingQueue or ArrayBlockingQueue causes tasks to be started in the order in which they arrived. For more control over task execution order, you can use a PriorityBlockingQueue, which

---

4. This is analogous to flow control in communications networks: you may be willing to buffer a certain amount of data, but eventually you need to find a way to get the other side to stop sending you data, or throw the excess data on the floor and hope the sender retransmits it when you're not so busy.

orders tasks according to priority. Priority can be defined by natural order (if tasks implement `Comparable`) or by a `Comparator`.

> The `newCachedThreadPool` factory is a good default choice for an Executor, providing better queuing performance than a fixed thread pool.[5] A fixed size thread pool is a good choice when you need to limit the number of concurrent tasks for resource-management purposes, as in a server application that accepts requests from network clients and would otherwise be vulnerable to overload.

Bounding either the thread pool or the work queue is suitable only when tasks are independent. With tasks that depend on other tasks, bounded thread pools or queues can cause thread starvation deadlock; instead, use an unbounded pool configuration like `newCachedThreadPool`.[6]

8.3.3 Saturation policies

When a bounded work queue fills up, the *saturation policy* comes into play. The saturation policy for a `ThreadPoolExecutor` can be modified by calling `setRejectedExecutionHandler`. (The saturation policy is also used when a task is submitted to an `Executor` that has been shut down.) Several implementations of `RejectedExecutionHandler` are provided, each implementing a different saturation policy: `AbortPolicy`, `CallerRunsPolicy`, `DiscardPolicy`, and `DiscardOldestPolicy`.

The default policy, *abort*, causes `execute` to throw the unchecked `RejectedExecutionException`; the caller can catch this exception and implement its own overflow handling as it sees fit. The *discard* policy silently discards the newly submitted task if it cannot be queued for execution; the *discard-oldest* policy discards the task that would otherwise be executed next and tries to resubmit the new task. (If the work queue is a priority queue, this discards the highest-priority element, so the combination of a discard-oldest saturation policy and a priority queue is not a good one.)

The *caller-runs* policy implements a form of throttling that neither discards tasks nor throws an exception, but instead tries to slow down the flow of new tasks by pushing some of the work back to the caller. It executes the newly submitted task not in a pool thread, but in the thread that calls `execute`. If we modified our `WebServer` example to use a bounded queue and the caller-runs policy, after all the pool threads were occupied and the work queue filled up the next task would be executed in the main thread during the call to `execute`. Since

---

5. This performance difference comes from the use of `SynchronousQueue` instead of `LinkedBlockingQueue`. `SynchronousQueue` was replaced in Java 6 with a new nonblocking algorithm that improved throughput in `Executor` benchmarks by a factor of three over the Java 5.0 `SynchronousQueue` implementation (Scherer et al., 2006).

6. An alternative configuration for tasks that submit other tasks and wait for their results is to use a bounded thread pool, a `SynchronousQueue` as the work queue, and the caller-runs saturation policy.

this would probably take some time, the main thread cannot submit any more tasks for at least a little while, giving the worker threads some time to catch up on the backlog. The main thread would also not be calling accept during this time, so incoming requests will queue up in the TCP layer instead of in the application. If the overload persisted, eventually the TCP layer would decide it has queued enough connection requests and begin discarding connection requests as well. As the server becomes overloaded, the overload is gradually pushed outward—from the pool threads to the work queue to the application to the TCP layer, and eventually to the client—enabling more graceful degradation under load.

Choosing a saturation policy or making other changes to the execution policy can be done when the Executor is created. Listing 8.3 illustrates creating a fixed-size thread pool with the caller-runs saturation policy.

```
ThreadPoolExecutor executor
    = new ThreadPoolExecutor(N_THREADS, N_THREADS,
        0L, TimeUnit.MILLISECONDS,
        new LinkedBlockingQueue<Runnable>(CAPACITY));
executor.setRejectedExecutionHandler(
    new ThreadPoolExecutor.CallerRunsPolicy());
```

LISTING 8.3. Creating a fixed-sized thread pool with a bounded queue and the caller-runs saturation policy.

There is no predefined saturation policy to make execute block when the work queue is full. However, the same effect can be accomplished by using a Semaphore to bound the task injection rate, as shown in BoundedExecutor in Listing 8.4. In such an approach, use an unbounded queue (there's no reason to bound both the queue size and the injection rate) and set the bound on the semaphore to be equal to the pool size *plus* the number of queued tasks you want to allow, since the semaphore is bounding the number of tasks both currently executing and awaiting execution.

8.3.4 Thread factories

Whenever a thread pool needs to create a thread, it does so through a *thread factory* (see Listing 8.5). The default thread factory creates a new, nondaemon thread with no special configuration. Specifying a thread factory allows you to customize the configuration of pool threads. ThreadFactory has a single method, newThread, that is called whenever a thread pool needs to create a new thread.

There are a number of reasons to use a custom thread factory. You might want to specify an UncaughtExceptionHandler for pool threads, or instantiate an instance of a custom Thread class, such as one that performs debug logging. You might want to modify the priority (generally not a very good idea; see Section 10.3.1) or set the daemon status (again, not all that good an idea; see Section 7.4.2) of pool threads. Or maybe you just want to give pool threads more meaningful names to simplify interpreting thread dumps and error logs.

```
@ThreadSafe
public class BoundedExecutor {
    private final Executor exec;
    private final Semaphore semaphore;

    public BoundedExecutor(Executor exec, int bound) {
        this.exec = exec;
        this.semaphore = new Semaphore(bound);
    }

    public void submitTask(final Runnable command)
            throws InterruptedException {
        semaphore.acquire();
        try {
            exec.execute(new Runnable() {
                public void run() {
                    try {
                        command.run();
                    } finally {
                        semaphore.release();
                    }
                }
            });
        } catch (RejectedExecutionException e) {
            semaphore.release();
        }
    }
}
```

LISTING 8.4. Using a Semaphore to throttle task submission.

```
public interface ThreadFactory {
    Thread newThread(Runnable r);
}
```

LISTING 8.5. ThreadFactory interface.

MyThreadFactory in Listing 8.6 illustrates a custom thread factory. It instantiates a new MyAppThread, passing a pool-specific name to the constructor so that threads from each pool can be distinguished in thread dumps and error logs. MyAppThread can also be used elsewhere in the application so that all threads can take advantage of its debugging features.

```
public class MyThreadFactory implements ThreadFactory {
    private final String poolName;

    public MyThreadFactory(String poolName) {
        this.poolName = poolName;
    }

    public Thread newThread(Runnable runnable) {
        return new MyAppThread(runnable, poolName);
    }
}
```

LISTING 8.6. Custom thread factory.

The interesting customization takes place in MyAppThread, shown in Listing 8.7, which lets you provide a thread name, sets a custom UncaughtException-Handler that writes a message to a Logger, maintains statistics on how many threads have been created and destroyed, and optionally writes a debug message to the log when a thread is created or terminates.

If your application takes advantage of *security policies* to grant permissions to particular codebases, you may want to use the privilegedThreadFactory factory method in Executors to construct your thread factory. It creates pool threads that have the same permissions, AccessControlContext, and contextClassLoader as the thread creating the privilegedThreadFactory. Otherwise, threads created by the thread pool inherit permissions from whatever client happens to be calling execute or submit at the time a new thread is needed, which could cause confusing security-related exceptions.

8.3.5 Customizing ThreadPoolExecutor after construction

Most of the options passed to the ThreadPoolExecutor constructors can also be modified after construction via setters (such as the core thread pool size, maximum thread pool size, keep-alive time, thread factory, and rejected execution handler). If the Executor is created through one of the factory methods in Executors (except newSingleThreadExecutor), you can cast the result to ThreadPoolExecutor to access the setters as in Listing 8.8.

Executors includes a factory method, unconfigurableExecutorService, which takes an existing ExecutorService and wraps it with one exposing only the methods of ExecutorService so it cannot be further configured. Unlike the pooled implementations, newSingleThreadExecutor returns an ExecutorService wrapped in this manner, rather than a raw ThreadPoolExecutor. While

```
public class MyAppThread extends Thread {
    public static final String DEFAULT_NAME = "MyAppThread";
    private static volatile boolean debugLifecycle = false;
    private static final AtomicInteger created = new AtomicInteger();
    private static final AtomicInteger alive = new AtomicInteger();
    private static final Logger log = Logger.getAnonymousLogger();

    public MyAppThread(Runnable r) { this(r, DEFAULT_NAME); }

    public MyAppThread(Runnable runnable, String name) {
        super(runnable, name + "-" + created.incrementAndGet());
        setUncaughtExceptionHandler(
            new Thread.UncaughtExceptionHandler() {
                public void uncaughtException(Thread t,
                                              Throwable e) {
                    log.log(Level.SEVERE,
                        "UNCAUGHT in thread " + t.getName(), e);
                }
            });
    }

    public void run() {
        // Copy debug flag to ensure consistent value throughout.
        boolean debug = debugLifecycle;
        if (debug) log.log(Level.FINE, "Created "+getName());
        try {
            alive.incrementAndGet();
            super.run();
        } finally {
            alive.decrementAndGet();
            if (debug) log.log(Level.FINE, "Exiting "+getName());
        }
    }

    public static int getThreadsCreated() { return created.get(); }
    public static int getThreadsAlive() { return alive.get(); }
    public static boolean getDebug() { return debugLifecycle; }
    public static void setDebug(boolean b) { debugLifecycle = b; }
}
```

LISTING 8.7. Custom thread base class.

```
ExecutorService exec = Executors.newCachedThreadPool();
if (exec instanceof ThreadPoolExecutor)
    ((ThreadPoolExecutor) exec).setCorePoolSize(10);
else
    throw new AssertionError("Oops, bad assumption");
```

LISTING 8.8. Modifying an Executor created with the standard factories.

a single-threaded executor is actually implemented as a thread pool with one thread, it also promises not to execute tasks concurrently. If some misguided code were to increase the pool size on a single-threaded executor, it would undermine the intended execution semantics.

You can use this technique with your own executors to prevent the execution policy from being modified. If you will be exposing an ExecutorService to code you don't trust not to modify it, you can wrap it with an unconfigurableExecutorService.

8.4   Extending ThreadPoolExecutor

ThreadPoolExecutor was designed for extension, providing several "hooks" for subclasses to override—beforeExecute, afterExecute, and terminated—that can be used to extend the behavior of ThreadPoolExecutor.

The beforeExecute and afterExecute hooks are called in the thread that executes the task, and can be used for adding logging, timing, monitoring, or statistics gathering. The afterExecute hook is called whether the task completes by returning normally from run or by throwing an Exception. (If the task completes with an Error, afterExecute is not called.) If beforeExecute throws a RuntimeException, the task is not executed and afterExecute is not called.

The terminated hook is called when the thread pool completes the shutdown process, after all tasks have finished and all worker threads have shut down. It can be used to release resources allocated by the Executor during its lifecycle, perform notification or logging, or finalize statistics gathering.

8.4.1   Example: adding statistics to a thread pool

TimingThreadPool in Listing 8.9 shows a custom thread pool that uses beforeExecute, afterExecute, and terminated to add logging and statistics gathering. To measure a task's runtime, beforeExecute must record the start time and store it somewhere afterExecute can find it. Because execution hooks are called in the thread that executes the task, a value placed in a ThreadLocal by beforeExecute can be retrieved by afterExecute. TimingThreadPool uses a pair of AtomicLongs to keep track of the total number of tasks processed and the total processing time, and uses the terminated hook to print a log message showing the average task time.

```java
public class TimingThreadPool extends ThreadPoolExecutor {
    private final ThreadLocal<Long> startTime
            = new ThreadLocal<Long>();
    private final Logger log = Logger.getLogger("TimingThreadPool");
    private final AtomicLong numTasks = new AtomicLong();
    private final AtomicLong totalTime = new AtomicLong();

    protected void beforeExecute(Thread t, Runnable r) {
        super.beforeExecute(t, r);
        log.fine(String.format("Thread %s: start %s", t, r));
        startTime.set(System.nanoTime());
    }

    protected void afterExecute(Runnable r, Throwable t) {
        try {
            long endTime = System.nanoTime();
            long taskTime = endTime - startTime.get();
            numTasks.incrementAndGet();
            totalTime.addAndGet(taskTime);
            log.fine(String.format("Thread %s: end %s, time=%dns",
                    t, r, taskTime));
        } finally {
            super.afterExecute(r, t);
        }
    }

    protected void terminated() {
        try {
            log.info(String.format("Terminated: avg time=%dns",
                    totalTime.get() / numTasks.get()));
        } finally {
            super.terminated();
        }
    }
}
```

LISTING 8.9. Thread pool extended with logging and timing.

8.5 Parallelizing recursive algorithms

The page rendering examples in Section 6.3 went through a series of refinements in search of exploitable parallelism. The first attempt was entirely sequential; the second used two threads but still performed all the image downloads sequentially; the final version treated each image download as a separate task to achieve greater parallelism. Loops whose bodies contain nontrivial computation or perform potentially blocking I/O are frequently good candidates for parallelization, as long as the iterations are independent.

If we have a loop whose iterations are independent and we don't need to wait for all of them to complete before proceeding, we can use an Executor to transform a sequential loop into a parallel one, as shown in processSequentially and processInParallel in Listing 8.10.

```
void processSequentially(List<Element> elements) {
    for (Element e : elements)
        process(e);
}

void processInParallel(Executor exec, List<Element> elements) {
    for (final Element e : elements)
        exec.execute(new Runnable() {
            public void run() { process(e); }
        });
}
```

LISTING 8.10. Transforming sequential execution into parallel execution.

A call to processInParallel returns more quickly than a call to processSequentially because it returns as soon as all the tasks are queued to the Executor, rather than waiting for them all to complete. If you want to submit a set of tasks and wait for them all to complete, you can use ExecutorService.invokeAll; to retrieve the results as they become available, you can use a CompletionService, as in Renderer on page 130.

> Sequential loop iterations are suitable for parallelization when each iteration is independent of the others and the work done in each iteration of the loop body is significant enough to offset the cost of managing a new task.

Loop parallelization can also be applied to some recursive designs; there are often sequential loops within the recursive algorithm that can be parallelized in the same manner as Listing 8.10. The easier case is when each iteration does not require the results of the recursive iterations it invokes. For example, sequentialRecursive in Listing 8.11 does a depth-first traversal of a tree, performing a calculation on each node and placing the result in a collection. The transformed version, `parallelRecursive`, also does a depth-first traversal, but instead of computing the result as each node is visited, it submits a task to compute the node result.

```
public<T> void sequentialRecursive(List<Node<T>> nodes,
                                    Collection<T> results) {
    for (Node<T> n : nodes) {
        results.add(n.compute());
        sequentialRecursive(n.getChildren(), results);
    }
}

public<T> void parallelRecursive(final Executor exec,
                                 List<Node<T>> nodes,
                                 final Collection<T> results) {
    for (final Node<T> n : nodes) {
        exec.execute(new Runnable() {
            public void run() {
                results.add(n.compute());
            }
        });
        parallelRecursive(exec, n.getChildren(), results);
    }
}
```

LISTING 8.11. *Transforming sequential tail-recursion into parallelized recursion.*

When `parallelRecursive` returns, each node in the tree has been visited (the traversal is still sequential: only the calls to `compute` are executed in parallel) and the computation for each node has been queued to the Executor. Callers of `parallelRecursive` can wait for all the results by creating an Executor specific to the traversal and using `shutdown` and `awaitTermination`, as shown in Listing 8.12.

```
public<T> Collection<T> getParallelResults(List<Node<T>> nodes)
        throws InterruptedException {
    ExecutorService exec = Executors.newCachedThreadPool();
    Queue<T> resultQueue = new ConcurrentLinkedQueue<T>();
    parallelRecursive(exec, nodes, resultQueue);
    exec.shutdown();
    exec.awaitTermination(Long.MAX_VALUE, TimeUnit.SECONDS);
    return resultQueue;
}
```

LISTING 8.12. *Waiting for results to be calculated in parallel.*

8.5.1 Example: A puzzle framework

An appealing application of this technique is solving puzzles that involve finding a sequence of transformations from some initial state to reach a goal state, such as the familiar "sliding block puzzles",[7] "Hi-Q", "Instant Insanity", and other solitaire puzzles.

We define a "puzzle" as a combination of an initial position, a goal position, and a set of rules that determine valid moves. The rule set has two parts: computing the list of legal moves from a given position and computing the result of applying a move to a position. Puzzle in Listing 8.13 shows our puzzle abstraction; the type parameters P and M represent the classes for a position and a move. From this interface, we can write a simple sequential solver that searches the puzzle space until a solution is found or the puzzle space is exhausted.

```
public interface Puzzle<P, M> {
    P initialPosition();
    boolean isGoal(P position);
    Set<M> legalMoves(P position);
    P move(P position, M move);
}
```

LISTING 8.13. Abstraction for puzzles like the "sliding blocks puzzle".

Node in Listing 8.14 represents a position that has been reached through some series of moves, holding a reference to the move that created the position and the previous Node. Following the links back from a Node lets us reconstruct the sequence of moves that led to the current position.

SequentialPuzzleSolver in Listing 8.15 shows a sequential solver for the puzzle framework that performs a depth-first search of the puzzle space. It terminates when it finds a solution (which is not necessarily the shortest solution).

Rewriting the solver to exploit concurrency would allow us to compute next moves and evaluate the goal condition in parallel, since the process of evaluating one move is mostly independent of evaluating other moves. (We say "mostly" because tasks share some mutable state, such as the set of seen positions.) If multiple processors are available, this could reduce the time it takes to find a solution.

ConcurrentPuzzleSolver in Listing 8.16 uses an inner SolverTask class that extends Node and implements Runnable. Most of the work is done in run: evaluating the set of possible next positions, pruning positions already searched, evaluating whether success has yet been achieved (by this task or by some other task), and submitting unsearched positions to an Executor.

To avoid infinite loops, the sequential version maintained a Set of previously searched positions; ConcurrentPuzzleSolver uses a ConcurrentHashMap for this purpose. This provides thread safety and avoids the race condition inherent in conditionally updating a shared collection by using putIfAbsent to atomically

---

7. See http://www.puzzleworld.org/SlidingBlockPuzzles.

```
@Immutable
static class Node<P, M> {
    final P pos;
    final M move;
    final Node<P, M> prev;

    Node(P pos, M move, Node<P, M> prev) {...}

    List<M> asMoveList() {
        List<M> solution = new LinkedList<M>();
        for (Node<P, M> n = this; n.move != null; n = n.prev)
            solution.add(0, n.move);
        return solution;
    }
}
```

LISTING 8.14. Link node for the puzzle solver framework.

add a position only if it was not previously known. ConcurrentPuzzleSolver uses the internal work queue of the thread pool instead of the call stack to hold the state of the search.

The concurrent approach also trades one form of limitation for another that might be more suitable to the problem domain. The sequential version performs a depth-first search, so the search is bounded by the available stack size. The concurrent version performs a breadth-first search and is therefore free of the stack size restriction (but can still run out of memory if the set of positions to be searched or already searched exceeds the available memory).

In order to stop searching when we find a solution, we need a way to determine whether any thread has found a solution yet. If we want to accept the first solution found, we also need to update the solution only if no other task has already found one. These requirements describe a sort of *latch* (see Section 5.5.1) and in particular, a *result-bearing latch*. We could easily build a blocking result-bearing latch using the techniques in Chapter 14, but it is often easier and less error-prone to use existing library classes rather than low-level language mechanisms. ValueLatch in Listing 8.17 uses a CountDownLatch to provide the needed latching behavior, and uses locking to ensure that the solution is set only once.

Each task first consults the solution latch and stops if a solution has already been found. The main thread needs to wait until a solution is found; getValue in ValueLatch blocks until some thread has set the value. ValueLatch provides a way to hold a value such that only the first call actually sets the value, callers can test whether it has been set, and callers can block waiting for it to be set. On the first call to setValue, the solution is updated and the CountDownLatch is decremented, releasing the main solver thread from getValue.

The first thread to find a solution also shuts down the Executor, to prevent new tasks from being accepted. To avoid having to deal with RejectedExecu-

```
public class SequentialPuzzleSolver<P, M> {
    private final Puzzle<P, M> puzzle;
    private final Set<P> seen = new HashSet<P>();

    public SequentialPuzzleSolver(Puzzle<P, M> puzzle) {
        this.puzzle = puzzle;
    }

    public List<M> solve() {
        P pos = puzzle.initialPosition();
        return search(new Node<P, M>(pos, null, null));
    }

    private List<M> search(Node<P, M> node) {
        if (!seen.contains(node.pos)) {
            seen.add(node.pos);
            if (puzzle.isGoal(node.pos))
                return node.asMoveList();
            for (M move : puzzle.legalMoves(node.pos)) {
                P pos = puzzle.move(node.pos, move);
                Node<P, M> child = new Node<P, M>(pos, move, node);
                List<M> result = search(child);
                if (result != null)
                    return result;
            }
        }
        return null;
    }

    static class Node<P, M> { /* Listing 8.14 */ }
}
```

LISTING 8.15. Sequential puzzle solver.

```
public class ConcurrentPuzzleSolver<P, M> {
    private final Puzzle<P, M> puzzle;
    private final ExecutorService exec;
    private final ConcurrentMap<P, Boolean> seen;
    final ValueLatch<Node<P, M>> solution
            = new ValueLatch<Node<P, M>>();
    ...
    public List<M> solve() throws InterruptedException {
        try {
            P p = puzzle.initialPosition();
            exec.execute(newTask(p, null, null));
            // block until solution found
            Node<P, M> solnNode = solution.getValue();
            return (solnNode == null) ? null : solnNode.asMoveList();
        } finally {
            exec.shutdown();
        }
    }

    protected Runnable newTask(P p, M m, Node<P,M> n) {
        return new SolverTask(p, m, n);
    }

    class SolverTask extends Node<P, M> implements Runnable {
        ...
        public void run() {
            if (solution.isSet()
                    || seen.putIfAbsent(pos, true) != null)
                return; // already solved or seen this position
            if (puzzle.isGoal(pos))
                solution.setValue(this);
            else
                for (M m : puzzle.legalMoves(pos))
                    exec.execute(
                        newTask(puzzle.move(pos, m), m, this));
        }
    }
}
```

LISTING 8.16. Concurrent version of puzzle solver.

```
@ThreadSafe
public class ValueLatch<T> {
    @GuardedBy("this") private T value = null;
    private final CountDownLatch done = new CountDownLatch(1);

    public boolean isSet() {
        return (done.getCount() == 0);
    }

    public synchronized void setValue(T newValue) {
        if (!isSet()) {
            value = newValue;
            done.countDown();
        }
    }

    public T getValue() throws InterruptedException {
        done.await();
        synchronized (this) {
            return value;
        }
    }
}
```

LISTING 8.17. Result-bearing latch used by `ConcurrentPuzzleSolver`.

tionException, the rejected execution handler should be set to discard submitted tasks. Then, all unfinished tasks eventually run to completion and any subsequent attempts to execute new tasks fail silently, allowing the executor to terminate. (If the tasks took longer to run, we might want to interrupt them instead of letting them finish.)

ConcurrentPuzzleSolver does not deal well with the case where there is no solution: if all possible moves and positions have been evaluated and no solution has been found, solve waits forever in the call to getSolution. The sequential version terminated when it had exhausted the search space, but getting concurrent programs to terminate can sometimes be more difficult. One possible solution is to keep a count of active solver tasks and set the solution to null when the count drops to zero, as in Listing 8.18.

Finding the solution may also take longer than we are willing to wait; there are several additional termination conditions we could impose on the solver. One is a time limit; this is easily done by implementing a timed getValue in ValueLatch (which would use the timed version of await), and shutting down the Executor and declaring failure if getValue times out. Another is some sort of puzzle-specific metric such as searching only up to a certain number of positions. Or we can provide a cancellation mechanism and let the client make its own

```
public class PuzzleSolver<P,M> extends ConcurrentPuzzleSolver<P,M> {
    ...
    private final AtomicInteger taskCount = new AtomicInteger(0);

    protected Runnable newTask(P p, M m, Node<P,M> n) {
        return new CountingSolverTask(p, m, n);
    }

    class CountingSolverTask extends SolverTask {
        CountingSolverTask(P pos, M move, Node<P, M> prev) {
            super(pos, move, prev);
            taskCount.incrementAndGet();
        }
        public void run() {
            try {
                super.run();
            } finally {
                if (taskCount.decrementAndGet() == 0)
                    solution.setValue(null);
            }
        }
    }
}
```

LISTING 8.18. Solver that recognizes when no solution exists.

decision about when to stop searching.

Summary

The Executor framework is a powerful and flexible framework for concurrently executing tasks. It offers a number of tuning options, such as policies for creating and tearing down threads, handling queued tasks, and what to do with excess tasks, and provides several hooks for extending its behavior. As in most powerful frameworks, however, there are combinations of settings that do not work well together; some types of tasks require specific execution policies, and some combinations of tuning parameters may produce strange results.

Chapter 9

GUI Applications

If you've tried to write even a simple GUI application using Swing, you know that GUI applications have their own peculiar threading issues. To maintain safety, certain tasks must run in the Swing event thread. But you cannot execute long-running tasks in the event thread, lest the UI become unresponsive. And Swing data structures are not thread-safe, so you must be careful to confine them to the event thread.

Nearly all GUI toolkits, including Swing and SWT, are implemented as *single-threaded subsystems* in which all GUI activity is confined to a single thread. If you are not planning to write a totally single-threaded program, there will be activities that run partially in an application thread and partially in the event thread. Like many other threading bugs, getting this division wrong may not necessarily make your program crash immediately; instead, it could behave oddly under hard-to-identify conditions. Even though the GUI frameworks themselves are single-threaded subsystems, your application may not be, and you still need to consider threading issues carefully when writing GUI code.

9.1 Why are GUIs single-threaded?

In the old days, GUI applications were single-threaded and GUI events were processed from a "main event loop". Modern GUI frameworks use a model that is only slightly different: they create a dedicated *event dispatch thread* (EDT) for handling GUI events.

Single-threaded GUI frameworks are not unique to Java; Qt, NextStep, MacOS Cocoa, X Windows, and many others are also single-threaded. This is not for lack of trying; there have been many attempts to write multithreaded GUI frameworks, but because of persistent problems with race conditions and deadlock, they all eventually arrived at the single-threaded event queue model in which a dedicated thread fetches events off a queue and dispatches them to application-defined event handlers. (AWT originally tried to support a greater degree of multithreaded access, and the decision to make Swing single-threaded was based largely on experience with AWT.)

Multithreaded GUI frameworks tend to be particularly susceptible to deadlock, partially because of the unfortunate interaction between input event processing and any sensible object-oriented modeling of GUI components. Actions initiated by the user tend to "bubble up" from the OS to the application—a mouse click is detected by the OS, is turned into a "mouse click" event by the toolkit, and is eventually delivered to an application listener as a higher level event such as a "button pressed" event. On the other hand, application-initiated actions "bubble down" from the application to the OS—changing the background color of a component originates in the application and is dispatched to a specific component class and eventually into the OS for rendering. Combining this tendency for activities to access the same GUI objects in the opposite order with the requirement of making each object thread-safe yields a recipe for inconsistent lock ordering, which leads to deadlock (see Chapter 10). And this is exactly what nearly every GUI toolkit development effort rediscovered through experience.

Another factor leading to deadlock in multithreaded GUI frameworks is the prevalence of the model-view-control (MVC) pattern. Factoring user interactions into cooperating model, view, and controller objects greatly simplifies implementing GUI applications, but again raises the risk of inconsistent lock ordering. The controller calls into the model, which notifies the view that something has changed. But the controller can also call into the view, which may in turn call back into the model to query the model state. The result is again inconsistent lock ordering, with the attendant risk of deadlock.

In his weblog,[1] Sun VP Graham Hamilton nicely sums up the challenges, describing why the multithreaded GUI toolkit is one of the recurring "failed dreams" of computer science.

> I believe you can program successfully with multithreaded GUI toolkits if the toolkit is very carefully designed; if the toolkit exposes its locking methodology in gory detail; if you are very smart, very careful, and have a global understanding of the whole structure of the toolkit. If you get one of these things slightly wrong, things will mostly work, but you will get occasional hangs (due to deadlocks) or glitches (due to races). This multithreaded approach works best for people who have been intimately involved in the design of the toolkit.

> Unfortunately, I don't think this set of characteristics scales to widespread commercial use. What you tend to end up with is normal smart programmers building apps that don't quite work reliably for reasons that are not at all obvious. So the authors get very disgruntled and frustrated and use bad words on the poor innocent toolkit.

Single-threaded GUI frameworks achieve thread safety via thread confinement; all GUI objects, including visual components and data models, are accessed exclusively from the event thread. Of course, this just pushes some of the thread safety burden back onto the application developer, who must make sure these objects are properly confined.

---

1. http://weblogs.java.net/blog/kgh/archive/2004/10

9.1.1 Sequential event processing

GUI applications are oriented around processing fine-grained *events* such as mouse clicks, key presses, or timer expirations. Events are a kind of task; the event handling machinery provided by AWT and Swing is structurally similar to an Executor.

Because there is only a single thread for processing GUI tasks, they are processed sequentially—one task finishes before the next one begins, and no two tasks overlap. Knowing this makes writing task code easier—you don't have to worry about interference from other tasks.

The downside of sequential task processing is that if one task takes a long time to execute, other tasks must wait until it is finished. If those other tasks are responsible for responding to user input or providing visual feedback, the application will appear to have frozen. If a lengthy task is running in the event thread, the user cannot even click "Cancel" because the cancel button listener is not called until the lengthy task completes. Therefore, tasks that execute in the event thread must return control to the event thread quickly. To initiate a long-running task such as spell-checking a large document, searching the file system, or fetching a resource over a network, you must run that task in another thread so control can return quickly to the event thread. To update a progress indicator while a long-running task executes or provide visual feedback when it completes, you again need to execute code in the event thread. This can get complicated quickly.

9.1.2 Thread confinement in Swing

All Swing components (such as JButton and JTable) and data model objects (such as TableModel and TreeModel) are confined to the event thread, so any code that accesses these objects must run in the event thread. GUI objects are kept consistent not by synchronization, but by thread confinement. The upside is that tasks that run in the event thread need not worry about synchronization when accessing presentation objects; the downside is that you cannot access presentation objects from outside the event thread at all.

> The *Swing single-thread rule*: Swing components and models should be created, modified, and queried only from the event-dispatching thread.

As with all rules, there are a few exceptions. A small number of Swing methods may be called safely from any thread; these are clearly identified in the Javadoc as being thread-safe. Other exceptions to the single-thread rule include:

- SwingUtilities.isEventDispatchThread, which determines whether the current thread is the event thread;

- SwingUtilities.invokeLater, which schedules a Runnable for execution on the event thread (callable from any thread);

- `SwingUtilities.invokeAndWait`, which schedules a `Runnable` task for exe-cution on the event thread and blocks the current thread until it completes (callable *only* from a non-GUI thread);

- methods to enqueue a repaint or revalidation request on the event queue (callable from any thread); and

- methods for adding and removing listeners (can be called from any thread, but listeners will always be invoked in the event thread).

The `invokeLater` and `invokeAndWait` methods function a lot like an `Executor`. In fact, it is trivial to implement the threading-related methods from `SwingUtil-ities` using a single-threaded `Executor`, as shown in Listing 9.1. This is not how `SwingUtilities` is actually implemented, as Swing predates the `Executor` framework, but is probably how it would be if Swing were being implemented today.

The Swing event thread can be thought of as a single-threaded `Executor` that processes tasks from the event queue. As with thread pools, sometimes the worker thread dies and is replaced by a new one, but this should be transpar-ent to tasks. Sequential, single-threaded execution is a sensible execution policy when tasks are short-lived, scheduling predictability is not important, or it is imperative that tasks not execute concurrently.

`GuiExecutor` in Listing 9.2 is an `Executor` that delegates tasks to `SwingUtil-ities` for execution. It could be implemented in terms of other GUI frameworks as well; for example, SWT provides the `Display.asyncExec` method, which is similar to Swing's `invokeLater`.

9.2   Short-running GUI tasks

In a GUI application, events originate in the event thread and bubble up to ap-plication-provided listeners, which will probably perform some computation that affects the presentation objects. For simple, short-running tasks, the entire action can stay in the event thread; for longer-running tasks, some of the processing should be offloaded to another thread.

In the simple case, confining presentation objects to the event thread is com-pletely natural. Listing 9.3 creates a button whose color changes randomly when pressed. When the user clicks on the button, the toolkit delivers an `ActionEvent` in the event thread to all registered action listeners. In response, the action lis-tener picks a new color and changes the button's background color. So the event originates in the GUI toolkit and is delivered to the application, and the applica-tion modifies the GUI in response to the user's action. Control never has to leave the event thread, as illustrated in Figure 9.1.

This trivial example characterizes the majority of interactions between GUI applications and GUI toolkits. So long as tasks are short-lived and access only GUI objects (or other thread-confined or thread-safe application objects), you can almost totally ignore threading concerns and do everything from the event thread, and the right thing happens.

```
public class SwingUtilities {
    private static final ExecutorService exec =
        Executors.newSingleThreadExecutor(new SwingThreadFactory());
    private static volatile Thread swingThread;

    private static class SwingThreadFactory implements ThreadFactory {
        public Thread newThread(Runnable r) {
            swingThread = new Thread(r);
            return swingThread;
        }
    }

    public static boolean isEventDispatchThread() {
        return Thread.currentThread() == swingThread;
    }

    public static void invokeLater(Runnable task) {
        exec.execute(task);
    }

    public static void invokeAndWait(Runnable task)
            throws InterruptedException, InvocationTargetException {
        Future f = exec.submit(task);
        try {
            f.get();
        } catch (ExecutionException e) {
            throw new InvocationTargetException(e);
        }
    }
}
```

LISTING 9.1. Implementing SwingUtilities using an Executor.

```
public class GuiExecutor extends AbstractExecutorService {
    // Singletons have a private constructor and a public factory
    private static final GuiExecutor instance = new GuiExecutor();

    private GuiExecutor() { }

    public static GuiExecutor instance() { return instance; }

    public void execute(Runnable r) {
        if (SwingUtilities.isEventDispatchThread())
            r.run();
        else
            SwingUtilities.invokeLater(r);
    }

    // Plus trivial implementations of lifecycle methods
}
```

LISTING 9.2. Executor built atop `SwingUtilities`.

```
final Random random = new Random();
final JButton button = new JButton("Change Color");
...
button.addActionListener(new ActionListener() {
    public void actionPerformed(ActionEvent e) {
        button.setBackground(new Color(random.nextInt()));
    }
});
```

LISTING 9.3. Simple event listener.

FIGURE 9.1. Control flow of a simple button click.

A slightly more complicated version of this same scenario, illustrated in Figure 9.2, involves the use of a formal data model such as a `TableModel` or `TreeModel`. Swing splits most visual components into two objects, a model and a view. The data to be displayed resides in the model and the rules governing how it is displayed reside in the view. The model objects can fire events indicating that the model data has changed, and views subscribe to these events. When the view receives an event indicating the model data may have changed, it queries the model for the new data and updates the display. So in a button listener that

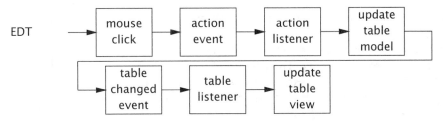

FIGURE 9.2. Control flow with separate model and view objects.

modifies the contents of a table, the action listener would update the model and call one of the fireXxx methods, which would in turn invoke the view's table model listeners, which would update the view. Again, control never leaves the event thread. (The Swing data model fireXxx methods always call the model listeners directly rather than submitting a new event to the event queue, so the fireXxx methods must be called only from the event thread.)

9.3   Long-running GUI tasks

If all tasks were short-running (and the application had no significant non-GUI portion), then the entire application could run within the event thread and you wouldn't have to pay any attention to threads at all. However, sophisticated GUI applications may execute tasks that may take longer than the user is willing to wait, such as spell checking, background compilation, or fetching remote resources. These tasks must run in another thread so that the GUI remains responsive while they run.

Swing makes it easy to have a task run in the event thread, but (prior to Java 6) doesn't provide any mechanism for helping GUI tasks execute code in other threads. But we don't need Swing to help us here: we can create our own Executor for processing long-running tasks. A cached thread pool is a good choice for long-running tasks; only rarely do GUI applications initiate a large number of long-running tasks, so there is little risk of the pool growing without bound.

We start with a simple task that does not support cancellation or progress indication and that does not update the GUI on completion, and then add those features one by one. Listing 9.4 shows an action listener, bound to a visual component, that submits a long-running task to an Executor. Despite the two layers of inner classes, having a GUI task initiate a task in this manner is fairly straightforward: the UI action listener is called in the event thread and submits a Runnable to execute in the thread pool.

This example gets the long-running task out of the event thread in a "fire and forget" manner, which is probably not very useful. There is usually some sort of visual feedback when a long-running task completes. But you cannot access presentation objects from the background thread, so on completion the task must submit another task to run in the event thread to update the user interface.

```
ExecutorService backgroundExec = Executors.newCachedThreadPool();
...
button.addActionListener(new ActionListener() {
    public void actionPerformed(ActionEvent e) {
        backgroundExec.execute(new Runnable() {
            public void run() { doBigComputation(); }
        });
}});
```

LISTING 9.4. Binding a long-running task to a visual component.

Listing 9.5 illustrates the obvious way to do this, which is starting to get complicated; we're now up to three layers of inner classes. The action listener first dims the button and sets a label indicating that a computation is in progress, then submits a task to the background executor. When that task finishes, it queues another task to run in the event thread, which reenables the button and restores the label text.

```
button.addActionListener(new ActionListener() {
    public void actionPerformed(ActionEvent e) {
        button.setEnabled(false);
        label.setText("busy");
        backgroundExec.execute(new Runnable() {
            public void run() {
                try {
                    doBigComputation();
                } finally {
                    GuiExecutor.instance().execute(new Runnable() {
                        public void run() {
                            button.setEnabled(true);
                            label.setText("idle");
                        }
                    });
                }
            }
        });
    }
});
```

LISTING 9.5. Long-running task with user feedback.

The task triggered when the button is pressed is composed of three sequential subtasks whose execution alternates between the event thread and the background thread. The first subtask updates the user interface to show that a long-running operation has begun and starts the second subtask in a background thread. Upon completion, the second subtask queues the third subtask to run again in the event thread, which updates the user interface to reflect that the operation has completed. This sort of "thread hopping" is typical of handling long-running tasks in GUI applications.

9.3.1 Cancellation

Any task that takes long enough to run in another thread probably also takes long enough that the user might want to cancel it. You could implement cancellation directly using thread interruption, but it is much easier to use Future, which was designed to manage cancellable tasks.

When you call cancel on a Future with mayInterruptIfRunning set to true, the Future implementation interrupts the thread that is executing the task if it is currently running. If your task is written to be responsive to interruption, it can return early if it is cancelled. Listing 9.6 illustrates a task that polls the thread's interrupted status and returns early on interruption.

```
Future<?> runningTask = null;   // thread-confined
...
startButton.addActionListener(new ActionListener() {
    public void actionPerformed(ActionEvent e) {
        if (runningTask == null) {
            runningTask = backgroundExec.submit(new Runnable() {
                public void run() {
                    while (moreWork()) {
                        if (Thread.currentThread().isInterrupted()) {
                            cleanUpPartialWork();
                            break;
                        }
                        doSomeWork();
                    }
                }
            });
        };
}});

cancelButton.addActionListener(new ActionListener() {
    public void actionPerformed(ActionEvent event) {
        if (runningTask != null)
            runningTask.cancel(true);
}});
```

LISTING 9.6. Cancelling a long-running task.

Because runningTask is confined to the event thread, no synchronization is required when setting or checking it, and the start button listener ensures that only one background task is running at a time. However, it would be better to be notified when the task completes so that, for example, the cancel button could be disabled. We address this in the next section.

9.3.2 Progress and completion indication

Using a Future to represent a long-running task greatly simplified implementing cancellation. FutureTask also has a done hook that similarly facilitates completion notification. After the background Callable completes, done is called. By having done trigger a completion task in the event thread, we can construct a Back-groundTask class providing an onCompletion hook that is called in the event thread, as shown in Listing 9.7.

BackgroundTask also supports progress indication. The compute method can call setProgress, indicating progress in numerical terms. This causes onProgress to be called from the event thread, which can update the user interface to indicate progress visually.

To implement a BackgroundTask you need only implement compute, which is called in the background thread. You also have the option of overriding onCompletion and onProgress, which are invoked in the event thread.

Basing BackgroundTask on FutureTask also simplifies cancellation. Rather than having to poll the thread's interrupted status, compute can call Future.isCancelled. Listing 9.8 recasts the example from Listing 9.6 using Background-Task.

9.3.3 SwingWorker

We've built a simple framework using FutureTask and Executor to execute long-running tasks in background threads without undermining the responsiveness of the GUI. These techniques can be applied to any single-threaded GUI framework, not just Swing. In Swing, many of the features developed here are provided by the SwingWorker class, including cancellation, completion notification, and progress indication. Various versions of SwingWorker have been published in *The Swing Connection* and *The Java Tutorial*, and an updated version is included in Java 6.

9.4 Shared data models

Swing presentation objects, including data model objects such as TableModel or TreeModel, are confined to the event thread. In simple GUI programs, all the mutable state is held in the presentation objects and the only thread besides the event thread is the main thread. In these programs enforcing the single-thread rule is easy: don't access the data model or presentation components from the main thread. More complicated programs may use other threads to move data to or from a persistent store, such as a file system or database, so as not to compromise responsiveness.

In the simplest case, the data in the data model is entered by the user or loaded statically from a file or other data source at application startup, in which case the data is never touched by any thread other than the event thread. But sometimes

```java
abstract class BackgroundTask<V> implements Runnable, Future<V> {
    private final FutureTask<V> computation = new Computation();

    private class Computation extends FutureTask<V> {
        public Computation() {
            super(new Callable<V>() {
                public V call() throws Exception {
                    return BackgroundTask.this.compute();
                }
            });
        }
        protected final void done() {
            GuiExecutor.instance().execute(new Runnable() {
                public void run() {
                    V value = null;
                    Throwable thrown = null;
                    boolean cancelled = false;
                    try {
                        value = get();
                    } catch (ExecutionException e) {
                        thrown = e.getCause();
                    } catch (CancellationException e) {
                        cancelled = true;
                    } catch (InterruptedException consumed) {
                    } finally {
                        onCompletion(value, thrown, cancelled);
                    }
                };
            });
        }
    }
    protected void setProgress(final int current, final int max) {
        GuiExecutor.instance().execute(new Runnable() {
            public void run() { onProgress(current, max); }
        });
    }
    // Called in the background thread
    protected abstract V compute() throws Exception;
    // Called in the event thread
    protected void onCompletion(V result, Throwable exception,
                                boolean cancelled) { }
    protected void onProgress(int current, int max) { }
    // Other Future methods forwarded to computation
}
```

LISTING 9.7. Background task class supporting cancellation, completion notification, and progress notification.

```
startButton.addActionListener(new ActionListener() {
    public void actionPerformed(ActionEvent e) {
        class CancelListener implements ActionListener {
            BackgroundTask<?> task;
            public void actionPerformed(ActionEvent event) {
                if (task != null)
                    task.cancel(true);
            }
        }

        final CancelListener listener = new CancelListener();
        listener.task = new BackgroundTask<Void>() {
            public Void compute() {
                while (moreWork() && !isCancelled())
                    doSomeWork();
                return null;
            }
            public void onCompletion(boolean cancelled, String s,
                                     Throwable exception) {
                cancelButton.removeActionListener(listener);
                label.setText("done");
            }
        };

        cancelButton.addActionListener(listener);
        backgroundExec.execute(listener.task);
    }
});
```

LISTING 9.8. Initiating a long-running, cancellable task with BackgroundTask.

the presentation model object is only a view onto another data source, such as a database, file system, or remote service. In this case, more than one thread is likely to touch the data as it goes into or out of the application.

For example, you might display the contents of a remote file system using a tree control. You wouldn't want to enumerate the entire file system before you can display the tree control—that would take too much time and memory. Instead, the tree can be lazily populated as nodes are expanded. Enumerating even a single directory on a remote volume can take a long time, so you may want to do the enumeration in a background task. When the background task completes, you have to get the data into the tree model somehow. This could be done by using a thread-safe tree model, by "pushing" the data from the background task to the event thread by posting a task with invokeLater, or by having the event thread poll to see if the data is available.

9.4.1 Thread-safe data models

As long as responsiveness is not unduly affected by blocking, the problem of multiple threads operating on the data can be addressed with a thread-safe data model. If the data model supports fine-grained concurrency, the event thread and background threads should be able to share it without responsiveness problems. For example, `DelegatingVehicleTracker` on page 65 uses an underlying `ConcurrentHashMap` whose retrieval operations offer a high degree of concurrency. The downside is that it does not offer a consistent snapshot of the data, which may or may not be a requirement. Thread-safe data models must also generate events when the model has been updated, so that views can be updated when the data changes.

It may sometimes be possible to get thread safety, consistency and good responsiveness with a *versioned data model* such as `CopyOnWriteArrayList` [CPJ 2.2.3.3]. When you acquire an iterator for a copy-on-write collection, that iterator traverses the collection as it existed when the iterator was created. However, copy-on-write collections offer good performance only when traversals greatly outnumber modifications, which would probably not be the case in, say, a vehicle tracking application. More specialized versioned data structures may avoid this restriction, but building versioned data structures that provide both efficient concurrent access and do not retain old versions of data longer than needed is not easy, and thus should be considered only when other approaches are not practical.

9.4.2 Split data models

From the perspective of the GUI, the Swing table model classes like `TableModel` and `TreeModel` are the official repository for data to be displayed. However, these model objects are often themselves "views" of other objects managed by the application. A program that has both a presentation-domain and an application-domain data model is said to have a *split-model* design (Fowler, 2005).

In a split-model design, the presentation model is confined to the event thread and the other model, the *shared model*, is thread-safe and may be accessed by both the event thread and application threads. The presentation model registers listeners with the shared model so it can be notified of updates. The presentation model can then be updated from the shared model by embedding a snapshot of the relevant state in the update message or by having the presentation model retrieve the data directly from the shared model when it receives an update event.

The snapshot approach is simple, but has limitations. It works well when the data model is small, updates are not too frequent, and the structure of the two models is similar. If the data model is large or updates are very frequent, or if one or both sides of the split contain information that is not visible to the other side, it can be more efficient to send incremental updates instead of entire snapshots. This approach has the effect of serializing updates on the shared model and recreating them in the event thread against the presentation model. Another advantage of incremental updates is that finer-grained information about what changed can improve the perceived quality of the display—if only one vehicle moves, we don't have to repaint the entire display, just the affected regions.

> Consider a split-model design when a data model must be shared by more than one thread and implementing a thread-safe data model would be inadvisable because of blocking, consistency, or complexity reasons.

9.5   Other forms of single-threaded subsystems

Thread confinement is not restricted to GUIs: it can be used whenever a facility is implemented as a single-threaded subsystem. Sometimes thread confinement is forced on the developer for reasons that have nothing to do with avoiding synchronization or deadlock. For example, some native libraries require that all access to the library, even loading the library with `System.loadLibrary`, be made from the same thread.

Borrowing from the approach taken by GUI frameworks, you can easily create a dedicated thread or single-threaded executor for accessing the native library, and provide a proxy object that intercepts calls to the thread-confined object and submits them as tasks to the dedicated thread. `Future` and `newSingleThreadExecutor` work together to make this easy; the proxy method can `submit` the task and immediately call `Future.get` to wait for the result. (If the class to be thread-confined implements an interface, you can automate the process of having each method submit a `Callable` to a background thread executor and waiting for the result using dynamic proxies.)

Summary

GUI frameworks are nearly always implemented as single-threaded subsystems in which all presentation-related code runs as tasks in an event thread. Because there is only a single event thread, long-running tasks can compromise responsiveness and so should be executed in background threads. Helper classes like `SwingWorker` or the `BackgroundTask` class built here, which provide support for cancellation, progress indication, and completion indication, can simplify the development of long-running tasks that have both GUI and non-GUI components.

Part III

Liveness, Performance, and Testing

CHAPTER 10

Avoiding Liveness Hazards

There is often a tension between safety and liveness. We use locking to ensure thread safety, but indiscriminate use of locking can cause *lock-ordering deadlocks*. Similarly, we use thread pools and semaphores to bound resource consumption, but failure to understand the activities being bounded can cause *resource deadlocks*. Java applications do not recover from deadlock, so it is worthwhile to ensure that your design precludes the conditions that could cause it. This chapter explores some of the causes of liveness failures and what can be done to prevent them.

10.1 Deadlock

Deadlock is illustrated by the classic, if somewhat unsanitary, "dining philosophers" problem. Five philosophers go out for Chinese food and are seated at a circular table. There are five chopsticks (not five pairs), one placed between each pair of diners. The philosophers alternate between thinking and eating. Each needs to acquire two chopsticks for long enough to eat, but can then put the chopsticks back and return to thinking. There are some chopstick-management algorithms that let everyone eat on a more or less timely basis (a hungry philosopher tries to grab both adjacent chopsticks, but if one is not available, puts down the one that is available and waits a minute or so before trying again), and some that can result in some or all of the philosophers dying of hunger (each philosopher immediately grabs the chopstick to his left and waits for the chopstick to his right to be available before putting down the left). The latter situation, where each has a resource needed by another and is waiting for a resource held by another, and will not release the one they hold until they acquire the one they don't, illustrates deadlock.

When a thread holds a lock forever, other threads attempting to acquire that lock will block forever waiting. When thread *A* holds lock *L* and tries to acquire lock *M*, but at the same time thread *B* holds *M* and tries to acquire *L*, *both* threads will wait forever. This situation is the simplest case of deadlock (or *deadly embrace*), where multiple threads wait forever due to a cyclic locking dependency. (Think of the threads as the nodes of a directed graph whose edges represent the relation

"Thread *A* is waiting for a resource held by thread *B*". If this graph is cyclical, there is a deadlock.)

Database systems are designed to detect and recover from deadlock. A transaction may acquire many locks, and locks are held until the transaction commits. So it is quite possible, and in fact not uncommon, for two transactions to deadlock. Without intervention, they would wait forever (holding locks that are probably required by other transactions as well). But the database server is not going to let this happen. When it detects that a set of transactions is deadlocked (which it does by searching the *is-waiting-for* graph for cycles), it picks a victim and aborts that transaction. This releases the locks held by the victim, allowing the other transactions to proceed. The application can then retry the aborted transaction, which may be able to complete now that any competing transactions have completed.

The JVM is not nearly as helpful in resolving deadlocks as database servers are. When a set of Java threads deadlock, that's the end of the game—those threads are permanently out of commission. Depending on what those threads do, the application may stall completely, or a particular subsystem may stall, or performance may suffer. The only way to restore the application to health is to abort and restart it—and hope the same thing doesn't happen again.

Like many other concurrency hazards, deadlocks rarely manifest themselves immediately. The fact that a class has a potential deadlock doesn't mean that it ever *will* deadlock, just that it can. When deadlocks do manifest themselves, it is often at the worst possible time—under heavy production load.

10.1.1 Lock-ordering deadlocks

LeftRightDeadlock in Listing 10.1 is at risk for deadlock. The leftRight and rightLeft methods each acquire the left and right locks. If one thread calls leftRight and another calls rightLeft, and their actions are interleaved as shown in Figure 10.1, they will deadlock.

The deadlock in LeftRightDeadlock came about because the two threads attempted to acquire the same locks in a *different order*. If they asked for the locks in the same order, there would be no cyclic locking dependency and therefore no deadlock. If you can guarantee that every thread that needs locks *L* and *M* at the same time always acquires *L* and *M* in the same order, there will be no deadlock.

> A program will be free of lock-ordering deadlocks if all threads acquire the locks they need in a fixed global order.

Verifying consistent lock ordering requires a global analysis of your program's locking behavior. It is not sufficient to inspect code paths that acquire multiple locks individually; both leftRight and rightLeft are "reasonable" ways to acquire the two locks, they are just not compatible. When it comes to locking, the left hand needs to know what the right hand is doing.

```
// Warning: deadlock-prone!
public class LeftRightDeadlock {
    private final Object left = new Object();
    private final Object right = new Object();

    public void leftRight() {
        synchronized (left) {
            synchronized (right) {
                doSomething();
            }
        }
    }

    public void rightLeft() {
        synchronized (right) {
            synchronized (left) {
                doSomethingElse();
            }
        }
    }
}
```

LISTING 10.1. Simple lock-ordering deadlock. *Don't do this.*

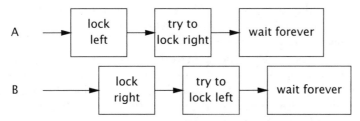

FIGURE 10.1. Unlucky timing in `LeftRightDeadlock`.

10.1.2 Dynamic lock order deadlocks

Sometimes it is not obvious that you have sufficient control over lock ordering to prevent deadlocks. Consider the harmless-looking code in Listing 10.2 that transfers funds from one account to another. It acquires the locks on both Account objects before executing the transfer, ensuring that the balances are updated atomically and without violating invariants such as "an account cannot have a negative balance".

How can `transferMoney` deadlock? It may appear as if all the threads acquire their locks in the same order, but in fact the lock order depends on the order of arguments passed to `transferMoney`, and these in turn might depend on external inputs. Deadlock can occur if two threads call `transferMoney` at the same time,

```
// Warning: deadlock-prone!
public void transferMoney(Account fromAccount,
                          Account toAccount,
                          DollarAmount amount)
        throws InsufficientFundsException {
    synchronized (fromAccount) {
        synchronized (toAccount) {
            if (fromAccount.getBalance().compareTo(amount) < 0)
                throw new InsufficientFundsException();
            else {
                fromAccount.debit(amount);
                toAccount.credit(amount);
            }
        }
    }
}
```

LISTING 10.2. Dynamic lock-ordering deadlock. *Don't do this.*

one transferring from X to Y, and the other doing the opposite:

```
A: transferMoney(myAccount, yourAccount, 10);
B: transferMoney(yourAccount, myAccount, 20);
```

With unlucky timing, A will acquire the lock on myAccount and wait for the lock on yourAccount, while B is holding the lock on yourAccount and waiting for the lock on myAccount.

Deadlocks like this one can be spotted the same way as in Listing 10.1—look for nested lock acquisitions. Since the order of arguments is out of our control, to fix the problem we must *induce* an ordering on the locks and acquire them according to the induced ordering consistently throughout the application.

One way to induce an ordering on objects is to use System.identityHashCode, which returns the value that would be returned by Object.hashCode. Listing 10.3 shows a version of transferMoney that uses System.identityHashCode to induce a lock ordering. It involves a few extra lines of code, but eliminates the possibility of deadlock.

In the rare case that two objects have the same hash code, we must use an arbitrary means of ordering the lock acquisitions, and this reintroduces the possibility of deadlock. To prevent inconsistent lock ordering in this case, a third "tie breaking" lock is used. By acquiring the tie-breaking lock before acquiring either Account lock, we ensure that only one thread at a time performs the risky task of acquiring two locks in an arbitrary order, eliminating the possibility of deadlock (so long as this mechanism is used consistently). If hash collisions were common, this technique might become a concurrency bottleneck (just as having a single, program-wide lock would), but because hash collisions with System.identity-HashCode are vanishingly infrequent, this technique provides that last bit of safety at little cost.

```
private static final Object tieLock = new Object();

public void transferMoney(final Account fromAcct,
                          final Account toAcct,
                          final DollarAmount amount)
        throws InsufficientFundsException {
    class Helper {
        public void transfer() throws InsufficientFundsException {
            if (fromAcct.getBalance().compareTo(amount) < 0)
                throw new InsufficientFundsException();
            else {
                fromAcct.debit(amount);
                toAcct.credit(amount);
            }
        }
    }
    int fromHash = System.identityHashCode(fromAcct);
    int toHash = System.identityHashCode(toAcct);

    if (fromHash < toHash) {
        synchronized (fromAcct) {
            synchronized (toAcct) {
                new Helper().transfer();
            }
        }
    } else if (fromHash > toHash) {
        synchronized (toAcct) {
            synchronized (fromAcct) {
                new Helper().transfer();
            }
        }
    } else {
        synchronized (tieLock) {
            synchronized (fromAcct) {
                synchronized (toAcct) {
                    new Helper().transfer();
                }
            }
        }
    }
}
```

LISTING 10.3. *Inducing a lock ordering to avoid deadlock.*

If Account has a unique, immutable, comparable key such as an account number, inducing a lock ordering is even easier: order objects by their key, thus eliminating the need for the tie-breaking lock.

You may think we're overstating the risk of deadlock because locks are usually
held only briefly, but deadlocks are a serious problem in real systems. A production application may perform billions of lock acquire-release cycles per day. Only
one of those needs to be timed just wrong to bring the application to deadlock,
and even a thorough load-testing regimen may not disclose all latent deadlocks.[1]
DemonstrateDeadlock in Listing 10.4[2] deadlocks fairly quickly on most systems.

```
public class DemonstrateDeadlock {
    private static final int NUM_THREADS = 20;
    private static final int NUM_ACCOUNTS = 5;
    private static final int NUM_ITERATIONS = 1000000;

    public static void main(String[] args) {
        final Random rnd = new Random();
        final Account[] accounts = new Account[NUM_ACCOUNTS];

        for (int i = 0; i < accounts.length; i++)
            accounts[i] = new Account();

        class TransferThread extends Thread {
            public void run() {
                for (int i=0; i<NUM_ITERATIONS; i++) {
                    int fromAcct = rnd.nextInt(NUM_ACCOUNTS);
                    int toAcct = rnd.nextInt(NUM_ACCOUNTS);
                    DollarAmount amount =
                        new DollarAmount(rnd.nextInt(1000));
                    transferMoney(accounts[fromAcct],
                                  accounts[toAcct], amount);
                }
            }
        }
        for (int i = 0; i < NUM_THREADS; i++)
            new TransferThread().start();
    }
}
```

LISTING 10.4. *Driver loop that induces deadlock under typical conditions.*

1. Ironically, holding locks for short periods of time, as you are supposed to do to reduce lock contention, increases the likelihood that testing will not disclose latent deadlock risks.
2. For simplicity, DemonstrateDeadlock ignores the issue of negative account balances.

10.1.3 Deadlocks between cooperating objects

Multiple lock acquisition is not always as obvious as in LeftRightDeadlock or transferMoney; the two locks need not be acquired by the same method. Consider the cooperating classes in Listing 10.5, which might be used in a taxicab dispatching application. Taxi represents an individual taxi with a location and a destination; Dispatcher represents a fleet of taxis.

While no method *explicitly* acquires two locks, callers of setLocation and getImage can acquire two locks just the same. If a thread calls setLocation in response to an update from a GPS receiver, it first updates the taxi's location and then checks to see if it has reached its destination. If it has, it informs the dispatcher that it needs a new destination. Since both setLocation and notifyAvailable are synchronized, the thread calling setLocation acquires the Taxi lock and then the Dispatcher lock. Similarly, a thread calling getImage acquires the Dispatcher lock and then each Taxi lock (one at at time). Just as in LeftRightDeadlock, two locks are acquired by two threads in different orders, risking deadlock.

It was easy to spot the deadlock possibility in LeftRightDeadlock or transferMoney by looking for methods that acquire two locks. Spotting the deadlock possibility in Taxi and Dispatcher is a little harder: the warning sign is that an *alien* method (defined on page 40) is being called while holding a lock.

> Invoking an alien method with a lock held is asking for liveness trouble. The alien method might acquire other locks (risking deadlock) or block for an unexpectedly long time, stalling other threads that need the lock you hold.

10.1.4 Open calls

Of course, Taxi and Dispatcher didn't *know* that they were each half of a deadlock waiting to happen. And they shouldn't have to; a method call is an abstraction barrier intended to shield you from the details of what happens on the other side. But because you don't know what is happening on the other side of the call, *calling an alien method with a lock held is difficult to analyze and therefore risky*.

Calling a method with no locks held is called an *open call* [CPJ 2.4.1.3], and classes that rely on open calls are more well-behaved and composable than classes that make calls with locks held. Using open calls to avoid deadlock is analogous to using encapsulation to provide thread safety: while one can certainly construct a thread-safe program without any encapsulation, the thread safety analysis of a program that makes effective use of encapsulation is far easier than that of one that does not. Similarly, the liveness analysis of a program that relies exclusively on open calls is far easier than that of one that does not. Restricting yourself to

```
// Warning: deadlock-prone!
class Taxi {
    @GuardedBy("this") private Point location, destination;
    private final Dispatcher dispatcher;

    public Taxi(Dispatcher dispatcher) {
        this.dispatcher = dispatcher;
    }

    public synchronized Point getLocation() {
        return location;
    }

    public synchronized void setLocation(Point location) {
        this.location = location;
        if (location.equals(destination))
            dispatcher.notifyAvailable(this);
    }
}

class Dispatcher {
    @GuardedBy("this") private final Set<Taxi> taxis;
    @GuardedBy("this") private final Set<Taxi> availableTaxis;

    public Dispatcher() {
        taxis = new HashSet<Taxi>();
        availableTaxis = new HashSet<Taxi>();
    }

    public synchronized void notifyAvailable(Taxi taxi) {
        availableTaxis.add(taxi);
    }

    public synchronized Image getImage() {
        Image image = new Image();
        for (Taxi t : taxis)
            image.drawMarker(t.getLocation());
        return image;
    }
}
```

LISTING 10.5. Lock-ordering deadlock between cooperating objects. *Don't do this.*

open calls makes it far easier to identify the code paths that acquire multiple locks and therefore to ensure that locks are acquired in a consistent order.[3]

Taxi and Dispatcher in Listing 10.5 can be easily refactored to use open calls and thus eliminate the deadlock risk. This involves shrinking the synchronized blocks to guard only operations that involve shared state, as in Listing 10.6. Very often, the cause of problems like those in Listing 10.5 is the use of synchronized methods instead of smaller synchronized blocks for reasons of compact syntax or simplicity rather than because the entire method must be guarded by a lock. (As a bonus, shrinking the synchronized block may also improve scalability as well; see Section 11.4.1 for advice on sizing synchronized blocks.)

> Strive to use open calls throughout your program. Programs that rely on open calls are far easier to analyze for deadlock-freedom than those that allow calls to alien methods with locks held.

Restructuring a synchronized block to allow open calls can sometimes have undesirable consequences, since it takes an operation that was atomic and makes it not atomic. In many cases, the loss of atomicity is perfectly acceptable; there's no reason that updating a taxi's location and notifying the dispatcher that it is ready for a new destination need be an atomic operation. In other cases, the loss of atomicity is noticeable but the semantic changes are still acceptable. In the deadlock-prone version, getImage produces a complete snapshot of the fleet locations at that instant; in the refactored version, it fetches the location of each taxi at slightly different times.

In some cases, however, the loss of atomicity is a problem, and here you will have to use another technique to achieve atomicity. One such technique is to structure a concurrent object so that only one thread can execute the code path following the open call. For example, when shutting down a service, you may want to wait for in-progress operations to complete and then release resources used by the service. Holding the service lock while waiting for operations to complete is inherently deadlock-prone, but releasing the service lock before the service is shut down may let other threads start new operations. The solution is to hold the lock long enough to update the service state to "shutting down" so that other threads wanting to start new operations—including shutting down the service—see that the service is unavailable, and do not try. You can then wait for shutdown to complete, knowing that only the shutdown thread has access to the service state after the open call completes. Thus, rather than using locking to keep the other threads out of a critical section of code, this technique relies on constructing protocols so that other threads don't try to get in.

10.1.5 Resource deadlocks

Just as threads can deadlock when they are each waiting for a lock that the other holds and will not release, they can also deadlock when waiting for resources.

---

3. The need to rely on open calls and careful lock ordering reflects the fundamental messiness of composing synchronized objects rather than synchronizing composed objects.

```
@ThreadSafe
class Taxi {
    @GuardedBy("this") private Point location, destination;
    private final Dispatcher dispatcher;
    ...
    public synchronized Point getLocation() {
        return location;
    }

    public void setLocation(Point location) {
        boolean reachedDestination;
        synchronized (this) {
            this.location = location;
            reachedDestination = location.equals(destination);
        }
        if (reachedDestination)
            dispatcher.notifyAvailable(this);
    }
}

@ThreadSafe
class Dispatcher {
    @GuardedBy("this") private final Set<Taxi> taxis;
    @GuardedBy("this") private final Set<Taxi> availableTaxis;
    ...
    public synchronized void notifyAvailable(Taxi taxi) {
        availableTaxis.add(taxi);
    }

    public Image getImage() {
        Set<Taxi> copy;
        synchronized (this) {
            copy = new HashSet<Taxi>(taxis);
        }
        Image image = new Image();
        for (Taxi t : copy)
            image.drawMarker(t.getLocation());
        return image;
    }
}
```

LISTING 10.6. Using open calls to avoiding deadlock between cooperating objects.

Say you have two pooled resources, such as connection pools for two different databases. Resource pools are usually implemented with semaphores (see Section 5.5.3) to facilitate blocking when the pool is empty. If a task requires connections to both databases and the two resources are not always requested in the same order, thread A could be holding a connection to database D_1 while waiting for a connection to database D_2, and thread B could be holding a connection to D_2 while waiting for a connection to D_1. (The larger the pools are, the less likely this is to occur; if each pool has N connections, deadlock requires N sets of cyclically waiting threads and a lot of unlucky timing.)

Another form of resource-based deadlock is *thread-starvation deadlock*. We saw an example of this hazard in Section 8.1.1, where a task that submits a task and waits for its result executes in a single-threaded Executor. In that case, the first task will wait forever, permanently stalling that task and all others waiting to execute in that Executor. Tasks that wait for the results of other tasks are the primary source of thread-starvation deadlock; bounded pools and interdependent tasks do not mix well.

10.2 Avoiding and diagnosing deadlocks

A program that never acquires more than one lock at a time cannot experience lock-ordering deadlock. Of course, this is not always practical, but if you can get away with it, it's a lot less work. If you must acquire multiple locks, lock ordering must be a part of your design: try to minimize the number of potential locking interactions, and follow and document a lock-ordering protocol for locks that may be acquired together.

In programs that use fine-grained locking, audit your code for deadlock freedom using a two-part strategy: first, identify where multiple locks could be acquired (try to make this a small set), and then perform a global analysis of all such instances to ensure that lock ordering is consistent across your entire program. Using open calls wherever possible simplifies this analysis substantially. With no non-open calls, finding instances where multiple locks are acquired is fairly easy, either by code review or by automated bytecode or source code analysis.

10.2.1 Timed lock attempts

Another technique for detecting and recovering from deadlocks is to use the timed tryLock feature of the explicit Lock classes (see Chapter 13) instead of intrinsic locking. Where intrinsic locks wait forever if they cannot acquire the lock, explicit locks let you specify a timeout after which tryLock returns failure. By using a timeout that is much longer than you expect acquiring the lock to take, you can regain control when something unexpected happens. (Listing 13.3 on page 280 shows an alternative implementation of transferMoney using the polled tryLock with retries for probabilistic deadlock avoidance.)

When a timed lock attempt fails, you do not necessarily know *why*. Maybe there was a deadlock; maybe a thread erroneously entered an infinite loop while holding that lock; or maybe some activity is just running a lot slower than you expected. Still, at least you have the opportunity to record that your attempt failed, log any useful information about what you were trying to do, and restart the computation somewhat more gracefully than killing the entire process.

Using timed lock acquisition to acquire multiple locks can be effective against deadlock even when timed locking is not used consistently throughout the program. If a lock acquisition times out, you can release the locks, back off and wait for a while, and try again, possibly clearing the deadlock condition and allowing the program to recover. (This technique works only when the two locks are acquired together; if multiple locks are acquired due to the nesting of method calls, you cannot just release the outer lock, even if you know you hold it.)

10.2.2 Deadlock analysis with thread dumps

While preventing deadlocks is mostly your problem, the JVM can help identify them when they do happen using *thread dumps*. A thread dump includes a stack trace for each running thread, similar to the stack trace that accompanies an exception. Thread dumps also include locking information, such as which locks are held by each thread, in which stack frame they were acquired, and which lock a blocked thread is waiting to acquire.[4] Before generating a thread dump, the JVM searches the is-waiting-for graph for cycles to find deadlocks. If it finds one, it includes deadlock information identifying which locks and threads are involved, and where in the program the offending lock acquisitions are.

To trigger a thread dump, you can send the JVM process a SIGQUIT signal (kill -3) on Unix platforms, or press the Ctrl-\ key on Unix or Ctrl-Break on Windows platforms. Many IDEs can request a thread dump as well.

If you are using the explicit Lock classes instead of intrinsic locking, Java 5.0 has no support for associating Lock information with the thread dump; explicit Locks do not show up at all in thread dumps. Java 6 does include thread dump support and deadlock detection with explicit Locks, but the information on where Locks are acquired is necessarily less precise than for intrinsic locks. Intrinsic locks are associated with the stack frame in which they were acquired; explicit Locks are associated only with the acquiring thread.

Listing 10.7 shows portions of a thread dump taken from a production J2EE application. The failure that caused the deadlock involves three components—a J2EE application, a J2EE container, and a JDBC driver, each from different vendors. (The names have been changed to protect the guilty.) All three were commercial products that had been through extensive testing cycles; each had a bug that was harmless until they all interacted and caused a fatal server failure.

We've shown only the portion of the thread dump relevant to identifying the deadlock. The JVM has done a lot of work for us in diagnosing the deadlock—which locks are causing the problem, which threads are involved, which other locks they hold, and whether other threads are being indirectly inconvenienced. One thread holds the lock on the MumbleDBConnection and is waiting to acquire

---

4. This information is useful for debugging even when you don't have a deadlock; periodically triggering thread dumps lets you observe your program's locking behavior.

```
Found one Java-level deadlock:
=============================
"ApplicationServerThread":
  waiting to lock monitor 0x080f0cdc (a MumbleDBConnection),
  which is held by "ApplicationServerThread"
"ApplicationServerThread":
  waiting to lock monitor 0x080f0ed4 (a MumbleDBCallableStatement),
  which is held by "ApplicationServerThread"

Java stack information for the threads listed above:
"ApplicationServerThread":
        at MumbleDBConnection.remove_statement
        - waiting to lock <0x650f7f30> (a MumbleDBConnection)
        at MumbleDBStatement.close
        - locked <0x6024ffb0> (a MumbleDBCallableStatement)
    ...

"ApplicationServerThread":
        at MumbleDBCallableStatement.sendBatch
        - waiting to lock <0x6024ffb0> (a MumbleDBCallableStatement)
        at MumbleDBConnection.commit
        - locked <0x650f7f30> (a MumbleDBConnection)
    ...
```

LISTING 10.7. Portion of thread dump after deadlock.

the lock on the MumbleDBCallableStatement; the other holds the lock on the Mum-bleDBCallableStatement and is waiting for the lock on the MumbleDBConnection.

The JDBC driver being used here clearly has a lock-ordering bug: different call chains through the JDBC driver acquire multiple locks in different orders. But this problem would not have manifested itself were it not for another bug: multiple threads were trying to use the same JDBC Connection at the same time. This was not how the application was supposed to work—the developers were surprised to see the same Connection used concurrently by two threads. There's nothing in the JDBC specification that requires a Connection to be thread-safe, and it is common to confine use of a Connection to a single thread, as was intended here. This vendor tried to deliver a thread-safe JDBC driver, as evidenced by the synchronization on multiple JDBC objects within the driver code. Unfortunately, because the vendor did not take lock ordering into account, the driver was prone to deadlock, but it was only the interaction of the deadlock-prone driver and the incorrect Connection sharing by the application that disclosed the problem. Because neither bug was fatal in isolation, both persisted despite extensive testing.

10.3 Other liveness hazards

While deadlock is the most widely encountered liveness hazard, there are several other liveness hazards you may encounter in concurrent programs including starvation, missed signals, and livelock. (Missed signals are covered in Section 14.2.3.)

10.3.1 Starvation

Starvation occurs when a thread is perpetually denied access to resources it needs in order to make progress; the most commonly starved resource is CPU cycles. Starvation in Java applications can be caused by inappropriate use of thread priorities. It can also be caused by executing nonterminating constructs (infinite loops or resource waits that do not terminate) with a lock held, since other threads that need that lock will never be able to acquire it.

The thread priorities defined in the Thread API are merely scheduling hints. The Thread API defines ten priority levels that the JVM can map to operating system scheduling priorities as it sees fit. This mapping is platform-specific, so two Java priorities can map to the same OS priority on one system and different OS priorities on another. Some operating systems have fewer than ten priority levels, in which case multiple Java priorities map to the same OS priority.

Operating system schedulers go to great lengths to provide scheduling fairness and liveness beyond that required by the Java Language Specification. In most Java applications, all application threads have the same priority, Thread. NORM_PRIORITY. The thread priority mechanism is a blunt instrument, and it's not always obvious what effect changing priorities will have; boosting a thread's priority might do nothing or might always cause one thread to be scheduled in preference to the other, causing starvation.

It is generally wise to resist the temptation to tweak thread priorities. As soon as you start modifying priorities, the behavior of your application becomes platform-specific and you introduce the risk of starvation. You can often spot a program that is trying to recover from priority tweaking or other responsiveness problems by the presence of Thread.sleep or Thread.yield calls in odd places, in an attempt to give more time to lower-priority threads.[5]

> Avoid the temptation to use thread priorities, since they increase platform dependence and can cause liveness problems. Most concurrent applications can use the default priority for all threads.

---

5. The semantics of Thread.yield (and Thread.sleep(0)) are undefined [JLS 17.9]; the JVM is free to implement them as no-ops or treat them as scheduling hints. In particular, they are *not* required to have the semantics of sleep(0) on Unix systems—put the current thread at the end of the run queue for that priority, yielding to other threads of the same priority—though some JVMs implement yield in this way.

10.3.2   Poor responsiveness

One step removed from starvation is poor responsiveness, which is not uncommon in GUI applications using background threads. Chapter 9 developed a framework for offloading long-running tasks onto background threads so as not to freeze the user interface. CPU-intensive background tasks can still affect responsiveness because they can compete for CPU cycles with the event thread. This is one case where altering thread priorities makes sense; when compute-intensive background computations would affect responsiveness. If the work done by other threads are truly background tasks, lowering their priority can make the foreground tasks more responsive.

Poor responsiveness can also be caused by poor lock management. If a thread holds a lock for a long time (perhaps while iterating a large collection and performing substantial work for each element), other threads that need to access that collection may have to wait a very long time.

10.3.3   Livelock

Livelock is a form of liveness failure in which a thread, while not blocked, still cannot make progress because it keeps retrying an operation that will always fail. Livelock often occurs in transactional messaging applications, where the messaging infrastructure rolls back a transaction if a message cannot be processed successfully, and puts it back at the head of the queue. If a bug in the message handler for a particular type of message causes it to fail, every time the message is dequeued and passed to the buggy handler, the transaction is rolled back. Since the message is now back at the head of the queue, the handler is called over and over with the same result. (This is sometimes called the *poison message* problem.) The message handling thread is not blocked, but it will never make progress either. This form of livelock often comes from overeager error-recovery code that mistakenly treats an unrecoverable error as a recoverable one.

Livelock can also occur when multiple cooperating threads change their state in response to the others in such a way that no thread can ever make progress. This is similar to what happens when two overly polite people are walking in opposite directions in a hallway: each steps out of the other's way, and now they are again in each other's way. So they both step aside again, and again, and again...

The solution for this variety of livelock is to introduce some randomness into the retry mechanism. For example, when two stations in an ethernet network try to send a packet on the shared carrier at the same time, the packets collide. The stations detect the collision, and each tries to send their packet again later. If they each retry *exactly* one second later, they collide over and over, and neither packet ever goes out, even if there is plenty of available bandwidth. To avoid this, we make each wait an amount of time that includes a random component. (The ethernet protocol also includes exponential backoff after repeated collisions, reducing both congestion and the risk of repeated failure with multiple colliding stations.) Retrying with random waits and backoffs can be equally effective for avoiding livelock in concurrent applications.

Summary

Liveness failures are a serious problem because there is no way to recover from them short of aborting the application. The most common form of liveness failure is lock-ordering deadlock. Avoiding lock ordering deadlock starts at design time: ensure that when threads acquire multiple locks, they do so in a consistent order. The best way to do this is by using open calls throughout your program. This greatly reduces the number of places where multiple locks are held at once, and makes it more obvious where those places are.

CHAPTER 11

Performance and Scalability

One of the primary reasons to use threads is to improve performance.[1] Using threads can improve resource utilization by letting applications more easily exploit available processing capacity, and can improve responsiveness by letting applications begin processing new tasks immediately while existing tasks are still running.

This chapter explores techniques for analyzing, monitoring, and improving the performance of concurrent programs. Unfortunately, many of the techniques for improving performance also increase complexity, thus increasing the likelihood of safety and liveness failures. Worse, some techniques intended to improve performance are actually counterproductive or trade one sort of performance problem for another. While better performance is often desirable—and improving performance can be very satisfying—safety always comes first. First make your program right, then make it fast—and then only if your performance requirements and measurements tell you it needs to be faster. In designing a concurrent application, squeezing out the last bit of performance is often the least of your concerns.

11.1 Thinking about performance

Improving performance means doing more work with fewer resources. The meaning of "resources" can vary; for a given activity, some specific resource is usually in shortest supply, whether it is CPU cycles, memory, network bandwidth, I/O bandwidth, database requests, disk space, or any number of other resources. When the performance of an activity is limited by availability of a particular resource, we say it is *bound* by that resource: CPU-bound, database-bound, etc.

While the goal may be to improve performance overall, using multiple threads always introduces some performance costs compared to the single-threaded approach. These include the overhead associated with coordinating between threads (locking, signaling, and memory synchronization), increased context switching,

---

1. Some might argue this is the *only* reason we put up with the complexity threads introduce.

thread creation and teardown, and scheduling overhead. When threading is employed effectively, these costs are more than made up for by greater throughput, responsiveness, or capacity. On the other hand, a poorly designed concurrent application can perform even worse than a comparable sequential one.[2]

In using concurrency to achieve better performance, we are trying to do two things: utilize the processing resources we have more effectively, and enable our program to exploit additional processing resources if they become available. From a performance monitoring perspective, this means we are looking to keep the CPUs as busy as possible. (Of course, this doesn't mean burning cycles with useless computation; we want to keep the CPUs busy with *useful* work.) If the program is compute-bound, then we may be able to increase its capacity by adding more processors; if it can't even keep the processors we have busy, adding more won't help. Threading offers a means to keep the CPU(s) "hotter" by decomposing the application so there is always work to be done by an available processor.

11.1.1 Performance versus scalability

Application performance can be measured in a number of ways, such as service time, latency, throughput, efficiency, scalability, or capacity. Some of these (service time, latency) are measures of "how fast" a given unit of work can be processed or acknowledged; others (capacity, throughput) are measures of "how much" work can be performed with a given quantity of computing resources.

> *Scalability* describes the ability to improve throughput or capacity when additional computing resources (such as additional CPUs, memory, storage, or I/O bandwidth) are added.

Designing and tuning concurrent applications for scalability can be very different from traditional performance optimization. When tuning for performance, the goal is usually to do the *same* work with *less* effort, such as by reusing previously computed results through caching or replacing an $O(n^2)$ algorithm with an $O(n \log n)$ one. When tuning for scalability, you are instead trying to find ways to parallelize the problem so you can take advantage of additional processing resources to do *more* work with *more* resources.

These two aspects of performance—*how fast* and *how much*—are completely separate, and sometimes even at odds with each other. In order to achieve higher scalability or better hardware utilization, we often end up *increasing* the amount of work done to process each *individual* task, such as when we divide tasks into multiple "pipelined" subtasks. Ironically, many of the tricks that improve performance in single-threaded programs are bad for scalability (see Section 11.4.4 for an example).

---

2. A colleague provided this amusing anecdote: he had been involved in the testing of an expensive and complex application that managed its work via a tunable thread pool. After the system was complete, testing showed that the optimal number of threads for the pool was ... 1. This should have been obvious from the outset; the target system was a single-CPU system and the application was almost entirely CPU-bound.

The familiar three-tier application model—in which presentation, business logic, and persistence are separated and may be handled by different systems—illustrates how improvements in scalability often come at the expense of performance. A monolithic application where presentation, business logic, and persistence are intertwined would almost certainly provide better performance for the *first* unit of work than would a well-factored multitier implementation distributed over multiple systems. How could it not? The monolithic application would not have the network latency inherent in handing off tasks between tiers, nor would it have to pay the costs inherent in separating a computational process into distinct abstracted layers (such as queuing overhead, coordination overhead, and data copying).

However, when the monolithic system reaches its processing capacity, we could have a serious problem: it may be prohibitively difficult to significantly increase capacity. So we often accept the performance costs of longer service time or greater computing resources used per unit of work so that our application can scale to handle greater load by adding more resources.

Of the various aspects of performance, the "how much" aspects—scalability, throughput, and capacity—are usually of greater concern for server applications than the "how fast" aspects. (For interactive applications, latency tends to be more important, so that users need not wait for indications of progress and wonder what is going on.) This chapter focuses primarily on scalability rather than raw single-threaded performance.

11.1.2 Evaluating performance tradeoffs

Nearly all engineering decisions involve some form of tradeoff. Using thicker steel in a bridge span may increase its capacity and safety, but also its construction cost. While software engineering decisions don't usually involve tradeoffs between money and risk to human life, we often have less information with which to make the right tradeoffs. For example, the "quicksort" algorithm is highly efficient for large data sets, but the less sophisticated "bubble sort" is actually more efficient for small data sets. If you are asked to implement an efficient sort routine, you need to know something about the sizes of data sets it will have to process, along with metrics that tell you whether you are trying to optimize average-case time, worst-case time, or predictability. Unfortunately, that information is often not part of the requirements given to the author of a library sort routine. This is one of the reasons why most optimizations are premature: *they are often undertaken before a clear set of requirements is available.*

> Avoid premature optimization. First make it right, then make it fast—*if* it is not already fast enough.

When making engineering decisions, sometimes you are trading one form of cost for another (service time versus memory consumption); sometimes you are trading cost for safety. Safety doesn't necessarily mean risk to human lives, as it did in the bridge example. Many performance optimizations come at the cost of readability or maintainability—the more "clever" or nonobvious code is, the harder it is to understand and maintain. Sometimes optimizations entail compromising good object-oriented design principles, such as breaking encapsulation; sometimes they involve greater risk of error, because faster algorithms are usually more complicated. (If you can't spot the costs or risks, you probably haven't thought it through carefully enough to proceed.)

Most performance decisions involve multiple variables and are highly situational. Before deciding that one approach is "faster" than another, ask yourself some questions:

- What do you mean by "faster"?

- Under what conditions will this approach *actually* be faster? Under light or heavy load? With large or small data sets? Can you support your answer with measurements?

- How often are these conditions likely to arise in your situation? Can you support your answer with measurements?

- Is this code likely to be used in other situations where the conditions may be different?

- What hidden costs, such as increased development or maintenance risk, are you trading for this improved performance? Is this a good tradeoff?

These considerations apply to any performance-related engineering decision, but this is a book about concurrency. Why are we recommending such a conservative approach to optimization? *The quest for performance is probably the single greatest source of concurrency bugs.* The belief that synchronization was "too slow" led to many clever-looking but dangerous idioms for reducing synchronization (such as double-checked locking, discussed in Section 16.2.4), and is often cited as an excuse for not following the rules regarding synchronization. Because concurrency bugs are among the most difficult to track down and eliminate, however, anything that risks introducing them must be undertaken very carefully.

Worse, when you trade safety for performance, you may get neither. Especially when it comes to concurrency, the intuition of many developers about where a performance problem lies or which approach will be faster or more scalable is often incorrect. It is therefore imperative that any performance tuning exercise be accompanied by concrete performance requirements (so you know both when to tune and when to *stop* tuning) and with a measurement program in place using a realistic configuration and load profile. Measure again after tuning to verify that you've achieved the desired improvements. The safety and maintenance risks associated with many optimizations are bad enough—you don't want to pay these costs if you don't need to—and you definitely don't want to pay them if you don't even get the desired benefit.

> Measure, don't guess.

There are sophisticated profiling tools on the market for measuring performance and tracking down performance bottlenecks, but you don't have to spend a lot of money to figure out what your program is doing. For example, the free perfbar application can give you a good picture of how busy the CPUs are, and since your goal is usually to keep the CPUs busy, this is a very good way to evaluate whether you need performance tuning or how effective your tuning has been.

11.2 Amdahl's law

Some problems can be solved faster with more resources—the more workers available for harvesting crops, the faster the harvest can be completed. Other tasks are fundamentally serial—no number of additional workers will make the crops grow any faster. If one of our primary reasons for using threads is to harness the power of multiple processors, we must also ensure that the problem is amenable to parallel decomposition and that our program effectively exploits this potential for parallelization.

Most concurrent programs have a lot in common with farming, consisting of a mix of parallelizable and serial portions. *Amdahl's law* describes how much a program can theoretically be sped up by additional computing resources, based on the proportion of parallelizable and serial components. If F is the fraction of the calculation that must be executed serially, then Amdahl's law says that on a machine with N processors, we can achieve a speedup of at most:

$$Speedup \leq \frac{1}{F + \frac{(1-F)}{N}}$$

As N approaches infinity, the maximum speedup converges to $1/F$, meaning that a program in which fifty percent of the processing must be executed serially can be sped up only by a factor of two, regardless of how many processors are available, and a program in which ten percent must be executed serially can be sped up by at most a factor of ten. Amdahl's law also quantifies the efficiency cost of serialization. With ten processors, a program with 10% serialization can achieve at most a speedup of 5.3 (at 53% utilization), and with 100 processors it can achieve at most a speedup of 9.2 (at 9% utilization). It takes a lot of inefficiently utilized CPUs to never get to that factor of ten.

Figure 11.1 shows the maximum possible processor utilization for varying degrees of serial execution and numbers of processors. (Utilization is defined as the speedup divided by the number of processors.) It is clear that as processor counts increase, even a small percentage of serialized execution limits how much throughput can be increased with additional computing resources.

Chapter 6 explored identifying logical boundaries for decomposing applications into tasks. But in order to predict what kind of speedup is possible from running your application on a multiprocessor system, you also need to identify the sources of serialization in your tasks.

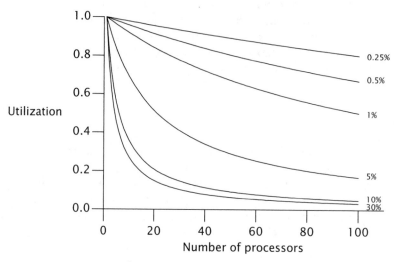

FIGURE 11.1. Maximum utilization under Amdahl's law for various serialization percentages.

Imagine an application where N threads execute doWork in Listing 11.1, fetching tasks from a shared work queue and processing them; assume that tasks do not depend on the results or side effects of other tasks. Ignoring for a moment how the tasks get onto the queue, how well will this application scale as we add processors? At first glance, it may appear that the application is completely parallelizable: tasks do not wait for each other, and the more processors available, the more tasks can be processed concurrently. However, there is a serial component as well—fetching the task from the work queue. The work queue is shared by all the worker threads, and it will require some amount of synchronization to maintain its integrity in the face of concurrent access. If locking is used to guard the state of the queue, then while one thread is dequeing a task, other threads that need to dequeue their next task must wait—and this is where task processing is serialized.

The processing time of a single task includes not only the time to execute the task Runnable, but also the time to dequeue the task from the shared work queue. If the work queue is a LinkedBlockingQueue, the dequeue operation may block less than with a synchronized LinkedList because LinkedBlockingQueue uses a more scalable algorithm, but accessing any shared data structure fundamentally introduces an element of serialization into a program.

This example also ignores another common source of serialization: result handling. All useful computations produce some sort of result or side effect—if not, they can be eliminated as dead code. Since Runnable provides for no explicit result handling, these tasks must have some sort of side effect, say writing their results to a log file or putting them in a data structure. Log files and result containers are usually shared by multiple worker threads and therefore are also a

```
public class WorkerThread extends Thread {
    private final BlockingQueue<Runnable> queue;

    public WorkerThread(BlockingQueue<Runnable> queue) {
        this.queue = queue;
    }

    public void run() {
        while (true) {
            try {
                Runnable task = queue.take();
                task.run();
            } catch (InterruptedException e) {
                break; /* Allow thread to exit */
            }
        }
    }
}
```

LISTING 11.1. Serialized access to a task queue.

source of serialization. If instead each thread maintains its own data structure for results that are merged after all the tasks are performed, then the final merge is a source of serialization.

> All concurrent applications have some sources of serialization; if you think yours does not, look again.

11.2.1 Example: serialization hidden in frameworks

To see how serialization can be hidden in the structure of an application, we can compare throughput as threads are added and infer differences in serialization based on observed differences in scalability. Figure 11.2 shows a simple application in which multiple threads repeatedly remove an element from a shared Queue and process it, similar to Listing 11.1. The processing step involves only thread-local computation. If a thread finds the queue is empty, it puts a batch of new elements on the queue so that other threads have something to process on their next iteration. Accessing the shared queue clearly entails some degree of serialization, but the processing step is entirely parallelizable since it involves no shared data.

The curves in Figure 11.2 compare throughput for two thread-safe Queue implementations: a LinkedList wrapped with synchronizedList, and a ConcurrentLinkedQueue. The tests were run on an 8-way Sparc V880 system running

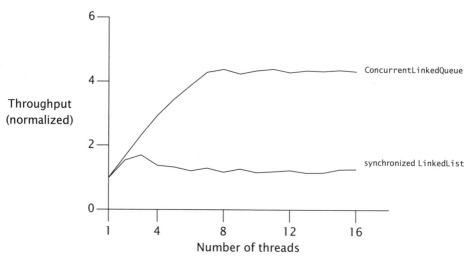

FIGURE 11.2. Comparing queue implementations.

Solaris. While each run represents the same amount of "work", we can see that merely changing queue implementations can have a big impact on scalability.

The throughput of ConcurrentLinkedQueue continues to improve until it hits the number of processors and then remains mostly constant. On the other hand, the throughput of the synchronized LinkedList shows some improvement up to three threads, but then falls off as synchronization overhead increases. By the time it gets to four or five threads, contention is so heavy that every access to the queue lock is contended and throughput is dominated by context switching.

The difference in throughput comes from differing degrees of serialization between the two queue implementations. The synchronized LinkedList guards the entire queue state with a single lock that is held for the duration of the offer or remove call; ConcurrentLinkedQueue uses a sophisticated nonblocking queue algorithm (see Section 15.4.2) that uses atomic references to update individual link pointers. In one, the entire insertion or removal is serialized; in the other, only updates to individual pointers are serialized.

11.2.2   Applying Amdahl's law qualitatively

Amdahl's law quantifies the possible speedup when more computing resources are available, if we can accurately estimate the fraction of execution that is serialized. Although measuring serialization directly can be difficult, Amdahl's law can still be useful without such measurement.

Since our mental models are influenced by our environment, many of us are used to thinking that a multiprocessor system has two or four processors, or maybe (if we've got a big budget) as many as a few dozen, because this is the technology that has been widely available in recent years. But as multicore CPUs become mainstream, systems will have hundreds or even thousands of process-ors.[3] Algorithms that seem scalable on a four-way system may have hidden scal-ability bottlenecks that have just not yet been encountered.

When evaluating an algorithm, thinking "in the limit" about what would hap-pen with hundreds or thousands of processors can offer some insight into where scaling limits might appear. For example, Sections 11.4.2 and 11.4.3 discuss two techniques for reducing lock granularity: lock splitting (splitting one lock into two) and lock striping (splitting one lock into many). Looking at them through the lens of Amdahl's law, we see that splitting a lock in two does not get us very far towards exploiting many processors, but lock striping seems much more promising because the size of the stripe set can be increased as processor count increases. (Of course, performance optimizations should always be considered in light of actual performance requirements; in some cases, splitting a lock in two may be enough to meet the requirements.)

11.3 Costs introduced by threads

Single-threaded programs incur neither scheduling nor synchronization over-head, and need not use locks to preserve the consistency of data structures. Scheduling and interthread coordination have performance costs; for threads to offer a performance improvement, the performance benefits of parallelization must outweigh the costs introduced by concurrency.

11.3.1 Context switching

If the main thread is the only schedulable thread, it will almost never be sched-uled out. On the other hand, if there are more runnable threads than CPUs, eventually the OS will preempt one thread so that another can use the CPU. This causes a *context switch*, which requires saving the execution context of the cur-rently running thread and restoring the execution context of the newly scheduled thread.

Context switches are not free; thread scheduling requires manipulating shared data structures in the OS and JVM. The OS and JVM use the same CPUs your pro-gram does; more CPU time spent in JVM and OS code means less is available for your program. But OS and JVM activity is not the only cost of context switches. When a new thread is switched in, the data it needs is unlikely to be in the local processor cache, so a context switch causes a flurry of cache misses, and thus threads run a little more slowly when they are first scheduled. This is one of the reasons that schedulers give each runnable thread a certain minimum time quantum even when many other threads are waiting: it amortizes the cost of the context switch and its consequences over more uninterrupted execution time, improving overall throughput (at some cost to responsiveness).

---

3. Market update: at this writing, Sun is shipping low-end server systems based on the 8-core Niagara processor, and Azul is shipping high-end server systems (96, 192, and 384-way) based on the 24-core Vega processor.

```
synchronized (new Object()) {
    // do something
}
```

LISTING 11.2. Synchronization that has no effect. *Don't do this.*

When a thread blocks because it is waiting for a contended lock, the JVM usually suspends the thread and allows it to be switched out. If threads block frequently, they will be unable to use their full scheduling quantum. A program that does more blocking (blocking I/O, waiting for contended locks, or waiting on condition variables) incurs more context switches than one that is CPU-bound, increasing scheduling overhead and reducing throughput. (Nonblocking algorithms can also help reduce context switches; see Chapter 15.)

The actual cost of context switching varies across platforms, but a good rule of thumb is that a context switch costs the equivalent of 5,000 to 10,000 clock cycles, or several microseconds on most current processors.

The `vmstat` command on Unix systems and the `perfmon` tool on Windows systems report the number of context switches and the percentage of time spent in the kernel. High kernel usage (over 10%) often indicates heavy scheduling activity, which may be caused by blocking due to I/O or lock contention.

11.3.2 Memory synchronization

The performance cost of synchronization comes from several sources. The visibility guarantees provided by `synchronized` and `volatile` may entail using special instructions called *memory barriers* that can flush or invalidate caches, flush hardware write buffers, and stall execution pipelines. Memory barriers may also have indirect performance consequences because they inhibit other compiler optimizations; most operations cannot be reordered with memory barriers.

When assessing the performance impact of synchronization, it is important to distinguish between *contended* and *uncontended* synchronization. The `synchronized` mechanism is optimized for the uncontended case (`volatile` is always uncontended), and at this writing, the performance cost of a "fast-path" uncontended synchronization ranges from 20 to 250 clock cycles for most systems. While this is certainly not zero, the effect of needed, uncontended synchronization is rarely significant in overall application performance, and the alternative involves compromising safety and potentially signing yourself (or your successor) up for some very painful bug hunting later.

Modern JVMs can reduce the cost of incidental synchronization by optimizing away locking that can be proven never to contend. If a lock object is accessible only to the current thread, the JVM is permitted to optimize away a lock acquisition because there is no way another thread could synchronize on the same lock. For example, the lock acquisition in Listing 11.2 can always be eliminated by the JVM.

More sophisticated JVMs can use *escape analysis* to identify when a local object reference is never published to the heap and is therefore thread-local. In get-

StoogeNames in Listing 11.3, the only reference to the List is the local variable
stooges, and stack-confined variables are automatically thread-local. A naive
execution of getStoogeNames would acquire and release the lock on the Vector
four times, once for each call to add or toString. However, a smart runtime
compiler can inline these calls and then see that stooges and its internal state
never escape, and therefore that all four lock acquisitions can be eliminated.[4]

```
public String getStoogeNames() {
    List<String> stooges = new Vector<String>();
    stooges.add("Moe");
    stooges.add("Larry");
    stooges.add("Curly");
    return stooges.toString();
}
```

LISTING 11.3. Candidate for lock elision.

Even without escape analysis, compilers can also perform *lock coarsening*, the
merging of adjacent synchronized blocks using the same lock. For getStooge-
Names, a JVM that performs lock coarsening might combine the three calls to add
and the call to toString into a single lock acquisition and release, using heuristics
on the relative cost of synchronization versus the instructions inside the synchronized block.[5] Not only does this reduce the synchronization overhead, but it
also gives the optimizer a much larger block to work with, likely enabling other
optimizations.

> Don't worry excessively about the cost of uncontended synchronization.
> The basic mechanism is already quite fast, and JVMs can perform addi-
> tional optimizations that further reduce or eliminate the cost. Instead,
> focus optimization efforts on areas where lock contention actually occurs.

Synchronization by one thread can also affect the performance of other
threads. Synchronization creates traffic on the shared memory bus; this bus
has a limited bandwidth and is shared across all processors. If threads must
compete for synchronization bandwidth, all threads using synchronization will
suffer.[6]

4. This compiler optimization, called *lock elision*, is performed by the IBM JVM and is expected in
HotSpot as of Java 7.
5. A smart dynamic compiler can figure out that this method always returns the same string, and
after the first execution recompile getStoogeNames to simply return the value returned by the first
execution.
6. This aspect is sometimes used to argue against the use of nonblocking algorithms without some
sort of backoff, because under heavy contention, nonblocking algorithms generate more synchronization traffic than lock-based ones. See Chapter 15.

11.3.3   Blocking

Uncontended synchronization can be handled entirely within the JVM (Bacon et al., 1998); contended synchronization may require OS activity, which adds to the cost. When locking is contended, the losing thread(s) must block. The JVM can implement blocking either via *spin-waiting* (repeatedly trying to acquire the lock until it succeeds) or by *suspending* the blocked thread through the operating system. Which is more efficient depends on the relationship between context switch overhead and the time until the lock becomes available; spin-waiting is preferable for short waits and suspension is preferable for long waits. Some JVMs choose between the two adaptively based on profiling data of past wait times, but most just suspend threads waiting for a lock.

Suspending a thread because it could not get a lock, or because it blocked on a condition wait or blocking I/O operation, entails two additional context switches and all the attendant OS and cache activity: the blocked thread is switched out before its quantum has expired, and is then switched back in later after the lock or other resource becomes available. (Blocking due to lock contention also has a cost for the thread holding the lock: when it releases the lock, it must then ask the OS to resume the blocked thread.)

11.4   Reducing lock contention

We've seen that serialization hurts scalability and that context switches hurt performance. Contended locking causes both, so reducing lock contention can improve both performance and scalability.

Access to resources guarded by an exclusive lock is serialized—only one thread at a time may access it. Of course, we use locks for good reasons, such as preventing data corruption, but this safety comes at a price. Persistent contention for a lock limits scalability.

> The principal threat to scalability in concurrent applications is the exclusive resource lock.

Two factors influence the likelihood of contention for a lock: how often that lock is requested and how long it is held once acquired.[7] If the product of these factors is sufficiently small, then most attempts to acquire the lock will be uncontended, and lock contention will not pose a significant scalability impediment. If, however, the lock is in sufficiently high demand, threads will block waiting for it; in the extreme case, processors will sit idle even though there is plenty of work to do.

---

7. This is a corollary of *Little's law*, a result from queueing theory that says "the average number of customers in a stable system is equal to their average arrival rate multiplied by their average time in the system". (Little, 1961)

There are three ways to reduce lock contention:
- Reduce the duration for which locks are held;
- Reduce the frequency with which locks are requested; or
- Replace exclusive locks with coordination mechanisms that permit greater concurrency.

11.4.1 Narrowing lock scope ("Get in, get out")

An effective way to reduce the likelihood of contention is to hold locks as briefly as possible. This can be done by moving code that doesn't require the lock out of synchronized blocks, especially for expensive operations and potentially blocking operations such as I/O.

It is easy to see how holding a "hot" lock for too long can limit scalability; we saw an example of this in SynchronizedFactorizer in Chapter 2. If an operation holds a lock for 2 milliseconds and every operation requires that lock, throughput can be no greater than 500 operations per second, no matter how many processors are available. Reducing the time the lock is held to 1 millisecond improves the lock-induced throughput limit to 1000 operations per second.[8]

AttributeStore in Listing 11.4 shows an example of holding a lock longer than necessary. The userLocationMatches method looks up the user's location in a Map and uses regular expression matching to see if the resulting value matches the supplied pattern. The entire userLocationMatches method is synchronized, but the only portion of the code that actually needs the lock is the call to Map.get.

```
@ThreadSafe
public class AttributeStore {
    @GuardedBy("this") private final Map<String, String>
            attributes = new HashMap<String, String>();

    public synchronized boolean userLocationMatches(String name,
                                                    String regexp) {
        String key = "users." + name + ".location";
        String location = attributes.get(key);
        if (location == null)
            return false;
        else
            return Pattern.matches(regexp, location);
    }
}
```

LISTING 11.4. Holding a lock longer than necessary.

---

8. Actually, this calculation *understates* the cost of holding locks for too long because it doesn't take into account the context switch overhead generated by increased lock contention.

BetterAttributeStore in Listing 11.5 rewrites AttributeStore to reduce significantly the lock duration. The first step is to construct the Map key associated with the user's location, a string of the form users.*name*.location. This entails instantiating a StringBuilder object, appending several strings to it, and instantiating the result as a String. After the location has been retrieved, the regular expression is matched against the resulting location string. Because constructing the key string and processing the regular expression do not access shared state, they need not be executed with the lock held. BetterAttributeStore factors these steps out of the synchronized block, thus reducing the time the lock is held.

```
@ThreadSafe
public class BetterAttributeStore {
    @GuardedBy("this") private final Map<String, String>
            attributes = new HashMap<String, String>();

    public boolean userLocationMatches(String name, String regexp) {
        String key = "users." + name + ".location";
        String location;
        synchronized (this) {
            location = attributes.get(key);
        }
        if (location == null)
            return false;
        else
            return Pattern.matches(regexp, location);
    }
}
```

LISTING 11.5. Reducing lock duration.

Reducing the scope of the lock in userLocationMatches substantially reduces the number of instructions that are executed with the lock held. By Amdahl's law, this removes an impediment to scalability because the amount of serialized code is reduced.

Because AttributeStore has only one state variable, attributes, we can improve it further by the technique of *delegating thread safety* (Section 4.3). By replacing attributes with a thread-safe Map (a Hashtable, synchronizedMap, or ConcurrentHashMap), AttributeStore can delegate all its thread safety obligations to the underlying thread-safe collection. This eliminates the need for explicit synchronization in AttributeStore, reduces the lock scope to the duration of the Map access, and removes the risk that a future maintainer will undermine thread safety by forgetting to acquire the appropriate lock before accessing attributes.

While shrinking synchronized blocks can improve scalability, a synchronized block can be *too* small—operations that need to be atomic (such updating multiple variables that participate in an invariant) must be contained in a single synchronized block. And because the cost of synchronization is nonzero, breaking one synchronized block into multiple synchronized blocks (correctness permitting) at some point becomes counterproductive in terms of performance.[9] The ideal balance is of course platform-dependent, but in practice it makes sense to worry about the size of a synchronized block only when you can move "substantial" computation or blocking operations out of it. ·

11.4.2 Reducing lock granularity

The other way to reduce the fraction of time that a lock is held (and therefore the likelihood that it will be contended) is to have threads ask for it less often. This can be accomplished by *lock splitting* and *lock striping*, which involve using separate locks to guard multiple independent state variables previously guarded by a single lock. These techniques reduce the granularity at which locking occurs, potentially allowing greater scalability—but using more locks also increases the risk of deadlock.

As a thought experiment, imagine what would happen if there was *only one* lock for the entire application instead of a separate lock for each object. Then execution of all synchronized blocks, regardless of their lock, would be serialized. With many threads competing for the global lock, the chance that two threads want the lock at the same time increases, resulting in more contention. So if lock requests were instead distributed over a *larger* set of locks, there would be less contention. Fewer threads would be blocked waiting for locks, thus increasing scalability.

If a lock guards more than one *independent* state variable, you may be able to improve scalability by splitting it into multiple locks that each guard different variables. This results in each lock being requested less often.

ServerStatus in Listing 11.6 shows a portion of the monitoring interface for a database server that maintains the set of currently logged-on users and the set of currently executing queries. As a user logs on or off or query execution begins or ends, the ServerStatus object is updated by calling the appropriate add or remove method. The two types of information are completely independent; ServerStatus could even be split into two separate classes with no loss of functionality.

Instead of guarding both users and queries with the ServerStatus lock, we can instead guard each with a separate lock, as shown in Listing 11.7. After splitting the lock, each new finer-grained lock will see less locking traffic than the original coarser lock would have. (Delegating to a thread-safe Set implementation for users and queries instead of using explicit synchronization would implicitly provide lock splitting, as each Set would use a different lock to guard its state.)

Splitting a lock into two offers the greatest possibility for improvement when the lock is experiencing moderate but not heavy contention. Splitting locks that are experiencing little contention yields little net improvement in performance or throughput, although it might increase the load threshold at which performance starts to degrade due to contention. Splitting locks experiencing moderate con-

---

9. If the JVM performs lock coarsening, it may undo the splitting of synchronized blocks anyway.

```
@ThreadSafe
public class ServerStatus {
    @GuardedBy("this") public final Set<String> users;
    @GuardedBy("this") public final Set<String> queries;
    ...
    public synchronized void addUser(String u) { users.add(u); }
    public synchronized void addQuery(String q) { queries.add(q); }
    public synchronized void removeUser(String u) {
        users.remove(u);
    }
    public synchronized void removeQuery(String q) {
        queries.remove(q);
    }
}
```

LISTING 11.6. Candidate for lock splitting.

```
@ThreadSafe
public class ServerStatus {
    @GuardedBy("users") public final Set<String> users;
    @GuardedBy("queries") public final Set<String> queries;
    ...
    public void addUser(String u) {
        synchronized (users) {
            users.add(u);
        }
    }

    public void addQuery(String q) {
        synchronized (queries) {
            queries.add(q);
        }
    }
    // remove methods similarly refactored to use split locks
}
```

LISTING 11.7. ServerStatus refactored to use split locks.

tention might actually turn them into mostly uncontended locks, which is the most desirable outcome for both performance and scalability.

11.4.3 Lock striping

Splitting a heavily contended lock into two is likely to result in two heavily contended locks. While this will produce a small scalability improvement by enabling two threads to execute concurrently instead of one, it still does not dramatically improve prospects for concurrency on a system with many processors. The lock splitting example in the ServerStatus classes does not offer any obvious opportunity for splitting the locks further.

Lock splitting can sometimes be extended to partition locking on a variable-sized set of independent objects, in which case it is called *lock striping*. For example, the implementation of ConcurrentHashMap uses an array of 16 locks, each of which guards 1/16 of the hash buckets; bucket N is guarded by lock N mod 16. Assuming the hash function provides reasonable spreading characteristics and keys are accessed uniformly, this should reduce the demand for any given lock by approximately a factor of 16. It is this technique that enables ConcurrentHashMap to support up to 16 concurrent writers. (The number of locks could be increased to provide even better concurrency under heavy access on high-processor-count systems, but the number of stripes should be increased beyond the default of 16 only when you have evidence that concurrent writers are generating enough contention to warrant raising the limit.)

One of the downsides of lock striping is that locking the collection for exclusive access is more difficult and costly than with a single lock. Usually an operation can be performed by acquiring at most one lock, but occasionally you need to lock the entire collection, as when ConcurrentHashMap needs to expand the map and rehash the values into a larger set of buckets. This is typically done by acquiring all of the locks in the stripe set.[10]

StripedMap in Listing 11.8 illustrates implementing a hash-based map using lock striping. There are N_LOCKS locks, each guarding a subset of the buckets. Most methods, like get, need acquire only a single bucket lock. Some methods may need to acquire all the locks but, as in the implementation for clear, may not need to acquire them all simultaneously.[11]

11.4.4 Avoiding hot fields

Lock splitting and lock striping can improve scalability because they enable different threads to operate on different data (or different portions of the same data structure) without interfering with each other. A program that would benefit from lock splitting necessarily exhibits contention for a *lock* more often than for the *data*

---

10. The only way to acquire an arbitrary set of intrinsic locks is via recursion.

11. Clearing the Map in this way is not atomic, so there is not necessarily a time when the Striped-Map is actually empty if other threads are concurrently adding elements; making the operation atomic would require acquiring all the locks at once. However, for concurrent collections that clients typically cannot lock for exclusive access, the result of methods like size or isEmpty may be out of date by the time they return anyway, so this behavior, while perhaps somewhat surprising, is usually acceptable.

```
@ThreadSafe
public class StripedMap {
    // Synchronization policy: buckets[n] guarded by locks[n%N_LOCKS]
    private static final int N_LOCKS = 16;
    private final Node[] buckets;
    private final Object[] locks;

    private static class Node { ... }

    public StripedMap(int numBuckets) {
        buckets = new Node[numBuckets];
        locks = new Object[N_LOCKS];
        for (int i = 0; i < N_LOCKS; i++)
            locks[i] = new Object();
    }

    private final int hash(Object key) {
        return Math.abs(key.hashCode() % buckets.length);
    }

    public Object get(Object key) {
        int hash = hash(key);
        synchronized (locks[hash % N_LOCKS]) {
            for (Node m = buckets[hash]; m != null; m = m.next)
                if (m.key.equals(key))
                    return m.value;
        }
        return null;
    }

    public void clear() {
        for (int i = 0; i < buckets.length; i++) {
            synchronized (locks[i % N_LOCKS]) {
                buckets[i] = null;
            }
        }
    }
    ...
}
```

LISTING 11.8. Hash-based map using lock striping.

guarded by that lock. If a lock guards two independent variables X and Y, and thread A wants to access X while B wants to access Y (as would be the case if one thread called addUser while another called addQuery in ServerStatus), then the two threads are not contending for any data, even though they are contending for a lock.

Lock granularity cannot be reduced when there are variables that are required for every operation. This is yet another area where raw performance and scalability are often at odds with each other; common optimizations such as caching frequently computed values can introduce "hot fields" that limit scalability.

If you were implementing HashMap, you would have a choice of how size computes the number of entries in the Map. The simplest approach is to count the number of entries every time it is called. A common optimization is to update a separate counter as entries are added or removed; this slightly increases the cost of a put or remove operation to keep the counter up-to-date, but reduces the cost of the size operation from $O(n)$ to $O(1)$.

Keeping a separate count to speed up operations like size and isEmpty works fine for a single-threaded or fully synchronized implementation, but makes it much harder to improve the scalability of the implementation because every operation that modifies the map must now update the shared counter. Even if you use lock striping for the hash chains, synchronizing access to the counter reintroduces the scalability problems of exclusive locking. What looked like a performance optimization—caching the results of the size operation—has turned into a scalability liability. In this case, the counter is called a *hot field* because every mutative operation needs to access it.

ConcurrentHashMap avoids this problem by having size enumerate the stripes and add up the number of elements in each stripe, instead of maintaining a global count. To avoid enumerating every element, ConcurrentHashMap maintains a separate count field for each stripe, also guarded by the stripe lock.[12]

11.4.5   Alternatives to exclusive locks

A third technique for mitigating the effect of lock contention is to forego the use of exclusive locks in favor of a more concurrency-friendly means of managing shared state. These include using the concurrent collections, read-write locks, immutable objects and atomic variables.

ReadWriteLock (see Chapter 13) enforces a multiple-reader, single-writer locking discipline: more than one reader can access the shared resource concurrently so long as none of them wants to modify it, but writers must acquire the lock excusively. For read-mostly data structures, ReadWriteLock can offer greater concurrency than exclusive locking; for read-only data structures, immutability can eliminate the need for locking entirely.

Atomic variables (see Chapter 15) offer a means of reducing the cost of updating "hot fields" such as statistics counters, sequence generators, or the reference

---

12. If size is called frequently compared to mutative operations, striped data structures can optimize for this by caching the collection size in a volatile whenever size is called and invalidating the cache (setting it to -1) whenever the collection is modified. If the cached value is nonnegative on entry to size, it is accurate and can be returned; otherwise it is recomputed.

to the first node in a linked data structure. (We used `AtomicLong` to maintain the hit counter in the servlet examples in Chapter 2.) The atomic variable classes provide very fine-grained (and therefore more scalable) atomic operations on integers or object references, and are implemented using low-level concurrency primitives (such as compare-and-swap) provided by most modern processors. If your class has a small number of hot fields that do not participate in invariants with other variables, replacing them with atomic variables may improve scalability. (Changing your algorithm to have fewer hot fields might improve scalability even more—atomic variables reduce the cost of updating hot fields, but they don't eliminate it.)

11.4.6   Monitoring CPU utilization

When testing for scalability, the goal is usually to keep the processors fully utilized. Tools like `vmstat` and `mpstat` on Unix systems or `perfmon` on Windows systems can tell you just how "hot" the processors are running.

If the CPUs are asymmetrically utilized (some CPUs are running hot but others are not) your first goal should be to find increased parallelism in your program. Asymmetric utilization indicates that most of the computation is going on in a small set of threads, and your application will not be able to take advantage of additional processors.

If the CPUs are not fully utilized, you need to figure out why. There are several likely causes:

Insufficent load. It may be that the application being tested is just not subjected to enough load. You can test for this by increasing the load and measuring changes in utilization, response time, or service time. Generating enough load to saturate an application can require substantial computer power; the problem may be that the client systems, not the system being tested, are running at capacity.

I/O-bound. You can determine whether an application is disk-bound using `iostat` or `perfmon`, and whether it is bandwidth-limited by monitoring traffic levels on your network.

Externally bound. If your application depends on external services such as a database or web service, the bottleneck may not be in your code. You can test for this by using a profiler or database administration tools to determine how much time is being spent waiting for answers from the external service.

Lock contention. Profiling tools can tell you how much lock contention your application is experiencing and which locks are "hot". You can often get the same information without a profiler through random sampling, triggering a few thread dumps and looking for threads contending for locks. If a thread is blocked waiting for a lock, the appropriate stack frame in the thread dump indicates "waiting to lock monitor ... " Locks that are mostly uncontended rarely show up in a thread dump; a heavily contended lock will almost always have at least one thread waiting to acquire it and so will frequently appear in thread dumps.

If your application is keeping the CPUs sufficiently hot, you can use monitoring tools to infer whether it would benefit from additional CPUs. A program with only four threads may be able to keep a 4-way system fully utilized, but is unlikely to see a performance boost if moved to an 8-way system since there would need to be waiting runnable threads to take advantage of the additional processors. (You may also be able to reconfigure the program to divide its workload over more threads, such as adjusting a thread pool size.) One of the columns reported by `vmstat` is the number of threads that are runnable but not currently running because a CPU is not available; if CPU utilization is high and there are always runnable threads waiting for a CPU, your application would probably benefit from more processors.

11.4.7 Just say no to object pooling

In early JVM versions, object allocation and garbage collection were slow,[13] but their performance has improved substantially since then. In fact, allocation in Java is now faster than `malloc` is in C: the common code path for `new Object` in HotSpot 1.4.x and 5.0 is approximately ten machine instructions.

To work around "slow" object lifecycles, many developers turned to object pooling, where objects are recycled instead of being garbage collected and allocated anew when needed. Even taking into account its reduced garbage collection overhead, object pooling has been shown to be a performance loss[14] for all but the most expensive objects (and a serious loss for light- and medium-weight objects) in single-threaded programs (Click, 2005).

In concurrent applications, pooling fares even worse. When threads allocate new objects, very little inter-thread coordination is required, as allocators typically use thread-local allocation blocks to eliminate most synchronization on heap data structures. But if those threads instead request an object from a pool, some synchronization is necessary to coordinate access to the pool data structure, creating the possibility that a thread will block. Because blocking a thread due to lock contention is hundreds of times more expensive than an allocation, even a small amount of pool-induced contention would be a scalability bottleneck. (Even an uncontended synchronization is usually more expensive than allocating an object.) This is yet another technique intended as a performance optimization but that turned into a scalability hazard. Pooling has its uses,[15] but is of limited utility as a performance optimization.

---

13. As was everything else—synchronization, graphics, JVM startup, reflection—predictably so in the first version of an experimental technology.

14. In addition to being a loss in terms of CPU cycles, object pooling has a number of other problems, among them the challenge of setting pool sizes correctly (too small, and pooling has no effect; too large, and it puts pressure on the garbage collector, retaining memory that could be used more effectively for something else); the risk that an object will not be properly reset to its newly allocated state, introducing subtle bugs; the risk that a thread will return an object to the pool but continue using it; and that it makes more work for generational garbage collectors by encouraging a pattern of old-to-young references.

15. In constrained environments, such as some J2ME or RTSJ targets, object pooling may still be required for effective memory management or to manage responsiveness.

> Allocating objects is usually cheaper than synchronizing.

11.5 Example: Comparing Map performance

The single-threaded performance of ConcurrentHashMap is slightly better than that of a synchronized HashMap, but it is in concurrent use that it really shines. The implementation of ConcurrentHashMap assumes the most common operation is retrieving a value that already exists, and is therefore optimized to provide highest performance and concurrency for successful get operations.

The major scalability impediment for the synchronized Map implementations is that there is a single lock for the entire map, so only one thread can access the map at a time. On the other hand, ConcurrentHashMap does no locking for most successful read operations, and uses lock striping for write operations and those few read operations that do require locking. As a result, multiple threads can access the Map concurrently without blocking.

Figure 11.3 illustrates the differences in scalability between several Map implementations: ConcurrentHashMap, ConcurrentSkipListMap, and HashMap and TreeMap wrapped with synchronizedMap. The first two are thread-safe by design; the latter two are made thread-safe by the synchronized wrapper. In each run, N threads concurrently execute a tight loop that selects a random key and attempts to retrieve the value corresponding to that key. If the value is not present, it is added to the Map with probability $p = .6$, and if it is present, is removed with probability $p = .02$. The tests were run under a pre-release build of Java 6 on an 8-way Sparc V880, and the graph displays throughput normalized to the one-thread case for ConcurrentHashMap. (The scalability gap between the concurrent and synchronized collections is even larger on Java 5.0.)

The data for ConcurrentHashMap and ConcurrentSkipListMap shows that they scale well to large numbers of threads; throughput continues to improve as threads are added. While the numbers of threads in Figure 11.3 may not seem large, this test program generates more contention per thread than a typical application because it does little other than pound on the Map; a real program would do additional thread-local work in each iteration.

The numbers for the synchronized collections are not as encouraging. Performance for the one-thread case is comparable to ConcurrentHashMap, but once the load transitions from mostly uncontended to mostly contended—which happens here at two threads—the synchronized collections suffer badly. This is common behavior for code whose scalability is limited by lock contention. So long as contention is low, time per operation is dominated by the time to actually do the work and throughput may improve as threads are added. Once contention becomes significant, time per operation is dominated by context switch and scheduling delays, and adding more threads has little effect on throughput.

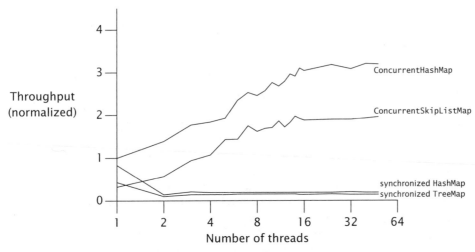

FIGURE 11.3. Comparing scalability of Map implementations.

11.6   Reducing context switch overhead

Many tasks involve operations that may block; transitioning between the running and blocked states entails a context switch. One source of blocking in server applications is generating log messages in the course of processing requests; to illustrate how throughput can be improved by reducing context switches, we'll analyze the scheduling behavior of two logging approaches.

Most logging frameworks are thin wrappers around println; when you have something to log, just write it out right then and there. Another approach was shown in LogWriter on page 152: the logging is performed in a dedicated background thread instead of by the requesting thread. From the developer's perspective, both approaches are roughly equivalent. But there may be a difference in performance, depending on the volume of logging activity, how many threads are doing logging, and other factors such as the cost of context switching.[16]

The service time for a logging operation includes whatever computation is associated with the I/O stream classes; if the I/O operation blocks, it also includes the duration for which the thread is blocked. The operating system will deschedule the blocked thread until the I/O completes, and probably a little longer. When the I/O completes, other threads are probably active and will be allowed to finish out their scheduling quanta, and threads may already be waiting ahead of us on

---

16. Building a logger that moves the I/O to another thread may improve performance, but it also introduces a number of design complications, such as interruption (what happens if a thread blocked in a logging operation is interrupted?), service guarantees (does the logger guarantee that a successfully queued log message will be logged prior to service shutdown?), saturation policy (what happens when the producers log messages faster than the logger thread can handle them?), and service lifecycle (how do we shut down the logger, and how do we communicate the service state to producers?).

the scheduling queue—further adding to service time. Alternatively, if multiple threads are logging simultaneously, there may be contention for the output stream lock, in which case the result is the same as with blocking I/O—the thread blocks waiting for the lock and gets switched out. Inline logging involves I/O and locking, which can lead to increased context switching and therefore increased service times.

Increasing request service time is undesirable for several reasons. First, service time affects quality of service: longer service times mean someone is waiting longer for a result. But more significantly, longer service times in this case mean more lock contention. The "get in, get out" principle of Section 11.4.1 tells us that we should hold locks as briefly as possible, because the longer a lock is held, the more likely that lock will be contended. If a thread blocks waiting for I/O while holding a lock, another thread is more likely to want the lock while the first thread is holding it. Concurrent systems perform much better when most lock acquisitions are uncontended, because contended lock acquisition means more context switches. A coding style that encourages more context switches thus yields lower overall throughput.

Moving the I/O out of the request-processing thread is likely to shorten the mean service time for request processing. Threads calling log no longer block waiting for the output stream lock or for I/O to complete; they need only queue the message and can then return to their task. On the other hand, we've introduced the possibility of contention for the message queue, but the put operation is lighter-weight than the logging I/O (which might require system calls) and so is less likely to block in actual use (as long as the queue is not full). Because the request thread is now less likely to block, it is less likely to be context-switched out in the middle of a request. What we've done is turned a complicated and uncertain code path involving I/O and possible lock contention into a straight-line code path.

To some extent, we are just moving the work around, moving the I/O to a thread where its cost isn't perceived by the user (which may in itself be a win). But by moving *all* the logging I/O to a single thread, we also eliminate the chance of contention for the output stream and thus eliminate a source of blocking. This improves overall throughput because fewer resources are consumed in scheduling, context switching, and lock management.

Moving the I/O from many request-processing threads to a single logger thread is similar to the difference between a bucket brigade and a collection of individuals fighting a fire. In the "hundred guys running around with buckets" approach, you have a greater chance of contention at the water source and at the fire (resulting in overall less water delivered to the fire), plus greater inefficiency because each worker is continuously switching modes (filling, running, dumping, running, etc.). In the bucket-brigade approach, the flow of water from the source to the burning building is constant, less energy is expended transporting the water to the fire, and each worker focuses on doing one job continuously. Just as interruptions are disruptive and productivity-reducing to humans, blocking and context switching are disruptive to threads.

Summary

Because one of the most common reasons to use threads is to exploit multiple processors, in discussing the performance of concurrent applications, we are usually more concerned with throughput or scalability than we are with raw service time. Amdahl's law tells us that the scalability of an application is driven by the proportion of code that must be executed serially. Since the primary source of serialization in Java programs is the exclusive resource lock, scalability can often be improved by spending less time holding locks, either by reducing lock granularity, reducing the duration for which locks are held, or replacing exclusive locks with nonexclusive or nonblocking alternatives.

CHAPTER 12

Testing Concurrent Programs

Concurrent programs employ similar design principles and patterns to sequential programs. The difference is that concurrent programs have a degree of nondeterminism that sequential programs do not, increasing the number of potential interactions and failure modes that must be planned for and analyzed.

Similarly, testing concurrent programs uses and extends ideas from testing sequential ones. The same techniques for testing correctness and performance in sequential programs can be applied to concurrent programs, but with concurrent programs the space of things that can go wrong is much larger. The major challenge in constructing tests for concurrent programs is that potential failures may be rare probabalistic occurrences rather than deterministic ones; tests that disclose such failures must be more extensive and run for longer than typical sequential tests.

Most tests of concurrent classes fall into one or both of the classic categories of *safety* and *liveness*. In Chapter 1, we defined safety as "nothing bad ever happens" and liveness as "something good eventually happens".

Tests of safety, which verify that a class's behavior conforms to its specification, usually take the form of testing invariants. For example, in a linked list implementation that caches the size of the list every time it is modified, one safety test would be to compare the cached count against the actual number of elements in the list. In a single-threaded program this is easy, since the list contents do not change while you are testing its properties. But in a concurrent program, such a test is likely to be fraught with races unless you can observe the count field and count the elements in a single atomic operation. This can be done by locking the list for exclusive access, employing some sort of "atomic snapshot" feature provided by the implementation, or by using "test points" provided by the implementation that let tests assert invariants or execute test code atomically.

In this book, we've used timing diagrams to depict "unlucky" interactions that could cause failures in incorrectly constructed classes; test programs attempt to search enough of the state space that such bad luck eventually occurs. Unfortunately, test code can introduce timing or synchronization artifacts that can mask bugs that might otherwise manifest themselves.[1]

---

1. Bugs that disappear when you add debugging or test code are playfully called *Heisenbugs*.

Liveness properties present their own testing challenges. Liveness tests include tests of progress and nonprogress, which are hard to quantify—how do you verify that a method is blocking and not merely running slowly? Similarly, how do you test that an algorithm does *not* deadlock? How long should you wait before you declare it to have failed?

Related to liveness tests are performance tests. Performance can be measured in a number of ways, including:

Throughput: the rate at which a set of concurrent tasks is completed;

Responsiveness: the delay between a request for and completion of some action (also called *latency*); or

Scalability: the improvement in throughput (or lack thereof) as more resources (usually CPUs) are made available.

12.1 Testing for correctness

Developing unit tests for a concurrent class starts with the same analysis as for a sequential class—identifying invariants and postconditions that are amenable to mechanical checking. If you are lucky, many of these are present in the specification; the rest of the time, writing tests is an adventure in iterative specification discovery.

As a concrete illustration, we're going to build a set of test cases for a bounded buffer. Listing 12.1 shows our BoundedBuffer implementation, using Semaphore to implement the required bounding and blocking.

BoundedBuffer implements a fixed-length array-based queue with blocking put and take methods controlled by a pair of counting semaphores. The availableItems semaphore represents the number of elements that can be *removed* from the buffer, and is initially zero (since the buffer is initially empty). Similarly, availableSpaces represents how many items can be *inserted* into the buffer, and is initialized to the size of the buffer.

A take operation first requires that a permit be obtained from availableItems. This succeeds immediately if the buffer is nonempty, and otherwise blocks until the buffer becomes nonempty. Once a permit is obtained, the next element from the buffer is removed and a permit is released to the availableSpaces semaphore.[2] The put operation is defined conversely, so that on exit from either the put or take methods, the sum of the counts of both semaphores always equals the bound. (In practice, if you need a bounded buffer you should use ArrayBlockingQueue or LinkedBlockingQueue rather than rolling your own, but the technique used here illustrates how insertions and removals can be controlled in other data structures as well.)

---

2. In a counting semaphore, the permits are not represented explicitly or associated with an owning thread; a release operation creates a permit and an acquire operation consumes one.

```
@ThreadSafe
public class BoundedBuffer<E> {
    private final Semaphore availableItems, availableSpaces;
    @GuardedBy("this") private final E[] items;
    @GuardedBy("this") private int putPosition = 0, takePosition = 0;

    public BoundedBuffer(int capacity) {
        availableItems = new Semaphore(0);
        availableSpaces = new Semaphore(capacity);
        items = (E[]) new Object[capacity];
    }
    public boolean isEmpty() {
        return availableItems.availablePermits() == 0;
    }
    public boolean isFull() {
        return availableSpaces.availablePermits() == 0;
    }

    public void put(E x) throws InterruptedException {
        availableSpaces.acquire();
        doInsert(x);
        availableItems.release();
    }
    public E take() throws InterruptedException {
        availableItems.acquire();
        E item = doExtract();
        availableSpaces.release();
        return item;
    }

    private synchronized void doInsert(E x) {
        int i = putPosition;
        items[i] = x;
        putPosition = (++i == items.length)? 0 : i;
    }
    private synchronized E doExtract() {
        int i = takePosition;
        E x = items[i];
        items[i] = null;
        takePosition = (++i == items.length)? 0 : i;
        return x;
    }
}
```

LISTING 12.1. Bounded buffer using Semaphore.

12.1.1   Basic unit tests

The most basic unit tests for BoundedBuffer are similar to what we'd use in a sequential context—create a bounded buffer, call its methods, and assert post-conditions and invariants. Some invariants that quickly come to mind are that a freshly created buffer should identify itself as empty, and also as not full. A similar but slightly more complicated safety test is to insert N elements into a buffer with capacity N (which should succeed without blocking), and test that the buffer recognizes that it is full (and not empty). JUnit test methods for these properties are shown in Listing 12.2.

```
class BoundedBufferTest extends TestCase {
    void testIsEmptyWhenConstructed() {
        BoundedBuffer<Integer> bb = new BoundedBuffer<Integer>(10);
        assertTrue(bb.isEmpty());
        assertFalse(bb.isFull());
    }

    void testIsFullAfterPuts() throws InterruptedException {
        BoundedBuffer<Integer> bb = new BoundedBuffer<Integer>(10);
        for (int i = 0; i < 10; i++)
            bb.put(i);
        assertTrue(bb.isFull());
        assertFalse(bb.isEmpty());
    }
}
```

LISTING 12.2. Basic unit tests for BoundedBuffer.

These simple test methods are entirely sequential. Including a set of sequential tests in your test suite is often helpful, since they can disclose when a problem is *not* related to concurrency issues before you start looking for data races.

12.1.2   Testing blocking operations

Tests of essential concurrency properties require introducing more than one thread. Most testing frameworks are not very concurrency-friendly: they rarely include facilities to create threads or monitor them to ensure that they do not die unexpectedly. If a helper thread created by a test case discovers a failure, the framework usually does not know with which test the thread is associated, so some work may be required to relay success or failure information back to the main test runner thread so it can be reported.

For the conformance tests for java.util.concurrent, it was important that failures be clearly associated with a specific test. Hence the JSR 166 Expert Group created a base class[3] that provided methods to relay and report failures during

---

3. http://gee.cs.oswego.edu/cgi-bin/viewcvs.cgi/jsr166/src/test/tck/JSR166TestCase.java

tearDown, following the convention that every test must wait until all the threads it created terminate. You may not need to go to such lengths; the key requirements are that it be clear whether the tests passed and that failure information is reported somewhere for use in diagnosing the problem.

If a method is supposed to block under certain conditions, then a test for that behavior should succeed only if the thread does *not* proceed. Testing that a method blocks is similar to testing that a method throws an exception; if the method returns normally, the test has failed.

Testing that a method blocks introduces an additional complication: once the method successfully blocks, you have to convince it somehow to unblock. The obvious way to do this is via interruption—start a blocking activity in a separate thread, wait until the thread blocks, interrupt it, and then assert that the blocking operation completed. Of course, this requires your blocking methods to respond to interruption by returning early or throwing InterruptedException.

The "wait until the thread blocks" part is easier said than done; in practice, you have to make an arbitrary decision about how long the few instructions being executed could possibly take, and wait longer than that. You should be prepared to increase this value if you are wrong (in which case you will see spurious test failures).

Listing 12.3 shows an approach to testing blocking operations. It creates a "taker" thread that attempts to take an element from an empty buffer. If take succeeds, it registers failure. The test runner thread starts the taker thread, waits a long time, and then interrupts it. If the taker thread has correctly blocked in the take operation, it will throw InterruptedException, and the catch block for this exception treats this as success and lets the thread exit. The main test runner thread then attempts to join with the taker thread and verifies that the join returned successfully by calling Thread.isAlive; if the taker thread responded to the interrupt, the join should complete quickly.

The timed join ensures that the test completes even if take gets stuck in some unexpected way. This test method tests several properties of take—not only that it blocks but that, when interrupted, it throws InterruptedException. This is one of the few cases in which it is appropriate to subclass Thread explicitly instead of using a Runnable in a pool: in order to test proper termination with join. The same approach can be used to test that the taker thread unblocks after an element is placed in the queue by the main thread.

It is tempting to use Thread.getState to verify that the thread is actually blocked on a condition wait, but this approach is not reliable. There is nothing that requires a blocked thread *ever* to enter the WAITING or TIMED_WAITING states, since the JVM can choose to implement blocking by spin-waiting instead. Similarly, because spurious wakeups from Object.wait or Condition.await are permitted (see Chapter 14), a thread in the WAITING or TIMED_WAITING state may temporarily transition to RUNNABLE even if the condition for which it is waiting is not yet true. Even ignoring these implementation options, it may take some time for the target thread to settle into a blocking state. *The result of Thread.getState should not be used for concurrency control, and is of limited usefulness for testing—its primary utility is as a source of debugging information.*

```
void testTakeBlocksWhenEmpty() {
    final BoundedBuffer<Integer> bb = new BoundedBuffer<Integer>(10);
    Thread taker = new Thread() {
        public void run() {
            try {
                int unused = bb.take();
                fail(); // if we get here, it's an error
            } catch (InterruptedException success) { }
        }};
    try {
        taker.start();
        Thread.sleep(LOCKUP_DETECT_TIMEOUT);
        taker.interrupt();
        taker.join(LOCKUP_DETECT_TIMEOUT);
        assertFalse(taker.isAlive());
    } catch (Exception unexpected) {
        fail();
    }
}
```

LISTING 12.3. Testing blocking and responsiveness to interruption.

12.1.3   Testing safety

The tests in Listings 12.2 and 12.3 test important properties of the bounded buffer, but are unlikely to disclose errors stemming from data races. To test that a concurrent class performs correctly under unpredictable concurrent access, we need to set up multiple threads performing put and take operations over some amount of time and then somehow test that nothing went wrong.

Constructing tests to disclose safety errors in concurrent classes is a chicken-and-egg problem: the test programs themselves are concurrent programs. Developing good concurrent tests can be more difficult than developing the classes they test.

> The challenge to constructing effective safety tests for concurrent classes is identifying easily checked properties that will, with high probability, fail if something goes wrong, while at the same time not letting the failure-auditing code limit concurrency artificially. It is best if checking the test property does not require any synchronization.

One approach that works well with classes used in producer-consumer designs (like BoundedBuffer) is to check that everything put into a queue or buffer comes out of it, and that nothing else does. A naive implementation of this approach would insert the element into a "shadow" list when it is put on the queue, remove it from the list when it is removed from the queue, and assert that the shadow list is empty when the test has finished. But this approach would distort the scheduling of the test threads because modifying the shadow list would require synchronization and possibly blocking.

A better approach is to compute checksums of the elements that are enqueued and dequeued using an order-sensitive checksum function, and compare them. If they match, the test passes. This approach works best when there is a single producer putting elements into the buffer and a single consumer taking them out, because it can test not only that the right elements (probably) came out but that they came out in the right order.

Extending this approach to a multiple-producer, multiple-consumer situation requires using a checksum function that is *insensitive* to the order in which the elements are combined, so that multiple checksums can be combined after the test. Otherwise, synchronizing access to a shared checksum field could become a concurrency bottleneck or distort the timing of the test. (Any commutative operation, such as addition or XOR, meets these requirements.)

To ensure that your test actually tests what you think it does, it is important that the checksums themselves not be guessable by the compiler. It would be a bad idea to use consecutive integers as your test data because then the result would always be the same, and a smart compiler could conceivably just precompute it.

To avoid this problem, test data should be generated randomly, but many otherwise effective tests are compromised by a poor choice of random number generator (RNG). Random number generation can create couplings between classes and timing artifacts because most random number generator classes are thread-safe and therefore introduce additional synchronization.[4] Giving each thread its own RNG allows a non-thread-safe RNG to be used.

Rather than using a general-purpose RNG, it is better to use simple pseudorandom functions. You don't need high-quality randomness; all you need is enough randomness to ensure the numbers change from run to run. The xorShift function in Listing 12.4 (Marsaglia, 2003) is among the cheapest medium-quality random number functions. Starting it off with values based on hashCode and nanoTime makes the sums both unguessable and almost always different for each run.

```
static int xorShift(int y) {
    y ^= (y << 6);
    y ^= (y >>> 21);
    y ^= (y << 7);
    return y;
}
```

LISTING 12.4. Medium-quality random number generator suitable for testing.

---

4. Many benchmarks are, unbeknownst to their developers or users, simply tests of how great a concurrency bottleneck the RNG is.

PutTakeTest in Listings 12.5 and 12.6 starts N producer threads that generate elements and enqueue them, and N consumer threads that dequeue them. Each thread updates the checksum of the elements as they go in or out, using a per-thread checksum that is combined at the end of the test run so as to add no more synchronization or contention than required to test the buffer.

Depending on your platform, creating and starting a thread can be a moderately heavyweight operation. If your thread is short-running and you start a number of threads in a loop, the threads run sequentially rather than concurrently in the worst case. Even in the not-quite-worst case, the fact that the first thread has a head start on the others means that you may get fewer interleavings than expected: the first thread runs by itself for some amount of time, and then the first two threads run concurrently for some amount of time, and only eventually are all the threads running concurrently. (The same thing happens at the end of the run: the threads that got a head start also finish early.)

We presented a technique for mitigating this problem in Section 5.5.1, using a CountDownLatch as a starting gate and another as a finish gate. Another way to get the same effect is to use a CyclicBarrier, initialized with the number of worker threads plus one, and have the worker threads and the test driver wait at the barrier at the beginning and end of their run. This ensures that all threads are up and running before any start working. PutTakeTest uses this technique to coordinate starting and stopping the worker threads, creating more potential concurrent interleavings. We still can't guarantee that the scheduler won't run each thread to completion sequentially, but making the runs long enough reduces the extent to which scheduling distorts our results.

The final trick employed by PutTakeTest is to use a deterministic termination criterion so that no additional inter-thread coordination is needed to figure out when the test is finished. The test method starts exactly as many producers as consumers and each of them puts or takes the same number of elements, so the total number of items added and removed is the same.

Tests like PutTakeTest tend to be good at finding safety violations. For example, a common error in implementing semaphore-controlled buffers is to forget that the code actually doing the insertion and extraction requires mutual exclusion (using synchronized or ReentrantLock). A sample run of PutTakeTest with a version of BoundedBuffer that omits making doInsert and doExtract synchronized fails fairly quickly. Running PutTakeTest with a few dozen threads iterating a few million times on buffers of various capacity on various systems increases our confidence about the lack of data corruption in put and take.

Tests should be run on multiprocessor systems to increase the diversity of potential interleavings. However, having more than a few CPUs does not necessarily make tests more effective. To maximize the chance of detecting timing-sensitive data races, there should be more active threads than CPUs, so that at any given time some threads are running and some are switched out, thus reducing the predicatability of interactions between threads.

```
public class PutTakeTest {
    private static final ExecutorService pool
            = Executors.newCachedThreadPool();
    private final AtomicInteger putSum = new AtomicInteger(0);
    private final AtomicInteger takeSum = new AtomicInteger(0);
    private final CyclicBarrier barrier;
    private final BoundedBuffer<Integer> bb;
    private final int nTrials, nPairs;

    public static void main(String[] args) {
        new PutTakeTest(10, 10, 100000).test(); // sample parameters
        pool.shutdown();
    }

    PutTakeTest(int capacity, int npairs, int ntrials) {
        this.bb = new BoundedBuffer<Integer>(capacity);
        this.nTrials = ntrials;
        this.nPairs = npairs;
        this.barrier = new CyclicBarrier(npairs * 2 + 1);
    }

    void test() {
        try {
            for (int i = 0; i < nPairs; i++) {
                pool.execute(new Producer());
                pool.execute(new Consumer());
            }
            barrier.await(); // wait for all threads to be ready
            barrier.await(); // wait for all threads to finish
            assertEquals(putSum.get(), takeSum.get());
        } catch (Exception e) {
            throw new RuntimeException(e);
        }
    }

    class Producer implements Runnable { /* Listing 12.6 */ }

    class Consumer implements Runnable { /* Listing 12.6 */ }
}
```

LISTING 12.5. Producer-consumer test program for BoundedBuffer.

```
/* inner classes of PutTakeTest (Listing 12.5) */
class Producer implements Runnable {
    public void run() {
        try {
            int seed = (this.hashCode() ^ (int)System.nanoTime());
            int sum = 0;
            barrier.await();
            for (int i = nTrials; i > 0; --i) {
                bb.put(seed);
                sum += seed;
                seed = xorShift(seed);
            }
            putSum.getAndAdd(sum);
            barrier.await();
        } catch (Exception e) {
            throw new RuntimeException(e);
        }
    }
}

class Consumer implements Runnable {
    public void run() {
        try {
            barrier.await();
            int sum = 0;
            for (int i = nTrials; i > 0; --i) {
                sum += bb.take();
            }
            takeSum.getAndAdd(sum);
            barrier.await();
        } catch (Exception e) {
            throw new RuntimeException(e);
        }
    }
}
```

LISTING 12.6. Producer and consumer classes used in PutTakeTest.

In tests that run until they complete a fixed number of operations, it is possible that the test case will never finish if the code being tested encounters an exception due to a bug. The most common way to handle this is to have the test framework abort tests that do not terminate within a certain amount of time; how long to wait should be determined empirically, and failures must then be analyzed to ensure that the problem wasn't just that you didn't wait long enough. (This problem is not unique to testing concurrent classes; sequential tests must also distinguish between long-running and infinite loops.)

12.1.4 Testing resource management

The tests so far have been concerned with a class's adherence to its specification—that it does what it is supposed to do. A secondary aspect to test is that it does *not* do things it is *not* supposed to do, such as leak resources. Any object that holds or manages other objects should not continue to maintain references to those objects longer than necessary. Such storage leaks prevent garbage collectors from reclaiming memory (or threads, file handles, sockets, database connections, or other limited resources) and can lead to resource exhaustion and application failure.

Resource management issues are especially important for classes like Bound-edBuffer—the entire reason for bounding a buffer is to prevent application failure due to resource exhaustion when producers get too far ahead of consumers. Bounding causes overly productive producers to block rather than continue to create work that will consume more and more memory or other resources.

Undesirable memory retention can be easily tested with heap-inspection tools that measure application memory usage; a variety of commercial and open-source heap-profiling tools can do this. The testLeak method in Listing 12.7 contains placeholders for a heap-inspection tool to snapshot the heap, which forces a garbage collection[5] and then records information about the heap size and memory usage.

The testLeak method inserts several large objects into a bounded buffer and then removes them; memory usage at heap snapshot #2 should be approximately the same as at heap snapshot #1. On the other hand, if doExtract forgot to null out the reference to the returned element (items[i]=null), the reported memory usage at the two snapshots would definitely not be the same. (This is one of the few times where explicit nulling is necessary; most of the time, it is either not helpful or actually harmful [EJ Item 5].)

12.1.5 Using callbacks

Callbacks to client-provided code can be helpful in constructing test cases; callbacks are often made at known points in an object's lifecycle that are good opportunities to assert invariants. For example, ThreadPoolExecutor makes calls to the task Runnables and to the ThreadFactory.

---

5. Technically, it is impossible to *force* a garbage collection; System.gc only *suggests* to the JVM that this might be a good time to perform a garbage collection. HotSpot can be instructed to ignore System.gc calls with -XX:+DisableExplicitGC.

```
class Big { double[] data = new double[100000]; }

void testLeak() throws InterruptedException {
    BoundedBuffer<Big> bb = new BoundedBuffer<Big>(CAPACITY);
    int heapSize1 = /* snapshot heap */;
    for (int i = 0; i < CAPACITY; i++)
        bb.put(new Big());
    for (int i = 0; i < CAPACITY; i++)
        bb.take();
    int heapSize2 = /* snapshot heap */;
    assertTrue(Math.abs(heapSize1-heapSize2) < THRESHOLD);
}
```

LISTING 12.7. Testing for resource leaks.

Testing a thread pool involves testing a number of elements of execution policy: that additional threads are created when they are supposed to, but not when they are not supposed to; that idle threads get reaped when they are supposed to, etc. Constructing a comprehensive test suite that covers all the possibilities is a major effort, but many of them can be tested fairly simply individually.

We can instrument thread creation by using a custom thread factory. TestingThreadFactory in Listing 12.8 maintains a count of created threads; test cases can then verify the number of threads created during a test run. TestingThreadFactory could be extended to return a custom Thread that also records when the thread terminates, so that test cases can verify that threads are reaped in accordance with the execution policy.

```
class TestingThreadFactory implements ThreadFactory {
    public final AtomicInteger numCreated = new AtomicInteger();
    private final ThreadFactory factory
            = Executors.defaultThreadFactory();

    public Thread newThread(Runnable r) {
        numCreated.incrementAndGet();
        return factory.newThread(r);
    }
}
```

LISTING 12.8. Thread factory for testing ThreadPoolExecutor.

If the core pool size is smaller than the maximum size, the thread pool should grow as demand for execution increases. Submitting long-running tasks to the pool makes the number of executing tasks stay constant for long enough to make a few assertions, such as testing that the pool is expanded as expected, as shown in Listing 12.9.

```
public void testPoolExpansion() throws InterruptedException {
    int MAX_SIZE = 10;
    ExecutorService exec = Executors.newFixedThreadPool(MAX_SIZE);

    for (int i = 0; i < 10 * MAX_SIZE; i++)
        exec.execute(new Runnable() {
            public void run() {
                try {
                    Thread.sleep(Long.MAX_VALUE);
                } catch (InterruptedException e) {
                    Thread.currentThread().interrupt();
                }
            }
        });
    for (int i = 0;
         i < 20 && threadFactory.numCreated.get() < MAX_SIZE;
         i++)
        Thread.sleep(100);
    assertEquals(threadFactory.numCreated.get(), MAX_SIZE);
    exec.shutdownNow();
}
```

LISTING 12.9. Test method to verify thread pool expansion.

12.1.6 Generating more interleavings

Since many of the potential failures in concurrent code are low-probability events, testing for concurrency errors is a numbers game, but there are some things you can do to improve your chances. We've already mentioned how running on multiprocessor systems with fewer processors than active threads can generate more interleavings than either a single-processor system or one with many processors. Similarly, testing on a variety of systems with different processor counts, operating systems, and processor architectures can disclose problems that might not occur on all systems.

A useful trick for increasing the number of interleavings, and therefore more effectively exploring the state space of your programs, is to use Thread.yield to encourage more context switches during operations that access shared state. (The effectiveness of this technique is platform-specific, since the JVM is free to treat Thread.yield as a no-op [JLS 17.9]; using a short but nonzero sleep would be slower but more reliable.) The method in Listing 12.10 transfers credits from one account to another; between the two update operations, invariants such as "sum of all accounts equals zero" do not hold. By sometimes yielding in the middle of an operation, you may activate timing-sensitive bugs in code that does not use adequate synchronization to access state. The inconvenience of adding these calls for testing and removing them for production can be reduced by adding them using aspect-oriented programming (AOP) tools.

```
public synchronized void transferCredits(Account from,
                                         Account to,
                                         int amount) {
    from.setBalance(from.getBalance() - amount);
    if (random.nextInt(1000) > THRESHOLD)
        Thread.yield();
    to.setBalance(to.getBalance() + amount);
}
```

LISTING 12.10. *Using* Thread.yield *to generate more interleavings.*

12.2 Testing for performance

Performance tests are often extended versions of functionality tests. In fact, it is almost always worthwhile to include some basic functionality testing within performance tests to ensure that you are not testing the performance of broken code.

While there is definitely overlap between performance and functionality tests, they have different goals. Performance tests seek to measure end-to-end performance metrics for representative use cases. Picking a reasonable set of usage scenarios is not always easy; ideally, tests should reflect how the objects being tested are actually used in your application.

In some cases an appropriate test scenario is obvious. Bounded buffers are nearly always used in producer-consumer designs, so it is sensible to measure the throughput of producers feeding data to consumers. We can easily extend PutTakeTest to become a performance test for this scenario.

A common secondary goal of performance testing is to select sizings empirically for various bounds—numbers of threads, buffer capacities, and so on. While these values might turn out to be sensitive enough to platform characteristics (such as processor type or even processor stepping level, number of CPUs, or memory size) to require dynamic configuration, it is equally common that reasonable choices for these values work well across a wide range of systems.

12.2.1 Extending PutTakeTest to add timing

The primary extension we have to make to PutTakeTest is to measure the time taken for a run. Rather than attempting to measure the time for a single operation, we get a more accurate measure by timing the entire run and dividing by the number of operations to get a per-operation time. We are already using a CyclicBarrier to start and stop the worker threads, so we can extend this by using a barrier action that measures the start and end time, as shown in Listing 12.11.

We can modify the initialization of the barrier to use this barrier action by using the constructor for CyclicBarrier that accepts a barrier action:

```
this.timer = new BarrierTimer();
this.barrier = new CyclicBarrier(npairs * 2 + 1, timer);
```

```
public class BarrierTimer implements Runnable {
    private boolean started;
    private long startTime, endTime;

    public synchronized void run() {
        long t = System.nanoTime();
        if (!started) {
            started = true;
            startTime = t;
        } else
            endTime = t;
    }
    public synchronized void clear() {
        started = false;
    }
    public synchronized long getTime() {
        return endTime - startTime;
    }
}
```

LISTING 12.11. Barrier-based timer.

The modified `test` method using the barrier-based timer is shown in Listing 12.12.

We can learn several things from running `TimedPutTakeTest`. One is the throughput of the producer-consumer handoff operation for various combinations of parameters; another is how the bounded buffer scales with different numbers of threads; a third is how we might select the bound size. Answering these questions requires running the test for various combinations of parameters, so we'll need a main test driver, shown in Listing 12.13.

Figure 12.1 shows some sample results on a 4-way machine, using buffer capacities of 1, 10, 100, and 1000. We see immediately that a buffer size of one causes very poor throughput; this is because each thread can make only a tiny bit of progress before blocking and waiting for another thread. Increasing buffer size to ten helps dramatically, but increases past ten offer diminishing returns.

It may be somewhat puzzling at first that adding a lot more threads degrades performance only slightly. The reason is hard to see from the data, but easy to see on a CPU performance meter such as `perfbar` while the test is running: even with many threads, not much computation is going on, and most of it is spent blocking and unblocking threads. So there is plenty of CPU slack for more threads to do the same thing without hurting performance very much.

However, be careful about concluding from this data that you can always add more threads to a producer-consumer program that uses a bounded buffer. This test is fairly artificial in how it simulates the *application*; the producers do almost no work to generate the item placed on the queue, and the consumers do almost no work with the item retrieved. If the worker threads in a real producer-

```
public void test() {
    try {
        timer.clear();
        for (int i = 0; i < nPairs; i++) {
            pool.execute(new Producer());
            pool.execute(new Consumer());
        }
        barrier.await();
        barrier.await();
        long nsPerItem = timer.getTime() / (nPairs * (long)nTrials);
        System.out.print("Throughput: " + nsPerItem + " ns/item");
        assertEquals(putSum.get(), takeSum.get());
    } catch (Exception e) {
        throw new RuntimeException(e);
    }
}
```

LISTING 12.12. Testing with a barrier-based timer.

```
public static void main(String[] args) throws Exception {
    int tpt = 100000; // trials per thread
    for (int cap = 1; cap <= 1000; cap *= 10) {
        System.out.println("Capacity: " + cap);
        for (int pairs = 1; pairs <= 128; pairs *= 2) {
            TimedPutTakeTest t =
                new TimedPutTakeTest(cap, pairs, tpt);
            System.out.print("Pairs: " + pairs + "\t");
            t.test();
            System.out.print("\t");
            Thread.sleep(1000);
            t.test();
            System.out.println();
            Thread.sleep(1000);
        }
    }
    pool.shutdown();
}
```

LISTING 12.13. Driver program for TimedPutTakeTest.

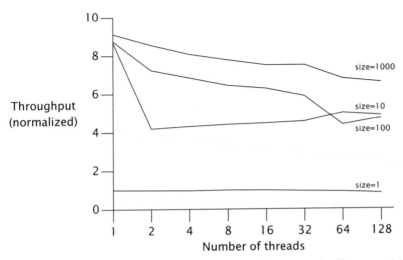

FIGURE 12.1. `TimedPutTakeTest` with various buffer capacities.

consumer application do some nontrivial work to produce and consume items (as is generally the case), then this slack would disappear and the effects of having too many threads could be very noticeable. The primary purpose of this test is to measure what constraints the producer-consumer handoff via the bounded buffer imposes on overall throughput.

12.2.2 Comparing multiple algorithms

While `BoundedBuffer` is a fairly solid implementation that performs reasonably well, it turns out to be no match for either `ArrayBlockingQueue` or `LinkedBlock-ingQueue` (which explains why this buffer algorithm wasn't selected for inclusion in the class library). The `java.util.concurrent` algorithms have been selected and tuned, in part using tests just like those described here, to be as efficient as we know how to make them, while still offering a wide range of functionality.[6] The main reason `BoundedBuffer` fares poorly is that put and take each have multiple operations that could encouter contention—acquire a semaphore, acquire a lock, release a semaphore. Other implementation approaches have fewer points at which they might contend with another thread.

Figure 12.2 shows comparative throughput on a dual hyperthreaded machine for all three classes with 256-element buffers, using a variant of `TimedPutTake-Test`. This test suggests that `LinkedBlockingQueue` scales better than `Array-BlockingQueue`. This may seem odd at first: a linked queue must allocate a link node object for each insertion, and hence seems to be doing more work than the array-based queue. However, even though it has more allocation and

---

6. You might be able to outperform them if you both are a concurrency expert and can give up some of the provided functionality.

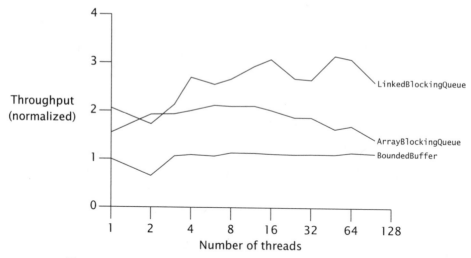

FIGURE 12.2. Comparing blocking queue implementations.

GC overhead, a linked queue allows more concurrent access by puts and takes than an array-based queue because the best linked queue algorithms allow the head and tail to be updated independently. Because allocation is usually thread-local, algorithms that can reduce contention by doing more allocation usually scale better. (This is another instance in which intuition based on traditional performance tuning runs counter to what is needed for scalability.)

12.2.3 Measuring responsiveness

So far we have focused on measuring throughput, which is usually the most important performance metric for concurrent programs. But sometimes it is more important to know how long an individual action might take to complete, and in this case we want to measure the *variance* of service time. Sometimes it makes sense to allow a longer average service time if it lets us obtain a smaller variance; predictability is a valuable performance characteristic too. Measuring variance allows us to estimate the answers to quality-of-service questions like "What percentage of operations will succeed in under 100 milliseconds?"

Histograms of task completion times are normally the best way to visualize variance in service time. Variances are only slightly more difficult to measure than averages—you need to keep track of per-task completion times in addition to aggregate completion time. Since timer granularity can be a factor in measuring individual task time (an individual task may take less than or close to the smallest "timer tick", which would distort measurements of task duration), to avoid measurement artifacts we can measure the run time of small batches of put and take operations instead.

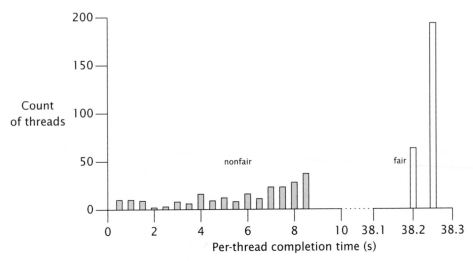

FIGURE 12.3. Completion time histogram for `TimedPutTakeTest` with default (nonfair) and fair semaphores.

Figure 12.3 shows the per-task completion times of a variant of `TimedPutTake-Test` using a buffer size of 1000 in which each of 256 concurrent tasks iterates only 1000 items for nonfair (shaded bars) and fair semaphores (open bars). (Section 13.3 explains fair versus nonfair queueing for locks and semaphores.) Completion times for nonfair semaphores range from 104 to 8,714 ms, a factor of over eighty. It is possible to reduce this range by forcing more fairness in concurrency control; this is easy to do in `BoundedBuffer` by initializing the semaphores to fair mode. As Figure 12.3 shows, this succeeds in greatly reducing the variance (now ranging only from 38,194 to 38,207 ms), but unfortunately also greatly reduces the throughput. (A longer-running test with more typical kinds of tasks would probably show an even larger throughput reduction.)

We saw before that very small buffer sizes cause heavy context switching and poor throughput even in nonfair mode, because nearly every operation involves a context switch. As an indication that the cost of fairness results primarily from blocking threads, we can rerun this test with a buffer size of one and see that nonfair semaphores now perform comparably to fair semaphores. Figure 12.4 shows that fairness doesn't make the average much worse or the variance much better in this case.

So, unless threads are continually blocking anyway because of tight synchronization requirements, nonfair semaphores provide much better throughput and fair semaphores provides lower variance. Because the results are so dramatically different, `Semaphore` forces its clients to decide which of the two factors to optimize for.

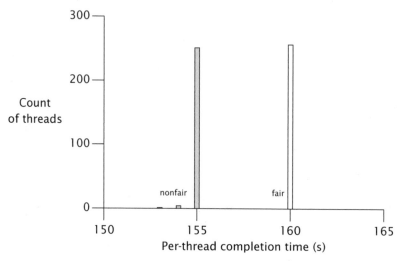

FIGURE 12.4. Completion time histogram for `TimedPutTakeTest` with single-item buffers.

12.3 Avoiding performance testing pitfalls

In theory, developing performance tests is easy—find a typical usage scenario, write a program that executes that scenario many times, and time it. In practice, you have to watch out for a number of coding pitfalls that prevent performance tests from yielding meaningful results.

12.3.1 Garbage collection

The timing of garbage collection is unpredictable, so there is always the possibility that the garbage collector will run during a measured test run. If a test program performs N iterations and triggers no garbage collection but iteration $N+1$ would trigger a garbage collection, a small variation in the size of the run could have a big (but spurious) effect on the measured time per iteration.

There are two strategies for preventing garbage collection from biasing your results. One is to ensure that garbage collection does not run at all during your test (you can invoke the JVM with `-verbose:gc` to find out); alternatively, you can make sure that the garbage collector runs a number of times during your run so that the test program adequately reflects the cost of ongoing allocation and garbage collection. The latter strategy is often better—it requires a longer test and is more likely to reflect real-world performance.

Most producer-consumer applications involve a fair amount of allocation and garbage collection—producers allocate new objects that are used and discarded by consumers. Running the bounded buffer test for long enough to incur multiple garbage collections yields more accurate results.

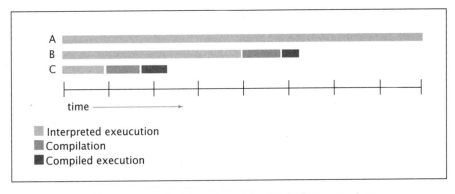

FIGURE 12.5. Results biased by dynamic compilation.

12.3.2 Dynamic compilation

Writing and interpreting performance benchmarks for dynamically compiled languages like Java is far more difficult than for statically compiled languages like C or C++. The HotSpot JVM (and other modern JVMs) uses a combination of bytecode interpretation and dynamic compilation. When a class is first loaded, the JVM executes it by interpreting the bytecode. At some point, if a method is run often enough, the dynamic compiler kicks in and converts it to machine code; when compilation completes, it switches from interpretation to direct execution.

The timing of compilation is unpredictable. Your timing tests should run only after all code has been compiled; there is no value in measuring the speed of the interpreted code since most programs run long enough that all frequently executed code paths are compiled. Allowing the compiler to run during a measured test run can bias test results in two ways: compilation consumes CPU resources, and measuring the run time of a combination of interpreted and compiled code is not a meaningful performance metric. Figure 12.5 shows how this can bias your results. The three timelines represent the execution of the same number of iterations: timeline *A* represents all interpreted execution, *B* represents compilation halfway through the run, and *C* represents compilation early in the run. The point at which compilation runs seriously affects the measured per-operation runtime.[7]

Code may also be decompiled (reverting to interpreted execution) and recompiled for various reasons, such as loading a class that invalidates assumptions made by prior compilations, or gathering sufficient profiling data to decide that a code path should be recompiled with different optimizations.

One way to to prevent compilation from biasing your results is to run your program for a long time (at least several minutes) so that compilation and interpreted execution represent a small fraction of the total run time. Another approach is to use an unmeasured "warm-up" run, in which your code is executed enough to be fully compiled when you actually start timing. On HotSpot, running your program with -XX:+PrintCompilation prints out a message when

---

7. The JVM may choose to perform compilation in the application thread or in the background thread; each can bias timing results in different ways.

dynamic compilation runs, so you can verify that this is prior to, rather than during, measured test runs.

Running the same test several times in the same JVM instance can be used to validate the testing methodology. The first group of results should be discarded as warm-up; seeing inconsistent results in the remaining groups suggests that the test should be examined further to determine why the timing results are not repeatable.

The JVM uses various background threads for housekeeping tasks. When measuring multiple *unrelated* computationally intensive activities in a single run, it is a good idea to place explicit pauses between the measured trials to give the JVM a chance to catch up with background tasks with minimal interference from measured tasks. (When measuring multiple related activities, however, such as multiple runs of the same test, excluding JVM background tasks in this way may give unrealistically optimistic results.)

12.3.3 Unrealistic sampling of code paths

Runtime compilers use profiling information to help optimize the code being compiled. The JVM is permitted to use information specific to the execution in order to produce better code, which means that compiling method M in one program may generate different code than compiling M in another. In some cases, the JVM may make optimizations based on assumptions that may only be true temporarily, and later back them out by invalidating the compiled code if they become untrue.[8]

As a result, it is important that your test programs not only adequately approximate the usage patterns of a typical application, but also approximate the set of code paths used by such an application. Otherwise, a dynamic compiler could make special optimizations to a purely single-threaded test program that could not be applied in real applications containing at least occasional parallelism. Therefore, tests of multithreaded performance should normally be mixed with tests of single-threaded performance, even if you want to measure only single-threaded performance. (This issue does not arise in TimedPutTakeTest because even the smallest test case uses two threads.)

12.3.4 Unrealistic degrees of contention

Concurrent applications tend to interleave two very different sorts of work: accessing shared data, such as fetching the next task from a shared work queue, and thread-local computation (executing the task, assuming the task itself does not access shared data). Depending on the relative proportions of the two types of work, the application will experience different levels of contention and exhibit different performance and scaling behaviors.

If N threads are fetching tasks from a shared work queue and executing them, and the tasks are compute-intensive and long-running (and do not access shared

---

8. For example, the JVM can use *monomorphic call transformation* to convert a virtual method call to a direct method call if no classes currently loaded override that method, but it invalidates the compiled code if a class is subsequently loaded that overrides the method.

data very much), there will be almost no contention; throughput is dominated by the availability of CPU resources. On the other hand, if the tasks are very short-lived, there will be a lot of contention for the work queue and throughput is dominated by the cost of synchronization.

To obtain realistic results, concurrent performance tests should try to approximate the thread-local computation done by a typical application in addition to the concurrent coordination under study. If the the work done for each task in an application is significantly different in nature or scope from the test program, it is easy to arrive at unwarranted conclusions about where the performance bottlenecks lie. We saw in Section 11.5 that, for lock-based classes such as the synchronized `Map` implementations, whether access to the lock is mostly contended or mostly uncontended can have a dramatic effect on throughput. The tests in that section do nothing but pound on the `Map`; even with two threads, all attempts to access the `Map` are contended. However, if an application did a significant amount of thread-local computation for each time it accesses the shared data structure, the contention level might be low enough to offer good performance.

In this regard, `TimedPutTakeTest` may be a poor model for some applications. Since the worker threads do not do very much, throughput is dominated by coordination overhead, and this is not necessarily the case in all applications that exchange data between producers and consumers via bounded buffers.

12.3.5 Dead code elimination

One of the challenges of writing good benchmarks (in any language) is that optimizing compilers are adept at spotting and eliminating dead code—code that has no effect on the outcome. Since benchmarks often don't compute anything, they are an easy target for the optimizer. Most of the time, it is a good thing when the optimizer prunes dead code from a program, but for a benchmark this is a big problem because then you are measuring less execution than you think. If you're lucky, the optimizer will prune away your *entire* program, and then it will be obvious that your data is bogus. If you're unlucky, dead-code elimination will just speed up your program by some factor that *could* be explained by other means.

Dead-code elimination is a problem in benchmarking statically compiled languages too, but detecting that the compiler has eliminated a good chunk of your benchmark is a lot easier because you can look at the machine code and see that a part of your program is missing. With dynamically compiled languages, that information is not easily accessible.

Many microbenchmarks perform much "better" when run with HotSpot's `-server` compiler than with `-client`, not just because the server compiler can produce more efficient code, but also because it is more adept at optimizing dead code. Unfortunately, the dead-code elimination that made such short work of your benchmark won't do quite as well with code that actually does something. But you should still prefer `-server` to `-client` for both production and testing on multiprocessor systems—you just have to write your tests so that they are not susceptible to dead-code elimination.

Writing effective performance tests requires tricking the optimizer into not optimizing away your benchmark as dead code. This requires every computed result to be used somehow by your program—in a way that does not require synchronization or substantial computation.

In PutTakeTest, we compute the checksum of elements added to and removed from the queue and combine these checksums across all the threads, but this could still be optimized away if we do not actually *use* the checksum value. We happen to need it to verify the correctness of the algorithm, but you can ensure that a value is used by printing it out. However, you should avoid doing I/O while the test is actually running, so as not to distort the run time measurement.

A cheap trick for preventing a calculation from being optimized away without introducing too much overhead is to compute the hashCode of the field of some derived object, compare it to an arbitrary value such as the current value of System.nanoTime, and print a useless and ignorable message if they happen to match:

```
if (foo.x.hashCode() == System.nanoTime())
    System.out.print(" ");
```

The comparison will rarely succeed, and if it does, its only effect will be to insert a harmless space character into the output. (The print method buffers output until println is called, so in the rare case that hashCode and System.nanoTime are equal no I/O is actually performed.)

Not only should every computed result be used, but results should also be unguessable. Otherwise, a smart dynamic optimizing compiler is allowed to replace actions with precomputed results. We addressed this in the construction of PutTakeTest, but any test program whose input is static data is vulnerable to this optimization.

12.4 Complementary testing approaches

While we'd like to believe that an effective testing program should "find all the bugs", this is an unrealistic goal. NASA devotes more of its engineering resources to testing (it is estimated they employ 20 testers for each developer) than any commercial entity could afford to—and the code produced is still not free of defects. In complex programs, no amount of testing can find all coding errors.

The goal of testing is not so much to *find errors* as it is to *increase confidence* that the code works as expected. Since it is unrealistic to assume you can find all the bugs, the goal of a quality assurance (QA) plan should be to achieve the greatest possible confidence given the testing resources available. More things can go wrong in a concurrent program than in a sequential one, and therefore more testing is required to achieve the same level of confidence. So far we've focused primarily on techniques for constructing effective unit and performance tests. Testing is critically important for building confidence that concurrent classes behave correctly, but should be only one of the QA methologies you employ.

Different QA methodologies are more effective at finding some types of defects and less effective at finding others. By employing complementary testing methodologies such as code review and static analysis, you can achieve greater confidence than you could with any single approach.

12.4.1 Code review

As effective and important as unit and stress tests are for finding concurrency bugs, they are no substitute for rigorous code review by multiple people. (On the other hand, code review is no substitute for testing either.) You can and should design tests to maximize their chances of discovering safety errors, and you should run them frequently, but you should not neglect to have concurrent code reviewed carefully by someone besides its author. Even concurrency experts make mistakes; taking the time to have someone else review the code is almost always worthwhile. Expert concurrent programmers are better at finding subtle races than are most test programs. (Also, platform issues such as JVM implementation details or processor memory models can prevent bugs from showing up on particular hardware or software configurations.) Code review also has other benefits; not only can it find errors, but it often improves the quality of comments describing the implementation details, thus reducing future maintenence cost and risk.

12.4.2 Static analysis tools

As of this writing, *static analysis tools* are rapidly emerging as an effective complement to formal testing and code review. Static code analysis is the process of analyzing code without executing it, and code auditing tools can analyze classes to look for instances of common *bug patterns*. Static analysis tools such as the open-source FindBugs[9] contain *bug-pattern detectors* for many common coding errors, many of which can easily be missed by testing or code review.

Static analysis tools produce a list of warnings that must be examined by hand to determine whether they represent actual errors. Historically, tools like `lint` produced so many false warnings as to scare developers away, but tools like FindBugs have been tuned to produce many fewer false alarms. Static analysis tools are still somewhat primitive (especially in their integration with development tools and lifecycle), but they are already effective enough to be a valuable addition to the testing process.

As of this writing, FindBugs includes detectors for the following concurrency-related bug patterns, and more are being added all the time:

Inconsistent synchronization. Many objects follow the synchronization policy of guarding all variables with the object's intrinsic lock. If a field is accessed frequently but not always with the `this` lock held, this may indicate that the synchronization policy is not being consistently followed.

Analysis tools must guess at the synchronization policy because Java classes do not have formal concurrency specifications. In the future, if annotations

---
9. `http://findbugs.sourceforge.net`

such as @GuardedBy are standardized, auditing tools could interpret annotations rather than having to guess at the relationship between variables and locks, thus improving the quality of analysis.

Invoking Thread.run. Thread implements Runnable and therefore has a run method. However, it is almost always a mistake to call Thread.run directly; usually the programmer meant to call Thread.start.

Unreleased lock. Unlike intrinsic locks, explicit locks (see Chapter 13) are not automatically released when control exits the scope in which they were acquired. The standard idiom is to release the lock from a finally block; otherwise the lock can remain unreleased in the event of an Exception.

Empty synchronized block. While empty synchronized blocks do have semantics under the Java Memory Model, they are frequently used incorrectly, and there are usually better solutions to whatever problem the developer was trying to solve.

Double-checked locking. Double-checked locking is a broken idiom for reducing synchronization overhead in lazy initialization (see Section 16.2.4) that involves reading a shared mutable field without appropriate synchronization.

Starting a thread from a constructor. Starting a thread from a constructor introduces the risk of subclassing problems, and can allow the this reference to escape the constructor.

Notification errors. The notify and notifyAll methods indicate that an object's state may have changed in a way that would unblock threads that are waiting on the associated condition queue. These methods should be called only when the state associated with the condition queue has changed. A synchronized block that calls notify or notifyAll but does not modify any state is likely to be an error. (See Chapter 14.)

Condition wait errors. When waiting on a condition queue, Object.wait or Condition.await should be called in a loop, with the appropriate lock held, after testing some state predicate (see Chapter 14). Calling Object.wait or Condition.await without the lock held, not in a loop, or without testing some state predicate is almost certainly an error.

Misuse of Lock and Condition. Using a Lock as the lock argument for a synchronized block is likely to be a typo, as is calling Condition.wait instead of await (though the latter would likely be caught in testing, since it would throw an IllegalMonitorStateException the first time it was called).

Sleeping or waiting while holding a lock. Calling Thread.sleep with a lock held can prevent other threads from making progress for a long time and is therefore a potentially serious liveness hazard. Calling Object.wait or Condition.await with two locks held poses a similar hazard.

Spin loops. Code that does nothing but spin (busy wait) checking a field for an expected value can waste CPU time and, if the field is not volatile, is not guaranteed to terminate. Latches or condition waits are often a better technique when waiting for a state transition to occur.

12.4.3 Aspect-oriented testing techniques

As of this writing, aspect-oriented programming (AOP) techniques have only limited applicability to concurrency, because most popular AOP tools do not yet support pointcuts at synchronization points. However, AOP can be applied to assert invariants or some aspects of compliance with synchronization policies. For example, (Laddad, 2003) provides an example of using an aspect to wrap all calls to non-thread-safe Swing methods with the assertion that the call is occurring in the event thread. As it requires no code changes, this technique is easy to apply and can disclose subtle publication and thread-confinement errors.

12.4.4 Profilers and monitoring tools

Most commercial profiling tools have some support for threads. They vary in feature set and effectiveness, but can often provide insight into what your program is doing (although profiling tools are usually intrusive and can substantially affect program timing and behavior). Most offer a display showing a timeline for each thread with different colors for the various thread states (runnable, blocked waiting for a lock, blocked waiting for I/O, etc.). Such a display can show how effectively your program is utilizing the available CPU resources, and if it is doing badly, where to look for the cause. (Many profilers also claim features for identifying which locks are causing contention, but in practice these features are often a blunter instrument than is desired for analyzing a program's locking behavior.)

The built-in JMX agent also offers some limited features for monitoring thread behavior. The `ThreadInfo` class includes the thread's current state and, if the thread is blocked, the lock or condition queue on which it is blocked. If the "thread contention monitoring" feature is enabled (it is disabled by default because of its performance impact), `ThreadInfo` also includes the number of times that the thread has blocked waiting for a lock or notification, and the cumulative amount of time it has spent waiting.

Summary

Testing concurrent programs for correctness can be extremely challenging because many of the possible failure modes of concurrent programs are low-probability events that are sensitive to timing, load, and other hard-to-reproduce conditions. Further, the testing infrastructure can introduce additional synchronization or timing constraints that can mask concurrency problems in the code being tested. Testing concurrent programs for performance can be equally challenging; Java programs are more difficult to test than programs written in statically compiled languages like C, because timing measurements can be affected by dynamic compilation, garbage collection, and adaptive optimization.

To have the best chance of finding latent bugs before they occur in production, combine traditional testing techniques (being careful to avoid the pitfalls discussed here) with code reviews and automated analysis tools. Each of these techniques finds problems that the others are likely to miss.

PART IV

Advanced Topics

CHAPTER 13

Explicit Locks

Before Java 5.0, the only mechanisms for coordinating access to shared data were synchronized and volatile. Java 5.0 adds another option: ReentrantLock. Contrary to what some have written, ReentrantLock is not a replacement for intrinsic locking, but rather an alternative with advanced features for when intrinsic locking proves too limited.

13.1 Lock and ReentrantLock

The Lock interface, shown in Listing 13.1, defines a number of abstract locking operations. Unlike intrinsic locking, Lock offers a choice of unconditional, polled, timed, and interruptible lock acquisition, and all lock and unlock operations are explicit. Lock implementations must provide the same memory-visibility semantics as intrinsic locks, but can differ in their locking semantics, scheduling algorithms, ordering guarantees, and performance characteristics. (Lock.newCondition is covered in Chapter 14.)

```
public interface Lock {
    void lock();
    void lockInterruptibly() throws InterruptedException;
    boolean tryLock();
    boolean tryLock(long timeout, TimeUnit unit)
        throws InterruptedException;
    void unlock();
    Condition newCondition();
}
```

LISTING 13.1. Lock interface.

ReentrantLock implements Lock, providing the same mutual exclusion and memory-visibility guarantees as synchronized. Acquiring a ReentrantLock has the same memory semantics as entering a synchronized block, and releasing a ReentrantLock has the same memory semantics as exiting a synchronized block.

(Memory visibility is covered in Section 3.1 and in Chapter 16.) And, like synchronized, ReentrantLock offers reentrant locking semantics (see Section 2.3.2). ReentrantLock supports all of the lock-acquisition modes defined by Lock, providing more flexibility for dealing with lock unavailability than does synchronized.

Why create a new locking mechanism that is so similar to intrinsic locking? Intrinsic locking works fine in most situations but has some functional limitations—it is not possible to interrupt a thread waiting to acquire a lock, or to attempt to acquire a lock without being willing to wait for it forever. Intrinsic locks also must be released in the same block of code in which they are acquired; this simplifies coding and interacts nicely with exception handling, but makes non-block-structured locking disciplines impossible. None of these are reasons to abandon synchronized, but in some cases a more flexible locking mechanism offers better liveness or performance.

Listing 13.2 shows the canonical form for using a Lock. This idiom is somewhat more complicated than using intrinsic locks: the lock *must* be released in a finally block. Otherwise, the lock would never be released if the guarded code were to throw an exception. When using locking, you must also consider what happens if an exception is thrown out of the try block; if it is possible for the object to be left in an inconsistent state, additional try-catch or try-finally blocks may be needed. (You should always consider the effect of exceptions when using any form of locking, including intrinsic locking.)

Failing to use finally to release a Lock is a ticking time bomb. When it goes off, you will have a hard time tracking down its origin as there will be no record of where or when the Lock should have been released. This is one reason not to use ReentrantLock as a blanket substitute for synchronized: it is more "dangerous" because it doesn't automatically clean up the lock when control leaves the guarded block. While remembering to release the lock from a finally block is not all that difficult, it is also not impossible to forget.[1]

```
Lock lock = new ReentrantLock();
...
lock.lock();
try {
    // update object state
    // catch exceptions and restore invariants if necessary
} finally {
    lock.unlock();
}
```

LISTING 13.2. Guarding object state using ReentrantLock.

---

1. FindBugs has an "unreleased lock" detector identifying when a Lock is not released in all code paths out of the block in which it was acquired.

13.1.1 Polled and timed lock acquisition

The timed and polled lock-acqusition modes provided by tryLock allow more sophisticated error recovery than unconditional acquisition. With intrinsic locks, a deadlock is fatal—the only way to recover is to restart the application, and the only defense is to construct your program so that inconsistent lock ordering is impossible. Timed and polled locking offer another option: probabalistic deadlock avoidance.

Using timed or polled lock acquisition (tryLock) lets you regain control if you cannot acquire all the required locks, release the ones you did acquire, and try again (or at least log the failure and do something else). Listing 13.3 shows an alternate way of addressing the dynamic ordering deadlock from Section 10.1.2: use tryLock to attempt to acquire both locks, but back off and retry if they cannot both be acquired. The sleep time has a fixed component and a random component to reduce the likelihood of livelock. If the locks cannot be acquired within the specified time, transferMoney returns a failure status so that the operation can fail gracefully. (See [CPJ 2.5.1.2] and [CPJ 2.5.1.3] for more examples of using polled locks for deadlock avoidance.)

Timed locks are also useful in implementing activities that manage a time budget (see Section 6.3.7). When an activity with a time budget calls a blocking method, it can supply a timeout corresponding to the remaining time in the budget. This lets activities terminate early if they cannot deliver a result within the desired time. With intrinsic locks, there is no way to cancel a lock acquisition once it is started, so intrinsic locks put the ability to implement time-budgeted activities at risk.

The travel portal example in Listing 6.17 on page 134 creates a separate task for each car-rental company from which it was soliciting bids. Soliciting a bid probably involves some sort of network-based request mechanism, such as a web service request. But soliciting a bid might also require exclusive access to a scarce resource, such as a direct communications line to the company.

We saw one way to ensure serialized access to a resource in Section 9.5: a single-threaded executor. Another approach is to use an exclusive lock to guard access to the resource. The code in Listing 13.4 tries to send a message on a shared communications line guarded by a Lock, but fails gracefully if it cannot do so within its time budget. The timed tryLock makes it practical to incorporate exclusive locking into such a time-limited activity.

13.1.2 Interruptible lock acquisition

Just as timed lock acquisition allows exclusive locking to be used within time-limited activities, interruptible lock acquisition allows locking to be used within cancellable activities. Section 7.1.6 identified several mechanisms, such as acquiring an intrinsic lock, that are not responsive to interruption. These non-interruptible blocking mechanisms complicate the implementation of cancellable tasks. The lockInterruptibly method allows you to try to acquire a lock while remaining responsive to interruption, and its inclusion in Lock avoids creating another category of non-interruptible blocking mechanisms.

```
public boolean transferMoney(Account fromAcct,
                             Account toAcct,
                             DollarAmount amount,
                             long timeout,
                             TimeUnit unit)
        throws InsufficientFundsException, InterruptedException {
    long fixedDelay = getFixedDelayComponentNanos(timeout, unit);
    long randMod = getRandomDelayModulusNanos(timeout, unit);
    long stopTime = System.nanoTime() + unit.toNanos(timeout);

    while (true) {
        if (fromAcct.lock.tryLock()) {
            try {
                if (toAcct.lock.tryLock()) {
                    try {
                        if (fromAcct.getBalance().compareTo(amount)
                                < 0)
                            throw new InsufficientFundsException();
                        else {
                            fromAcct.debit(amount);
                            toAcct.credit(amount);
                            return true;
                        }
                    } finally {
                        toAcct.lock.unlock();
                    }
                }
            } finally {
                fromAcct.lock.unlock();
            }
        }
        if (System.nanoTime() > stopTime)
            return false;
        NANOSECONDS.sleep(fixedDelay + rnd.nextLong() % randMod);
    }
}
```

LISTING 13.3. Avoiding lock-ordering deadlock using tryLock.

```
public boolean trySendOnSharedLine(String message,
                                    long timeout, TimeUnit unit)
                                    throws InterruptedException {
    long nanosToLock = unit.toNanos(timeout)
                        - estimatedNanosToSend(message);
    if (!lock.tryLock(nanosToLock, NANOSECONDS))
        return false;
    try {
        return sendOnSharedLine(message);
    } finally {
        lock.unlock();
    }
}
```

LISTING 13.4. *Locking with a time budget.*

The canonical structure of interruptible lock acquisition is slightly more complicated than normal lock acquisition, as two `try` blocks are needed. (If the interruptible lock acquisition can throw `InterruptedException`, the standard `try-finally` locking idiom works.) Listing 13.5 uses `lockInterruptibly` to implement `sendOnSharedLine` from Listing 13.4 so that we can call it from a cancellable task. The timed `tryLock` is also responsive to interruption and so can be used when you need both timed and interruptible lock acquisition.

```
public boolean sendOnSharedLine(String message)
        throws InterruptedException {
    lock.lockInterruptibly();
    try {
        return cancellableSendOnSharedLine(message);
    } finally {
        lock.unlock();
    }
}

private boolean cancellableSendOnSharedLine(String message)
    throws InterruptedException { ... }
```

LISTING 13.5. *Interruptible lock acquisition.*

13.1.3 Non-block-structured locking

With intrinsic locks, acquire-release pairs are block-structured—a lock is always released in the same basic block in which it was acquired, regardless of how control exits the block. Automatic lock release simplifies analysis and prevents potential coding errors, but sometimes a more flexible locking discipline is needed.

In Chapter 11, we saw how reducing lock granularity can enhance scalability. Lock striping allows different hash chains in a hash-based collection to use different locks. We can apply a similar principle to reduce locking granularity in a linked list by using a separate lock for *each link node*, allowing different threads to operate independently on different portions of the list. The lock for a given node guards the link pointers and the data stored in that node, so when traversing or modifying the list we must hold the lock on one node until we acquire the lock on the next node; only then can we release the lock on the first node. An example of this technique, called *hand-over-hand locking* or *lock coupling*, appears in [CPJ 2.5.1.4].

13.2   Performance considerations

When ReentrantLock was added in Java 5.0, it offered far better contended performance than intrinsic locking. For synchronization primitives, contended performance is the key to scalability: if more resources are expended on lock management and scheduling, fewer are available for the application. A better lock implementation makes fewer system calls, forces fewer context switches, and initiates less memory-synchronization traffic on the shared memory bus, operations that are time-consuming and divert computing resources from the program.

Java 6 uses an improved algorithm for managing intrinsic locks, similar to that used by ReentrantLock, that closes the scalability gap considerably. Figure 13.1 shows the performance difference between intrinsic locks and ReentrantLock on Java 5.0 and on a prerelease build of Java 6 on a four-way Opteron system running Solaris. The curves represent the "speedup" of ReentrantLock over intrinsic locking on a single JVM version. On Java 5.0, ReentrantLock offers considerably better throughput, but on Java 6, the two are quite close.[2] The test program is the same one used in Section 11.5, this time comparing the throughput of a HashMap guarded by an intrinsic lock and by a ReentrantLock.

On Java 5.0, the performance of intrinsic locking drops dramatically in going from one thread (no contention) to more than one thread; the performance of ReentrantLock drops far less, showing its better scalability. But on Java 6, it is a different story—intrinsic locks no longer fall apart under contention, and the two scale fairly similarly.

Graphs like Figure 13.1 remind us that statements of the form "X is faster than Y" are at best short-lived. Performance and scalability are sensitive to platform factors such as CPU, processor count, cache size, and JVM characteristics, all of which can change over time.[3]

---

2. Though this particular graph doesn't show it, the scalability difference between Java 5.0 and Java 6 really does come from improvement in intrinsic locking, rather than from regression in Reentrant-Lock.

3. When we started this book, ReentrantLock seemed the last word in lock scalability. Less than a year later, intrinsic locking gives it a good run for its money. Performance is not just a moving target, it can be a fast-moving target.

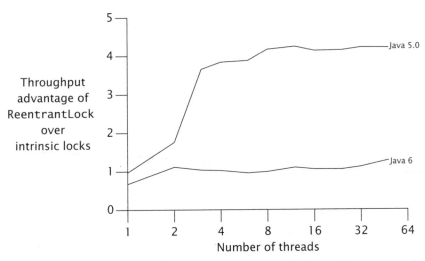

FIGURE 13.1. Intrinsic locking versus `ReentrantLock` performance on Java 5.0 and Java 6.

Performance is a moving target; yesterday's benchmark showing that *X* is faster than *Y* may already be out of date today.

13.3 Fairness

The `ReentrantLock` constructor offers a choice of two *fairness* options: create a *nonfair* lock (the default) or a *fair* lock. Threads acquire a fair lock in the order in which they requested it, whereas a nonfair lock permits *barging*: threads requesting a lock can jump ahead of the queue of waiting threads if the lock happens to be available when it is requested. (`Semaphore` also offers the choice of fair or nonfair acquisition ordering.) Nonfair `ReentrantLocks` do not go out of their way to promote barging—they simply don't prevent a thread from barging if it shows up at the right time. With a fair lock, a newly requesting thread is queued if the lock is held by another thread or if threads are queued waiting for the lock; with a nonfair lock, the thread is queued only if the lock is currently held.[4]

Wouldn't we want all locks to be fair? After all, fairness is good and unfairness is bad, right? (Just ask your kids.) When it comes to locking, though, fairness has a significant performance cost because of the overhead of suspending and resuming threads. In practice, a statistical fairness guarantee—promising that a blocked thread will *eventually* acquire the lock—is often good enough, and is far less expensive to deliver. Some algorithms rely on fair queueing to ensure their

---

4. The polled `tryLock` always barges, even for fair locks.

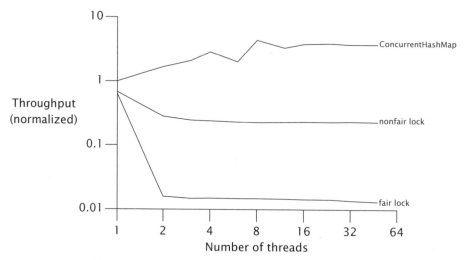

FIGURE 13.2. Fair versus nonfair lock performance.

correctness, but these are unusual. In most cases, the performance benefits of nonfair locks outweigh the benefits of fair queueing.

Figure 13.2 shows another run of the Map performance test, this time comparing HashMap wrapped with fair and nonfair ReentrantLocks on a four-way Opteron system running Solaris, plotted on a log scale.[5] The fairness penalty is nearly two orders of magnitude. *Don't pay for fairness if you don't need it.*

One reason barging locks perform so much better than fair locks under heavy contention is that there can be a significant delay between when a suspended thread is resumed and when it actually runs. Let's say thread *A* holds a lock and thread *B* asks for that lock. Since the lock is busy, *B* is suspended. When *A* releases the lock, *B* is resumed so it can try again. In the meantime, though, if thread *C* requests the lock, there is a good chance that *C* can acquire the lock, use it, and release it before *B* even finishes waking up. In this case, everyone wins: *B* gets the lock no later than it otherwise would have, *C* gets it much earlier, and throughput is improved.

Fair locks tend to work best when they are held for a relatively long time or when the mean time between lock requests is relatively long. In these cases, the condition under which barging provides a throughput advantage—when the lock is unheld but a thread is currently waking up to claim it—is less likely to hold.

---

5. The graph for ConcurrentHashMap is fairly wiggly in the region between four and eight threads. These variations almost certainly come from measurement noise, which could be introduced by coincidental interactions with the hash codes of the elements, thread scheduling, map resizing, garbage collection or other memory-system effects, or by the OS deciding to run some periodic housekeeping task around the time that test case ran. The reality is that there are all sorts of variations in performance tests that usually aren't worth bothering to control. We made no attempt to clean up our graphs artificially, because real-world performance measurements are also full of noise.

Like the default `ReentrantLock`, intrinsic locking offers no deterministic fairness guarantees, but the statistical fairness guarantees of most locking implementations are good enough for almost all situations. The language specification does not require the JVM to implement intrinsic locks fairly, and no production JVMs do. `ReentrantLock` does not depress lock fairness to new lows—it only makes explicit something that was present all along.

13.4 Choosing between `synchronized` and `ReentrantLock`

`ReentrantLock` provides the same locking and memory semantics as intrinsic locking, as well as additional features such as timed lock waits, interruptible lock waits, fairness, and the ability to implement non-block-structured locking. The performance of `ReentrantLock` appears to dominate that of intrinsic locking, winning slightly on Java 6 and dramatically on Java 5.0. So why not deprecate `synchronized` and encourage all new concurrent code to use `ReentrantLock`? Some authors have in fact suggested this, treating `synchronized` as a "legacy" construct. But this is taking a good thing *way* too far.

Intrinsic locks still have significant advantages over explicit locks. The notation is familiar and compact, and many existing programs already use intrinsic locking—and mixing the two could be confusing and error-prone. `ReentrantLock` is definitely a more dangerous tool than synchronization; if you forget to wrap the `unlock` call in a `finally` block, your code will probably appear to run properly, but you've created a time bomb that may well hurt innocent bystanders. Save `ReentrantLock` for situations in which you need something `ReentrantLock` provides that intrinsic locking doesn't.

> `ReentrantLock` is an advanced tool for situations where intrinsic locking is not practical. Use it if you need its advanced features: timed, polled, or interruptible lock acquisition, fair queueing, or non-block-structured locking. Otherwise, prefer `synchronized`.

Under Java 5.0, intrinsic locking has another advantage over `ReentrantLock`: thread dumps show which call frames acquired which locks and can detect and identify deadlocked threads. The JVM knows nothing about which threads hold `ReentrantLock`s and therefore cannot help in debugging threading problems using `ReentrantLock`. This disparity is addressed in Java 6 by providing a management and monitoring interface with which locks can register, enabling locking information for `ReentrantLock`s to appear in thread dumps and through other management and debugging interfaces. The availability of this information for debugging is a substantial, if mostly temporary, advantage for `synchronized`; locking information in thread dumps has saved many programmers from utter consternation. The non-block-structured nature of `ReentrantLock` still means that lock acquisitions cannot be tied to specific stack frames, as they can with intrinsic locks.

Future performance improvements are likely to favor synchronized over ReentrantLock. Because synchronized is built into the JVM, it can perform optimizations such as lock elision for thread-confined lock objects and lock coarsening to eliminate synchronization with intrinsic locks (see Section 11.3.2); doing this with library-based locks seems far less likely. Unless you are deploying on Java 5.0 for the foreseeable future and you have a *demonstrated* need for ReentrantLock's scalability benefits on that platform, it is not a good idea to choose ReentrantLock over synchronized for performance reasons.

13.5 Read-write locks

ReentrantLock implements a standard mutual-exclusion lock: at most one thread at a time can hold a ReentrantLock. But mutual exclusion is frequently a stronger locking discipline than needed to preserve data integrity, and thus limits concurrency more than necessary. Mutual exclusion is a conservative locking strategy that prevents writer/writer and writer/reader overlap, but also prevents reader/reader overlap. In many cases, data structures are "read-mostly"—they are mutable and are sometimes modified, but most accesses involve only reading. In these cases, it would be nice to relax the locking requirements to allow multiple readers to access the data structure at once. As long as each thread is guaranteed an up-to-date view of the data and no other thread modifies the data while the readers are viewing it, there will be no problems. This is what read-write locks allow: a resource can be accessed by multiple readers or a single writer at a time, but not both.

ReadWriteLock, shown in Listing 13.6, exposes two Lock objects—one for reading and one for writing. To read data guarded by a ReadWriteLock you must first acquire the read lock, and to modify data guarded by a ReadWriteLock you must first acquire the write lock. While there may appear to be two separate locks, the read lock and write lock are simply different views of an integrated read-write lock object.

```
public interface ReadWriteLock {
    Lock readLock();
    Lock writeLock();
}
```

LISTING 13.6. ReadWriteLock interface.

The locking strategy implemented by read-write locks allows multiple simultaneous readers but only a single writer. Like Lock, ReadWriteLock admits multiple implementations that can vary in performance, scheduling guarantees, acquisition preference, fairness, or locking semantics.

Read-write locks are a performance optimization designed to allow greater concurrency in certain situations. In practice, read-write locks can improve performance for frequently accessed read-mostly data structures on multiprocessor systems; under other conditions they perform slightly worse than exclusive locks due to their greater complexity. Whether they are an improvement in any given situation is best determined via profiling; because ReadWriteLock uses Lock for the read and write portions of the lock, it is relatively easy to swap out a read-write lock for an exclusive one if profiling determines that a read-write lock is not a win.

The interaction between the read and write locks allows for a number of possible implementations. Some of the implementation options for a ReadWriteLock are:

Release preference. When a writer releases the write lock and both readers and writers are queued up, who should be given preference—readers, writers, or whoever asked first?

Reader barging. If the lock is held by readers but there are waiting writers, should newly arriving readers be granted immediate access, or should they wait behind the writers? Allowing readers to barge ahead of writers enhances concurrency but runs the risk of starving writers.

Reentrancy. Are the read and write locks reentrant?

Downgrading. If a thread holds the write lock, can it acquire the read lock without releasing the write lock? This would let a writer "downgrade" to a read lock without letting other writers modify the guarded resource in the meantime.

Upgrading. Can a read lock be upgraded to a write lock in preference to other waiting readers or writers? Most read-write lock implementations do not support upgrading, because without an explicit upgrade operation it is deadlock-prone. (If two readers simultaneously attempt to upgrade to a write lock, neither will release the read lock.)

ReentrantReadWriteLock provides reentrant locking semantics for both locks. Like ReentrantLock, a ReentrantReadWriteLock can be constructed as nonfair (the default) or fair. With a fair lock, preference is given to the thread that has been waiting the longest; if the lock is held by readers and a thread requests the write lock, no more readers are allowed to acquire the read lock until the writer has been serviced and releases the write lock. With a nonfair lock, the order in which threads are granted access is unspecified. Downgrading from writer to reader is permitted; upgrading from reader to writer is not (attempting to do so results in deadlock).

Like ReentrantLock, the write lock in ReentrantReadWriteLock has a unique owner and can be released only by the thread that acquired it. In Java 5.0, the read lock behaves more like a Semaphore than a lock, maintaining only the count of active readers, not their identities. This behavior was changed in Java 6 to keep track also of which threads have been granted the read lock.[6]

---

6. One reason for this change is that under Java 5.0, the lock implementation cannot distinguish between a thread requesting the read lock for the first time and a reentrant lock request, which would make fair read-write locks deadlock-prone.

Read-write locks can improve concurrency when locks are typically held for a moderately long time and most operations do not modify the guarded resources. ReadWriteMap in Listing 13.7 uses a ReentrantReadWriteLock to wrap a Map so that it can be shared safely by multiple readers and still prevent reader-writer or writer-writer conflicts.[7] In reality, ConcurrentHashMap's performance is so good that you would probably use it rather than this approach if all you needed was a concurrent hash-based map, but this technique would be useful if you want to provide more concurrent access to an alternate Map implementation such as LinkedHashMap.

```
public class ReadWriteMap<K,V> {
    private final Map<K,V> map;
    private final ReadWriteLock lock = new ReentrantReadWriteLock();
    private final Lock r = lock.readLock();
    private final Lock w = lock.writeLock();

    public ReadWriteMap(Map<K,V> map) {
        this.map = map;
    }

    public V put(K key, V value) {
        w.lock();
        try {
            return map.put(key, value);
        } finally {
            w.unlock();
        }
    }
    // Do the same for remove(), putAll(), clear()

    public V get(Object key) {
        r.lock();
        try {
            return map.get(key);
        } finally {
            r.unlock();
        }
    }
    // Do the same for other read-only Map methods
}
```

LISTING 13.7. Wrapping a Map with a read-write lock.

Figure 13.3 shows a throughput comparison between an ArrayList wrapped

7. ReadWriteMap does not implement Map because implementing the view methods such as entrySet and values would be difficult and the "easy" methods are usually sufficient.

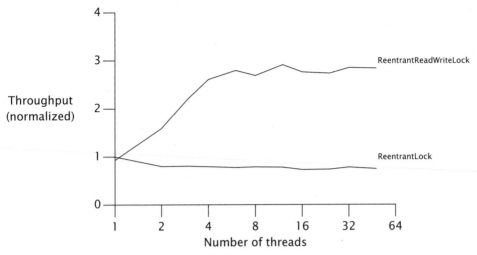

FIGURE 13.3. Read-write lock performance.

with a `ReentrantLock` and with a `ReadWriteLock` on a four-way Opteron system running Solaris. The test program used here is similar to the `Map` performance test we've been using throughout the book—each operation randomly selects a value and searches for it in the collection, and a small percentange of operations modify the contents of the collection.

Summary

Explicit `Lock`s offer an extended feature set compared to intrinsic locking, including greater flexibility in dealing with lock unavailability and greater control over queueing behavior. But `ReentrantLock` is not a blanket substitute for `synchronized`; use it only when you need features that `synchronized` lacks.

Read-write locks allow multiple readers to access a guarded object concurrently, offering the potential for improved scalability when accessing read-mostly data structures.

CHAPTER 14

Building Custom Synchronizers

The class libraries include a number of *state-dependent* classes—those having operations with *state-based preconditions*—such as FutureTask, Semaphore, and BlockingQueue. For example, you cannot remove an item from an empty queue or retrieve the result of a task that has not yet finished; before these operations can proceed, you must wait until the queue enters the "nonempty" state or the task enters the "completed" state.

The easiest way to construct a state-dependent class is usually to build on top of an existing state-dependent library class; we did this in ValueLatch on page 187, using a CountDownLatch to provide the required blocking behavior. But if the library classes do not provide the functionality you need, you can also build your own synchronizers using the low-level mechanisms provided by the language and libraries, including intrinsic *condition queues*, explicit Condition objects, and the AbstractQueuedSynchronizer framework. This chapter explores the various options for implementing state dependence and the rules for using the state dependence mechanisms provided by the platform.

14.1 Managing state dependence

In a single-threaded program, if a state-based precondition (like "the connection pool is nonempty") does not hold when a method is called, it will never become true. Therefore, classes in sequential programs can be coded to fail when their preconditions do not hold. But in a concurrent program, state-based conditions can change through the actions of other threads: a pool that was empty a few instructions ago can become nonempty because another thread returned an element. State-dependent methods on concurrent objects can sometimes get away with failing when their preconditions are not met, but there is often a better alternative: wait for the precondition to become true.

State-dependent operations that *block* until the operation can proceed are more convenient and less error-prone than those that simply fail. The built-in condition queue mechanism enables threads to block until an object has entered a state that allows progress and to wake blocked threads when they may be able to make further progress. We cover the details of condition queues in Section 14.2, but to motivate the value of an efficient condition wait mechanism, we first show how state dependence might be (painfully) tackled using polling and sleeping.

A blocking state-dependent action takes the form shown in Listing 14.1. The pattern of locking is somewhat unusual in that the lock is released and reacquired in the middle of the operation. The state variables that make up the precondition must be guarded by the object's lock, so that they can remain constant while the precondition is tested. But if the precondition does not hold, the lock must be released so another thread can modify the object state—otherwise the precondition will never become true. The lock must then be reacquired before testing the precondition again.

```
acquire lock on object state
while (precondition does not hold) {
    release lock
    wait until precondition might hold
    optionally fail if interrupted or timeout expires
    reacquire lock
}
perform action
release lock
```

LISTING 14.1. Structure of blocking state-dependent actions.

Bounded buffers such as `ArrayBlockingQueue` are commonly used in producer-consumer designs. A bounded buffer provides *put* and *take* operations, each of which has preconditions: you cannot take an element from an empty buffer, nor put an element into a full buffer. State dependent operations can deal with precondition failure by throwing an exception or returning an error status (making it the caller's problem), or by blocking until the object transitions to the right state.

We're going to develop several implementations of a bounded buffer that take different approaches to handling precondition failure. Each extends `BaseBoundedBuffer` in Listing 14.2, which implements a classic array-based circular buffer where the buffer state variables (`buf`, `head`, `tail`, and `count`) are guarded by the buffer's intrinsic lock. It provides synchronized `doPut` and `doTake` methods that are used by subclasses to implement the `put` and `take` operations; the underlying state is hidden from the subclasses.

14.1.1 Example: propagating precondition failure to callers

`GrumpyBoundedBuffer` in Listing 14.3 is a crude first attempt at implementing a bounded buffer. The `put` and `take` methods are `synchronized` to ensure exclusive access to the buffer state, since both employ check-then-act logic in accessing the buffer.

While this approach is easy enough to implement, it is annoying to use. Exceptions are supposed to be for exceptional conditions [EJ Item 39]. "Buffer is

```
@ThreadSafe
public abstract class BaseBoundedBuffer<V> {
    @GuardedBy("this") private final V[] buf;
    @GuardedBy("this") private int tail;
    @GuardedBy("this") private int head;
    @GuardedBy("this") private int count;

    protected BaseBoundedBuffer(int capacity) {
        this.buf = (V[]) new Object[capacity];
    }

    protected synchronized final void doPut(V v) {
        buf[tail] = v;
        if (++tail == buf.length)
            tail = 0;
        ++count;
    }

    protected synchronized final V doTake() {
        V v = buf[head];
        buf[head] = null;
        if (++head == buf.length)
            head = 0;
        --count;
        return v;
    }

    public synchronized final boolean isFull() {
        return count == buf.length;
    }

    public synchronized final boolean isEmpty() {
        return count == 0;
    }
}
```

LISTING 14.2. Base class for bounded buffer implementations.

```
@ThreadSafe
public class GrumpyBoundedBuffer<V> extends BaseBoundedBuffer<V> {
    public GrumpyBoundedBuffer(int size) { super(size); }

    public synchronized void put(V v) throws BufferFullException {
        if (isFull())
            throw new BufferFullException();
        doPut(v);
    }

    public synchronized V take() throws BufferEmptyException {
        if (isEmpty())
            throw new BufferEmptyException();
        return doTake();
    }
}
```

LISTING 14.3. *Bounded buffer that balks when preconditions are not met.*

full" is not an exceptional condition for a bounded buffer any more than "red" is an exceptional condition for a traffic signal. The simplification in implementing the buffer (forcing the caller to manage the state dependence) is more than made up for by the substantial complication in using it, since now the caller must be prepared to catch exceptions and possibly retry for every buffer operation.[1] A well-structured call to take is shown in Listing 14.4—not very pretty, especially if put and take are called throughout the program.

```
while (true) {
    try {
        V item = buffer.take();
        // use item
        break;
    } catch (BufferEmptyException e) {
        Thread.sleep(SLEEP_GRANULARITY);
    }
}
```

LISTING 14.4. *Client logic for calling* GrumpyBoundedBuffer.

A variant of this approach is to return an error value when the buffer is in the wrong state. This is a minor improvement in that it doesn't abuse the exception mechanism by throwing an exception that really means "sorry, try again",

---

[1]. Pushing the state dependence back to the caller also makes it nearly impossible to do things like preserve FIFO ordering; by forcing the caller to retry, you lose the information of who arrived first.

but it does not address the fundamental problem: that callers must deal with precondition failures themselves.[2]

The client code in Listing 14.4 is not the only way to implement the retry logic. The caller could retry the take immediately, without sleeping—an approach known as *busy waiting* or *spin waiting*. This could consume quite a lot of CPU time if the buffer state does not change for a while. On the other hand, if the caller decides to sleep so as not to consume so much CPU time, it could easily "oversleep" if the buffer state changes shortly after the call to sleep. So the client code is left with the choice between the poor CPU usage of spinning and the poor responsiveness of sleeping. (Somewhere between busy waiting and sleeping would be calling Thread.yield in each iteration, which is a hint to the scheduler that this would be a reasonable time to let another thread run. If you are waiting for another thread to do something, that something might happen faster if you yield the processor rather than consuming your full scheduling quantum.)

14.1.2 Example: crude blocking by polling and sleeping

SleepyBoundedBuffer in Listing 14.5 attempts to spare callers the inconvenience of implementing the retry logic on each call by encapsulating the same crude "poll and sleep" retry mechanism within the put and take operations. If the buffer is empty, take sleeps until another thread puts some data into the buffer; if the buffer is full, put sleeps until another thread makes room by removing some data. This approach encapsulates precondition management and simplifies using the buffer—definitely a step in the right direction.

The implementation of SleepyBoundedBuffer is more complicated than the previous attempt.[3] The buffer code must test the appropriate state condition with the buffer lock held, because the variables that represent the state condition are guarded by the buffer lock. If the test fails, the executing thread sleeps for a while, first releasing the lock so other threads can access the buffer.[4] Once the thread wakes up, it reacquires the lock and tries again, alternating between sleeping and testing the state condition until the operation can proceed.

From the perspective of the caller, this works nicely—if the operation can proceed immediately, it does, and otherwise it blocks—and the caller need not deal with the mechanics of failure and retry. Choosing the sleep granularity is a trade-off between responsiveness and CPU usage; the smaller the sleep granularity, the more responsive, but also the more CPU resources consumed. Figure 14.1 shows how sleep granularity can affect responsiveness: there may be a delay between when buffer space becomes available and when the thread wakes up and checks again.

---

2. Queue offers both of these options—poll returns null if the queue is empty, and remove throws an exception—but Queue is not intended for use in producer-consumer designs. BlockingQueue, whose operations block until the queue is in the right state to proceed, is a better choice when producers and consumers will execute concurrently.

3. We will spare you the details of Snow White's other five bounded buffer implementations, especially SneezyBoundedBuffer.

4. It is usually a bad idea for a thread to go to sleep or otherwise block with a lock held, but in this case is even worse because the desired condition (buffer is full/empty) can never become true if the lock is not released!

```
@ThreadSafe
public class SleepyBoundedBuffer<V> extends BaseBoundedBuffer<V> {
    public SleepyBoundedBuffer(int size) { super(size); }

    public void put(V v) throws InterruptedException {
        while (true) {
            synchronized (this) {
                if (!isFull()) {
                    doPut(v);
                    return;
                }
            }
            Thread.sleep(SLEEP_GRANULARITY);
        }
    }

    public V take() throws InterruptedException {
        while (true) {
            synchronized (this) {
                if (!isEmpty())
                    return doTake();
            }
            Thread.sleep(SLEEP_GRANULARITY);
        }
    }
}
```

LISTING 14.5. *Bounded buffer using crude blocking.*

SleepyBoundedBuffer also creates another requirement for the caller—dealing with InterruptedException. When a method blocks waiting for a condition to become true, the polite thing to do is to provide a cancellation mechanism (see Chapter 7). Like most well-behaved blocking library methods, SleepyBounded-Buffer supports cancellation through interruption, returning early and throwing InterruptedException if interrupted.

These attempts to synthesize a blocking operation from polling and sleeping were fairly painful. It would be nice to have a way of suspending a thread but ensuring that it is awakened promptly when a certain condition (such as the buffer being no longer full) becomes true. This is exactly what *condition queues* do.

14.1.3 Condition queues to the rescue

Condition queues are like the "toast is ready" bell on your toaster. If you are listening for it, you are notified promptly when your toast is ready and can drop what you are doing (or not, maybe you want to finish the newspaper first) and

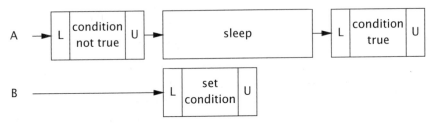

FIGURE 14.1. Thread oversleeping because the condition became true just after it went to sleep.

get your toast. If you are not listening for it (perhaps you went outside to get the newspaper), you could miss the notification, but on return to the kitchen you can observe the state of the toaster and either retrieve the toast if it is finished or start listening for the bell again if it is not.

A *condition queue* gets its name because it gives a group of threads—called the *wait set*—a way to wait for a specific condition to become true. Unlike typical queues in which the elements are data items, the elements of a condition queue are the threads waiting for the condition.

Just as each Java object can act as a lock, each object can also act as a condition queue, and the `wait`, `notify`, and `notifyAll` methods in `Object` constitute the API for intrinsic condition queues. An object's intrinsic lock and its intrinsic condition queue are related: in order to call any of the condition queue methods on object X, you must hold the lock on X. This is because the mechanism for waiting for state-based conditions is necessarily tightly bound to the mechanism for preserving state consistency: you cannot wait for a condition unless you can examine the state, and you cannot release another thread from a condition wait unless you can modify the state.

`Object.wait` atomically releases the lock and asks the OS to suspend the current thread, allowing other threads to acquire the lock and therefore modify the object state. Upon waking, it reacquires the lock before returning. Intuitively, calling `wait` means "I want to go to sleep, but wake me when something interesting happens", and calling the notification methods means "something interesting happened".

`BoundedBuffer` in Listing 14.6 implements a bounded buffer using `wait` and `notifyAll`. This is simpler than the sleeping version, and is both more efficient (waking up less frequently if the buffer state does not change) and more responsive (waking up promptly when an interesting state change happens). This is a big improvement, but note that the introduction of condition queues didn't change the semantics compared to the sleeping version. It is simply an optimization in several dimensions: CPU efficiency, context-switch overhead, and responsiveness. Condition queues don't let you do anything you can't do with sleeping and polling[5], but they make it a lot easier and more efficient to express and manage

---

5. This is not quite true; a *fair* condition queue can guarantee the relative order in which threads are released from the wait set. Intrinsic condition queues, like intrinsic locks, do not offer fair queueing; explicit `Conditions` offer a choice of fair or nonfair queueing.

state dependence.

```
@ThreadSafe
public class BoundedBuffer<V> extends BaseBoundedBuffer<V> {
    // CONDITION PREDICATE: not-full (!isFull())
    // CONDITION PREDICATE: not-empty (!isEmpty())

    public BoundedBuffer(int size) { super(size); }

    // BLOCKS-UNTIL: not-full
    public synchronized void put(V v) throws InterruptedException {
        while (isFull())
            wait();
        doPut(v);
        notifyAll();
    }

    // BLOCKS-UNTIL: not-empty
    public synchronized V take() throws InterruptedException {
        while (isEmpty())
            wait();
        V v = doTake();
        notifyAll();
        return v;
    }
}
```

LISTING 14.6. Bounded buffer using condition queues.

BoundedBuffer is finally good enough to use—it is easy to use and manages state dependence sensibly.[6] A production version should also include timed versions of put and take, so that blocking operations can time out if they cannot complete within a time budget. The timed version of Object.wait makes this easy to implement.

14.2   Using condition queues

Condition queues make it easier to build efficient and responsive state-dependent classes, but they are still easy to use incorrectly; there are a lot of rules regarding their proper use that are not enforced by the compiler or platform. (This is one of the reasons to build on top of classes like LinkedBlockingQueue, CountDown-Latch, Semaphore, and FutureTask when you can; if you can get away with it, it is a lot easier.)

6. ConditionBoundedBuffer in Section 14.3 is even better: it is more efficient because it can use single notification instead of notifyAll.

14.2.1 The condition predicate

The key to using condition queues correctly is identifying the *condition predicates* that the object may wait for. It is the condition predicate that causes much of the confusion surrounding `wait` and `notify`, because it has no instantiation in the API and nothing in either the language specification or the JVM implementation ensures its correct use. In fact, it is not mentioned directly at all in the language specification or the Javadoc. But without it, condition waits would not work.

The condition predicate is the precondition that makes an operation state-dependent in the first place. In a bounded buffer, `take` can proceed only if the buffer is not empty; otherwise it must wait. For `take`, the condition predicate is "the buffer is not empty", which `take` must test for before proceeding. Similarly, the condition predicate for `put` is "the buffer is not full". Condition predicates are expressions constructed from the state variables of the class; `BaseBoundedBuffer` tests for "buffer not empty" by comparing `count` to zero, and tests for "buffer not full" by comparing `count` to the buffer size.

> Document the condition predicate(s) associated with a condition queue and the operations that wait on them.

There is an important three-way relationship in a condition wait involving locking, the `wait` method, and a condition predicate. The condition predicate involves state variables, and the state variables are guarded by a lock, so before testing the condition predicate, we must hold that lock. The lock object and the condition queue object (the object on which `wait` and `notify` are invoked) must also be the same object.

In `BoundedBuffer`, the buffer state is guarded by the buffer lock and the buffer object is used as the condition queue. The `take` method acquires the buffer lock and then tests the condition predicate (that the buffer is nonempty). If the buffer is indeed nonempty, it removes the first element, which it can do because it still holds the lock guarding the buffer state.

If the condition predicate is not true (the buffer is empty), `take` must wait until another thread puts an object in the buffer. It does this by calling `wait` on the buffer's intrinsic condition queue, which requires holding the lock on the condition queue object. As careful design would have it, `take` already holds that lock, which it needed to test the condition predicate (and if the condition predicate was true, to modify the buffer state in the same atomic operation). The `wait` method releases the lock, blocks the current thread, and waits until the specified timeout expires, the thread is interrupted, or the thread is awakened by a notification. After the thread wakes up, `wait` reacquires the lock before returning. A thread waking up from `wait` gets no special priority in reacquiring the lock; it contends for the lock just like any other thread attempting to enter a `synchronized` block.

> Every call to wait is implicitly associated with a specific *condition predicate*. When calling wait regarding a particular condition predicate, the caller must already hold the lock associated with the condition queue, and that lock must also guard the state variables from which the condition predicate is composed.

14.2.2   Waking up too soon

As if the three-way relationship among the lock, the condition predicate, and the condition queue were not complicated enough, that wait returns does not necessarily mean that the condition predicate the thread is waiting for has become true.

A single intrinsic condition queue may be used with more than one condition predicate. When your thread is awakened because someone called notifyAll, that doesn't mean that the condition predicate *you* were waiting for is now true. (This is like having your toaster and coffee maker share a single bell; when it rings, you still have to look to see which device raised the signal.)[7] Additionally, wait is even allowed to return "spuriously"—not in response to any thread calling notify.[8]

When control re-enters the code calling wait, it has reacquired the lock associated with the condition queue. Is the condition predicate now true? Maybe. It might have been true at the time the notifying thread called notifyAll, but could have become false again by the time *you* reacquire the lock. Other threads may have acquired the lock and changed the object's state between when your thread was awakened and when wait reacquired the lock. Or maybe it hasn't been true at all since you called wait. You don't know why another thread called notify or notifyAll; maybe it was because *another* condition predicate associated with the same condition queue became true. Multiple condition predicates per condition queue are quite common—BoundedBuffer uses the same condition queue for both the "not full" and "not empty" predicates.[9]

For all these reasons, when you wake up from wait you must test the condition predicate *again*, and go back to waiting (or fail) if it is not yet true. Since you can wake up repeatedly without your condition predicate being true, you must therefore always call wait from within a loop, testing the condition predicate in each iteration. The canonical form for a condition wait is shown in Listing 14.7.

---

7. This situation actually describes Tim's kitchen pretty well; so many devices beep that when you hear one, you have to inspect the toaster, the microwave, the coffee maker, and several others to determine the cause of the signal.

8. To push the breakfast analogy way too far, this is like a toaster with a loose connection that makes the bell go off when the toast is ready but also sometimes when it is not ready.

9. It is actually possible for threads to be waiting for both "not full" and "not empty" at the same time! This can happen when the number of producers/consumers exceeds the buffer capacity.

```
void stateDependentMethod() throws InterruptedException {
    // condition predicate must be guarded by lock
    synchronized(lock) {
        while (!conditionPredicate())
            lock.wait();
        // object is now in desired state
    }
}
```

LISTING 14.7. Canonical form for state-dependent methods.

When using condition waits (`Object.wait` or `Condition.await`):
- Always have a condition predicate—some test of object state that must hold before proceeding;
- Always test the condition predicate before calling `wait`, and again after returning from `wait`;
- Always call `wait` in a loop;
- Ensure that the state variables making up the condition predicate are guarded by the lock associated with the condition queue;
- Hold the lock associated with the the condition queue when calling `wait`, `notify`, or `notifyAll`; and
- Do not release the lock after checking the condition predicate but before acting on it.

14.2.3   Missed signals

Chapter 10 discussed liveness failures such as deadlock and livelock. Another form of liveness failure is *missed signals*. A missed signal occurs when a thread must wait for a specific condition that is already true, but fails to check the condition predicate before waiting. Now the thread is waiting to be notified of an event that has already occurred. This is like starting the toast, going out to get the newspaper, having the bell go off while you are outside, and then sitting down at the kitchen table waiting for the toast bell. You could wait a long time—potentially forever.[10] Unlike the marmalade for your toast, notification is not "sticky"—if thread *A* notifies on a condition queue and thread *B* subsequently waits on that same condition queue, *B* does *not* immediately wake up—another notification is required to wake *B*. Missed signals are the result of coding errors like those warned against in the list above, such as failing to test the condition predicate before calling `wait`. If you structure your condition waits as in Listing 14.7, you will not have problems with missed signals.

---

10. In order to emerge from this wait, someone else would have to make toast, but this will just make matters worse; when the bell rings, you will then have a disagreement about toast ownership.

14.2.4   Notification

So far, we've described half of what goes on in a condition wait: waiting. The other half is notification. In a bounded buffer, `take` blocks if called when the buffer is empty. In order for `take` to *unblock* when the buffer becomes nonempty, we must ensure that *every* code path in which the buffer could become nonempty performs a notification. In `BoundedBuffer`, there is only one such place—after a put. So `put` calls `notifyAll` after successfully adding an object to the buffer. Similarly, `take` calls `notifyAll` after removing an element to indicate that the buffer may no longer be full, in case any threads are waiting on the "not full" condition.

> Whenever you wait on a condition, make sure that someone will perform a notification whenever the condition predicate becomes true.

There are two notification methods in the condition queue API—`notify` and `notifyAll`. To call either, you must hold the lock associated with the condition queue object. Calling `notify` causes the JVM to select one thread waiting on that condition queue to wake up; calling `notifyAll` wakes up *all* the threads waiting on that condition queue. Because you must hold the lock on the condition queue object when calling `notify` or `notifyAll`, and waiting threads cannot return from `wait` without reacquiring the lock, the notifying thread should release the lock quickly to ensure that the waiting threads are unblocked as soon as possible.

Because multiple threads could be waiting on the same condition queue for different condition predicates, using `notify` instead of `notifyAll` can be dangerous, primarily because single notification is prone to a problem akin to missed signals.

`BoundedBuffer` provides a good illustration of why `notifyAll` should be preferred to single `notify` in most cases. The condition queue is used for two different condition predicates: "not full" and "not empty". Suppose thread A waits on a condition queue for predicate P_A, while thread B waits on the same condition queue for predicate P_B. Now, suppose P_B becomes true and thread C performs a single `notify`: the JVM will wake up one thread of its own choosing. If A is chosen, it will wake up, see that P_A is not yet true, and go back to waiting. Meanwhile, B, which could now make progress, does not wake up. This is not exactly a missed signal—it's more of a "hijacked signal"—but the problem is the same: a thread is waiting for a signal that has (or should have) already occurred.

> Single notify can be used instead of notifyAll only when both of the following conditions hold:
>
> **Uniform waiters.** Only one condition predicate is associated with the condition queue, and each thread executes the same logic upon returning from wait; and
>
> **One-in, one-out.** A notification on the condition variable enables at most one thread to proceed.

BoundedBuffer meets the one-in, one-out requirement, but does not meet the uniform waiters requirement because waiting threads might be waiting for either the "not full" and "not empty" condition. A "starting gate" latch like that used in TestHarness on page 96, in which a single event releases a set of threads, does not meet the one-in, one-out requirement because opening the starting gate lets multiple threads proceed.

Most classes don't meet these requirements, so the prevailing wisdom is to use notifyAll in preference to single notify. While this may be inefficient, it is much easier to ensure that your classes behave correctly when using notifyAll instead of notify.

This "prevailing wisdom" makes some people uncomfortable, and for good reason. Using notifyAll when only one thread can make progress is inefficient—sometimes a little, sometimes grossly so. If ten threads are waiting on a condition queue, calling notifyAll causes each of them to wake up and contend for the lock; then most or all of them will go right back to sleep. This means a lot of context switches and a lot of contended lock acquisitions for each event that enables (maybe) a single thread to make progress. (In the worst case, using notify-All results in $O(n^2)$ wakeups where n would suffice.) This is another situation where performance concerns support one approach and safety concerns support the other.

The notification done by put and take in BoundedBuffer is conservative: a notification is performed every time an object is put into or removed from the buffer. This could be optimized by observing that a thread can be released from a wait only if the buffer goes from empty to not empty or from full to not full, and notifying only if a put or take effected one of these state transitions. This is called *conditional notification*. While conditional notification can improve performance, it is tricky to get right (and also complicates the implementation of subclasses) and so should be used carefully. Listing 14.8 illustrates using conditional notification in BoundedBuffer.put.

Single notification and conditional notification are optimizations. As always, follow the principle "First make it right, and then make it fast—*if* it is not already fast enough" when using these optimizations; it is easy to introduce strange liveness failures by applying them incorrectly.

```
public synchronized void put(V v) throws InterruptedException {
    while (isFull())
        wait();
    boolean wasEmpty = isEmpty();
    doPut(v);
    if (wasEmpty)
        notifyAll();
}
```

LISTING 14.8. Using conditional notification in `BoundedBuffer.put`.

14.2.5 Example: a gate class

The starting gate latch in `TestHarness` on page 96 was constructed with an initial count of one, creating a *binary latch*: one with two states, the initial state and the terminal state. The latch prevents threads from passing the starting gate until it is opened, at which point all the threads can pass through. While this latching mechanism is often exactly what is needed, sometimes it is a drawback that a gate constructed in this manner cannot be reclosed once opened.

It is easy to develop a recloseable `ThreadGate` class using condition waits, as shown in Listing 14.9. `ThreadGate` lets the gate be opened and closed, providing an `await` method that blocks until the gate is opened. The `open` method uses `notifyAll` because the semantics of this class fail the "one-in, one-out" test for single notification.

The condition predicate used by `await` is more complicated than simply testing `isOpen`. This is needed because if N threads are waiting at the gate at the time it is opened, they should all be allowed to proceed. But, if the gate is opened and closed in rapid succession, all threads might not be released if `await` examines only `isOpen`: by the time all the threads receive the notification, reacquire the lock, and emerge from `wait`, the gate may have closed again. So `ThreadGate` uses a somewhat more complicated condition predicate: every time the gate is closed, a "generation" counter is incremented, and a thread may pass `await` if the gate is open now or if the gate has opened since this thread arrived at the gate.

Since `ThreadGate` only supports waiting for the gate to open, it performs notification only in `open`; to support both "wait for open" and "wait for close" operations, it would have to notify in both `open` and `close`. This illustrates why state-dependent classes can be fragile to maintain—the addition of a new state-dependent operation may require modifying many code paths that modify the object state so that the appropriate notifications can be performed.

14.2.6 Subclass safety issues

Using conditional or single notification introduces constraints that can complicate subclassing [CPJ 3.3.3.3]. If you want to support subclassing at all, you must structure your class so subclasses can add the appropriate notification on behalf

```
@ThreadSafe
public class ThreadGate {
    // CONDITION-PREDICATE: opened-since(n) (isOpen || generation>n)
    @GuardedBy("this") private boolean isOpen;
    @GuardedBy("this") private int generation;

    public synchronized void close() {
        isOpen = false;
    }

    public synchronized void open() {
        ++generation;
        isOpen = true;
        notifyAll();
    }

    // BLOCKS-UNTIL: opened-since(generation on entry)
    public synchronized void await() throws InterruptedException {
        int arrivalGeneration = generation;
        while (!isOpen && arrivalGeneration == generation)
            wait();
    }
}
```

LISTING 14.9. Recloseable gate using `wait` and `notifyAll`.

of the base class if it is subclassed in a way that violates one of the requirements for single or conditional notification.

A state-dependent class should either fully expose (and document) its waiting and notification protocols to subclasses, or prevent subclasses from participating in them at all. (This is an extension of "design and document for inheritance, or else prohibit it" [EJ Item 15].) At the very least, designing a state-dependent class for inheritance requires exposing the condition queues and locks and documenting the condition predicates and synchronization policy; it may also require exposing the underlying state variables. (The worst thing a state-dependent class can do is expose its state to subclasses but *not* document its protocols for waiting and notification; this is like a class exposing its state variables but not documenting its invariants.)

One option for doing this is to effectively prohibit subclassing, either by making the class `final` or by hiding the condition queues, locks, and state variables from subclasses. Otherwise, if the subclass does something to undermine the way the base class uses `notify`, it needs to be able to repair the damage. Consider an unbounded blocking stack in which the pop operation blocks if the stack is empty but the push operation can always proceed. This meets the requirements for single notification. If this class uses single notification and a subclass adds a blocking "pop two consecutive elements" method, there are now two classes of waiters: those waiting to pop one element and those waiting to pop two. But if the base class exposes the condition queue and documents its protocols for using it, the subclass can override the push method to perform a notifyAll, restoring safety.

14.2.7 Encapsulating condition queues

It is generally best to encapsulate the condition queue so that it is not accessible outside the class hierarchy in which it is used. Otherwise, callers might be tempted to think they understand your protocols for waiting and notification and use them in a manner inconsistent with your design. (It is impossible to enforce the uniform waiters requirement for single notification unless the condition queue object is inaccessible to code you do not control; if alien code mistakenly waits on your condition queue, this could subvert your notification protocol and cause a hijacked signal.)

Unfortunately, this advice—to encapsulate objects used as condition queues— is not consistent with the most common design pattern for thread-safe classes, in which an object's intrinsic lock is used to guard its state. BoundedBuffer illustrates this common idiom, where the buffer object itself is the lock and condition queue. However, BoundedBuffer could be easily restructured to use a private lock object and condition queue; the only difference would be that it would no longer support any form of client-side locking.

14.2.8 Entry and exit protocols

Wellings (Wellings, 2004) characterizes the proper use of wait and notify in terms of *entry* and *exit protocols*. For each state-dependent operation and for each operation that modifies state on which another operation has a state dependency, you should define and document an entry and exit protocol. The entry protocol is the operation's condition predicate; the exit protocol involves examining any state variables that have been changed by the operation to see if they might have caused some other condition predicate to become true, and if so, notifying on the associated condition queue.

AbstractQueuedSynchronizer, upon which most of the state-dependent classes in java.util.concurrent are built (see Section 14.4), exploits the concept of exit protocol. Rather than letting synchronizer classes perform their own notification, it instead requires synchronizer methods to return a value indicating whether its action might have unblocked one or more waiting threads. This explicit API requirement makes it harder to "forget" to notify on some state transitions.

14.3 Explicit condition objects

As we saw in Chapter 13, explicit Locks can be useful in some situations where intrinsic locks are too inflexible. Just as Lock is a generalization of intrinsic locks, Condition (see Listing 14.10) is a generalization of intrinsic condition queues.

Intrinsic condition queues have several drawbacks. Each intrinsic lock can have only one associated condition queue, which means that in classes like Bound-edBuffer multiple threads might wait on the same condition queue for different condition predicates, and the most common pattern for locking involves exposing the condition queue object. Both of these factors make it impossible to enforce the uniform waiter requirement for using notify. If you want to write a concurrent object with multiple condition predicates, or you want to exercise more control over the visibility of the condition queue, the explicit Lock and Condition classes offer a more flexible alternative to intrinsic locks and condition queues.

A Condition is associated with a single Lock, just as a condition queue is associated with a single intrinsic lock; to create a Condition, call Lock.newCondition on the associated lock. And just as Lock offers a richer feature set than intrinsic locking, Condition offers a richer feature set than intrinsic condition queues: multiple wait sets per lock, interruptible and uninterruptible condition waits, deadline-based waiting, and a choice of fair or nonfair queueing.

```
public interface Condition {
    void await() throws InterruptedException;
    boolean await(long time, TimeUnit unit)
            throws InterruptedException;
    long awaitNanos(long nanosTimeout) throws InterruptedException;
    void awaitUninterruptibly();
    boolean awaitUntil(Date deadline) throws InterruptedException;

    void signal();
    void signalAll();
}
```

LISTING 14.10. Condition interface.

Unlike intrinsic condition queues, you can have as many Condition objects per Lock as you want. Condition objects inherit the fairness setting of their associated Lock; for fair locks, threads are released from Condition.await in FIFO order.

> Hazard warning: The equivalents of wait, notify, and notifyAll for Condition objects are await, signal, and signalAll. However, Condition extends Object, which means that it also has wait and notify methods. Be sure to use the proper versions—await and signal—instead!

Listing 14.11 shows yet another bounded buffer implementation, this time using two Conditions, notFull and notEmpty, to represent explicitly the "not full" and "not empty" condition predicates. When take blocks because the buffer is empty, it waits on notEmpty, and put unblocks any threads blocked in take by signaling on notEmpty.

The behavior of ConditionBoundedBuffer is the same as BoundedBuffer, but its use of condition queues is more readable—it is easier to analyze a class that uses multiple Conditions than one that uses a single intrinsic condition queue with multiple condition predicates. By separating the two condition predicates into separate wait sets, Condition makes it easier to meet the requirements for single notification. Using the more efficient signal instead of signalAll reduces the number of context switches and lock acquisitions triggered by each buffer operation.

Just as with built-in locks and condition queues, the three-way relationship among the lock, the condition predicate, and the condition variable must also hold when using explicit Locks and Conditions. The variables involved in the condition predicate must be guarded by the Lock, and the Lock must be held when testing the condition predicate and when calling await and signal.[11]

Choose between using explicit Conditions and intrinsic condition queues in the same way as you would choose between ReentrantLock and synchronized: use Condition if you need its advanced features such as fair queueing or multiple wait sets per lock, and otherwise prefer intrinsic condition queues. (If you already use ReentrantLock because you need its advanced features, the choice is already made.)

14.4 Anatomy of a synchronizer

The interfaces of ReentrantLock and Semaphore have a lot in common. Both classes act as a "gate", allowing only a limited number of threads to pass at a time; threads arrive at the gate and are allowed through (lock or acquire returns successfully), are made to wait (lock or acquire blocks), or are turned away (tryLock or tryAcquire returns false, indicating that the lock or permit did not become available in the time allowed). Further, both allow interruptible, uninterruptible, and timed acquisition attempts, and both allow a choice of fair or nonfair queueing of waiting threads.

Given this commonality, you might think that Semaphore was implemented on top of ReentrantLock, or perhaps ReentrantLock was implemented as a Semaphore with one permit. This would be entirely practical; it is a common exercise to prove that a counting semaphore can be implemented using a lock (as in SemaphoreOnLock in Listing 14.12) and that a lock can be implemented using a counting semaphore.

In actuality, they are both implemented using a common base class, Abstract-QueuedSynchronizer (AQS)—as are many other synchronizers. AQS is a framework for building locks and synchronizers, and a surprisingly broad range of synchronizers can be built easily and efficiently using it. Not only are ReentrantLock and Semaphore built using AQS, but so are CountDownLatch, ReentrantReadWriteLock, SynchronousQueue,[12] and FutureTask.

---

11. ReentrantLock requires that the Lock be held when calling signal or signalAll, but Lock implementations are permitted to construct Conditions that do not have this requirement.

12. Java 6 replaces the AQS-based SynchronousQueue with a (more scalable) nonblocking version.

```java
@ThreadSafe
public class ConditionBoundedBuffer<T> {
    protected final Lock lock = new ReentrantLock();
    // CONDITION PREDICATE: notFull (count < items.length)
    private final Condition notFull  = lock.newCondition();
    // CONDITION PREDICATE: notEmpty (count > 0)
    private final Condition notEmpty = lock.newCondition();
    @GuardedBy("lock")
    private final T[] items = (T[]) new Object[BUFFER_SIZE];
    @GuardedBy("lock") private int tail, head, count;

    // BLOCKS-UNTIL: notFull
    public void put(T x) throws InterruptedException {
        lock.lock();
        try {
            while (count == items.length)
                notFull.await();
            items[tail] = x;
            if (++tail == items.length)
                tail = 0;
            ++count;
            notEmpty.signal();
        } finally {
            lock.unlock();
        }
    }

    // BLOCKS-UNTIL: notEmpty
    public T take() throws InterruptedException {
        lock.lock();
        try {
            while (count == 0)
                notEmpty.await();
            T x = items[head];
            items[head] = null;
            if (++head == items.length)
                head = 0;
            --count;
            notFull.signal();
            return x;
        } finally {
            lock.unlock();
        }
    }
}
```

LISTING 14.11. *Bounded buffer using explicit condition variables.*

```
// Not really how java.util.concurrent.Semaphore is implemented
@ThreadSafe
public class SemaphoreOnLock {
    private final Lock lock = new ReentrantLock();
    // CONDITION PREDICATE: permitsAvailable (permits > 0)
    private final Condition permitsAvailable = lock.newCondition();
    @GuardedBy("lock") private int permits;

    SemaphoreOnLock(int initialPermits) {
        lock.lock();
        try {
            permits = initialPermits;
        } finally {
            lock.unlock();
        }
    }

    // BLOCKS-UNTIL: permitsAvailable
    public void acquire() throws InterruptedException {
        lock.lock();
        try {
            while (permits <= 0)
                permitsAvailable.await();
            --permits;
        } finally {
            lock.unlock();
        }
    }

    public void release() {
        lock.lock();
        try {
            ++permits;
            permitsAvailable.signal();
        } finally {
            lock.unlock();
        }
    }
}
```

LISTING 14.12. *Counting semaphore implemented using Lock.*

AQS handles many of the details of implementing a synchronizer, such as FIFO queuing of waiting threads. Individual synchronizers can define flexible criteria for whether a thread should be allowed to pass or be required to wait.

Using AQS to build synchronizers offers several benefits. Not only does it substantially reduce the implementation effort, but you also needn't pay for multiple points of contention, as you would when constructing one synchronizer on top of another. In `SemaphoreOnLock`, acquiring a permit has two places where it might block—once at the lock guarding the semaphore state, and then again if a permit is not available. Synchronizers built with AQS have only one point where they might block, reducing context-switch overhead and improving throughput. AQS was designed for scalability, and all the synchronizers in `java.util.concurrent` that are built with AQS benefit from this.

14.5 AbstractQueuedSynchronizer

Most developers will probably never use AQS directly; the standard set of synchronizers covers a fairly wide range of situations. But seeing how the standard synchronizers are implemented can help clarify how they work.

The basic operations that an AQS-based synchronizer performs are some variants of *acquire* and *release*. Acquisition is the state-dependent operation and can always block. With a lock or semaphore, the meaning of acquire is straightforward—acquire the lock or a permit—and the caller may have to wait until the synchronizer is in a state where that can happen. With `CountDownLatch`, acquire means "wait until the latch has reached its terminal state", and with `FutureTask`, it means "wait until the task has completed". Release is not a blocking operation; a release may allow threads blocked in acquire to proceed.

For a class to be state-dependent, it must have some state. AQS takes on the task of managing some of the state for the synchronizer class: it manages a single integer of state information that can be manipulated through the protected `getState`, `setState`, and `compareAndSetState` methods. This can be used to represent arbitrary state; for example, `ReentrantLock` uses it to represent the count of times the owning thread has acquired the lock, `Semaphore` uses it to represent the number of permits remaining, and `FutureTask` uses it to represent the state of the task (not yet started, running, completed, cancelled). Synchronizers can also manage additional state variables themselves; for example, `ReentrantLock` keeps track of the current lock owner so it can distinguish between reentrant and contended lock-acquisition requests.

Acquisition and release in AQS take the forms shown in Listing 14.13. Depending on the synchronizer, acquisition might be *exclusive*, as with `Reentrant-Lock`, or *nonexclusive*, as with `Semaphore` and `CountDownLatch`. An acquire operation has two parts. First, the synchronizer decides whether the current state permits acquisition; if so, the thread is allowed to proceed, and if not, the acquire blocks or fails. This decision is determined by the synchronizer semantics; for example, acquiring a lock can succeed if the lock is unheld, and acquiring a latch can succeed if the latch is in its terminal state.

The second part involves possibly updating the synchronizer state; one thread acquiring the synchronizer can affect whether other threads can acquire it. For example, acquiring a lock changes the lock state from "unheld" to "held", and acquiring a permit from a Semaphore reduces the number of permits left. On the other hand, the acquisition of a latch by one thread does not affect whether other threads can acquire it, so acquiring a latch does not change its state.

```
boolean acquire() throws InterruptedException {
    while (state does not permit acquire) {
        if (blocking acquisition requested) {
            enqueue current thread if not already queued
            block current thread
        }
        else
            return failure
    }
    possibly update synchronization state
    dequeue thread if it was queued
    return success
}

void release() {
    update synchronization state
    if (new state may permit a blocked thread to acquire)
        unblock one or more queued threads
}
```

Listing 14.13. Canonical forms for acquisition and release in AQS.

A synchronizer supporting exclusive acquisition should implement the protected methods tryAcquire, tryRelease, and isHeldExclusively, and those supporting shared acquisition should implement tryAcquireShared and tryReleaseShared. The acquire, acquireShared, release, and releaseShared methods in AQS call the try forms of these methods in the synchronizer subclass to determine if the operation can proceed. The synchronizer subclass can use getState, setState, and compareAndSetState to examine and update the state according to its acquire and release semantics, and informs the base class through the return status whether the attempt to acquire or release the synchronizer was successful. For example, returning a negative value from tryAcquireShared indicates acquisition failure; returning zero indicates the synchronizer was acquired exclusively; and returning a positive value indicates the synchronizer was acquired nonexclusively. The tryRelease and tryReleaseShared methods should return true if the release may have unblocked threads attempting to acquire the synchronizer.

To simplify implementation of locks that support condition queues (like ReentrantLock), AQS also provides machinery for constructing condition variables associated with synchronizers.

14.5.1 A simple latch

OneShotLatch in Listing 14.14 is a binary latch implemented using AQS. It has two public methods, await and signal, that correspond to acquisition and release. Initially, the latch is closed; any thread calling await blocks until the latch is opened. Once the latch is opened by a call to signal, waiting threads are released and threads that subsequently arrive at the latch will be allowed to proceed.

```
@ThreadSafe
public class OneShotLatch {
    private final Sync sync = new Sync();

    public void signal() { sync.releaseShared(0); }

    public void await() throws InterruptedException {
        sync.acquireSharedInterruptibly(0);
    }

    private class Sync extends AbstractQueuedSynchronizer {
        protected int tryAcquireShared(int ignored) {
            // Succeed if latch is open (state == 1), else fail
            return (getState() == 1) ? 1 : -1;
        }

        protected boolean tryReleaseShared(int ignored) {
            setState(1); // Latch is now open
            return true; // Other threads may now be able to acquire

        }
    }
}
```

LISTING 14.14. Binary latch using AbstractQueuedSynchronizer.

In OneShotLatch, the AQS state holds the latch state—closed (zero) or open (one). The await method calls acquireSharedInterruptibly in AQS, which in turn consults the tryAcquireShared method in OneShotLatch. The tryAcquireShared implementation must return a value indicating whether or not acquisition can proceed. If the latch has been previously opened, tryAcquireShared returns success, allowing the thread to pass; otherwise it returns a value indicating that the acquisition attempt failed. The acquireSharedInterruptibly method interprets failure to mean that the thread should be placed on the queue of waiting threads. Similarly, signal calls releaseShared, which causes tryReleaseShared to be consulted. The tryReleaseShared implementation unconditionally sets the latch state to open and indicates (through its return value) that the synchronizer is in a fully released state. This causes AQS to let all waiting threads attempt to reacquire the synchronizer, and acquisition will now succeed because tryAcquireShared returns success.

OneShotLatch is a fully functional, usable, performant synchronizer, implemented in only twenty or so lines of code. Of course, it is missing some useful features—such as timed acquisition or the ability to inspect the latch state—but these are easy to implement as well, since AQS provides timed versions of the acquisition methods and utility methods for common inspection operations.

OneShotLatch could have been implemented by extending AQS rather than delegating to it, but this is undesirable for several reasons [EJ Item 14]. Doing so would undermine the simple (two-method) interface of OneShotLatch, and while the public methods of AQS won't allow callers to corrupt the latch state, callers could easily use them incorrectly. None of the synchronizers in java.util.concurrent extends AQS directly—they all delegate to private inner subclasses of AQS instead.

14.6 AQS in java.util.concurrent synchronizer classes

Many of the blocking classes in java.util.concurrent, such as ReentrantLock, Semaphore, ReentrantReadWriteLock, CountDownLatch, SynchronousQueue, and FutureTask, are built using AQS. Without getting too deeply into the details (the source code is part of the JDK download[13]), let's take a quick look at how each of these classes uses AQS.

14.6.1 ReentrantLock

ReentrantLock supports only exclusive acquisition, so it implements tryAcquire, tryRelease, and isHeldExclusively; tryAcquire for the nonfair version is shown in Listing 14.15. ReentrantLock uses the synchronization state to hold the lock acquisition count, and maintains an owner variable holding the identity of the owning thread that is modified only when the current thread has just acquired the lock or is just about to release it.[14] In tryRelease, it checks the owner field to ensure that the current thread owns the lock before allowing an unlock to proceed; in tryAcquire, it uses this field to differentiate between a reentrant acquisition and a contended acquisition attempt.

When a thread attempts to acquire a lock, tryAcquire first consults the lock state. If it is unheld, it tries to update the lock state to indicate that it is held. Because the state could have changed since it was first inspected a few instructions ago, tryAcquire uses compareAndSetState to attempt to atomically update the state to indicate that the lock is now held and confirm that the state has not changed since last observed. (See the description of compareAndSet in Section 15.3.) If the lock state indicates that it is already held, if the current thread is the

---

13. Or with fewer licensing restrictions at http://gee.cs.oswego.edu/dl/concurrency-interest.
14. Because the protected state-manipulation methods have the memory semantics of a volatile read or write and ReentrantLock is careful to read the owner field only after calling getState and write it only before calling setState, ReentrantLock can piggyback on the memory semantics of the synchronization state, and thus avoid further synchronization—see Section 16.1.4.

```
protected boolean tryAcquire(int ignored) {
    final Thread current = Thread.currentThread();
    int c = getState();
    if (c == 0) {
        if (compareAndSetState(0, 1)) {
            owner = current;
            return true;
        }
    } else if (current == owner) {
        setState(c+1);
        return true;
    }
    return false;
}
```

LISTING 14.15. tryAcquire implementation from nonfair ReentrantLock.

owner of the lock, the acquisition count is incremented; if the current thread is not the owner of the lock, the acquisition attempt fails.

ReentrantLock also takes advantage of AQS's built-in support for multiple condition variables and wait sets. Lock.newCondition returns a new instance of ConditionObject, an inner class of AQS.

14.6.2 Semaphore and CountDownLatch

Semaphore uses the AQS synchronization state to hold the count of permits currently available. The tryAcquireShared method (see Listing 14.16) first computes the number of permits remaining, and if there are not enough, returns a value indicating that the acquire failed. If sufficient permits appear to be left, it attempts to atomically reduce the permit count using compareAndSetState. If that succeeds (meaning that the permit count had not changed since it last looked), it returns a value indicating that the acquire succeeded. The return value also encodes whether *other* shared acquisition attempts might succeed, in which case other waiting threads will also be unblocked.

The while loop terminates either when there are not enough permits or when tryAcquireShared can atomically update the permit count to reflect acquisition. While any given call to compareAndSetState may fail due to contention with another thread (see Section 15.3), causing it to retry, one of these two termination criteria will become true within a reasonable number of retries. Similarly, tryReleaseShared increases the permit count, potentially unblocking waiting threads, and retries until the update succeeds. The return value of tryReleaseShared indicates whether other threads might have been unblocked by the release.

CountDownLatch uses AQS in a similar manner to Semaphore: the synchronization state holds the current count. The countDown method calls release, which causes the counter to be decremented and unblocks waiting threads if the counter

```
protected int tryAcquireShared(int acquires) {
    while (true) {
        int available = getState();
        int remaining = available - acquires;
        if (remaining < 0
                || compareAndSetState(available, remaining))
            return remaining;
    }
}

protected boolean tryReleaseShared(int releases) {
    while (true) {
        int p = getState();
        if (compareAndSetState(p, p + releases))
            return true;
    }
}
```

LISTING 14.16. tryAcquireShared and tryReleaseShared from Semaphore.

has reached zero; await calls acquire, which returns immediately if the counter has reached zero and otherwise blocks.

14.6.3   FutureTask

At first glance, FutureTask doesn't even look like a synchronizer. But Future.get has semantics that are very similar to that of a latch—if some event (the completion or cancellation of the task represented by the FutureTask) has occurred, then threads can proceed, otherwise they are queued until that event occurs.

FutureTask uses the AQS synchronization state to hold the task status—running, completed, or cancelled. It also maintains additional state variables to hold the result of the computation or the exception it threw. It further maintains a reference to the thread that is running the computation (if it is currently in the running state), so that it can be interrupted if the task is cancelled.

14.6.4   ReentrantReadWriteLock

The interface for ReadWriteLock suggests there are two locks—a reader lock and a writer lock—but in the AQS-based implementation of ReentrantReadWriteLock, a single AQS subclass manages both read and write locking. ReentrantReadWriteLock uses 16 bits of the state for the write-lock count, and the other 16 bits for the read-lock count. Operations on the read lock use the shared acquire and release methods; operations on the write lock use the exclusive acquire and release methods.

Internally, AQS maintains a queue of waiting threads, keeping track of whether a thread has requested exclusive or shared access. In ReentrantRead-

WriteLock, when the lock becomes available, if the thread at the head of the queue was looking for write access it will get it, and if the thread at the head of the queue was looking for read access, all queued threads up to the first writer will get it.[15]

Summary

If you need to implement a state-dependent class—one whose methods must block if a state-based precondition does not hold—the best strategy is usually to build upon an existing library class such as Semaphore, BlockingQueue, or CountDownLatch, as in ValueLatch on page 187. However, sometimes existing library classes do not provide a sufficient foundation; in these cases, you can build your own synchronizers using intrinsic condition queues, explicit Condition objects, or AbstractQueuedSynchronizer. Intrinsic condition queues are tightly bound to intrinsic locking, since the mechanism for managing state dependence is necessarily tied to the mechanism for ensuring state consistency. Similarly, explicit Conditions are tightly bound to explicit Locks, and offer an extended feature set compared to intrinsic condition queues, including multiple wait sets per lock, interruptible or uninterruptible condition waits, fair or nonfair queuing, and deadline-based waiting.

---

15. This mechanism does not permit the choice of a reader-preference or writer-preference policy, as some read-write lock implementations do. For that, either the AQS wait queue would need to be something other than a FIFO queue, or two queues would be needed. However, such a strict ordering policy is rarely needed in practice; if the nonfair version of ReentrantReadWriteLock does not offer acceptable liveness, the fair version usually provides satisfactory ordering and guarantees nonstarvation of readers and writers.

Chapter 15

Atomic Variables and Nonblocking Synchronization

Many of the classes in `java.util.concurrent`, such as `Semaphore` and `Concur-rentLinkedQueue`, provide better performance and scalability than alternatives using `synchronized`. In this chapter, we take a look at the primary source of this performance boost: atomic variables and nonblocking synchronization.

Much of the recent research on concurrent algorithms has focused on *nonblocking algorithms*, which use low-level atomic machine instructions such as *compare-and-swap* instead of locks to ensure data integrity under concurrent access. Nonblocking algorithms are used extensively in operating systems and JVMs for thread and process scheduling, garbage collection, and to implement locks and other concurrent data structures.

Nonblocking algorithms are considerably more complicated to design and implement than lock-based alternatives, but they can offer significant scalability and liveness advantages. They coordinate at a finer level of granularity and can greatly reduce scheduling overhead because they don't block when multiple threads contend for the same data. Further, they are immune to deadlock and other liveness problems. In lock-based algorithms, other threads cannot make progress if a thread goes to sleep or spins while holding a lock, whereas nonblocking algorithms are impervious to individual thread failures. As of Java 5.0, it is possible to build efficient nonblocking algorithms in Java using the *atomic variable classes* such as `AtomicInteger` and `AtomicReference`.

Atomic variables can also be used as "better volatile variables" even if you are not developing nonblocking algorithms. Atomic variables offer the same memory semantics as volatile variables, but with additional support for atomic updates—making them ideal for counters, sequence generators, and statistics gathering while offering better scalability than lock-based alternatives.

15.1 Disadvantages of locking

Coordinating access to shared state using a consistent locking protocol ensures that whichever thread holds the lock guarding a set of variables has exclusive access to those variables, and that any changes made to those variables are visible to other threads that subsequently acquire the lock.

Modern JVMs can optimize uncontended lock acquisition and release fairly effectively, but if multiple threads request the lock at the same time the JVM enlists the help of the operating system. If it gets to this point, some unfortunate thread will be suspended and have to be resumed later.[1] When that thread is resumed, it may have to wait for other threads to finish their scheduling quanta before it is actually scheduled. Suspending and resuming a thread has a lot of overhead and generally entails a lengthy interruption. For lock-based classes with fine-grained operations (such as the synchronized collections classes, where most methods contain only a few operations), the ratio of scheduling overhead to useful work can be quite high *when the lock is frequently contended.*

Volatile variables are a lighter-weight synchronization mechanism than locking because they do not involve context switches or thread scheduling. However, volatile variables have some limitations compared to locking: while they provide similar visibility guarantees, they cannot be used to construct atomic compound actions. This means that volatile variables cannot be used when one variable depends on another, or when the new value of a variable depends on its old value. This limits when volatile variables are appropriate, since they cannot be used to reliably implement common tools such as counters or mutexes.[2]

For example, while the increment operation (++i) may *look* like an atomic operation, it is actually three distinct operations—fetch the current value of the variable, add one to it, and then write the updated value back. In order to not lose an update, the entire read-modify-write operation must be atomic. So far, the only way we've seen to do this is with locking, as in `Counter` on page 56.

`Counter` is thread-safe, and in the presence of little or no contention performs just fine. But under contention, performance suffers because of context-switch overhead and scheduling delays. When locks are held so briefly, being put to sleep is a harsh penalty for asking for the lock at the wrong time.

Locking has a few other disadvantages. When a thread is waiting for a lock, it cannot do anything else. If a thread holding a lock is delayed (due to a page fault, scheduling delay, or the like), then no thread that needs that lock can make progress. This can be a serious problem if the blocked thread is a high-priority thread but the thread holding the lock is a lower-priority thread—a performance hazard known as *priority inversion.* Even though the higher-priority thread should have precedence, it must wait until the lock is released, and this effectively downgrades its priority to that of the lower-priority thread. If a thread holding a lock is permanently blocked (due to an infinite loop, deadlock, livelock, or other liveness failure), any threads waiting for that lock can never make progress.

Even ignoring these hazards, locking is simply a heavyweight mechanism for fine-grained operations such as incrementing a counter. It would be nice to have a finer-grained technique for managing contention between threads—something

---

1. A smart JVM need not necessarily suspend a thread if it contends for a lock; it could use profiling data to decide adaptively between suspension and spin locking based on how long the lock has been held during previous acquisitions.

2. It is theoretically possible, though wholly impractical, to use the semantics of `volatile` to construct mutexes and other synchronizers; see (Raynal, 1986).

like volatile variables, but offering the possibility of atomic updates as well. Happily, modern processors offer us precisely such a mechanism.

15.2 Hardware support for concurrency

Exclusive locking is a *pessimistic* technique—it assumes the worst (if you don't lock your door, gremlins will come in and rearrange your stuff) and doesn't proceed until you can guarantee, by acquiring the appropriate locks, that other threads will not interfere.

For fine-grained operations, there is an alternate approach that is often more efficient—the *optimistic* approach, whereby you proceed with an update, hopeful that you can complete it without interference. This approach relies on *collision detection* to determine if there has been interference from other parties during the update, in which case the operation fails and can be retried (or not). The optimistic approach is like the old saying, "It is easier to obtain forgiveness than permission", where "easier" here means "more efficient".

Processors designed for multiprocessor operation provide special instructions for managing concurrent access to shared variables. Early processors had atomic *test-and-set*, *fetch-and-increment*, or *swap* instructions sufficient for implementing mutexes that could in turn be used to implement more sophisticated concurrent objects. Today, nearly every modern processor has some form of atomic read-modify-write instruction, such as *compare-and-swap* or *load-linked/store-conditional*. Operating systems and JVMs use these instructions to implement locks and concurrent data structures, but until Java 5.0 they had not been available directly to Java classes.

15.2.1 Compare and swap

The approach taken by most processor architectures, including IA32 and Sparc, is to implement a *compare-and-swap* (CAS) instruction. (Other processors, such as PowerPC, implement the same functionality with a pair of instructions: *load-linked* and *store-conditional*.) CAS has three operands—a memory location V on which to operate, the expected old value A, and the new value B. CAS atomically updates V to the new value B, but only if the value in V matches the expected old value A; otherwise it does nothing. In either case, it returns the value currently in V. (The variant called compare-and-set instead returns whether the operation succeeded.) CAS means "I think V should have the value A; if it does, put B there, otherwise don't change it but tell me I was wrong." CAS is an optimistic technique—it proceeds with the update in the hope of success, and can detect failure if another thread has updated the variable since it was last examined. SimulatedCAS in Listing 15.1 illustrates the semantics (but not the implementation or performance) of CAS.

When multiple threads attempt to update the same variable simultaneously using CAS, one wins and updates the variable's value, and the rest lose. But the losers are not punished by suspension, as they could be if they failed to acquire a lock; instead, they are told that they didn't win the race this time but

```
@ThreadSafe
public class SimulatedCAS {
    @GuardedBy("this") private int value;

    public synchronized int get() { return value; }

    public synchronized int compareAndSwap(int expectedValue,
                                           int newValue) {
        int oldValue = value;
        if (oldValue == expectedValue)
            value = newValue;
        return oldValue;
    }

    public synchronized boolean compareAndSet(int expectedValue,
                                              int newValue) {
        return (expectedValue
                == compareAndSwap(expectedValue, newValue));
    }
}
```

LISTING 15.1. Simulated CAS operation.

can try again. Because a thread that loses a CAS is not blocked, it can decide whether it wants to try again, take some other recovery action, or do nothing.[3] This flexibility eliminates many of the liveness hazards associated with locking (though in unusual cases can introduce the risk of *livelock*—see Section 10.3.3).

The typical pattern for using CAS is first to read the value A from V, derive the new value B from A, and then use CAS to atomically change V from A to B so long as no other thread has changed V to another value in the meantime. CAS addresses the problem of implementing atomic read-modify-write sequences without locking, because it can detect interference from other threads.

15.2.2   A nonblocking counter

CasCounter in Listing 15.2 implements a thread-safe counter using CAS. The increment operation follows the canonical form—fetch the old value, transform it to the new value (adding one), and use CAS to set the new value. If the CAS fails, the operation is immediately retried. Retrying repeatedly is usually a reasonable strategy, although in cases of extreme contention it might be desirable to wait or back off before retrying to avoid livelock.

---

3. Doing nothing may be a perfectly sensible response to a failed CAS; in some nonblocking algorithms, such as the linked queue algorithm in Section 15.4.2, a failed CAS means that someone else already did the work you were planning to do.

CasCounter does not block, though it may have to retry several[4] times if other threads are updating the counter at the same time. (In practice, if all you need is a counter or sequence generator, just use AtomicInteger or AtomicLong, which provide atomic increment and other arithmetic methods.)

```
@ThreadSafe
public class CasCounter {
    private SimulatedCAS value;

    public int getValue() {
        return value.get();
    }

    public int increment() {
        int v;
        do {
            v = value.get();
        }
        while (v != value.compareAndSwap(v, v + 1));
        return v + 1;
    }
}
```

LISTING 15.2. Nonblocking counter using CAS.

At first glance, the CAS-based counter looks as if it should perform worse than a lock-based counter; it has more operations and a more complicated control flow, and depends on the seemingly complicated CAS operation. But in reality, CAS-based counters significantly outperform lock-based counters if there is even a small amount of contention, and often even if there is no contention. The fast path for uncontended lock acquisition typically requires at least one CAS plus other lock-related housekeeping, so more work is going on in the best case for a lock-based counter than in the normal case for the CAS-based counter. Since the CAS succeeds most of the time (assuming low to moderate contention), the hardware will correctly predict the branch implicit in the while loop, minimizing the overhead of the more complicated control logic.

The language syntax for locking may be compact, but the work done by the JVM and OS to manage locks is not. Locking entails traversing a relatively complicated code path in the JVM and may entail OS-level locking, thread suspension, and context switches. In the best case, locking requires at least one CAS, so using locks moves the CAS out of sight but doesn't save any actual execution cost. On the other hand, executing a CAS from within the program involves no JVM code, system calls, or scheduling activity. What looks like a longer code path at the application level is in fact a much shorter code path when JVM and OS activity are

4. Theoretically, it could have to retry arbitrarily many times if other threads keep winning the CAS race; in practice, this sort of starvation rarely happens.

taken into account. The primary disadvantage of CAS is that it forces the caller to deal with contention (by retrying, backing off, or giving up), whereas locks deal with contention automatically by blocking until the lock is available.[5]

CAS performance varies widely across processors. On a single-CPU system, a CAS typically takes on the order of a handful of clock cycles, since no synchronization across processors is necessary. As of this writing, the cost of an uncontended CAS on multiple CPU systems ranges from about ten to about 150 cycles; CAS performance is a rapidly moving target and varies not only across architectures but even across versions of the same processor. Competitive forces will likely result in continued CAS performance improvement over the next several years. A good rule of thumb is that the cost of the "fast path" for *uncontended* lock acquisition and release on most processors is approximately twice the cost of a CAS.

15.2.3 CAS support in the JVM

So, how does Java code convince the processor to execute a CAS on its behalf? Prior to Java 5.0, there was no way to do this short of writing native code. In Java 5.0, low-level support was added to expose CAS operations on int, long, and object references, and the JVM compiles these into the most efficient means provided by the underlying hardware. On platforms supporting CAS, the runtime inlines them into the appropriate machine instruction(s); in the worst case, if a CAS-like instruction is not available the JVM uses a spin lock. This low-level JVM support is used by the atomic variable classes (AtomicXxx in java.util.concurrent.atomic) to provide an efficient CAS operation on numeric and reference types; these atomic variable classes are used, directly or indirectly, to implement most of the classes in java.util.concurrent.

15.3   Atomic variable classes

Atomic variables are finer-grained and lighter-weight than locks, and are critical for implementing high-performance concurrent code on multiprocessor systems. Atomic variables limit the scope of contention to a single variable; this is as fine-grained as you can get (assuming your algorithm can even be implemented using such fine granularity). The fast (uncontended) path for updating an atomic variable is no slower than the fast path for acquiring a lock, and usually faster; the slow path is definitely faster than the slow path for locks because it does not involve suspending and rescheduling threads. With algorithms based on atomic variables instead of locks, threads are more likely to be able to proceed without delay and have an easier time recovering if they do experience contention.

The atomic variable classes provide a generalization of volatile variables to support atomic conditional read-modify-write operations. AtomicInteger represents an int value, and provides get and set methods with the same memory

---

5. Actually, the biggest disadvantage of CAS is the difficulty of constructing the surrounding algorithms correctly.

semantics as reads and writes to a volatile `int`. It also provides an atomic compareAndSet method (which if successful has the memory effects of both reading and writing a volatile variable) and, for convenience, atomic add, increment, and decrement methods. `AtomicInteger` bears a superficial resemblance to an extended `Counter` class, but offers far greater scalability under contention because it can directly exploit underlying hardware support for concurrency.

There are twelve atomic variable classes, divided into four groups: scalars, field updaters, arrays, and compound variables. The most commonly used atomic variables are the scalars: `AtomicInteger`, `AtomicLong`, `AtomicBoolean`, and `AtomicReference`. All support CAS; the `Integer` and `Long` versions support arithmetic as well. (To simulate atomic variables of other primitive types, you can cast `short` or `byte` values to and from `int`, and use `floatToIntBits` or `doubleToLongBits` for floating-point numbers.)

The atomic array classes (available in `Integer`, `Long`, and `Reference` versions) are arrays whose elements can be updated atomically. The atomic array classes provide volatile access semantics to the elements of the array, a feature not available for ordinary arrays—a `volatile` array has `volatile` semantics only for the array reference, not for its elements. (The other types of atomic variables are discussed in Sections 15.4.3 and 15.4.4.)

While the atomic scalar classes extend `Number`, they do not extend the primitive wrapper classes such as `Integer` or `Long`. In fact, they cannot: the primitive wrapper classes are immutable whereas the atomic variable classes are mutable. The atomic variable classes also do not redefine `hashCode` or `equals`; each instance is distinct. Like most mutable objects, they are not good candidates for keys in hash-based collections.

15.3.1   Atomics as "better volatiles"

In Section 3.4.2, we used a `volatile` reference to an immutable object to update multiple state variables atomically. That example relied on check-then-act, but in that particular case the race was harmless because we did not care if we occasionally lost an update. In most other situations, such a check-then-act would not be harmless and could compromise data integrity. For example, `NumberRange` on page 67 could not be implemented safely with a `volatile` reference to an immutable holder object for the upper and lower bounds, nor with using atomic integers to store the bounds. Because an invariant constrains the two numbers and they cannot be updated simultaneously while preserving the invariant, a number range class using `volatile` references or multiple atomic integers will have unsafe check-then-act sequences.

We can combine the technique from `OneValueCache` with atomic references to close the race condition by *atomically* updating the reference to an immutable object holding the lower and upper bounds. `CasNumberRange` in Listing 15.3 uses an `AtomicReference` to an `IntPair` to hold the state; by using compareAndSet it can update the upper or lower bound without the race conditions of `NumberRange`.

```java
public class CasNumberRange {
    @Immutable
    private static class IntPair {
        final int lower; // Invariant: lower <= upper
        final int upper;
        ...
    }
    private final AtomicReference<IntPair> values =
        new AtomicReference<IntPair>(new IntPair(0, 0));

    public int getLower() { return values.get().lower; }
    public int getUpper() { return values.get().upper; }

    public void setLower(int i) {
        while (true) {
            IntPair oldv = values.get();
            if (i > oldv.upper)
                throw new IllegalArgumentException(
                    "Can't set lower to " + i + " > upper");
            IntPair newv = new IntPair(i, oldv.upper);
            if (values.compareAndSet(oldv, newv))
                return;
        }
    }
    // similarly for setUpper
}
```

LISTING 15.3. Preserving multivariable invariants using CAS.

15.3.2 Performance comparison: locks versus atomic variables

To demonstrate the differences in scalability between locks and atomic variables, we constructed a benchmark comparing several implementations of a pseudo-random number generator (PRNG). In a PRNG, the next "random" number is a deterministic function of the previous number, so a PRNG must remember the previous number as part of its state.

Listings 15.4 and 15.5 show two implementations of a thread-safe PRNG, one using ReentrantLock and the other using AtomicInteger. The test driver invokes each repeatedly; each iteration generates a random number (which fetches and modifies the shared seed state) and also performs a number of "busy-work" iterations that operate strictly on thread-local data. This simulates typical operations that include some portion of operating on shared state and some portion of operating on thread-local state.

Figures 15.1 and 15.2 show throughput with low and moderate levels of simulated work in each iteration. With a low level of thread-local computation, the lock or atomic variable experiences heavy contention; with more thread-local compu-

```
@ThreadSafe
public class ReentrantLockPseudoRandom extends PseudoRandom {
    private final Lock lock = new ReentrantLock(false);
    private int seed;

    ReentrantLockPseudoRandom(int seed) {
        this.seed = seed;
    }

    public int nextInt(int n) {
        lock.lock();
        try {
            int s = seed;
            seed = calculateNext(s);
            int remainder = s % n;
            return remainder > 0 ? remainder : remainder + n;
        } finally {
            lock.unlock();
        }
    }
}
```

LISTING 15.4. Random number generator using `ReentrantLock`.

```
@ThreadSafe
public class AtomicPseudoRandom extends PseudoRandom {
    private AtomicInteger seed;

    AtomicPseudoRandom(int seed) {
        this.seed = new AtomicInteger(seed);
    }

    public int nextInt(int n) {
        while (true) {
            int s = seed.get();
            int nextSeed = calculateNext(s);
            if (seed.compareAndSet(s, nextSeed)) {
                int remainder = s % n;
                return remainder > 0 ? remainder : remainder + n;
            }
        }
    }
}
```

LISTING 15.5. Random number generator using `AtomicInteger`.

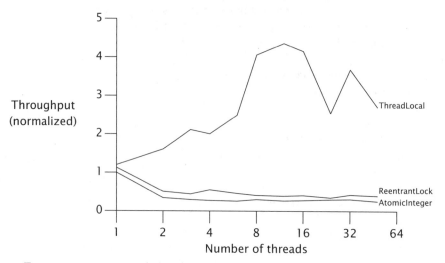

FIGURE 15.1. Lock and `AtomicInteger` performance under high contention.

tation, the lock or atomic variable experiences less contention since it is accessed less often by each thread.

As these graphs show, at high contention levels locking tends to outperform atomic variables, but at more realistic contention levels atomic variables outperform locks.[6] This is because a lock reacts to contention by suspending threads, reducing CPU usage and synchronization traffic on the shared memory bus. (This is similar to how blocking producers in a producer-consumer design reduces the load on consumers and thereby lets them catch up.) On the other hand, with atomic variables, contention management is pushed back to the calling class. Like most CAS-based algorithms, `AtomicPseudoRandom` reacts to contention by trying again immediately, which is usually the right approach but in a high-contention environment just creates more contention.

Before we condemn `AtomicPseudoRandom` as poorly written or atomic variables as a poor choice compared to locks, we should realize that the level of contention in Figure 15.1 is unrealistically high: no real program does nothing but contend for a lock or atomic variable. In practice, atomics tend to scale better than locks because atomics deal more effectively with typical contention levels.

The performance reversal between locks and atomics at differing levels of contention illustrates the strengths and weaknesses of each. With low to moderate contention, atomics offer better scalability; with high contention, locks offer better contention avoidance. (CAS-based algorithms also outperform lock-based ones on single-CPU systems, since a CAS always succeeds on a single-CPU system

---

6. The same holds true in other domains: traffic lights provide better throughput for high traffic but rotaries provide better throughput for low traffic; the contention scheme used by ethernet networks performs better at low traffic levels, but the token-passing scheme used by token ring networks does better with heavy traffic.

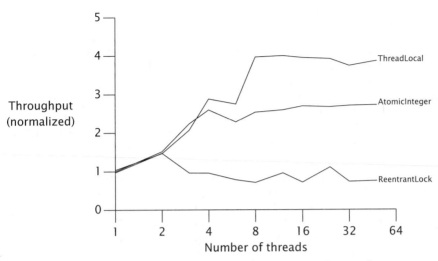

FIGURE 15.2. Lock and `AtomicInteger` performance under moderate contention.

except in the unlikely case that a thread is preempted in the middle of the read-modify-write operation.)

Figures 15.1 and 15.2 include a third curve; an implementation of `PseudoRandom` that uses a `ThreadLocal` for the PRNG state. This implementation approach changes the behavior of the class—each thread sees its own private sequence of pseudorandom numbers, instead of all threads sharing one sequence—but illustrates that it is often cheaper to not share state at all if it can be avoided. We can improve scalability by dealing more effectively with contention, but true scalability is achieved only by eliminating contention entirely.

15.4 Nonblocking algorithms

Lock-based algorithms are at risk for a number of liveness failures. If a thread holding a lock is delayed due to blocking I/O, page fault, or other delay, it is possible that no thread will make progress. An algorithm is called *nonblocking* if failure or suspension of any thread cannot cause failure or suspension of another thread; an algorithm is called *lock-free* if, at each step, *some* thread can make progress. Algorithms that use CAS exclusively for coordination between threads can, if constructed correctly, be both nonblocking and lock-free. An uncontended CAS always succeeds, and if multiple threads contend for a CAS, one always wins and therefore makes progress. Nonblocking algorithms are also immune to deadlock or priority inversion (though they can exhibit starvation or livelock because they can involve repeated retries). We've seen one nonblocking algorithm so far: `CasCounter`. Good nonblocking algorithms are known for many common data structures, including stacks, queues, priority queues, and hash tables—though designing new ones is a task best left to experts.

15.4.1   A nonblocking stack

Nonblocking algorithms are considerably more complicated than their lock-based equivalents. The key to creating nonblocking algorithms is figuring out how to limit the scope of atomic changes to a *single* variable while maintaining data consistency. In linked collection classes such as queues, you can sometimes get away with expressing state transformations as changes to individual links and using an AtomicReference to represent each link that must be updated atomically.

Stacks are the simplest linked data structure: each element refers to only one other element and each element is referred to by only one object reference. ConcurrentStack in Listing 15.6 shows how to construct a stack using atomic references. The stack is a linked list of Node elements, rooted at top, each of which contains a value and a link to the next element. The push method prepares a new link node whose next field refers to the current top of the stack, and then uses CAS to try to install it on the top of the stack. If the same node is still on the top of the stack as when we started, the CAS succeeds; if the top node has changed (because another thread has added or removed elements since we started), the CAS fails and push updates the new node based on the current stack state and tries again. In either case, the stack is still in a consistent state after the CAS.

CasCounter and ConcurrentStack illustrate characteristics of all nonblocking algorithms: some work is done speculatively and may have to be redone. In ConcurrentStack, when we construct the Node representing the new element, we are hoping that the value of the next reference will still be correct by the time it is installed on the stack, but are prepared to retry in the event of contention.

Nonblocking algorithms like ConcurrentStack derive their thread safety from the fact that, like locking, compareAndSet provides both atomicity and visibility guarantees. When a thread changes the state of the stack, it does so with a compareAndSet, which has the memory effects of a volatile write. When a thread examines the stack, it does so by calling get on the same AtomicReference, which has the memory effects of a volatile read. So any changes made by one thread are safely published to any other thread that examines the state of the list. And the list is modified with a compareAndSet that atomically either updates the top reference or fails if it detects interference from another thread.

15.4.2   A nonblocking linked list

The two nonblocking algorithms we've seen so far, the counter and the stack, illustrate the basic pattern of using CAS to update a value speculatively, retrying if the update fails. The trick to building nonblocking algorithms is to limit the scope of atomic changes to a single variable. With counters this is trivial, and with a stack it is straightforward enough, but for more complicated data structures such as queues, hash tables, or trees, it can get a lot trickier.

A linked queue is more complicated than a stack because it must support fast access to both the head and the tail. To do this, it maintains separate head and tail pointers. Two pointers refer to the node at the tail: the next pointer of the current

```java
@ThreadSafe
public class ConcurrentStack <E> {
    AtomicReference<Node<E>> top = new AtomicReference<Node<E>>();

    public void push(E item) {
        Node<E> newHead = new Node<E>(item);
        Node<E> oldHead;
        do {
            oldHead = top.get();
            newHead.next = oldHead;
        } while (!top.compareAndSet(oldHead, newHead));
    }

    public E pop() {
        Node<E> oldHead;
        Node<E> newHead;
        do {
            oldHead = top.get();
            if (oldHead == null)
                return null;
            newHead = oldHead.next;
        } while (!top.compareAndSet(oldHead, newHead));
        return oldHead.item;
    }

    private static class Node <E> {
        public final E item;
        public Node<E> next;

        public Node(E item) {
            this.item = item;
        }
    }
}
```

LISTING 15.6. Nonblocking stack using Treiber's algorithm (Treiber, 1986).

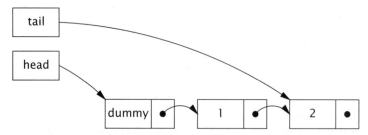

FIGURE 15.3. Queue with two elements in quiescent state.

last element, and the tail pointer. To insert a new element successfully, both of these pointers must be updated—atomically. At first glance, this cannot be done with atomic variables; separate CAS operations are required to update the two pointers, and if the first succeeds but the second one fails the queue is left in an inconsistent state. And, even if both operations succeed, another thread could try to access the queue between the first and the second. Building a nonblocking algorithm for a linked queue requires a plan for both these situations.

We need several tricks to develop this plan. The first is to ensure that the data structure is always in a consistent state, even in the middle of an multi-step update. That way, if thread A is in the middle of a update when thread B arrives on the scene, B can tell that an operation has been partially completed and knows not to try immediately to apply its own update. Then B can wait (by repeatedly examining the queue state) until A finishes, so that the two don't get in each other's way.

While this trick by itself would suffice to let threads "take turns" accessing the data structure without corrupting it, if one thread failed in the middle of an update, no thread would be able to access the queue at all. To make the algorithm nonblocking, we must ensure that the failure of a thread does not prevent other threads from making progress. Thus, the second trick is to make sure that if B arrives to find the data structure in the middle of an update by A, enough information is already embodied in the data structure for B to *finish the update for A*. If B "helps" A by finishing A's operation, B can proceed with its own operation without waiting for A. When A gets around to finishing its operation, it will find that B already did the job for it.

LinkedQueue in Listing 15.7 shows the insertion portion of the Michael-Scott nonblocking linked-queue algorithm (Michael and Scott, 1996), which is used by ConcurrentLinkedQueue. As in many queue algorithms, an empty queue consists of a "sentinel" or "dummy" node, and the head and tail pointers are initialized to refer to the sentinel. The tail pointer always refers to the sentinel (if the queue is empty), the last element in the queue, or (in the case that an operation is in mid-update) the second-to-last element. Figure 15.3 illustrates a queue with two elements in the normal, or *quiescent*, state.

Inserting a new element involves updating two pointers. The first links the new node to the end of the list by updating the next pointer of the current last element; the second swings the tail pointer around to point to the new last ele-

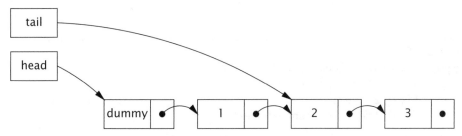

FIGURE 15.4. Queue in intermediate state during insertion.

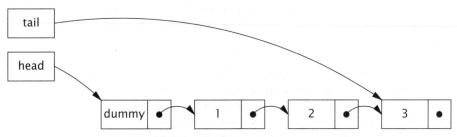

FIGURE 15.5. Queue again in quiescent state after insertion is complete.

ment. Between these two operations, the queue is in the *intermediate* state, shown in Figure 15.4. After the second update, the queue is again in the quiescent state, shown in Figure 15.5.

The key observation that enables both of the required tricks is that if the queue is in the quiescent state, the `next` field of the link node pointed to by `tail` is null, and if it is in the intermediate state, `tail.next` is non-null. So any thread can immediately tell the state of the queue by examining `tail.next`. Further, if the queue is in the intermediate state, it can be restored to the quiescent state by advancing the tail pointer forward one node, finishing the operation for whichever thread is in the middle of inserting an element.[7]

`LinkedQueue.put` first checks to see if the queue is in the intermediate state before attempting to insert a new element (step *A*). If it is, then some other thread is already in the process of inserting an element (between its steps *C* and *D*). Rather than wait for that thread to finish, the current thread helps it by finishing the operation for it, advancing the tail pointer (step *B*). It then repeats this check in case another thread has started inserting a new element, advancing the tail pointer until it finds the queue in the quiescent state so it can begin its own insertion.

The CAS at step *C*, which links the new node at the tail of the queue, could fail if two threads try to insert an element at the same time. In that case, no harm is done: no changes have been made, and the current thread can just reload the tail pointer and try again. Once *C* succeeds, the insertion is considered to have

---

7. For a full account of the correctness of this algorithm, see (Michael and Scott, 1996) or (Herlihy and Shavit, 2006).

```
@ThreadSafe
public class LinkedQueue <E> {
    private static class Node <E> {
        final E item;
        final AtomicReference<Node<E>> next;

        public Node(E item, Node<E> next) {
            this.item = item;
            this.next = new AtomicReference<Node<E>>(next);
        }
    }

    private final Node<E> dummy = new Node<E>(null, null);
    private final AtomicReference<Node<E>> head
            = new AtomicReference<Node<E>>(dummy);
    private final AtomicReference<Node<E>> tail
            = new AtomicReference<Node<E>>(dummy);

    public boolean put(E item) {
        Node<E> newNode = new Node<E>(item, null);
        while (true) {
            Node<E> curTail = tail.get();
            Node<E> tailNext = curTail.next.get();
            if (curTail == tail.get()) {
                if (tailNext != null) {                                    (A)
                    // Queue in intermediate state, advance tail
                    tail.compareAndSet(curTail, tailNext);                 (B)
                } else {
                    // In quiescent state, try inserting new node
                    if (curTail.next.compareAndSet(null, newNode)) {       (C)
                        // Insertion succeeded, try advancing tail
                        tail.compareAndSet(curTail, newNode);              (D)
                        return true;
                    }
                }
            }
        }
    }
}
```

LISTING 15.7.   Insertion in the Michael-Scott nonblocking queue algorithm (Michael and Scott, 1996).

taken effect; the second CAS (step *D*) is considered "cleanup", since it can be performed either by the inserting thread or by any other thread. If *D* fails, the inserting thread returns anyway rather than retrying the CAS, because no retry is needed—another thread has already finished the job in its step *B*! This works because before any thread tries to link a new node into the queue, it first checks to see if the queue needs cleaning up by checking if `tail.next` is non-null. If it is, it advances the tail pointer first (perhaps multiple times) until the queue is in the quiescent state.

15.4.3 Atomic field updaters

Listing 15.7 illustrates the algorithm used by `ConcurrentLinkedQueue`, but the actual implementation is a bit different. Instead of representing each `Node` with an atomic reference, `ConcurrentLinkedQueue` uses an ordinary volatile reference and updates it through the reflection-based `AtomicReferenceFieldUpdater`, as shown in Listing 15.8.

```
private class Node<E> {
    private final E item;
    private volatile Node<E> next;

    public Node(E item) {
        this.item = item;
    }
}

private static AtomicReferenceFieldUpdater<Node, Node> nextUpdater
        = AtomicReferenceFieldUpdater.newUpdater(
                Node.class, Node.class, "next");
```

LISTING 15.8. *Using atomic field updaters in* `ConcurrentLinkedQueue`.

The atomic field updater classes (available in `Integer`, `Long`, and `Reference` versions) represent a reflection-based "view" of an existing volatile field so that CAS can be used on existing volatile fields. The updater classes have no constructors; to create one, you call the `newUpdater` factory method, specifying the class and field name. The field updater classes are not tied to a specific instance; one can be used to update the target field for any instance of the target class. The atomicity guarantees for the updater classes are weaker than for the regular atomic classes because you cannot guarantee that the underlying fields will not be modified directly—the `compareAndSet` and arithmetic methods guarantee atomicity only with respect to other threads using the atomic field updater methods.

In `ConcurrentLinkedQueue`, updates to the `next` field of a `Node` are applied using the `compareAndSet` method of `nextUpdater`. This somewhat circuitous approach is used entirely for performance reasons. For frequently allocated, short-lived objects like queue link nodes, eliminating the creation of an `AtomicReference` for each `Node` is significant enough to reduce the cost of insertion operations.

However, in nearly all situations, ordinary atomic variables perform just fine—in only a few cases will the atomic field updaters be needed. (The atomic field updaters are also useful when you want to perform atomic updates while preserving the serialized form of an existing class.)

15.4.4   The ABA problem

The *ABA problem* is an anomaly that can arise from the naive use of compare-and-swap in algorithms where nodes can be recycled (primarily in environments without garbage collection). A CAS effectively asks "Is the value of V still A?", and proceeds with the update if so. In most situations, including the examples presented in this chapter, this is entirely sufficient. However, sometimes we really want to ask "Has the value of V changed since I last observed it to be A?" For some algorithms, changing V from A to B and then back to A still counts as a change that requires us to retry some algorithmic step.

This *ABA problem* can arise in algorithms that do their own memory management for link node objects. In this case, that the head of a list still refers to a previously observed node is not enough to imply that the contents of the list have not changed. If you cannot avoid the ABA problem by letting the garbage collector manage link nodes for you, there is still a relatively simple solution: instead of updating the value of a reference, update a *pair* of values, a reference and a version number. Even if the value changes from A to B and back to A, the version numbers will be different. `AtomicStampedReference` (and its cousin `AtomicMarkableReference`) provide atomic conditional update on a pair of variables. `AtomicStampedReference` updates an object reference-integer pair, allowing "versioned" references that are immune[8] to the ABA problem. Similarly, `AtomicMarkableReference` updates an object reference-boolean pair that is used by some algorithms to let a node remain in a list while being marked as deleted.[9]

Summary

Nonblocking algorithms maintain thread safety by using low-level concurrency primitives such as compare-and-swap instead of locks. These low-level primitives are exposed through the atomic variable classes, which can also be used as "better volatile variables" providing atomic update operations for integers and object references.

Nonblocking algorithms are difficult to design and implement, but can offer better scalability under typical conditions and greater resistance to liveness failures. Many of the advances in concurrent performance from one JVM version to the next come from the use of nonblocking algorithms, both within the JVM and in the platform libraries.

---

8. In practice, anyway; theoretically the counter could wrap.
9. Many processors provide a double-wide CAS (CAS2 or CASX) operation that can operate on a pointer-integer pair, which would make this operation reasonably efficient. As of Java 6, `Atomic-StampedReference` does not use double-wide CAS even on platforms that support it. (Double-wide CAS differs from DCAS, which operates on two unrelated memory locations; as of this writing, no current processor implements DCAS.)

CHAPTER 16

The Java Memory Model

Throughout this book, we've mostly avoided the low-level details of the Java Memory Model (JMM) and instead focused on higher-level design issues such as safe publication, specification of, and adherence to synchronization policies. These derive their safety from the JMM, and you may find it easier to use these mechanisms effectively when you understand *why* they work. This chapter pulls back the curtain to reveal the low-level requirements and guarantees of the Java Memory Model and the reasoning behind some of the higher-level design rules offered in this book.

16.1 What is a memory model, and why would I want one?

Suppose one thread assigns a value to aVariable:

```
aVariable = 3;
```

A memory model addresses the question "Under what conditions does a thread that reads aVariable see the value 3?" This may sound like a dumb question, but in the absence of synchronization, there are a number of reasons a thread might not immediately—or ever—see the results of an operation in another thread. Compilers may generate instructions in a different order than the "obvious" one suggested by the source code, or store variables in registers instead of in memory; processors may execute instructions in parallel or out of order; caches may vary the order in which writes to variables are committed to main memory; and values stored in processor-local caches may not be visible to other processors. These factors can prevent a thread from seeing the most up-to-date value for a variable and can cause memory actions in other threads to appear to happen out of order—if you don't use adequate synchronization.

In a single-threaded environment, all these tricks played on our program by the environment are hidden from us and have no effect other than to speed up execution. The Java Language Specification requires the JVM to maintain *within-thread as-if-serial semantics*: as long as the program has the same result as if it were executed in program order in a strictly sequential environment, all these games are permissible. And that's a good thing, too, because these rearrangements are responsible for much of the improvement in computing performance

337

in recent years. Certainly higher clock rates have contributed to improved performance, but so has increased parallelism—pipelined superscalar execution units, dynamic instruction scheduling, speculative execution, and sophisticated multilevel memory caches. As processors have become more sophisticated, so too have compilers, rearranging instructions to facilitate optimal execution and using sophisticated global register-allocation algorithms. And as processor manufacturers transition to multicore processors, largely because clock rates are getting harder to increase economically, hardware parallelism will only increase.

In a multithreaded environment, the illusion of sequentiality cannot be maintained without significant performance cost. Since most of the time threads within a concurrent application are each "doing their own thing", excessive inter-thread coordination would only slow down the application to no real benefit. It is only when multiple threads share data that it is necessary to coordinate their activities, and the JVM relies on the program to identify when this is happening by using synchronization.

The JMM specifies the minimal guarantees the JVM must make about when writes to variables become visible to other threads. It was designed to balance the need for predictability and ease of program development with the realities of implementing high-performance JVMs on a wide range of popular processor architectures. Some aspects of the JMM may be disturbing at first if you are not familiar with the tricks used by modern processors and compilers to squeeze extra performance out of your program.

16.1.1 Platform memory models

In a shared-memory multiprocessor architecture, each processor has its own cache that is periodically reconciled with main memory. Processor architectures provide varying degrees of *cache coherence*; some provide minimal guarantees that allow different processors to see different values for the same memory location at virtually any time. The operating system, compiler, and runtime (and sometimes, the program, too) must make up the difference between what the hardware provides and what thread safety requires.

Ensuring that every processor knows what every other processor is doing at all times is expensive. Most of the time this information is not needed, so processors relax their memory-coherency guarantees to improve performance. An architecture's *memory model* tells programs what guarantees they can expect from the memory system, and specifies the special instructions required (called *memory barriers* or *fences*) to get the additional memory coordination guarantees required when sharing data. In order to shield the Java developer from the differences between memory models across architectures, Java provides its own memory model, and the JVM deals with the differences between the JMM and the underlying platform's memory model by inserting memory barriers at the appropriate places.

One convenient mental model for program execution is to imagine that there is a single order in which the operations happen in a program, regardless of what processor they execute on, and that each read of a variable will see the last write in the execution order to that variable by any processor. This happy, if unrealistic, model is called *sequential consistency*. Software developers often mistakenly assume sequential consistency, but no modern multiprocessor offers sequential consistency and the JMM does not either. The classic sequential computing model, the von Neumann model, is only a vague approximation of how modern multiprocessors behave.

The bottom line is that modern shared-memory multiprocessors (and compilers) can do some surprising things when data is shared across threads, unless you've told them not to through the use of memory barriers. Fortunately, Java programs need not specify the placement of memory barriers; they need only identify when shared state is being accessed, through the proper use of synchronization.

16.1.2 Reordering

In describing race conditions and atomicity failures in Chapter 2, we used interaction diagrams depicting "unlucky timing" where the scheduler interleaved operations so as to cause incorrect results in insufficiently synchronized programs. To make matters worse, the JMM can permit actions to appear to execute in different orders from the perspective of different threads, making reasoning about ordering in the absence of synchronization even more complicated. The various reasons why operations might be delayed or appear to execute out of order can all be grouped into the general category of *reordering*.

PossibleReordering in Listing 16.1 illustrates how difficult it is to reason about the behavior of even the simplest concurrent programs unless they are correctly synchronized. It is fairly easy to imagine how PossibleReordering could print $(1,0)$, or $(0,1)$, or $(1,1)$: thread A could run to completion before B starts, B could run to completion before A starts, or their actions could be interleaved. But, strangely, PossibleReordering can also print $(0,0)$! The actions in each thread have no dataflow dependence on each other, and accordingly can be executed out of order. (Even if they are executed in order, the timing by which caches are flushed to main memory can make it appear, from the perspective of B, that the assignments in A occurred in the opposite order.) Figure 16.1 shows a possible interleaving with reordering that results in printing $(0,0)$.

PossibleReordering is a trivial program, and it is still surprisingly tricky to enumerate its possible results. Reordering at the memory level can make programs behave unexpectedly. It is prohibitively difficult to reason about ordering in the absence of synchronization; it is much easier to ensure that your program uses synchronization appropriately. Synchronization inhibits the compiler, runtime, and hardware from reordering memory operations in ways that would violate the visibility guarantees provided by the JMM.[1]

16.1.3 The Java Memory Model in 500 words or less

The Java Memory Model is specified in terms of *actions*, which include reads and writes to variables, locks and unlocks of monitors, and starting and joining with

---

1. On most popular processor architectures, the memory model is strong enough that the performance cost of a volatile read is in line with that of a nonvolatile read.

```
public class PossibleReordering {
    static int x = 0, y = 0;
    static int a = 0, b = 0;

    public static void main(String[] args)
            throws InterruptedException {
        Thread one = new Thread(new Runnable() {
            public void run() {
                a = 1;
                x = b;
            }
        });
        Thread other = new Thread(new Runnable() {
            public void run() {
                b = 1;
                y = a;
            }
        });
        one.start(); other.start();
        one.join();  other.join();
        System.out.println("( "+ x + "," + y + ")");
    }
}
```

LISTING 16.1. Insufficiently synchronized program that can have surprising results. *Don't do this.*

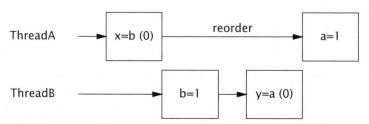

FIGURE 16.1. Interleaving showing reordering in `PossibleReordering`.

threads. The JMM defines a partial ordering[2] called *happens-before* on all actions
within the program. To guarantee that the thread executing action *B* can see the
results of action *A* (whether or not *A* and *B* occur in different threads), there must
be a *happens-before* relationship between *A* and *B*. In the absence of a *happens-before*
ordering between two operations, the JVM is free to reorder them as it pleases.

---

2. A partial ordering $\prec$ is a relation on a set that is antisymmetric, reflexive, and transitive, but for
any two elements x and y, it need not be the case that $x \prec y$ or $y \prec x$. We use partial orderings every
day to express preferences; we may prefer sushi to cheeseburgers and Mozart to Mahler, but we don't
necessarily have a clear preference between cheeseburgers and Mozart.

A *data race* occurs when a variable is read by more than one thread, and written by at least one thread, but the reads and writes are not ordered by *happens-before*. A *correctly synchronized program* is one with no data races; correctly synchronized programs exhibit sequential consistency, meaning that all actions within the program appear to happen in a fixed, global order.

The rules for *happens-before* are:

Program order rule. Each action in a thread *happens-before* every action in that thread that comes later in the program order.

Monitor lock rule. An unlock on a monitor lock *happens-before* every subsequent lock on that same monitor lock.[3]

Volatile variable rule. A write to a volatile field *happens-before* every subsequent read of that same field.[4]

Thread start rule. A call to Thread.start on a thread *happens-before* every action in the started thread.

Thread termination rule. Any action in a thread *happens-before* any other thread detects that thread has terminated, either by successfully return from Thread.join or by Thread.isAlive returning false.

Interruption rule. A thread calling interrupt on another thread *happens-before* the interrupted thread detects the interrupt (either by having InterruptedException thrown, or invoking isInterrupted or interrupted).

Finalizer rule. The end of a constructor for an object *happens-before* the start of the finalizer for that object.

Transitivity. If A *happens-before* B, and B *happens-before* C, then A *happens-before* C.

Even though actions are only partially ordered, synchronization actions—lock acquisition and release, and reads and writes of volatile variables—are totally ordered. This makes it sensible to describe *happens-before* in terms of "subsequent" lock acquisitions and reads of volatile variables.

Figure 16.2 illustrates the *happens-before* relation when two threads synchronize using a common lock. All the actions within thread *A* are ordered by the program

---

3. Locks and unlocks on explicit Lock objects have the same memory semantics as intrinsic locks.
4. Reads and writes of atomic variables have the same memory semantics as volatile variables.

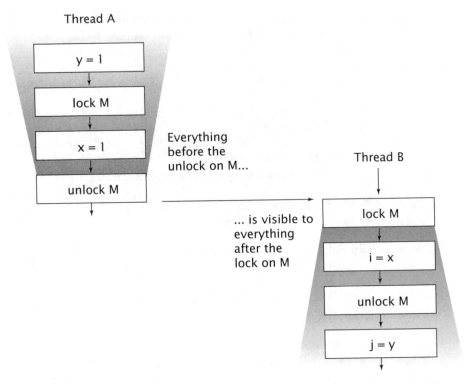

FIGURE 16.2. Illustration of *happens-before* in the Java Memory Model.

order rule, as are the actions within thread *B*. Because *A* releases lock *M* and *B* subsequently acquires *M*, all the actions in *A* before releasing the lock are therefore ordered before the actions in *B* after acquiring the lock. When two threads synchronize on *different* locks, we can't say anything about the ordering of actions between them—there is no *happens-before* relation between the actions in the two threads.

16.1.4 Piggybacking on synchronization

Because of the strength of the *happens-before* ordering, you can sometimes piggyback on the visibility properties of an existing synchronization. This entails combining the program order rule for *happens-before* with one of the other ordering rules (usually the monitor lock or volatile variable rule) to order accesses to a variable not otherwise guarded by a lock. This technique is very sensitive to the order in which statements occur and is therefore quite fragile; it is an advanced technique that should be reserved for squeezing the last drop of performance out of the most performance-critical classes like ReentrantLock.

The implementation of the protected AbstractQueuedSynchronizer methods in FutureTask illustrates piggybacking. AQS maintains an integer of synchronizer state that FutureTask uses to store the task state: running, completed, or cancelled. But FutureTask also maintains additional variables, such as the result of the computation. When one thread calls set to save the result and another thread calls get to retrieve it, the two had better be ordered by *happens-before*. This could be done by making the reference to the result volatile, but it is possible to exploit existing synchronization to achieve the same result at lower cost.

FutureTask is carefully crafted to ensure that a successful call to tryReleaseShared always *happens-before* a subsequent call to tryAcquireShared; tryReleaseShared always writes to a volatile variable that is read by tryAcquireShared. Listing 16.2 shows the innerSet and innerGet methods that are called when the result is saved or retrieved; since innerSet writes result before calling releaseShared (which calls tryReleaseShared) and innerGet reads result after calling acquireShared (which calls tryAcquireShared), the program order rule combines with the volatile variable rule to ensure that the write of result in innerGet *happens-before* the read of result in innerGet.

```java
// Inner class of FutureTask
private final class Sync extends AbstractQueuedSynchronizer {
    private static final int RUNNING = 1, RAN = 2, CANCELLED = 4;
    private V result;
    private Exception exception;

    void innerSet(V v) {
        while (true) {
            int s = getState();
            if (ranOrCancelled(s))
                return;
            if (compareAndSetState(s, RAN))
                break;
        }
        result = v;
        releaseShared(0);
        done();
    }

    V innerGet() throws InterruptedException, ExecutionException {
        acquireSharedInterruptibly(0);
        if (getState() == CANCELLED)
            throw new CancellationException();
        if (exception != null)
            throw new ExecutionException(exception);
        return result;
    }
}
```

Listing 16.2. Inner class of FutureTask illustrating synchronization piggybacking.

We call this technique "piggybacking" because it uses an existing *happens-before* ordering that was created for some other reason to ensure the visibility of object X, rather than creating a *happens-before* ordering specifically for publishing X.

Piggybacking of the sort employed by FutureTask is quite fragile and should not be undertaken casually. However, in some cases piggybacking is perfectly reasonable, such as when a class commits to a *happens-before* ordering between methods as part of its specification. For example, safe publication using a BlockingQueue is a form of piggybacking. One thread putting an object on a queue and another thread subsequently retrieving it constitutes safe publication because there is guaranteed to be sufficient internal synchronization in a BlockingQueue implementation to ensure that the enqueue *happens-before* the dequeue.

Other *happens-before* orderings guaranteed by the class library include:

- Placing an item in a thread-safe collection *happens-before* another thread retrieves that item from the collection;

- Counting down on a CountDownLatch *happens-before* a thread returns from await on that latch;

- Releasing a permit to a Semaphore *happens-before* acquiring a permit from that same Semaphore;

- Actions taken by the task represented by a Future *happens-before* another thread successfully returns from Future.get;

- Submitting a Runnable or Callable to an Executor *happens-before* the task begins execution; and

- A thread arriving at a CyclicBarrier or Exchanger *happens-before* the other threads are released from that same barrier or exchange point. If Cyclic-Barrier uses a barrier action, arriving at the barrier *happens-before* the barrier action, which in turn *happens-before* threads are released from the barrier.

16.2   Publication

Chapter 3 explored how an object could be safely or improperly published. The safe publication techniques described there derive their safety from guarantees provided by the JMM; the risks of improper publication are consequences of the absence of a *happens-before* ordering between publishing a shared object and accessing it from another thread.

16.2.1   Unsafe publication

The possibility of reordering in the absence of a *happens-before* relationship explains why publishing an object without adequate synchronization can allow another thread to see a *partially constructed object* (see Section 3.5). Initializing a new object involves writing to variables—the new object's fields. Similarly, publishing a reference involves writing to another variable—the reference to the new object.

If you do not ensure that publishing the shared reference *happens-before* another thread loads that shared reference, then the write of the reference to the new object can be reordered (from the perspective of the thread consuming the object) with the writes to its fields. In that case, another thread could see an up-to-date value for the object reference but *out-of-date values for some or all of that object's state*—a partially constructed object.

Unsafe publication can happen as a result of an incorrect lazy initialization, as shown in Figure 16.3. At first glance, the only problem here seems to be the race condition described in Section 2.2.2. Under certain circumstances, such as when all instances of the Resource are identical, you might be willing to overlook these (along with the inefficiency of possibly creating the Resource more than once). Unfortunately, even if these defects are overlooked, UnsafeLazyInitialization is still not safe, because another thread could observe a reference to a partially constructed Resource.

```
@NotThreadSafe
public class UnsafeLazyInitialization {
    private static Resource resource;

    public static Resource getInstance() {
        if (resource == null)
            resource = new Resource(); // unsafe publication
        return resource;
    }
}
```

LISTING 16.3. Unsafe lazy initialization. *Don't do this.*

Suppose thread *A* is the first to invoke getInstance. It sees that resource is null, instantiates a new Resource, and sets resource to reference it. When thread *B* later calls getInstance, it might see that resource already has a non-null value and just use the already constructed Resource. This might look harmless at first, but *there is no happens-before ordering between the writing of resource in A and the reading of resource in B*. A data race has been used to publish the object, and therefore *B* is not guaranteed to see the correct state of the Resource.

The Resource constructor changes the fields of the freshly allocated Resource from their default values (written by the Object constructor) to their initial values. Since neither thread used synchronization, *B* could possibly see *A*'s actions in a different order than *A* performed them. So even though *A* initialized the Resource before setting resource to reference it, *B* could see the write to resource as occurring *before* the writes to the fields of the Resource. *B* could thus see a partially constructed Resource that may well be in an invalid state—and whose state may unexpectedly change later.

> With the exception of immutable objects, it is not safe to use an object that
> has been initialized by another thread unless the publication *happens-before* the consuming thread uses it.

16.2.2 Safe publication

The safe-publication idioms described in Chapter 3 ensure that the published
object is visible to other threads because they ensure the publication *happens-before* the consuming thread loads a reference to the published object. If thread *A*
places *X* on a BlockingQueue (and no thread subsequently modifies it) and thread
B retrieves it from the queue, *B* is guaranteed to see *X* as *A* left it. This is because
the BlockingQueue implementations have sufficient internal synchronization to
ensure that the put *happens-before* the take. Similarly, using a shared variable
guarded by a lock or a shared volatile variable ensures that reads and writes of
that variable are ordered by *happens-before*.

This *happens-before* guarantee is actually a stronger promise of visibility and
ordering than made by safe publication. When *X* is safely published from *A* to *B*,
the safe publication guarantees visibility of the state of *X*, but not of the state of
other variables *A* may have touched. But if *A* putting *X* on a queue *happens-before*
B fetches *X* from that queue, not only does *B* see *X* in the state that *A* left it
(assuming that *X* has not been subsequently modified by *A* or anyone else), but
B sees *everything* *A* did before the handoff (again, subject to the same caveat).[5]

Why did we focus so heavily on @GuardedBy and safe publication, when the
JMM already provides us with the more powerful *happens-before*? Thinking in
terms of handing off object ownership and publication fits better into most program designs than thinking in terms of visibility of individual memory writes.
The *happens-before* ordering operates at the level of individual memory accesses—
it is a sort of "concurrency assembly language". Safe publication operates at a
level closer to that of your program's design.

16.2.3 Safe initialization idioms

It sometimes makes sense to defer initialization of objects that are expensive to
initialize until they are actually needed, but we have seen how the misuse of
lazy initialization can lead to trouble. UnsafeLazyInitialization can be fixed
by making the getResource method synchronized, as shown in Listing 16.4. Because the code path through getInstance is fairly short (a test and a predicted
branch), if getInstance is not called frequently by many threads, there is little enough contention for the SafeLazyInitialization lock that this approach
offers adequate performance.

The treatment of static fields with initializers (or fields whose value is initialized in a static initialization block [JPL 2.2.1 and 2.5.3]) is somewhat special and

---

5. The JMM guarantees that *B* sees a value at least as up-to-date as the value that *A* wrote; subsequent
writes may or may not be visible.

```
@ThreadSafe
public class SafeLazyInitialization {
    private static Resource resource;

    public synchronized static Resource getInstance() {
        if (resource == null)
            resource = new Resource();
        return resource;
    }
}
```

LISTING 16.4. Thread-safe lazy initialization.

offers additional thread-safety guarantees. Static initializers are run by the JVM at class initialization time, after class loading but before the class is used by any thread. Because the JVM acquires a lock during initialization [JLS 12.4.2] and this lock is acquired by each thread at least once to ensure that the class has been loaded, memory writes made during static initialization are automatically visible to all threads. Thus statically initialized objects require no explicit synchronization either during construction or when being referenced. However, this applies only to the *as-constructed* state—if the object is mutable, synchronization is still required by both readers and writers to make subsequent modifications visible and to avoid data corruption.

```
@ThreadSafe
public class EagerInitialization {
    private static Resource resource = new Resource();

    public static Resource getResource() { return resource; }
}
```

LISTING 16.5. Eager initialization.

Using eager initialization, shown in Listing 16.5, eliminates the synchronization cost incurred on each call to getInstance in SafeLazyInitialization. This technique can be combined with the JVM's lazy class loading to create a lazy initialization technique that does not require synchronization on the common code path. The *lazy initialization holder class* idiom [EJ Item 48] in Listing 16.6 uses a class whose only purpose is to initialize the Resource. The JVM defers initializing the ResourceHolder class until it is actually used [JLS 12.4.1], and because the Resource is initialized with a static initializer, no additional synchronization is needed. The first call to getResource by any thread causes ResourceHolder to be loaded and initialized, at which time the initialization of the Resource happens through the static initializer.

```
@ThreadSafe
public class ResourceFactory {
    private static class ResourceHolder {
        public static Resource resource = new Resource();
    }

    public static Resource getResource() {
        return ResourceHolder.resource;
    }
}
```

LISTING 16.6. *Lazy initialization holder class idiom.*

16.2.4   Double-checked locking

No book on concurrency would be complete without a discussion of the infamous double-checked locking (DCL) antipattern, shown in Listing 16.7. In very early JVMs, synchronization, even uncontended synchronization, had a significant performance cost. As a result, many clever (or at least clever-looking) tricks were invented to reduce the impact of synchronization—some good, some bad, and some ugly. DCL falls into the "ugly" category.

Again, because the performance of early JVMs left something to be desired, lazy initialization was often used to avoid potentially unnecessary expensive operations or reduce application startup time. A properly written lazy initialization method requires synchronization. But at the time, synchronization was slow and, more importantly, not completely understood: the exclusion aspects were well enough understood, but the visibility aspects were not.

DCL purported to offer the best of both worlds—lazy initialization without paying the synchronization penalty on the common code path. The way it worked was first to check whether initialization was needed without synchronizing, and if the resource reference was not null, use it. Otherwise, synchronize and check again if the Resource is initialized, ensuring that only one thread actually initializes the shared Resource. The common code path—fetching a reference to an already constructed Resource—doesn't use synchronization. And that's where the problem is: as described in Section 16.2.1, it is possible for a thread to see a partially constructed Resource.

The real problem with DCL is the assumption that the worst thing that can happen when reading a shared object reference without synchronization is to erroneously see a stale value (in this case, null); in that case the DCL idiom compensates for this risk by trying again with the lock held. But the worst case is actually considerably worse—it is possible to see a current value of the reference but stale values for the object's state, meaning that the object could be seen to be in an invalid or incorrect state.

Subsequent changes in the JMM (Java 5.0 and later) have enabled DCL to work *if* resource is made volatile, and the performance impact of this is small since volatile reads are usually only slightly more expensive than nonvolatile reads.

```
@NotThreadSafe
public class DoubleCheckedLocking {
    private static Resource resource;

    public static Resource getInstance() {
        if (resource == null) {
            synchronized (DoubleCheckedLocking.class) {
                if (resource == null)
                    resource = new Resource();
            }
        }
        return resource;
    }
}
```

LISTING 16.7. Double-checked-locking antipattern. *Don't do this.*

However, this is an idiom whose utility has largely passed—the forces that motivated it (slow uncontended synchronization, slow JVM startup) are no longer in play, making it less effective as an optimization. The lazy initialization holder idiom offers the same benefits and is easier to understand.

16.3 Initialization safety

The guarantee of *initialization safety* allows properly constructed *immutable* objects to be safely shared across threads without synchronization, regardless of how they are published—even if published using a data race. (This means that UnsafeLazyInitialization is actually safe *if* Resource is immutable.)

Without initialization safety, supposedly immutable objects like String can appear to change their value if synchronization is not used by both the publishing and consuming threads. The security architecture relies on the immutability of String; the lack of initialization safety could create security vulnerabilities that allow malicious code to bypass security checks.

> Initialization safety guarantees that for *properly constructed* objects, all threads will see the correct values of final fields that were set by the constructor, regardless of how the object is published. Further, any variables that can be *reached* through a final field of a properly constructed object (such as the elements of a final array or the contents of a HashMap referenced by a final field) are also guaranteed to be visible to other threads.[6]

---

6. This applies only to objects that are reachable *only* through final fields of the object under construction.

For objects with final fields, initialization safety prohibits reordering any part of construction with the initial load of a reference to that object. All writes to final fields made by the constructor, as well as to any variables reachable through those fields, become "frozen" when the constructor completes, and any thread that obtains a reference to that object is guaranteed to see a value that is at least as up to date as the frozen value. Writes that initialize variables reachable through final fields are not reordered with operations following the post-construction freeze.

Initialization safety means that SafeStates in Listing 16.8 could be safely published even through unsafe lazy initialization or stashing a reference to a Safe-States in a public static field with no synchronization, even though it uses no synchronization and relies on the non-thread-safe HashSet.

```
@ThreadSafe
public class SafeStates {
    private final Map<String, String> states;

    public SafeStates() {
        states = new HashMap<String, String>();
        states.put("alaska", "AK");
        states.put("alabama", "AL");
        ...
        states.put("wyoming", "WY");
    }

    public String getAbbreviation(String s) {
        return states.get(s);
    }
}
```

LISTING 16.8. *Initialization safety for immutable objects.*

However, a number of small changes to SafeStates would take away its thread safety. If states were not final, or if any method other than the constructor modified its contents, initialization safety would not be strong enough to safely access SafeStates without synchronization. If SafeStates had other nonfinal fields, other threads might still see incorrect values of those fields. And allowing the object to escape during construction invalidates the initialization-safety guarantee.

> Initialization safety makes visibility guarantees only for the values that are reachable through final fields as of the time the constructor finishes. For values reachable through nonfinal fields, or values that may change after construction, you must use synchronization to ensure visibility.

Summary

The Java Memory Model specifies when the actions of one thread on memory are guaranteed to be visible to another. The specifics involve ensuring that operations are ordered by a partial ordering called *happens-before*, which is specified at the level of individual memory and synchronization operations. In the absence of sufficient synchronization, some very strange things can happen when threads access shared data. However, the higher-level rules offered in Chapters 2 and 3, such as @GuardedBy and safe publication, can be used to ensure thread safety without resorting to the low-level details of *happens-before*.

APPENDIX A

Annotations for Concurrency

We've used annotations such as @GuardedBy and @ThreadSafe to show how thread-safety promises and synchronization policies can be documented. This appendix documents these annotations; their source code can be downloaded from this book's website. (There are, of course, additional thread-safety promises and implementation details that should be documented but that are not captured by this minimal set of annotations.)

A.1 Class annotations

We use three class-level annotations to describe a class's *intended* thread-safety promises: @Immutable, @ThreadSafe, and @NotThreadSafe. @Immutable means, of course, that the class is immutable, and implies @ThreadSafe. @NotThreadSafe is optional—if a class is not annotated as thread-safe, it should be presumed not to be thread-safe, but if you want to make it extra clear, use @NotThreadSafe.

These annotations are relatively unintrusive and are beneficial to both users and maintainers. Users can see immediately whether a class is thread-safe, and maintainers can see immediately whether thread-safety guarantees must be preserved. Annotations are also useful to a third constituency: tools. Static code-analysis tools may be able to verify that the code complies with the contract indicated by the annotation, such as verifying that a class annotated with @Immutable actually is immutable.

A.2 Field and method annotations

The class-level annotations above are part of the public documentation for the class. Other aspects of a class's thread-safety strategy are entirely for maintainers and are not part of its public documentation.

Classes that use locking should document which state variables are guarded with which locks, and which locks are used to guard those variables. A common source of inadvertent non-thread-safety is when a thread-safe class consistently uses locking to guard its state, but is later modified to add either new state variables that are not adequately guarded by locking, or new methods that do not use locking properly to guard the existing state variables. Documenting which variables are guarded by which locks can help prevent both types of omissions.

@GuardedBy(lock) documents that a field or method should be accessed only with a specific lock held. The lock argument identifies the lock that should be held when accessing the annotated field or method. The possible values for lock are:

- @GuardedBy("this"), meaning the intrinsic lock on the containing object (the object of which the method or field is a member);

- @GuardedBy("*fieldName*"), meaning the lock associated with the object referenced by the named field, either an intrinsic lock (for fields that do not refer to a Lock) or an explicit Lock (for fields that refer to a Lock);

- @GuardedBy("*ClassName.fieldName*"), like @GuardedBy("*fieldName*"), but referencing a lock object held in a static field of another class;

- @GuardedBy("*methodName*()"), meaning the lock object that is returned by calling the named method;

- @GuardedBy("*ClassName*.class"), meaning the class literal object for the named class.

Using @GuardedBy to identify each state variable that needs locking and which lock guards it can assist in maintenance and code reviews, and can help automated analysis tools spot potential thread-safety errors.

Bibliography

Ken Arnold, James Gosling, and David Holmes. *The Java Programming Language*, Fourth Edition. Addison–Wesley, 2005.

David F. Bacon, Ravi B. Konuru, Chet Murthy, and Mauricio J. Serrano. Thin Locks: Featherweight Synchronization for Java. In *SIGPLAN Conference on Programming Language Design and Implementation*, pages 258–268, 1998. URL http://citeseer.ist.psu.edu/bacon98thin.html.

Joshua Bloch. *Effective Java Programming Language Guide*. Addison–Wesley, 2001.

Joshua Bloch and Neal Gafter. *Java Puzzlers*. Addison–Wesley, 2005.

Hans Boehm. Destructors, Finalizers, and Synchronization. In *POPL '03: Proceedings of the 30th ACM SIGPLAN-SIGACT Symposium on Principles of Programming Languages*, pages 262–272. ACM Press, 2003. URL http://doi.acm.org/10.1145/604131.604153.

Hans Boehm. Finalization, Threads, and the Java Memory Model. JavaOne presentation, 2005. URL http://developers.sun.com/learning/javaoneonline/2005/coreplatform/TS-3281.pdf.

Joseph Bowbeer. The Last Word in Swing Threads, 2005. URL http://java.sun.com/products/jfc/tsc/articles/threads/threads3.html.

Cliff Click. Performance Myths Exposed. JavaOne presentation, 2003.

Cliff Click. Performance Myths Revisited. JavaOne presentation, 2005. URL http://developers.sun.com/learning/javaoneonline/2005/coreplatform/TS-3268.pdf.

Martin Fowler. Presentation Model, 2005. URL http://www.martinfowler.com/eaaDev/PresentationModel.html.

Erich Gamma, Richard Helm, Ralph Johnson, and John Vlissides. *Design Patterns*. Addison–Wesley, 1995.

Martin Gardner. The fantastic combinations of John Conway's new solitaire game 'Life'. *Scientific American*, October 1970.

James Gosling, Bill Joy, Guy Steele, and Gilad Bracha. *The Java Language Specification*, Third Edition. Addison–Wesley, 2005.

Tim Harris and Keir Fraser. Language Support for Lightweight Transactions. In *OOPSLA '03: Proceedings of the 18th Annual ACM SIGPLAN Conference on Object-Oriented Programming, Systems, Languages, and Applications*, pages 388–402. ACM Press, 2003. URL http://doi.acm.org/10.1145/949305.949340.

Tim Harris, Simon Marlow, Simon Peyton-Jones, and Maurice Herlihy. Composable Memory Transactions. In *PPoPP '05: Proceedings of the Tenth ACM SIGPLAN Symposium on Principles and Practice of Parallel Programming*, pages 48–60. ACM Press, 2005. URL http://doi.acm.org/10.1145/1065944.1065952.

Maurice Herlihy. Wait-Free Synchronization. *ACM Transactions on Programming Languages and Systems*, 13(1):124–149, 1991. URL http://doi.acm.org/10.1145/114005.102808.

Maurice Herlihy and Nir Shavit. *Multiprocessor Synchronization and Concurrent Data Structures*. Morgan-Kaufman, 2006.

C. A. R. Hoare. Monitors: An Operating System Structuring Concept. *Communications of the ACM*, 17(10):549–557, 1974. URL http://doi.acm.org/10.1145/355620.361161.

David Hovemeyer and William Pugh. Finding Bugs is Easy. *SIGPLAN Notices*, 39 (12):92–106, 2004. URL http://doi.acm.org/10.1145/1052883.1052895.

Ramnivas Laddad. *AspectJ in Action*. Manning, 2003.

Doug Lea. *Concurrent Programming in Java*, Second Edition. Addison–Wesley, 2000.

Doug Lea. JSR-133 Cookbook for Compiler Writers. URL http://gee.cs.oswego.edu/dl/jmm/cookbook.html.

J. D. C. Little. A proof of the Queueing Formula $L = \lambda W$". *Operations Research*, 9: 383–387, 1961.

Jeremy Manson, William Pugh, and Sarita V. Adve. The Java Memory Model. In *POPL '05: Proceedings of the 32nd ACM SIGPLAN-SIGACT Symposium on Principles of Programming Languages*, pages 378–391. ACM Press, 2005. URL http://doi.acm.org/10.1145/1040305.1040336.

George Marsaglia. XorShift RNGs. *Journal of Statistical Software*, 8(13), 2003. URL http://www.jstatsoft.org/v08/i14.

Maged M. Michael and Michael L. Scott. Simple, Fast, and Practical Non-Blocking and Blocking Concurrent Queue Algorithms. In *Symposium on Principles of Distributed Computing*, pages 267–275, 1996. URL http://citeseer.ist.psu.edu/michael96simple.html.

Mark Moir and Nir Shavit. *Concurrent Data Structures*, In *Handbook of Data Structures and Applications*, chapter 47. CRC Press, 2004.

William Pugh and Jeremy Manson. Java Memory Model and Thread Specification, 2004. URL `http://www.cs.umd.edu/~pugh/java/memoryModel/jsr133.pdf`.

M. Raynal. *Algorithms for Mutual Exclusion*. MIT Press, 1986.

William N. Scherer, Doug Lea, and Michael L. Scott. Scalable Synchronous Queues. In *11th ACM SIGPLAN Symposium on Principles and Practices of Parallel Programming (PPoPP)*, 2006.

R. K. Treiber. Systems Programming: Coping with Parallelism. Technical Report RJ 5118, IBM Almaden Research Center, April 1986.

Andrew Wellings. *Concurrent and Real-Time Programming in Java*. John Wiley & Sons, 2004.

Index

preservation of, as thread safety
requirement; 24
mutable; 15
objects
safe publication of; 54
state
managing access to, as thread
safety goal; 15
mutexes (mutual exclusion locks); 25
binary semaphore use as; 99
intrinsic locks as; 25
ReentrantLock capabilities; 277
MVC (model-view-controller) pattern
deadlock risks; 190
vehicle tracking example use of; 61

N

narrowing
lock scope
as lock contention reduction
strategy; 233–235
native code
finalizer use and limitations; 165
navigation
as compound action
in collection operations; 79
newTaskFor; 126$_{li}$
encapsulating non-standard cancellation; 148
nonatomic 64-bit operations; 36
nonblocking algorithms; 319, 329, 329–
336
backoff importance for; 231$_{fn}$
synchronization; 319–336
SynchronousQueue; 174$_{fn}$
thread-safe counter use; 322–324
nonfair semaphores
advantages of; 265
notification; 302–304
See also blocking; condition, queues;
event(s); listeners; notify;
notifyAll; sleeping; wait(s);
waking up;
completion
of long-running GUI task; 198
conditional; **303**
as optimization; 303
use; 304$_{li}$
errors
as concurrency bug pattern; 272
event notification systems

copy-on-write collection advantages; 87
notify
as optimization; 303
efficiency of; 298$_{fn}$
missed signal risk; 302
notifyAll vs.; 302
subclassing safety issues
documentation importance; 304
usage guidelines; 303
notifyAll
notify vs.; 302
@NotThreadSafe; 6, 353
NPTL threads package
Linux use; 4$_{fn}$
nulling out memory references
testing use; 257

O

object(s)
See also resource(s);
composing; 55–78
condition
explicit; 306–308
effectively immutable; **53**
guarded; **54**
immutable; **46**
initialization safety; 51
publication using volatile; 48–49
mutable
safe publication of; 54
pools
appropriate uses; 241$_{fn}$
bounded, semaphore management of; 99
disadvantages of; 241
serial thread confinement use; 90
references
and stack confinement; 44
sharing; 33–54
state; **55**
components of; 55
Swing
thread-confinement; 191–192
objects
guarded; **28**
open calls; 211, 211–213
See also encapsulation;
operating systems
concurrency use
historical role; 1

thread pool use of; 172–174
representation
  Runnable use for; 125
  with Future; 126
response-time sensitivity
  andexecution policy; 168
scheduling
  thread-per-task policy; 115
serialization sources
  identifying; 225
state
  effect on Future.get; 95
  intermediate, shutdown issues;
    158–161
thread(s) vs.
  interruption handling; 141
timed
  handling of; 123
two-party
  Exchanger management of; 101
TCK (Technology Compatibility Kit)
  concurrency testing requirements;
    250
teardown
  thread; 171–172
techniques
  See also design; guidelines; strate-
    gies;
temporary objects
  and ThreadLocal variables; 45
terminated
  ExecutorService state; 121
termination
  See also cancellation; interruption;
    lifecycle;
  puzzle-solving framework; 187
  safety test
    criteria for; 254, 257
  thread
    abnormal, handling; 161–163
    keep-alive time impact on; 172
    reasons for deprecation of; 135$_{fn}$
  timed locks use; 279
test example method; 262$_{li}$
testing
  See also instrumentation; logging;
    measurement; monitoring;
    quality assurance; statistics;
  concurrent programs; 247–274
  deadlock risks; 210$_{fn}$
  functionality

  vs. performance tests; 260
liveness
  criteria; 248
performance; 260–266
  criteria; 248
  goals; 260
pitfalls
  avoiding; 266–270
  dead code elimination; 269
  dynamic compilation; 267–268
  garbage collection; 266
  progress quantification; 248
  proving a negative; 248
  timing and synchronization arti-
    facts; 247
  unrealistic code path sampling;
    268
  unrealistic contention; 268–269
program correctness; 248–260
safety; 252–257
  criteria; 247
strategies; 270–274
testPoolExample example; 258$_{li}$
testTakeBlocksWhenEmpty example;
    252$_{li}$
this reference
  publication risks; 41
Thread
  join
    timed, problems with; 145
  getState
    use precautions; 251
  interruption methods; 138, 139$_{li}$
  usage precautions; 140
thread safety; **18**, 15–32
  and mutable data; 35
  and shutdown hooks; 164
  characteristics of; 17–19
  data models, GUI application han-
    dling; 201
  delegation; 62
  delegation of; **234**
  in puzzle-solving framework; 183
  issues, atomicity; 19–23
  issues, liveness and performance;
    29–32
  mechanisms, locking; 23–29
  risks; 5–8
thread(s); 2
  See also concurrent/concurrency;
    safety; synchronization;